THERAPEUTIC CONVERSATIONS

THERAPEUTIC CONVERSATIONS

Edited by

STEPHEN GILLIGAN

and

REESE PRICE

W.W. Norton & Company · New York · London

The text of this book is composed in Century Textbook
with the display set in Korinna. Composition by Bytheway Typesetting, Inc.
Manufacturing by Haddon Craftsmen.

Book design by Justine Burkat Trubey

Library of Congress Cataloging-in-Publication Data

Therapeutic conversations / edited by Stephen Gilligan and Reese
    Price.
        p.   cm.
    "A Norton professional book."
    Includes index.
    ISBN 0-393-70145-X
    1. Psychotherapy—Congresses.   2. Psychotherapist and patient—
Congresses.   I. Gilligan, Stephen G., 1954–   . II. Price, Reese,
1952–   .
RC480.5.T514   1993
616.89´14—dc20   92-31745   CIP

W. W. Norton & Company, Inc., 500 Fifth Avenue, New York, N.Y. 10110
W. W. Norton & Company Ltd., 10 Coptic Street, London WC1A 1PU

                    2 3 4 5 6 7 8 9 0

To my wife, Denise, and my daughter, Zoe, for the love and life they bring.

S. G.

To Ruth and Reese Price, whose love initiated my journey; to Bob, Mary, and Anne, whose loving guidance opened the door to this wonderful relationship called therapy; and to Chani, my partner in the dance of life and love.

R. P.

CONTRIBUTORS

Janet Adams-Westcott, Ph.D.
  Family & Children's Service, Inc., Tulsa, Oklahoma

Mia Andersson, Lic. Psychologist and Psychotherapist
  AGS-Institutet, Stockholm, Sweden

Jeff Chang, M.A.
  The Family Psychology Centre and Canada EAP Services Corporation, Calgary, Alberta

Gene Combs, M.D.
  Co-director, Evanston Family Therapy Center, Evanston, Illinois; Faculty, Chicago Center for Family Health, Chicago, Illinois

Thomas A. Dafforn, Ph.D.
  Domestic Violence Intervention Services, Inc., Tulsa, Oklahoma

Steve de Shazer
  Senior Research Associate, Brief Family Therapy Center, Milwaukee, Wisconsin

Victoria C. Dickerson, Ph.D.
Co-founder, Bay Area Family Therapy Training Associates, Cupertino, California; Research Associate and Teaching Faculty at the Mental Research Institute, Palo Alto; Adjunct Faculty, Santa Clara University

David Epston, M.A.
Co-director, the Family Therapy Centre, Auckland, New Zealand

Jill Freedman, M.S.W.
Co-director, Evanston Family Therapy Center, Evanston, Illinois; Faculty, Chicago Center for Family Health, Chicago, Illinois

Stephen Gilligan, Ph.D.
Director, Omega Institute for Ericksonian Psychotherapy, Encinitas, California

Klas Grevelius, Lic. Psychologist and Psychotherapist
AGS-Institutet, Stockholm, Sweden

James Griffith, M.D.
Associate Professor of Psychiatry; Co-director, Family Therapy Program, Department of Psychiatry, University of Mississippi School of Medicine, Jackson

Melissa Elliot Griffith, M.S.W.
Instructor in Clinical Psychiatry; Co-director, Family Therapy Program, Department of Psychiatry, University of Mississippi School of Medicine, Jackson

Stephen Patrick Madigan, Ph.D.
Director of Training, Yaletown Family Therapy, Vancouver, British Columbia

William Hudson O'Hanlon, M.S.
The Hudson Center for Brief Therapy, Omaha, Nebraska; Adjunct Professor of Psychology, Indiana University of Pennsylvania

Michele Phillips, Ph.D.
The Family Psychology Center, Calgary, Alberta

Reese Price, Ph.D.
Psychologist, Tulsa, Oklahoma

Ernst Salamon, Lic. Psychologist and Psychotherapist
AGS-Institutet, Stockholm, Sweden

Patricia Sterne, M.S.W., L.C.S.W.
Family & Children's Service, Inc., Tulsa, Oklahoma

Karl Tomm, M.D.
University of Calgary Medical School, Calgary, Alberta

John H. Weakland, Ch.E.
Senior Research Fellow, Mental Research Institute, Palo Alto, California

Michele Weiner-Davis, M.S.W.
Private practice, Woodstock, Illinois

Michael White, M.A.
Child, Marital, and Family Therapist, Dulwich Centre, Adelaide, South Australia

Jeffrey L. Zimmerman, Ph.D.
Co-founder of Bay Area Family Therapy Training Associates in Cupertino, California; Teaching Faculty, Mental Research Institute, Palo Alto; Clinical Faculty, Stanford University; teaches at Western and John F. Kennedy Universities

CONTENTS

II. CLINICAL APPLICATIONS

PREFACE

Reese Price

THE IDEA OF A conference centering around the notion of effective therapeutic conversation had its conception in early 1990. Over dinner, Bill O'Hanlon described a dream he had of sponsoring a conference bringing together some of the most innovative thinkers in the psychotherapy field in relation to solutions, possibilities, and the generating of a sense of authorship in one's life. The conversation was an exciting one, and I shared Bill's enthusiasm. Bill agreed to hand me the ball, and like any good quarterback, was content to let me run with it.

It was quite a learning experience enlisting a faculty of folk like Steve de Shazer, who put off his family's vacation, and other notables like John Weakland, Michael White, and Stephen Gilligan, to name a few. Particularly when they had to bank on an organization and an individual who had never done anything on a national level like this conference. But the idea and the spirit of a cooperative venture caught everyone's interest, and so a core faculty of John Weakland, Michael White, Stephen Gilligan, Bill O'Hanlon, Steve de Shazer, David Epston, Michele Weiner-Davis, and Karl Tomm took a chance on a conference representing a theme in which they believed.

And what a conference it turned out to be, as a crowd of approximately 375 people came together in Tulsa in June of 1991. The atmosphere from start to finish was one of cooperation and community, culminating in an impromptu meeting on the last night that was a true coming together of the conference as a community of people who share a deep belief in therapeutic possibilities.

In a project of this size, there are a lot of people to thank: the Tulsa more cooperative, aikido-like relationship. No attempt has been made to "integrate" these positions into a grand unifying framework. Rather, the differences serve to reinforce the stance of respect for multiple truths and multiple realities that is so integral to the new ideas represented in this book. I hope you benefit from these ideas as much as I have.

ACKNOWLEDGMENTS

Reese Price

THE MAKING OF this conference required the combined efforts of many people. I would like to acknowledge Gail Lapidus, Director of Family and Children Services, whose friendship with Karl Tomm, Michael White and David Epston was central in their decision to present. Also, thanks in this regard to Steve Terry and Janet Adams-Westcott, who aided and abetted Gail in the wooing of these presenters.

Many thanks to Peggy Martin for her tireless work on the phones and with registration. Also, my undying gratitude to Joanna Lee, whose magnificent organizational skills made this conference come together. Much appreciation also goes to a bevy of volunteers from Family and Children Services and Mental Health Care Services of Tulsa, and to the presenters whose papers appear in the book – innovative thinkers who took a chance on a conference sponsored by an unknown element in Tulsa, Oklahoma.

Finally, I would like to acknowledge the Tulsa Psychiatric Center, an organization founded to promote the education of the professional community, as well as to provide mental health care to the indigent. Its investment in this project provided the working capital that allowed the idea of this conference to become reality.

THERAPEUTIC CONVERSATIONS

Part I

THEORETICAL CONVERSATIONS

1

POSSIBILITY THERAPY:
FROM IATROGENIC INJURY
TO IATROGENIC HEALING

William Hudson O'Hanlon

IATROGENICS

I HAD A HAND in making up the faculty list for the conference from which these papers came. Over the years I had come across the work of the major faculty members and had found some commonalities in their approaches. Although they had different ideas and methods, there was something they all had in common: They respected their clients and collaborated with them in the change process. They had views that were co-constructivist. Clients and therapists were seen as creating in conversation and in interaction the focus for therapy and the view and experience that change was possible. In addition, all of the faculty members eschewed views that were pathologically-based or blaming towards clients. I was discussing this idea with my friend, Tapani Ahola, a therapist from Finland, and he said, "Oh, yes, the Fourth Wave." When I asked him what he meant by that phrase, he told me, "The First Wave in psychotherapy was pathology-based. The Second Wave was problem-focused or problem-solving therapy. The Third Wave was solution-focused or solution-oriented. The Fourth Wave is what is emerging now. Only no one has a good name for it yet."

Iatrogenic Injury and Iatrogenic Healing

Iatrogenic refers to treatment-caused problems. The word refers to injuries that are the result of the interventions done by the healing

3

agent. It was initially applied to medicine but has come to be used in therapy as well (Morgan, 1983). In 1961, Milton Erickson said, during a lecture in which he discussed the importance of iatrogenics, "While I have read a number of articles on this subject of iatrogenic disease, and have heard many discussions about it, there is one topic on which I haven't seen much written about and that is iatrogenic health. Iatrogenic health is a most important consideration – much more important than iatrogenic disease" (quoted in Rossi and Ryan, 1986, p. 140).

Iatrogenic injury (a term borrowed from my colleagues at the AGS Institute in Stockholm, Sweden) refers to methods, techniques, assessment procedures, explanations, or interventions that harm, discourage, invalidate, show disrespect, or close down the possibilities for change.

Iatrogenic healing refers to those methods, techniques, assessment procedures, explanations, or interventions that encourage, are respectful, and open up the possibilities for change.

The faculty and papers from this conference seem to me to be standing against iatrogenic injury in therapy and standing for iatrogenic health and healing. Taken together, I call these stances *possibility therapy*.

POSSIBILITY THERAPY:
A SHIFT IN THE WIND

For the past few years, I have been teaching an approach I call solution-oriented therapy (O'Hanlon and Weiner-Davis, 1989). It is a relative of de Shazer's and the BFTC team's work. We share an interest in exploring and emphasizing solutions, strengths, abilities, and exceptions. As I teach this method, though, I often get comments from workshop participants and supervisees along the line of: "I really like the *positive* approach you use; it's so refreshing." While I'm aware they are offering a compliment, I cringe when I hear this.

Of course, any approach which doesn't blame people or give them stigmatizing labels and which emphasizes workable aspects of people's lives looks positive compared to traditional therapy approaches. However, I am concerned about this word *positive*. To me it smells like either that gung-ho, "You-can-do-anything-you-set-your-mind-to," school of sales/motivation training or a New-Age Pollyanna view of life ("you can be wealthy if you write enough affirmations," and other such claptrap).

I don't like positive thinking because I think it minimizes the very real (you radical constructivists will excuse me for using that word) physical negative things that happen in the world and in the lives of the people with whom we work in therapy. I'm talking about things like rape, violence, poverty, malnutrition, job discrimination, and so forth. Positive thinking seems to me like putting gilding on the top of a pile of manure. It looks nice, but if you poke it very hard, you'll find the pleasantness does not go very deep. All the positive thinking, reframing, paradigm shifting, or whatever doesn't directly alter these difficult/harmful conditions.

At the same time, I'm not voting for negative thinking either. Negative thinking holds that everything *is* manure and there's not much you or I or anyone can do to change that. People *are* "narcissistic" or "borderline" or "sociopathic" personalities and they will *never* change. This is not a recommended stance for a change-agent.

So for now I have settled on the label "possibility therapy" for what I do. Possibility thinking does not claim that everything is (or will be) wonderful and successful or that it is (or will) be awful and futile.

Some years ago, I read a story about Dick Gregory, the American comedian turned social and nutritional activist. When someone asked him whether he thought we could achieve his hopes for eliminating hunger and starvation on this planet by the end of the 20th century, he replied that he had once chanced upon the scene of a building on fire. The fire fighters were struggling to fight the fire. Gregory asked the fire chief whether he thought they could save the building. The chief replied, "If there's a shift in the wind, we will. If not, we won't."

The possibility therapist recognizes the seriousness of clients' situations without taking a minimizing or Pollyanna view. She/he also recognizes the possibility that things won't change (the building will burn down), but works to be the shift in the wind in clients' lives.

My mother-in-law, Jessie Hudson, was once accused of being a pessimist. She replied, "I'm not a pessimist, I'm an experienced optimist." I am an experienced optimist when I approach clients. I know that there is a great deal of violence in this world and that there are economic problems, racial prejudice, and other difficulties to be faced. My view is that there are always possibilities, even within those difficult situations.

RADICAL CONSTRUCTIVISM AND SOCIAL/INTERACTIONAL CONSTRUCTIONISM

Radical constructivists and quantum physicists suggest that what we call reality is constructed/fabricated by our beliefs and our neurology (see Watzlawick, 1984). In this view, there is no such thing as reality (or truth either, which is another matter altogether and a compelling reason not to hire a radical constructivist to handle your cash).

Social/interactional constructionists take a different stance. They (or I should say, we, since I count myself in their numbers) hold that there is a physical reality out there but that our social reality, being influenced by language and interaction, is negotiable. This social reality can influence and be influenced by physical reality. For instance, if someone in a crowded hall yelled "Fire!" it would probably create the physical reality of people rushing for the exit. If someone was crushed to death in that rush, no amount of taking and interacting could change *that* reality.

This social reality is mutable, but within some limits – the constraints seem to be physical, environmental, and traditional/habitual. Traditions consist of typical ways of speaking, thinking about, perceiving, and doing things in a particular interactional group (family, subculture, culture). Habits consist of an individual's way of speaking, thinking about, perceiving, experiencing, and doing things.

One can't just waltz into a social situation and define it or reframe it as one likes. First, there is the physical environment, including our neurology and physiology, to be dealt with. Some frames just won't fit into these realities. Then there are traditions to be dealt with. Certain frames have held sway for many years and are not to be swept aside by a few clever phrases or questions. The social reality created in therapy interviews is just that – social. It is co-created by the therapist and clients, as well as by the culture and social system traditions that influence them. Thus, once a new or alternate reality is constructed, others must be "enrolled" in order for it to work.

ACKNOWLEDGMENT AND POSSIBILITY

I learned much of what I do in therapy from Milton Erickson. In the way that I have come to understand it, Erickson's work reminds me a great deal of the first model of counseling I learned in depth, the client-centered model of Carl Rogers.

I do hypnosis in the Erickson tradition. It is different from traditional hypnotic approaches in that it is more permissive, more inclusive, and more validating of whatever the "subject" is doing during the induction and however he or she responds while in trance.

I remember I was working with a client of mine who had terribly intrusive obsessions. He was rarely, if ever, free of them. For some time he had seen a psychoanalytic expert on obsessive-compulsive disorders, who pronounced the client the worst case of obsessiveness he had ever seen. I used hypnosis with the man and by the second session he was starting to develop fine trances. At the third session, I started the trance induction with my usual sort of spiel, "You can be where you are, feeling what you are feeling, thinking what you are thinking, obsessing about what you're obsessing about, and experiencing what you are experiencing. There's nothing to do to go into trance, no right way or wrong way to go into trance. So just let yourself be where you are, doing what you are doing, worrying that you won't go into trance." At that point, he popped his eyes open and said simply, "That's why I come here." "To go into trance, you mean?" I asked. "No," he replied, "to hear those words." He later explained that it was the only time in his life in which he could escape from the terrible sense that he was constantly doing his life incorrectly. He would also often be obsession-free during parts of the trance.

When this obsessive man said those words, something coalesced for me – something that I hadn't been articulating during my teaching about more directive ways of working with people. That is, you have to acknowledge, validate, and include people's experience before they will be open to new possibilities and directions.

If you only acknowledge, validate, and include, however, most clients won't move on very quickly, as we have seen from decades of experience with client-centered work. Twenty-seven sessions after the intake, you'll still be bobbing your head and reflecting back the client's depression or whatever. While clients may feel valued and heard, they likely won't have made many changes in their problematic situations.

So I think therapy is always a balance between acknowledgment of existing realities and the creation of new possibilities. If clients don't have a sense that you have heard, acknowledged, and valued them, they will either spend time trying to convince you of the legitimacy of their pain and suffering or they will leave therapy with you. Someone once asked me about the place of Carl Rogers' methods in my work and I replied, "That's the first five minutes. If you don't do that stuff, I don't think you're going to get anywhere with clients." In fact, I think people who work briefly generally have to be much better at acknowledging and joining people. If they are to be invited to move along rapidly, they must have the sense that you understand them.

I propose that the papers in this book and the faculty are creating a new tradition in therapy. Because therapy conversations can have different emphases and components, I will detail some of the components of traditional therapy conversations and some of the components of the new tradition that this conference represents.

TRADITIONAL THERAPY CONVERSATIONS

Conversations for Explanations

When I first went to study with Milton Erickson, I was a "true believer" in family systems theory. At the time, I worked in an agency in which the dominant model was psychodynamic. I was regularly getting into arguments with my colleagues during clinical case staffings. I would try to convince them that doing individual therapy was useless because they were just sending their clients back into their symptom-inducing systems, where they would again develop problems. I never seemed to sway them, though, as they would argue back just as vociferously that I was missing the clear, underlying psychodynamics of the situation.

Erickson had a way of pulling the rug out from under one's cherished theories. As I studied with him, he did that very effectively with me. He would bring up a clinical problem and ask me how I would handle it. I would usually spin out some impressive sounding systems psychobabble involving "entrenched coalitions," "enmeshment," and "triangulation." He would chastise me for attending to my theories more than to my clients, and then reorient my attention to what the clients were showing and telling me. He was big on observation and disdained theories. (I once asked him why he did not think that more people came to study with him, as I did not have to wait in line to see him in 1977. He replied, "Because I have no theory and some people think that's very wrong.")

By the time I finished studying with Erickson, I was no longer a true believer in systems theory. Unfortunately, my colleagues at the agency had gotten the family therapy religion and again there were clinical disagreements. They would try to convince me that people's problems were functions of systemic processes and I remained unconvinced. If I was not a psychodynamic therapist and not a family systems therapist, what was I? I was warped! I realized that I no longer believed any particular explanation of why people had problems. They all had some credibility, but they now seemed irrelevant to me. I went around for some years telling people I had no theory of psychotherapy. People would challenge me, of course. Just as you cannot not communicate, you cannot not have a theory. You have a theory, they would say, you have the theory of not having a theory. That didn't ring quite true to me and it seemed a little too pretentious. So I finally figured out that I had no *explanatory* theory, but I did have an *intervention* theory.

Typical conversations for explanations in traditional therapy include discussion and pursuit of the function of the symptom. Depending on the theory, the function is either benevolent or malevolent. The explanation is often pathologically-oriented, maintaining that the presenting concern is evidence of some underlying dysfunction or illness. Again, depending on the theory, the dysfunction is either individual or social (familial, cultural, etc.) or some combination of both.

Often traditional conversations focus on categorization according to some schema such as the *DSM-III-R*. Of course, not all categorization is iatrogenically harmful. I remember a time in therapy that I call B.B. – before borderlines and bulimics. When I first practiced therapy, neither of these was a common problem and one (bulimia) had not even been invented yet. I mention them because I think that these two labels show a contrast between labels that empower and labels that disempower and make the problem more difficult to resolve.

When I first treated someone who binged and vomited, I had never heard of bulimia. A woman came to therapy and asked me if I could help her stop this compulsive eating and vomiting pattern that she did. We worked out some ways for her to change and after a relatively short time she stopped eating such large quantities and making herself vomit. Some time later, I came across a book that named this disorder "bulimarexia" and distinguished it from anorexia (Boskind-White and White, 1983). I became interested in this problem and advertised in the local university newspaper describing the problem and announcing the formation of a treatment group for it. In the next few days, I received about 50 phone calls from young women regarding the group. Most cried on the phone and told me that they had never known there was a name for what they did, that they never knew anyone else did this, and that they were relieved to find that there was treatment for their problem. Many found that by the time they entered the group the knowledge that they were not alone and that there was help had enabled them to stop bingeing and vomiting or taking laxatives. This was a label that empowered and helped people to change.

When I first started hearing widespread reports of the epidemic of borderline personality disorder (Masterson, 1976), I was perplexed. I was traveling frequently to the east coast of the U.S. and teaching workshops. Participants in the workshops started asking with more and more regularity about how my approach would work with borderlines. I had heard of the disorder, but when I learned it, it was an obscure analytic concept that meant the person wasn't quite neurotic and not quite psychotic, but somewhere in between, on the border. A clinic in which I had worked in Arizona had a therapist who had seen one and the man had killed himself in the course of treatment. In Nebraska, where I worked at the time, there weren't any borderlines whom I had heard about and nobody ever asked questions about them in workshops. Since that time, of course, borderlines have become ubiquitous in the therapy field. Many books and workshops have spread this epidemic around the globe. We even have them in Nebraska now. There is a problem with the diagnosis, though. Most therapists have gotten the idea that these are very difficult "patients" to work with and that treatment necessarily takes years. When one gets a "borderline," one's colleagues commiserate and tell one not to expect much and not to get too many in one's caseload or one will burn out. This pessimism is often communicated to the client and can become part and parcel of the difficulty.

Sometimes traditional therapy conversations focus on a search for or discussion of causes and deterministic ideas. Current concerns are thought to be caused by past events or situations or by current events or situations, either inside or outside of the person.

Conversations for Expression of Emotion

Traditional therapy approaches often put an emphasis on the expression of emotion as a curative factor. The classic question is: "How do you feel about that?" I rarely, if ever, hear possibility therapists utter this question. My wife, Pat Hudson, who works in this new tradition, once had a client come in and appear very uncomfortable during the session. Pat had seen the woman for some time and knew something was up. She asked what was going on and the woman told her that she had something she needed to talk about but she was afraid to say. After much prompting, the woman still had not revealed her secret, so Pat started to guess. "Is it about sex?" Pat inquired. The woman nodded. "Do you have a man?" The woman shook her head. "Is it a woman?" Again the woman shook her head. Perplexed, Pat asked jokingly, "Well, what have you got, a big dog?" To Pat's surprise, the woman nodded. Pat was so shocked that all she could do was utter that timeless counselor phrase, "Well, how do you feel about that?" Usually, however, this phrase and others like it are more suited to the traditional therapist.

Conversations for Insight

Most therapists strive to give their clients insights and understandings into the nature and causes of their concerns. This idea, like the idea that expressing emotions is curative, is thought to be related to change in the presenting concern. This process is often guided by the therapists' interpretations or leading questions.

Conversations for Inability

Traditionally therapists have seen clients as somehow damaged or having deficits or inabilities. Clients are said to have an inability to tolerate ambiguity, conflict, or their feelings. They are said to be unable to assert themselves, to get in touch with their feelings, to control their violent actions or to live "normal" lives. Whatever the particulars, the overarching concept is that of inability, and that is communicated implicitly or explicitly to the clients and/or their families.

Conversations for Blame and Recrimination

If you've ever worked in a traditional psychiatric clinic or hospital, you've experienced the amount of blaming of patients/clients that goes on in these settings. The blaming is sometimes subtle, but sometimes very blatant: "This patient likes his illness." "She is playing a game with us, manipulating us." "He doesn't really want to change." "She's a borderline, don't expect much change." Blame takes two forms. One attributes bad or evil intentions to people (they don't want to change, they like their illness, they want to control or manipulate others, etc.). The other attributes bad or evil characteristics (narcissistic, selfish, sociopathic, resistant, etc.) to people.

Adversarial Conversations

Closely related to conversations for blame and recrimination are adversarial conversations. If the patient is seen to be resistant or has defenses that block him or her from cooperating or changing, the therapist must either confront those defenses (breaking through the denial, a specialty of drug and alcohol abuse treatment, but used in other treatment as well) or somehow find a way around the defenses. This can lead to trickery or deceit on the part of the therapist. If the therapist is open and aboveboard about his/her thoughts or agenda for therapy, the client might sabotage or thwart it.

This stance in therapy conversation arises in part from the idea that the therapist is the expert and the client is the nonexpert or amateur in psychological/emotional matters. The therapist knows best not only how to solve the clients concerns, but also what is really going on within the client. In addition, if the therapist's theory has a normative model within it, the therapist is then an expert on what "normal" is and how the client should live after therapy is over. For example, the idea that one should always express one's feelings was a popular idea for many years in therapy. Not only would this solve the present concern of the client, but it was in general a good rule for how to conduct one's daily life.

POSSIBILITY THERAPY CONVERSATIONS

Collaborative Conversations

In possibility therapy, clients and therapists are both considered experts. Clients are experts on their own experience, including their pain, suffering, and concerns. They also have expertise about their memories, goals, and responses. Therapists are expert at creating a conversational and interactional climate for change and results in therapy. Clients and therapists are partners in the change/therapy process and collaborate on deciding the focus for therapy, the goal to be sought, and when therapy should come to an end. Therapists attend carefully to clients' responses, both during the session and between sessions, to insure that the therapy fits for the client.

Conversations for Change/Difference

Therapists, because they are not living the lives of their clients, are able to notice and ask about differences and changes that may not at first be apparent to clients. The possibility therapist, like the solution-oriented therapist, highlights changes, exceptions to the problems, even changes that made the situation worse. In addition, the therapist introduces new distinctions into the conversation and attends carefully to notice which distinctions show up in clients' experience and/or actions. The possibility therapist also creates a sense of expectancy for change by his/her language and nonverbal behavior.

Conversations for Competence/Abilities

The possibility therapist presumes client competence and pursues evidence of it, always being careful not to invalidate clients or minimize their pain, suffering, or personal view of their concerns. This competence can be directly related to clients' concerns or perhaps derive from a different domain of clients' lives. For example, a golfer may find some golf knowledge that will help him approach his marriage in a new and more successful way.

Conversations for Possibilities

Possibility therapists focus the conversations on the possibilities of the future rather than on the problems of the past. The past may be discussed, but the emphasis will usually be on clients' goals and visions of the future. I teach workshops on working with people who were sexually abused. Once Steve de Shazer was hassling me for teaching them, saying that by focusing on the problem I was inadvertently being problem-focused. "I don't do therapy with people who have the problem of having been sexually abused," he told me, "I only do therapy with people who want things to happen in the future." He had a good point. The fact that they were sexually abused is certainly important background information, like the fact that they grew up in a rural or urban environment, that they were shy or outgoing, but the ultimate emphasis in therapy is on where people want to go in the future.

In addition to focusing on future possibilities, possibility therapists spend time searching for new possibilities in the past and the present as well. Some wit has said, "It's never too late to have a happy childhood." While that perhaps overstates the case, it points to the idea that one can change one's selection and interpretation of events in the past and thereby create a new sense of where one came from. A new narrative, in the current parlance.

New possibilities are introduced into the present by getting clients to change their actions (the doing, as I have called it) and their frames of reference and attention (the viewing) about their current situations and concerns.

Conversations for Goals/Results

Closely related to conversations for possibilities is focusing on how clients will know that they have achieved their therapeutic goals. Getting clear on when therapy should end according to the client not only minimizes the imposition of the therapist's ideas on the client, but often hastens the achievement of those goals. This also leaves the therapist with a clear sense of accountability for therapeutic reasons. If the goal is not achieved, the client is not blamed for lack of results. Goal setting is mutual and responsibility for results is mutual.

Conversations for Accountability/ Personal Agency

A strong thread that runs through many of the faculty members' work is the idea that people are accountable for their actions. "Mental dis-

orders" and "terrible childhoods" do not excuse people from accountability for their actions. This is distinct from blaming clients, which
was detailed in a previous section. Holding people accountable says
nothing about their intentions or character in performing those actions.

THE DISTINCTION BETWEEN
EXPERIENCE, ACTION,
AND STORIES

I make a distinction between three domains in people's lives.

The first is the domain of *experience*. That includes everything that
seems to happen inside the person's "bag of bones" (as Gregory Bateson used to call people's bodies). This includes feelings, sensations,
automatic thoughts, fantasies, neurology, and physiology. My stance
about experience is that there is nothing to change about it in therapy.
The therapist should acknowledge and validate clients' experiences
without trying to rid clients of those experiences directly. This is basically the Carl Rogers stance. Let people know that who they are and
what their "organismic selves" experience are acceptable and can be
valued.

This validation consists of:

1. Acknowledging – letting people know that you have noted their
   experience and points of view.
2. Validating/valuing – letting people know that their experiences
   and points of view are valid and valued.
3. Giving permission – letting people know that they can feel, experience, think, or do things.
4. Inclusion – incorporating whatever concerns, experiences, ob-
   jections, and barriers people show/express into the conversation without this becoming a block to moving on towards solution.

In this validating process, it is important to filter out blaming/
invalidating questions, statements, and labels. As we have discussed
above, blaming is attributing bad, sick, or evil intentions or character
traits to oneself or others. Some labels blame and invalidate and some
empower. It is also important not to invalidate the person or his/her
experience. Invalidating means minimizing, denying or undercutting

a person's felt experience, sense of self or point of view in a way that devalues them.

> I was consulting for a psychiatric inpatient unit and did an interview with a woman who I later learned had the label "borderline." After the interview, when I asked her how the interview had been for her, she told me that she had expected to be crucified and had been pleasantly surprised to find that she wasn't. Afterwards, in the discussion with the staff of the unit, I asked about her feelings of being crucified and they told me that she had made quite a scene after she was offered the wrong medication during the night shift. She complained to the nursing supervisor, who told her that it was a therapeutic issue and she should go confront the nurse. When the staff asked me what I would recommend, I said that first I would apologize to her for making the mistake. They all nodded and agreed. However, previously her complaint had seemed a symptom of her borderline personality. They had invalidated a legitimate complaint due to her diagnosis. She had also been encouraged to talk in group therapy and then, when she did, she was confronted about dominating the group. It's no wonder she felt crucified.

The second is the domain of *action*. Action consists of what people do that is actually or potentially under their deliberate influence. Whereas in the domain of experience, I give the client the message that everything is okay, in the realm of action I take a stand against actions that are harmful to the client him/herself or others and/or do not lead in the direction of results in therapy. After initially acknowledging the actions that clients have done or are doing, I start to sift the ones that are okay (not harmful, ethical, and lead towards the stated goals) from the ones that aren't okay (harmful, unethical, and lead away from the stated goals). I do my utmost to oppose "not okay" actions and lead clients and their intimates to "okay" actions.

The third domain is that of *stories*. This consists of the ideas, beliefs, frames of reference, and habits of language that the client and his/her intimates show in reference to the presenting concern in therapy. Again, I take a stance that some stories are okay (those that lead towards clients' goals and do not invalidate or close down possibilities for clients) and some aren't okay (those that lead away from the goal, block access to the goal, invalidate clients, or close down possibilities for them). I encourage okay stories and filter out, create doubt about, or gently challenge stories that aren't okay.

I prefer not to introduce explanations into my therapy sessions. My clients, of course, often introduce explanations into the conversation. I typically respond in several ways to such explanations. I either validate them as possible or create a little doubt as to their adequacy, relevance, or truth. If the explanations are not ones that blame them or their loved ones, invalidate them or their loved ones, or close down possibilities for change for them or their loved ones, I validate them. If they contain any of those elements of blame, invalidation, and closing possibilities, I create some uncertainty about them.

> During a marital therapy session, a woman told me that her husband, after ending an affair, suggested that she call him anytime he was at work to insure he was where he said he would be. She wondered aloud whether he was saying that because he didn't trust himself and wanted her to keep tabs on him or because he was trying to show her that he was now trustworthy and hoped she would check to find out he was not having affairs. Later in the session, when we discussed the matter again, she said, "I always look on the negative side of things." I replied, "Wait, I'm not so sure about that. I heard you say you had two ideas about why he suggested you check on him. One was positive and one was negative. It seems to me that you are a person who looks at both sides."

I was inviting her not to blame herself.

Since most of the interactions in therapy take place in the therapy session, conversation (both verbal and nonverbal) in the session then becomes the main fulcrum for influencing clients to develop stories and actions that further their goals and empower them. The session becomes like a filter separating the empowering from the disempowering, the useful from the harmful. This is why we called the conference "Generating Possibilities through Therapeutic Conversation."

The task of the possibility therapist, then, is threefold:

1. To *validate* the person and his/her experience;
2. To *change the doing* of the problem;
3. To *change the viewing* of the problem.

Possibility therapy is a method by which the client as a person, with all his or her past and current experiential realities, is validated and valued, as well as invited to change by co-creating new stories and opening the possibilities for new actions. All this is designed to empower clients, to remind them of their power. Possibility therapy seeks to avoid iatrogenic injury and to maximize iatrogenic healing and health. I hope that the reader has found both validation and possibility in reading this paper. I suspect that a lot of readers are working this way already and I have attempted in this paper to articulate and organize this emerging view.

Commentary

John H. Weakland

I WILL BE BRIEF, for several reasons. One, probably the most important one, is to leave time for general discussion of this paper. Another, rather a curious and unexpected reason, is that I find myself largely in agreement with what Bill has said. This does not leave me much room to raise hell—but there are a few points.

First of all, Bill said very early on that I would explain to you why his paper was not finished.* I am glad to do that; it's very simple. It is because although Bill had a good deal to say—as I think you can recognize without my underlining—he always has *more* to say. So naturally it was not finished.

"Positive thinking": While, as noted, I agree with much of what Bill has said, I often tend to think of matters in somewhat different terms. This is not necessarily a bad idea. It could be seen as a verbal analogue to Bateson's point about "binocular vision"; observation and description from two different standpoints can offer a "bonus," in Steve de Shazer's terms.

Bill appears to be recommending that in looking at the world—

---

*These comments were made at the time of the conference. Bill had apologized for not having gotten John a completed paper before the conference, as the paper was not yet completed.

particularly the troubles people bring to therapists – we might usefully find and utilize a position somewhere between two common views, that of the doomsayers (including especially therapists bent on finding pathology) on the one hand and the Pollyannas on the other. I would agree that this is desirable; this focus on "possibility" offers an escape route from a dichotomy that is prevalent, but apt to be misleading and certainly to be limiting. Moreover, I see this as just one instance of how to deal usefully with a quite general problem. Later on Bill himself mentions, less explicitly, another example. I'm proposing "let's not blame our clients – but let's hold them responsible"; he is really proposing not only that we avoid blame but also its unspecified opposite, excusing our clients wholesale, including accepting their excuses ("I can't do anything else") without question.

Dichotomization leads to thinking in absolutes, with an accompanying ignoring of context. This should be anathema to all systems thinkers, but it is not easy to avoid. We have been warned before, in various terms, by our mentors: Bateson emphasized that most human goods are matters of optimizing, not maximizing or minimizing. Erickson repeatedly pointed out that even "bad" attitudes presented by clients should be accepted and made useful – therefore "good" – by arranging appropriate contexts for them. We are indebted to Bill for further instruction on avoiding the traps of dichotomizing.

I could get into the issue of "function" of symptoms at some length – I certainly do differ from Haley, and in fact probably from most family therapists – but I will confine comment to what I see as basic. I would say that everything occurring in a social system can be seen as having a function; that's what being connected in a system of interaction means. But this is very different from the idea that everything has some sort of necessity about it, such that if you make a change there will be a great magnetic force pulling things back where they originally were. If you promote a change in a system, especially such that things are working better all around, I don't see any reason why people shouldn't settle for the new way.

I do have one difference with Bill, about his remarks on "adversarial communication." I do not see why having a "hidden agenda" is necessarily adversarial or disadvantageous to the client. Of course it could be, but I think this depends on whether the therapist is keeping his own counsel, in part, for his or her own advantage, or with the client's best interests in mind. Erickson has made this very distinction quite explicitly. And from another angle, it could be pointed out that a "hidden agenda" is necessarily present to some degree, unless a therapist always states his thoughts and reactions to whatever the client presents fully and immediately, without even selection of the phrasing. Is there *any* therapist who does this? But I don't think Bill and I are likely to settle this question in the few minutes left here, so let's just leave it as a matter for the future.

REFERENCES

Boskind-White, M., & White, W. (1983). *Bulimarexia: The binge-purge cycle.* New York: Norton.

Masterson, J. (1976). *Psychotherapy of the borderline adult: A developmental approach.* New York: Brunner/Mazel.

Morgan, R. (Ed.) (1983). *The iatrogenics handbook: A critical look at research and practice in the helping professions.* Toronto: IPI Publishing.

O'Hanlon, W. H., & Weiner-Davis, M. (1989). *In search of solutions: A new direction in psychotherapy.* New York: Norton.

Rossi, E., & Ryan, M. (1986). *Mind-body communication in hypnosis.* New York: Irvington.

Watzlawick, Paul (Ed.) (1984). *The invented reality: How do we know what we believe we know?* New York: Norton.

2

DECONSTRUCTION AND THERAPY

Michael White

LEST SOME READERS be disappointed, before proceeding with my discussion of deconstruction and therapy I should inform you that this paper is not about the deconstruction of the knowledges and the practices of specific and established models of therapy, or about the deconstruction of any particular therapy "movement." Rather, in this paper I have chosen to cast certain practices of therapy within the frame provided by deconstruction.

As the first and foremost concern of my professional life relates to what happens in the therapeutic context, at the outset of this paper I will present several stories of therapy. I would like to emphasize the fact that, due to space considerations, these stories are glossed. They do not adequately represent the disorderly process of therapy – the ups and downs of that adventure that we refer to as therapy. Thus, there is a simplicity reflected in these accounts that cannot be found in the work itself.

Elizabeth

Elizabeth, a sole parent,* initially consulted me about her two daughters, aged 12 and 15 years. She was concerned about their persistent

This paper first appeared in the *Dulwich Centre Newsletter*, 1991, *3*, 1–21.
*I prefer the description "sole parent" over the description "single parent." In our culture, it appears that "single" has so many negative connotations,

antagonism towards her, their frequent tantrums, their abuse of her, and their apparent unhappiness. These problems had been upsetting to Elizabeth for some considerable time, and she was concerned that she might never recover from the despair that she was experiencing. She had come to the interview alone because her children refused to accompany her. As Elizabeth described these problems to me, she revealed that she had begun to experience what she thought might be "hate" for them, and this had been distressing her all the more.

While discussing with Elizabeth her concerns, I first asked about how these problems were affecting the lives of family members, and about the extent to which they were interfering in family relationships. I then asked more specifically about how these problems had been influencing her thoughts about herself: What did she believe these problems reflected about her as a parent? What conclusions had she come to about herself as a mother? Tearfully, Elizabeth confessed that she had concluded that she was a failure as a mother. With this disclosure I began to understand something of the private story that Elizabeth had been living by.

I then inquired as to how the view that she was a failure was compelling of Elizabeth in her relationship with her children. In response to this question, she gave details of the guilt that she experienced over not having sustained a "more ideal" family environment, of her highly tenuous and apologetic interaction with her daughters, and of the extent to which she felt bound to submit herself to their evaluation of her.

Was the havoc that the view of failure, and its associated guilt, was wreaking in her life and her relationships acceptable to her? Or would Elizabeth feel more comfortable if she broke her life and her relationships free of the tyranny of this view and its associated guilt? In response to these questions, Elizabeth made it clear, in no uncertain terms, that the current status of her relationship with her children was quite untenable, and that it was time for her to intervene and have more to say about the direction of her life and the shape of this relationship.

---

including of incompleteness, of being unmarried, of failure – of not having made the grade. However, at least to my mind, the word "sole" conjures up something entirely different. It carries a recognition of the extraordinary responsibility that these parents face and of the strength necessary to achieve what they achieve. And, as well, a second meaning is not hard to discern – "soul." Soul is about essence, and for persons to refer to themselves as "soul parents" is for them to recognize the "heartfulness" that they provide, that their children depend upon to "see them through."

I encouraged Elizabeth to explore how she had been recruited into
this view that she was a failure as a mother and as a person, and
about the mechanisms by which her guilt had been provoked. What
experiences had been most instrumental in this recruitment? Did she
think that women were more vulnerable to being recruited into the
view that they had failed their children, or was it more likely that men
would be recruited into this view? On this point she had no doubt —
women!

The exploration of these questions brought forth some of the specifics of Elizabeth's recruitment into the view that she was a failure (for
example, her experience as the recipient of abuse at the hands of her
former husband),* and the wider context of the gender-specific nature
of this construction (for example, the inequitable social structures that
reinforce this view for sole parents who are women, and the prevalence
of mother-blaming in our culture).

As we explored the various ways that the view that she was a failure
had affected her life, and some of the details of how she was recruited
into this view, Elizabeth began to experience in herself an identity distinct in relation to this view — failure no longer spoke to her of her identity. This development cleared the way for us to distinguish some of the
areas of her life that had not been co-opted by this view.

I partly facilitated the identification of these distinctions by providing Elizabeth with an account of the myriad of ways that the idea of
failure, and its associated guilt, had tyrannized the lives of other
women with whom I had talked — other women who had been subject
to similar processes of recruitment. I then said that it was my understanding that this sort of tyrannization was never totally effective,
that it had never entirely succeeded in eclipsing the lives of these
women. I gave examples: "Some of these women had escaped the effects of this view of failure in their relationships with women friends,
and others had kept alive their hopes that things could be different."
In response to this, Elizabeth identified instances in several areas of
her life in which she had been able to resist this tyranny.

I asked Elizabeth whether she thought this resistance was a positive or negative development in her life. As she said that this was a
positive development, I inquired as to why she believed this to be
so. During our subsequent discussion, it was determined that these
instances reflected that she had not totally submitted to these nega-

---

*The work undertaken here did include exploration of the possibility that
the children may have been abused by their father. The findings disconfirmed
this as a possibility.

tive views of who she was, and that she had some resolve to challenge the tyranny of guilt. This provided Elizabeth with evidence that her life had not been dominated by failure.

Then, through a series of questions, I encouraged Elizabeth to trace the history of this refusal. In the process of this, she identified a couple of historical figures who had witnessed some developments in her capacity to protest certain injustices. In our subsequent discussion, Elizabeth put both of us in touch with alternative versions of who she might be, versions of herself that she clearly preferred. As these alternative and preferred versions emerged from the shadows through our discussion, they became more available to Elizabeth to enter her life into.

As Elizabeth's enthusiasm for this alternative knowledge of who she was as a person became more apparent, I discussed with her the importance of seizing the initiative in putting others in touch with what she had discovered. To this end, I encouraged her to identify persons who might provide an appropriate audience to this other version of who she might be, persons who might participate in the acknowledgment of and the authentication of this version.* We then discussed various ideas about how she might introduce this other version of herself to these persons, and ideas about how these persons could be invited to respond to what Elizabeth was enthusiastic about in regard to these discoveries.

As part of the exploration of other versions of who Elizabeth might be, I had asked her to identify what it was about herself that she would personally like to have in a mother. Having articulated some details of this, I suggested that it might be important to catch her children up with this. Would she be prepared to tell them what she had discovered about herself as a woman and as a mother that she could appreciate and to continue to remind them of this from time to time? This struck a chord. Elizabeth seemed rather joyful about the idea. I was quick to share my prediction that, in the first place, it was unlikely that Elizabeth's efforts to "reclaim her life" would be greeted with great enthusiasm by her children.

---

*In part, this work is premised on the narrative metaphor, which brings with it a specific non-essentialist account of authenticity. According to this metaphor, ordinarily persons achieve a sense of authenticity when (a) they perform particular claims about their lives, claims that relate to particular self-narratives, and when (b) this performance is witnessed by themselves and/ or others. This would suggest that there is a range of possible authenticities that persons might experience, and that this range is determined by the available stock of stories that persons have about their lives.

Elizabeth went away determined to have more to say about who she was and to decline her children's invitations for her to subject herself to their constant evaluation and surveillance. Initially, her daughters' response to her taking over the authorship of her own life was dramatic. They came up with some very creative ideas for turning back the clock. However, Elizabeth persevered through this, and then everyone's life went forward. She forged a new connection with her daughters, they became more enthusiastic about life, the abuse subsided, and Elizabeth reported that, for the first time, they had the sort of mother-daughter relationship that she had desired. They had become more connected as confidantes, able to discuss important matters of concern with each other.

Amy

Amy, age 23, sought help in her struggle with anorexia nervosa. This was a long-standing problem, and it had withstood many attempts to resolve it. I first reviewed with Amy the effects that anorexia nervosa was having in the various domains of her life—including the social, the emotional, the intellectual, and of course, the physical. In response to this review, the extent to which anorexia nervosa was making it difficult for her to make an appearance in any of these domains became apparent to both of us.

We then spent time exploring, in greater detail, how anorexia nervosa was affecting Amy's interactions with others. I wasn't surprised to learn that it had her constantly comparing herself to others, and that it had instilled in her a sense that she was being perpetually evaluated by others. Apart from this, it was enforcing a shroud of secrecy around her life and isolating her from others.

How was the anorexia nervosa affecting Amy's attitude towards, and interactions with, herself? What was it requiring her to do to herself? Predictably, it was requiring her to watch over herself, to police herself. I had her engaging in operations on her own body, attempting to forge it into a shape that might be considered acceptable—a "docile body." And it had her punishing her own body for its transgressions.

I then engaged Amy in an investigation of how she had been recruited into these various practices, procedures, and attitudes; these "disciplines of the self" according to gendered specifications for personhood; this hierarchical and disciplinary attitude and relationship to her own body. In this investigation, Amy was able to identify a history to this recruitment though familial, cultural, and social contexts. In our subsequent discussion, anorexia nervosa appeared as the embodiment of these attitudes, practices, and contexts.

Through this therapeutic process, anorexia nervosa was "unmasked," and Amy became increasingly alienated from it. The various taken-for-granted practices and attitudes that anorexia nervosa "relied upon for its survival" no longer spoke to her of the truth of who she was as a person. Would Amy be content to continue to submit to anorexia nervosa's claims on her life, to continue to defer to its requirements? Or was she more attracted to the idea of challenging its claims to her life and to the idea of taking her life over and making it her own?

Amy had no hesitation in stating that it was time to make her life her own, so together we reviewed the available evidence that she might be able to do so: events that reflected resistance to the practices and attitudes upon which that state of "the government of self" called anorexia nervosa depended. This led to the identification of various developments or events that were of an anti-anorectic nature.* I asked Amy to evaluate these anti-anorectic developments: Did she consider these to be the more attractive and desirable developments in her life, or did she consider them trivial and unappealing? In response, Amy judged these developments to be the preferred developments in her life. I then engaged her in a conversation about why she thought these developments were desirable, and about why she thought they personally suited her.

As Amy seemed to be more strongly supporting these anti-anorectic activities, I encouraged her to help me understand the basis or foundation of these in her life. I also encouraged her to reflect upon what these preferred developments said about what she believed was important for her life. During the ensuring discussion, Amy began to more fully articulate a preferred version of who she might be, one that incorporated alternative knowledges of life. This version gradually became available to her to enter her life into and to live by.

As Amy began to articulate and perform this alternative and preferred version of who she was, she took various steps to engage others in her project to reclaim her life. These steps were encouraged by my

---

*David Epston, of Auckland, New Zealand, has joined with a number of persons who have sought therapy for anorexia nervosa in establishing the "Anti-Anorexia League." The aims of this league are to unmask the "voice" of anorexia nervosa and to identify, document, and circulate knowledges and practices that are counter to those knowledges and practices upon which the anorexia nervosa depends.

observation that "fieldwork" was an integral part of any such project. I had asked Amy to identify who, of all those persons who had known her, might be the least inaccessible to this new view of who she was.* She decided to begin by re-introducing herself to those who were "far away" and contacted several school friends whom she had not seen for several years. Experiencing success in this, she moved to her more immediate social network, which included members of her family of origin, whom she began to invite along to the therapy session. Within the therapeutic context, these family members contributed significantly to the acknowledgment of, and the authentication of, Amy's preferred claims about her life and to Amy's ability to separate her life from anorexia nervosa.

Anne and John

John and Anne, a separating couple, sought therapy in an attempt to resolve their intense conflicts over custody and access in relation to their children and over property settlement. At the outset of the first meeting, they entered into a fierce dispute, each presenting various claims and counterclaims; only occasionally did they glance furtively in my direction. After a time, I interrupted, thanking them both for being so open about the problems they were having with each other and for providing such a clear demonstration of how things go for them.

After a pause, John and Anne launched into a fresh round of accusations. Fortunately, I was again able to interrupt, explaining that I believed I had a reasonable understanding of their experience of the relationship and informing them that further demonstrations of this would be unnecessary. Two more interruptions were necessary before the couple seemed convinced of this.

In the breathing space that followed, I asked to what extent this pattern of interacting – the adversarial one that they had just so clearly demonstrated – was dominating their relationship. How was this adversarial pattern influencing their perceptions of each other and of their relationship? And how were these perceptions of each other and of their relationship influencing their responses to each other? What did this adversarial pattern have them doing to each other that might be against their better judgment?

*Initial steps in fieldwork should not be overly ambitious. Questions like this contribute to more humble beginnings and to increased possibilities in terms of the circulation and the authentication of alternative knowledges of self.

After reviewing, with Anne and John, the extent to which this adversarial pattern had been dictating the terms of their relationship, I asked them if this had become their preferred way of responding to each other. Did they find this adversarial pattern captivating? Did this way of being with each other suit them best? Was this adversarial pattern of relating to each other tailor-made for them? Did they experience this way of being together as enriching their lives?

Both claimed that this was not their preferred way of relating to the other, and neither could resist adding that it did seem the preference of the other partner. Since John and Anne claimed that this was not their preferred way of going about things, I suggested that it was unlikely that they had invented it for themselves.

I then encouraged Anne and John to help me understand how they had been recruited into this pattern of responding to differences of opinion over particular issues, and to identify the history of this pattern. Where had they witnessed this pattern before? How were they originally introduced to these techniques for dealing with each other, and what situations first exposed them to these techniques? In what contexts would they expect to find these patterns commonplace, and what justifications are referred to most frequently in order to sustain them? How were they encouraged to subject their relationship to these patterns, to live their relationship out through these patterns?

During this discussion, as John and Anne articulated their experience of this adversarial pattern, it became apparent to them that their relationship was no longer at one with this pattern – they were able to think otherwise about their relationship. I asked them if they were prepared to leave what was left of their relationship to the designs of these patterns, or if they would prefer to intervene and have more to say about the direction of events – to determine a design for what was left of their relationship that would suit them both? In response to this question, John and Anne said that the adversarial pattern was impoverishing of their lives, and both indicated that they wanted to free themselves from its dictates.

We then worked to determine what basis there was for an attempt to retrieve what was left of their relationship and managed to identify several interactions that had not been dominated by the adversarial pattern. One of these related to the extent to which they had been able to evade this pattern for a good part of the interview. Did Anne and John find these interactions with each other more satisfying? Were they at all enthusiastic about these developments? Or were they more attracted to their more familiar ways of being with each other?

As they determined that they were more attracted to this alternative way of interacting with each other, I asked John and Anne what they thought this way of being together had going for it, and why they thought it would suit them to extend these developments. Following this I introduced questions that encouraged them to historicize these more positive developments in their relationship. In responding to these questions, Anne and John recalled a couple that they had befriended early in their marriage. This couple had witnessed several instances upon which they had been able to resolve a dispute satisfactorily and equitably. A review of this other couple's experience of John and Anne's relationship led to the resurrection of historically situated problem-solving knowledges; although the process was not without hitches, these became available to them to resolve their disputes over custody, access, and property.

Robert

Robert was referred to therapy over abusive behavior in relation to his partner and one of his children. This abuse had only been recently disclosed. He had agreed to leave the family home, and the appropriate police and court measures were in the process of being instituted.

During our early contact, discussion centered on Robert's responsibility for perpetrating the abuse,* on the identification of the survivors' experiences of abuse, on the real short-term and possible long-term traumatic effects of this on the life of the survivors, and on determining what he might do to take responsibility to mend what might be mended.

Following this work, I asked Robert whether he would be prepared to join me in some speculation about the conditions and the character of men's abusive behavior. This he agreed to do, so I asked him a series of questions within the category of those represented below:

- If a man wanted to control and to dominate another person, what sort of structures and conditions could he arrange that would make this possible?
- If a man desired to dominate another person, particularly a woman or a child, what sort of attitudes would be necessary in order to justify this?
- If a man decided to make someone his captive, particularly a

---

*I would refer readers to Alan Jenkin's book *Invitations to Responsibility* (1990), for an excellent discussion of this and other aspects of work with men who abuse others.

woman or a child, what sort of strategies and techniques of power would make this feasible?

During this speculation, particular knowledges about men's ways of being that are subjugating of others were articulated, techniques and strategies that men could rely upon to institute this subjugation were identified, and various structures and conditions that support abusive behavior were reviewed. I then asked Robert to determine which of these attitudes he had given his life to, which of these strategies had been dominant in shaping his relationships with others, and which of these conditions and structures had provided the framework for his life. This was followed by further discussion centered on a review of the historical processes through which Robert had been recruited into the life space that was fabricated of these attitudes, techniques, and structures.

Robert was invited to take a position on these attitudes, strategies, and structures. Would he continue to subject his life to this particular knowledge of men's way of being? To what extent did he think it was reasonable to live life as "power's instrument," as an instrument of terror? To what extent did he wish to cooperate with these strategies and tactics that so devastated the lives of others? In view of his developing understanding of the real effects of his actions, did he think it acceptable to depend upon these structures and conditions as a framework for his life?

As this work progressed, Robert began to experience a separation from these attitudes and an alienation from these structures and techniques of power and control. His previously familiar and taken-for-granted ways of being in relation to women and children – and for that matter, his previously familiar and taken-for-granted ways of being with other men – no longer spoke to him of the truth of who he was as a man. For Robert to challenge his abusive behavior no longer meant taking action against his own "nature," and he was now able to take entire responsibility for the abuse that he had perpetrated on others.

In the space that Robert stepped into as a result of this separation, we were able to find various unique outcomes, that is, occasions upon which his behavior had not been compelled by those previously familiar and taken-for-granted ways of being as a man. I asked Robert to evaluate these unique outcomes. Did he see these outcomes as desirable? Did he feel positively about them? Or were they of no consequence to him? As Robert concluded that these outcomes were desirable, I asked him to share with me how he had reached this conclusion.

As our work progressed, the identification of these unique outcomes

provided a point of entry for an "archeology" of alternative and preferred knowledges of men's ways of being, knowledges that Robert
began to enter. For example, in response to my encouragement to give
meaning to these unique outcomes, to determine what ways of "being"
as a man were reflected in them, Robert recalled an uncle who was
quite unlike other men in his family; this was a man who was certainly
compassionate and non-abusive. Robert subsequently did some home-
work on this uncle, and this contributed significantly to his knowledge
of some of the more intimate particularities of this alternative way of
being.

Robert's family had signaled a strong desire to explore the possibilities of reuniting.* As Robert had begun to separate from those attitudes and practices that had justified and supported his abusive behavior, and as he had entered into an exploration of alternative and
preferred knowledges of men's ways of being, the time seemed right to
convene a meeting with the family.** Understanding his responsibility to provide safeguards to family members, he agreed to participate
in certain structures that would contribute significantly to the security of family members. These included (a) a meeting with representa-
tives† of his partner and his child to disclose his responsibility for and
the nature of the abuse, (b) a willingness to participate in weekly escape from secrecy meetings‡ with his family and the nominated repre-

---

*The counseling of family members in relation to the abuse and other
issues was undertaken concurrently in a different context.

**I do not believe it is ever sufficient for men to take entire responsibility
for perpetrating abuse, to identify the experience of those abused, to get in
touch with the short-term and possible long-term effects of the abuse, to
develop a sincere apology, to work on ways of repairing what might be re-
paired, and to challenge the attitudes that justify such behavior and the
conditions and techniques of power that make abuse possible.

If that is where is ends, although the man may experience genuine remorse,
he is likely to re-offend because he has no other knowledges of men's ways of
being to live by. For there to be any semblance of security that this will not
occur, I believe that it is essential that these men be engaged in the identification and the performance of alternative knowledges of men's ways of being.

†These representatives must be nominated by the child and the non-
offending spouse. They can be relatives who do not have a history of abusive
behavior or persons known to them in the community.

‡Escape from secrecy meetings are held weekly in the first place, and gradually move to a monthly basis over a period of two years. At each of these
meetings, events of the past week or so are reviewed. Events which reflect a
reappearance of any of those attitudes, strategies, conditions, and structures
that provided the context for past abuse can be identified and challenged.
Different family members take turns at minute-taking for these meetings

sentatives, and (c) a preparedness to cooperate with other family members in the development of a contingency plan should any family member again feel threatened by abuse.

Over time, Robert traded a neglectful and strategic life for one that he, and others, considered to be caring, open, and direct.

An Interview With A Family

The interview had reached a point at which the therapist decided that it was time to hear from the team members who had been observing the interview from behind a one-way screen. The therapist and the family traded places with the team members; it was now their turn to be an audience to the team members' reflections. The team members first introduced themselves to the family. They then proceeded to share their responses to what family members had judged, or had seemed attracted to, as preferred developments in their lives and relationships.

It was the team members' task to relate to these preferred developments as one might relate to a mystery, a mystery that only family members could unravel. Initially, each observation from a team member was followed by questions that might encourage family members to account for these developments, and questions that might engage them in speculation about what these developments might mean. Team members also addressed questions to each other about these developments, inviting further speculation about them. In this way, the family members' fascination in relation to previously neglected aspects of their lived experience was engaged, and they were provoked to enlist their "knowledgeableness" in regard to their own lives.

Some team members then began to ask other team members about why they found a particular development interesting. These questions

---

and in the posting of these minutes to the therapist (frequently with the assistance of the representatives). The family member whose turn it is to take this responsibility is encouraged to append his or her confidential comments to these minutes. If the therapist does not receive the minutes of a meeting on schedule, s/he immediately follows this up. From time to time the therapist joins these meetings to review progress.

It is not possible to overemphasize the importance of local accountability in this work. State intervention can be highly effective in bringing about the immediate cessation of abuse, but local accountability structures are essential to the establishment of secure contexts.

For an excellent discussion of the significance of secrecy in structuring a context for abuse, I would refer readers to Amanda Kamsler and Lesley Laing's "Putting an end to secrecy" (1990).

encouraged team members to situate their reflections within the context of their personal experience and their imagination. Team members then invited each other to make transparent what they understood to be the intentions behind their reflections.

Following this, the family and the team again traded places, and the therapist proceeded to interview family members about their experience of the team's reflections, about what comments and questions family members found to be of interest and to the point, and about what comments and questions were not so. As family members began to relate those comments and questions that caught their interest, the therapist asked them to help her understand why they found these interesting and what realizations and/or conclusions accompanied these comments and questions. The therapist then encouraged family members' speculative assessment about how these realizations and conclusions could affect their day-to-day lives.

The therapist brought the interview to a close by inviting family members and the reflecting team to interview her about the interview, so that she might situate her comments and questions within the context of her own personal experience, imagination, and purposes.

DECONSTRUCTION

These stories about therapy portray a number of recurrent practices. I believe that most of these practices relate to what could be referred to as a "deconstructive method," which will be explicated in the following discussion.

I should preface this discussion of deconstruction with an admission—I am not an academic but, for the want of a better word, a therapist. It is my view that not being situated in the academic world allows me certain liberties, including the freedom to break some rules—for example, to use the term deconstruction in a way that may not be in accord with its strict Derridian sense—and to refer to writers who may not generally be considered to be proposing a deconstructivist method.

According to my rather loose definition, deconstruction has to do with procedures that subvert taken-for-granted realities and practices: those so-called "truths" that are split off from the conditions and the context of their production; those disembodied ways of speaking that hide their biases and prejudices; and those familiar practices of self and of relationship that are subjugating of persons' lives. Many of the methods of deconstruction render strange these familiar and everyday taken-for-granted realities and practices by objectifying them. In this sense, the methods of deconstruction are methods that "exoticize the domestic."

> The sociologist who chooses to study his (*sic*) own world in its nearest and most familiar aspects should not, as the ethnologist would, domesticate the exotic, but, if I may venture the expression, exoticize the domestic, through a break with his (*sic*) initial relation of intimacy with modes of life and thought which remain opaque to him (*sic*) because they are too familiar. In fact the movement towards the originary, and the ordinary, world should be the culmination of a movement toward alien and extraordinary worlds. (Bourdieu, 1988, pp. xi–xii)

According to Bourdieu, exoticizing the domestic through the objectification of a familiar and taken-for-granted world facilitates the "reappropriation" of the self. In referring to the reappropriation of the self, I do not believe that he is proposing an essentialist view of self, that in this re-appropriation persons will "find" themselves. Rather, he is suggesting that through the objectification of a familiar world, we might become more aware of the extent to which certain "modes of life and thought" shape our existence, and that we might then be in a position to choose to live by other "modes of life and thought."

If Bourdieu's work can be considered deconstructive, then it is so in a specific sense. His primary interest is in the extent to which a person's situation in a social structure – for example, in academia – is constituting of that person's stance on issues in life.

However, we can also consider deconstruction in other senses: for example, the deconstruction of self-narrative and the dominant cultural knowledges that persons live by; the deconstruction of practices of self and of relationship that are dominantly cultural; and the deconstruction of the discursive practices of our culture.

Deconstruction is premised on what is generally referred to as a "critical constructivist" or, as I would prefer, a "constitutionalist" perspective on the world. From this perspective, it is proposed that persons' lives are shaped by the meaning that they ascribe to their experience, by their situation in social structures, and by the language practices and cultural practices of self and of relationship that these lives are recruited into. This constitutionalist perspective is at variance with the dominant structuralist (behavior reflects the structure of the mind) and functionalist (behavior serves a purpose for the system) perspectives of the world of psychotherapy.

In the following discussion, I will consider first the deconstruction of narrative; second, the deconstruction of modern practices of power; and third, the deconstruction of discursive practices. However, I believe, with Michel Foucault (1980), that a domain of knowledge is a domain of power, and that a domain of power is a domain of knowledge. Thus, inasmuch as meaning relates to knowledge, and inasmuch as practices relate to power, I believe that meaning, structures, and practices are inseparable in their constitutive aspects.

NARRATIVE

Meaning

The idea that it is the meaning which persons attribute to their experience that is constitutive of those persons' lives has encouraged social scientists to explore the nature of the frames that facilitate the interpretation of experience. Many of these social scientists have proposed that it is the narrative or story that provides the primary frame for this interpretation, for the activity of meaning-making: that it is through the narratives or the stories that persons have about their own lives and the lives of others that they make sense of their experience. Not only do these stories determine the meaning that persons give to experience, it is argued, but these stories also largely determine which aspects of experience persons select out for expression. In addition, inasmuch as action is prefigured on meaning-making, these stories determine real effects in terms of the shaping of persons' lives.

This perspective should not be confused with that which proposes that stories function as a reflection of life or as a mirror for life. Instead, the narrative metaphor proposes that persons live their lives by stories—that these stories are shaping of life, and that they have real, not imagined, effects—and that these stories provide the structure of life.

In the family therapy literature there are many examples of the conflating of the narrative metaphor and of various conversation/linguistic metaphors. As these metaphors are situated in distinctly different traditions of thought, and as some are at variance with others, I will here present some further thoughts about the narrative metaphor that I hope will adequately distinguish it.

Narrative Structure

Bruner (1986), in referring to texts, proposed that stories are composed of dual landscapes—a "landscape of action" and a "landscape of consciousness." The landscape of action is constituted of (a) events that are linked together in (b) particular sequences through the (c) temporal dimension—through past, present and future—and according to (d) specific plots. In a text, the landscape of action provides the reader with a perspective on the thematic unfolding of events across time.

The landscape of consciousness is significantly constituted by the interpretations of the characters in the story, and also by those of the reader as s/he enters, at the invitation of the writer, the consciousness of these characters. The landscape of consciousness features the meanings derived by characters and readers through "reflection" on the events and plots as they unfold through the landscape of action. Perceptions, thoughts, speculation, realizations, and conclusions dominate this landscape, and many of these relate to:

(a) the determination of the desires and the preferences of the characters,
(b) the identification of their personal and relationship characteristics and qualities,
(c) the clarification of their intentional states—for example, their motives and their purposes—and
(d) the substantiation of the values and beliefs of these characters.

As these desires, qualities, intentional states and beliefs become sufficiently elaborated through the text, they coalesce into "commitments" that determine particular careers in life—"life-styles."

If we assume that there is an identity between the structure of texts and the structure of the stories or narratives that persons live by, and if we take as our interest the constitution of lives through stories, we might then consider the details of how persons live their lives through landscapes of action and landscapes of consciousness.

Determinacy

What is the origin of these stories or narratives that are constitutive of persons' lives? The stories that persons live by are rarely, if ever, "radically" constructed—it is not a matter of their being made up, "out of the blue," so to speak. Our culturally available and appropriate stories about personhood and about relationship have been historically constructed and negotiated in communities of persons and within the context of social structures and institutions. Inevitably, there is a canonical dimension to the stories that persons live by.

Thus, these stories are inevitably framed by our dominant cultural knowledges. These knowledges are not about discoveries regarding the "nature" of persons and of relationships, but are constructed knowledges that are specifying of a particular strain of personhood and of relationship. For example, in regard to dominant knowledges of personhood, in the West these establish a highly individual and gender distinct specification for ways of being in the world.

Indeterminacy Within Determinacy

If it is the case that the stories that persons have about their lives circumscribe the meanings that they give to experience, as well as the aspects of experience that they select out for expression, and if it is the case that these meanings have particular and real effects in persons' lives, then we have a strong argument for determinacy. And this argument for determinacy is strengthened upon consideration of the extent to which such stories are canonical in that they are co-authored within a community of persons, and in that they are historically constructed within the context of specific institutions and social structures.

However, despite the fact that these stories contribute a certain determinancy to life, rarely do they handle all of the contingencies that arise in "life as lived" in anything like an accomplished way. Just as with texts, in reference to life as lived, the stories that persons live by are full of gaps and inconsistencies, and, as well, these stories constantly run up against contradictions. It is the resolution of these gaps, inconsistencies, and contradictions that contributes to a certain indeterminacy of life; it is these gaps, inconsistencies, and contradictions that provoke persons to engage actively in the performance of unique meaning or, as Bruner (1990) would have it, in "meaning-making."

Thus, when considering the proposition that life is constituted through an ongoing storying and re-storying of experience, we are considering a process of "indeterminacy within determinacy"—or to what Geertz (1986) concludes to be a "copying that originates":

> The wrenching question, sour and disabused, that Lionel Trilling somewhere quotes an eighteenth-century aesthetician as asking—"How Comes It that we all start out Originals and end up Copies?"—finds . . . an answer that is surprisingly reassuring: it is the copying that originates. (p. 380)

THE DECONSTRUCTION OF
NARRATIVE

Externalizing Conversations

For the deconstruction of the stories that persons live by, I have proposed the objectification of the problems for which persons seek therapy (for example, White, 1984, 1986, 1989; White and Epston, 1990). This objectification engages persons in externalizing conversations in relation to that which they find problematic, rather than internalizing conversations. This externalizing conversation generates what might be called a counter-language or, as David Epston has recently proposed, an "anti-language" (personal communication).

These externalizing conversations "exoticize the domestic" in that they encourage persons to identify the private stories and the cultural knowledges that they live by; those stories and knowledges that guide their lives and that speak to them of their identity. These externalizing conversations assist persons to unravel, across time, the constitution of their self and of their relationships.

Externalizing conversations are initiated by encouraging persons to provide an account of the effects of the problem on their lives. This can include its effects on their emotional states, familial and peer relationships, social and work spheres, etc., with a special emphasis on how it has affected their "view" of themselves and of their relationships. Then, persons are invited to map the influence that these views or perceptions have on their lives, including on their interactions with others. This is often followed by some investigation of how persons have been recruited into these views.

As persons become engaged in these externalizing conversations, their private stories cease to speak to them of their identity and of the truth of their relationships — these private stories are no longer transfixing of persons' lives. Persons experience a separation from, and an alienation in relation to, these stories. In the space established by this separation, persons are free to explore alternative and preferred knowledges of who they might be, alternative and preferred knowledges into which they might enter their lives.

Unique Outcomes and Alternative Stories

How are these alternative knowledges generated and/or resurrected? What are the points of entry to these other versions of who persons might be? As persons separate from the dominant or "totalizing" stories that are constitutive of their lives, it becomes more possible for them to orient themselves to aspects of their experience that contradict these knowledges. Such contradictions are ever present, and, as well, they are many and varied. Previously, following Goffman, I have referred to these contradictions as "unique outcomes" (White, 1988a, 1989; White and Epston, 1990), and it is these that provide a gateway to what we might consider to be the alternative territories of a person's life.

For an event to comprise a unique outcome, it must be qualified as such by the person to whose life the event relates. Following the identification of events that are candidates for a unique outcome status, it is important that persons be invited to evaluate these events; are these events judged to be significant or to be irrelevant? Do these events represent preferred outcomes, or do they not? Do persons find these developments appealing? Are persons attracted to some of the new possibilities that might accompany these events? If these events are judged to represent preferred outcomes, then persons can be encouraged to give an account of why they believe this to be the case.

When it is established that particular events qualify as unique outcomes in that they are judged to be both significant and preferred, the therapist can facilitate the generation of and/or resurrection of alternative stories by orienting him/herself to these unique outcomes as one might orient oneself to a mystery. These stories are mysteries that only persons can unravel as they respond to the therapist's curiosity about them. As persons take up the task of unraveling such mysteries, they immediately engage in storytelling and meaning-making.

To facilitate this process, which I have called "reauthoring," the therapist can ask a variety of questions, including those that might be referred to as "landscape-of-action" questions and "landscape-of-consciousness" questions.* Landscape-of-action questions encourage persons to situate unique outcomes in sequences of events that unfold across time according to particular plots. Landscape-of-consciousness questions encourage persons to reflect on and to determine the meaning of those developments that occur in the landscape of action.

Landscape-of-Action Questions

Landscape-of-action questions can be referenced to the past, present, and future, and are effective in bringing forth alternative landscapes that stretch through these temporal domains. In the following discus-

---

*Elsewhere I have referred to landscape of action questions as "unique account" questions, and to landscape of consciousness questions as "unique redescription" questions (White, 1988a).

sion, due to considerations of space, I will focus mainly on those questions that resurrect and generate alternative historical landscapes, that is, questions that are historicizing of "unique outcomes." However, some future-oriented landscape-of-action questions will feature in some of the examples that I give.

Questions that historicize unique outcomes are particularly effective in bringing forth alternative landscapes of action. These questions bridge those preferred developments of the present with the past; they encourage persons to identify the history of unique outcomes by locating them within particular sequences of events that unfold through time. Often, these questions assist persons to plot the history of the alternative landscape of action to the extent that they reach back and predate the landscapes of action of the previously dominant and "problem-saturated" stories that persons have had about their lives.

Landscape-of-action questions can focus on both the recent history and the more distant history of unique outcomes. Those landscape-of-action questions that bring forth the recent history of the unique outcome mostly relate to its more immediate circumstances:

- How did you get yourself ready to take this step? What preparations led up to it?
- Just prior to taking this step, did you nearly turn back? If so, how did you stop yourself from doing so? Looking back from this vantage point, what did you notice yourself doing that might have contributed to this achievement?
- Could you give me some background to this? What were the circumstances surrounding this achievement? Did anyone else make a contribution? If so, would you describe this?
- What were you thinking at the time? Have you been advising yourself differently? What did you tell yourself that pulled you through on this occasion?
- What developments have occurred in other areas of your life that may relate to this? How do you think these developments prepared the way for you to take these steps?

The therapist can encourage the participation of other persons in this generation/resurrection of alternative and preferred landscapes of action. Including members of the community of persons who have participated historically in the negotiation of, and distribution of, the dominant story of the person's life is particularly helpful. For example, other family members can make particularly significant and authenticating contributions to these alternative landscapes of action:

- How do you think your parents managed to keep their act together in the face of this crisis?
- What have you witnessed Harry doing recently that could throw some light on how he was able to take this step?
- What did you see Sally doing leading up to this achievement? How does this contribute to an understanding of how she got ready for it?
- Would you describe to me the circumstances surrounding this development in your son's life? Did anyone else contribute to this, and if so, in what way?

The following questions provide examples of those that bring forth the more distant history of the unique outcome. These invite the identification of events and experiences that have a less immediate relation to the unique outcomes. As with those questions that bring forth the recent history of the unique outcome, it is helpful to engage, as co-authors, members of the community of persons who contributed historically to the negotiation and distribution of the dominant story that is repudiated in this reauthoring process.

- What can you tell me about your history that would help me to understand how you managed to take this step?
- Are you aware of any past achievements that might, in some way, provide the backdrop for this recent development?
- What have you witnessed in your life up to now that could have given you at least some hint that this was a possibility for you?
- I would like to get a better grasp of this development. What did you notice yourself doing, or thinking, as a younger person, that could have provided some vital clue that this development was on the horizon of your life?
- Please think about your son's recent feat and reflect on his life as you have known it. With hindsight, what do you recall him doing that could have foreshadowed this, that could have given you a lead on this?
- It seems that what Mary and Joe have recently accomplished is a manifestation of some behind-the-scenes work that they have been doing to retrieve their relationship. Were you aware of any signs that this work was taking place? If so, what were these signs?

These examples provide just some of the options for engaging persons in the generation/resurrection of alternative landscapes of action, and I believe that it is not possible to exhaust the choices for this sort of interaction with persons. For example, questions can be introduced to encourage persons to bring forth the recent history and distant history of those events in history that have foreshadowed the current unique outcomes.

As persons begin to articulate preferred events in these alternative landscapes of action, and as they become more engaged in the arrangement or linking of these events in particular sequences through time, they can be encouraged to explicitly name the alternative plot or the counterplot that is suggested by this arrangement. The naming of the alternative plot or counterplot is important, for it, among other things, (a) contributes very significantly to persons' sense of their life going forward in preferred ways; (b) makes possible the attribution of meaning to events or experiences that would otherwise be neglected or considered to be of little significance; (c) facilitates the session-by-session sorting and linking of the events that have taken place between sessions; and (d) provides for persons a sense of knowing what might be the next step in their preferred direction in life.

The alternative plot or counterplot is often named quite spontaneously in the process of this work. When it is not, the therapist can facilitate this by asking questions that encourage persons to generate descriptions in juxtaposition to the previously dominant plot. Through these questions, persons who have been concerned about "losing their relationship" (previously dominant plot), may determine that these developments in the alternative landscape of action suggest that they are on the path of "reclaiming their relationship" (alternative plot or counterplot). A person who concludes that "self-neglect" has been highly influential in his/her life (previously dominant plot) may decide that the developments in the alternative landscape of action reflect that s/he has been engaged in a "self-nurturing project" (alternative plot or counterplot).

Landscape-of-Consciousness Questions

Landscape-of-consciousness questions encourage persons to review the developments as they unfold through the alternative landscapes of action* and to determine what these might reveal about:

*Of course, the order of these questions can be reversed. Developments in the landscape of consciousness can be reviewed for what they might reveal about preferred developments in the landscape of consciousness. For example, "What did you see yourself doing that led you to this conclusion about your nature?" "What else have you witnessed yourself doing that reflects this belief?"

(a) the nature of their preferences and their desires,
(b) the character of various personal and relationship qualities,
(c) the constitution of their intentional states,
(d) the composition of their preferred values, beliefs, and lastly,
(e) the nature of their commitments.

Landscape-of-consciousness questions encourage the articulation and the performance of these alternative preferences, desires, personal and relationship qualities, and intentional states and beliefs, and this culminates in a "re-vision" of personal commitment in life.* It is through the performance of meaning in the landscape of consciousness that:

> ... people's beliefs and desires become sufficiently coherent and well organized as to merit being called "commitments" or "ways of life", and such coherences are seen as "dispositions" that characterize persons. (Bruner, 1990, p. 39)

The following questions provide an example of just some of the forms that landscape-of-consciousness questions might take. These invite persons to reflect on developments as they have unfolded in both the recent and the more distant history of the landscape of action.

- Let's reflect for a moment on these recent developments. What new conclusions might you reach about your tastes; about what is appealing to you; about what you are attracted to?
- What do these discoveries tell you about what you want for your life?
- I understand that you are more aware of the background of this turning point in Mary's life. How does this affect the picture that you have of her as a person?
- How would you describe the qualities that you experienced in your relationship at this earlier time, when you managed to support each other in the face of adversity?
- What do these developments inform you about what suits you as a person?

*The re-vision of intentional states is often begun ahead of the introduction of these landscape-of-consciousness questions with the institution of externalizing conversations in relation to the problem. This is achieved through questions like: "What does this problem have you doing that is against your better judgment/what you intend for your life/what you value/what you believe to be important?"

- In more fully appreciating what went into this achievement, what conclusions might you reach about what Harry intends for his life?
- It seems that we are both now more in touch with how you prepared yourself for this step. What does this reveal to you about your motives, or about the purposes you have for your life?
- What does this history of struggle suggest about what Jane believes to be important in life, about what she stands for?

As persons respond to landscape-of-action and landscape-of-consciousness questions, they engage in a reliving of experience and their lives are "retold." Alternative knowledges of self and of relationships are generated and/or resurrected; alternative modes of life and thought become available for persons to enter into. Throughout this reauthoring dialogue, the therapist plays a central role in challenging any early return to the canonical that would suggest that the unique outcome is self-explanatory.

Experience-of-Experience Questions

Experience-of-experience questions (White, 1988b) greatly facilitate the reauthoring of lives and relationships, and often they are more generative than those questions that encourage persons to reflect more directly on their lives. These questions encourage persons to provide an account of what they believe or imagine to be another person's experience of them. These experience-of-experience questions:

(a) invite persons to reach back into their stock of lived experience and to express certain aspects that have been forgotten or neglected with the passage of time, and
(b) recruit the imagination of persons in ways that are constitutive of alternative experiences of themselves.

Some examples of these experience-of-experience questions follow. In the examples, these questions are oriented first to alternative landscapes of action and second to alternative landscapes of consciousness. In the third place, examples are given of questions that encourage persons to bring forth the "intimate particularities" of future developments in these landscapes of action and landscapes of consciousness.

Of course, these questions are not asked in a barrage-like fashion. Instead, these questions are raised within the context of dialogue, and each is sensitively attuned to the responses triggered by the previous question.

(a) • If I had been a spectator to your life when you were a younger person, what do you think I might have witnessed you doing then that might help me to understand how you were able to achieve what you have recently achieved?
   • What do you think this tells me about what you have wanted for your life, and about what you have been trying for in your life?
   • How do you think that knowing this has affected my view of you as a person?
   • What do you think this might reveal to me about what you value most?
   • If you managed to keep this knowledge about who you are close to you over the next week or two, how would it affect the shape of your life?

(b) • Of all those persons who have known you, who would be least surprised that you have been able to take this step in challenging the problem's influence in your life?
   • What might they have witnessed you doing, in times past, that would have made it possible for them to predict that you could take such a step at this point in your life?*
   • What do you imagine this told them, at that time, about your capabilities?
   • What would they have assumed to be your purposes in taking this action at this point in your history?
   • How do you think this spoke to them of who you are, and about what you believe to be important?
   • Exactly what actions would you be committing yourself to if you were to more fully embrace this knowledge of who you are?

(c) • I would like to understand the foundations upon which this achievement rests. Of all those persons who have known you, who would be best placed to supply some details about these foundations?
   • What clues did this provide them with as to which developments in your life were most desirable to you?
   • What conclusions might they have reached about your intentions in building up these foundations?

*Daphne Hewson of the Macquarie University, Sydney, working from the perspectives of both narrative theory and social-cognitive psychology, has pioneered the development of prediction questions as a means of bringing forth the history of alternative stories.

- What could this have disclosed to them about the sort of life-style you are more suited to?
- If you were to side more strongly with this other view of who you are, and of what your life has been about, what difference would this make to your life on a day-to-day basis?

These examples serve only as an introduction to some of the options for developing questions that encourage the reauthoring of lives according to preferred stories. Among the many other options is the construction of questions that might bring forth future developments in the landscape of consciousness. These questions encourage a reflection on future events in the alternative landscape of action. For example:

- If you did witness yourself taking these steps, how might this confirm and extend on this preferred view of who you are as a person?

These questions can then be followed up by further landscape-of-action questions, and so on. For example:

- And what difference would the confirmation of this view make to how you lived your life?

Other Structures

In the shaping of suitable questions, it can be helpful for the therapist to refer to other structures in this work, including those derived from anthropology, drama and literature. For example, at times unique outcomes appear to mark turning points for which it is difficult to find any antecedents in distant history. Under these circumstances, persons can be encouraged to plot these unique outcomes into a "rite of passage" frame that structures transitions in life through the stages of separation, liminality, and reincorporation (van Gennep, 1960).

Alternatively, under these circumstances unique outcomes can be plotted into a "social drama" frame that structures transitions in life through the stages of steady state, breach, crisis, redress, and new steady state (Turner, 1980).

In regard to the borrowing of structures from literature, as I have discovered that the re-vision of motive that accompanies the resurrection of alternative stories and knowledges is particularly "liberating" for persons, I often refer to Burke's deconstruction of motive as a frame for this work:

We shall use five terms as generating principle of our investigation. They are: Act, Scene, Agent, Agency, Purpose. In a rounded statement about motives, you must have some word that names the act (names what took place, in thought or deed), and another that names the scene (the background of the act, the situation in which it occurred); also, you must indicate what person or kind of person (agent) performed the act, what means or instruments he (sic) used (agency), and the purpose . . . any complete statement about motives will offer some kind of answer to these five questions: what was done (act), when or where it was done (scene), who did it (agent), how he (sic) did it (agency), and why (purpose). (Burke, 1969, p. xv)

In relating experience-of-experience questions to alternative and historically situated motives, particular acts, scenes, agents, agency, and purposes can be brought forth.* This contributes "dramatically" to the archaeology of alternative knowledges of personhood and of relationship.

An example of the line of questioning that is informed by this structure follows:

(a) Okay, so your Aunt Mavis might have been best placed to predict such an achievement. Give me an example of the sort of event that she witnessed in your life that would have enabled her to predict this achievement.
(b) How might she have described the circumstances of the event?
(c) Would she have been aware of others who might have contributed to the event?
(d) If she had been asked to describe exactly how this was achieved, what do you imagine she would have said?
(e) What would she have construed your purposes to be in making this achievement? What do you think she might have learned about what you intended for your life?

Discussion

At the risk of belaboring the point, I want to emphasize that these landscape-of-action and landscape-of-consciousness questions are not simply questions about history. They are questions that historicize

---

*What's in a word? Answer—a world! And I believe that, for therapists, the dramatic terms "act," "scene," "agents," "agency," and "purpose" introduce a different world to that world introduced by the terms "what, where, who, how, and why." The terms *act* and *scene* impart a sense of the constructed and thematic nature of the world, the terms *agent* and *agency* invoke ideas

the unique outcome. And the reauthoring approach that I am describing here is not simply a process of "pointing out positives." Instead, this approach actively engages persons in unraveling mysteries that the therapist can't solve.

When I am teaching this work, following Bruner (1986), I often suggest to therapists that they envision an arch. The arch is a relatively recent development in history,* and it owes its extraordinary load-bearing performance to a specific and sequential arrangement of wedge-shaped stones. Each of these stones is uniquely placed; each stone owes its position to the particular arrangement of stones on either side of it, and in turn makes possible the particular arrangement of stones on either side of it.

The landscape of action can be represented as an arch. And the unique outcome as can be represented as one of the wedge-shaped stones, its existence understood to be contingent upon its place in a particular class and sequence of events that unfold through time, while at the same time contributing to the particular arrangements of events, across time, on either side of it. Questions that contextualize unique outcomes contribute significantly to bringing forth details about the unique arrangement of events of which the unique outcome is but a part.

A second arch can be envisaged above the first. The landscape of consciousness can be represented by this, and it interacts back and forth with the first arch, the landscape of action, through reflection.

Perhaps the approach that I have described here on the deconstruction of the stories and knowledges that persons live by is not entirely dissimilar to Derrida's work on the deconstruction of texts (1981).** Derrida's intention was to subvert texts and challenge the privileging of specific knowledges with methods that "deconstruct the opposition ... to overturn the hierarchy at a given moment." He achieved this by developing deconstructive methods that:

---

about specific "contributions" and a "know-how" that is related to intentional states, and the term *purpose* is suggestive of particular intentional states as explanatory notions.

*Debra Milinsky of Berkeley, who has a strong interest in the history of such matters, informs me that the Etruscans can be most fairly credited for the development of the modern aboveground arch.

**To my knowledge, there are a number of family therapists now undertaking a study of Derrida's work and exploring the implications of his ideas in terms of therapeutic practices. Ron Findlay of St. Kilda, Victoria, recently presented some of his thoughts on Derrida and therapy at a meeting at Dulwich Centre.

(a) brought forth the hidden contradictions in texts, rendering visible the repressed meanings – the "absent but implied" meanings,

(b) gave prominence to those knowledges "on the other side," those considered to be secondary, derivative, and worthless.

PRACTICES OF POWER

A good part of Michel Foucault's work is devoted to the analysis of the "practices of power" through which the modern "subject" is constituted (Foucault, 1980, 1984). He has traced the history of the "art of the government of persons" from the 17th century and detailed many of the practices of self and practices of relationship that persons are incited to enter their lives into. In that it is through these practices that persons shape their lives according to dominant specifications for being, they can be considered techniques of social control.

Constitutive Power

Foucault's (1980) conception was of a modern power that is constitutive or "positive" in its character and effects, not repressive or "negative," not a power that is dependent upon prohibitions and restrictions.

Rather than propose that the central mechanism of this modern form of power was containing or restricting, he proposed that its central mechanism was productive – persons' lives are actually constituted or made up through this form of power. According to Foucault (1979), the practices of this form of power permeate and fabricate persons' lives at the deepest levels – including their gestures, desires, bodies, habits, etc. – and he likened these practices to a form of "dressage."

Local Politics

Foucault was intent on exposing the operations of power at the microlevel and at the periphery of society: in clinics, prisons, families, etc. According to him, it was at these local sites that the practices of power were perfected; it is because of this that power can have its global effects. And, he argued, it is at these local sites that the workings of power are most evident.

So, for Foucault this modern system of power was decentered and "taken up," rather than centralized and exercised from the top down. Therefore, he argued that efforts to transform power relations in a society must address these practices of power at the local level – at the level of the everyday, taken-for-granted social practices.

Techniques of Power

In tracing the history of the apparatuses and institutions through which these practices were perfected, Foucault (1979) identifies Bentham's Panopticon as the "ideal" model for this form of power, for the "technologies of power, which determine the conduct of individuals and submit them to certain ends or domination, an objectivizing of the subject" (Foucault, 1988, p. 18). I have discussed Foucault's analysis of this model elsewhere (White, 1989). This model establishes a system of power in which:

- the source of power is invisible to those who experience it most intensely,
- persons are isolated in their experience of subjugation,
- persons are subject to the "gaze" and to "normalizing judgment,"
- it is impossible for persons to determine when they are the subject of surveillance and scrutiny and when they are not, and therefore they must assume this to always to be the case,
- persons are incited to perpetually evaluate themselves, to police themselves and to operate on their bodies and souls to forge them as docile,
- power is autonomous to the extent that those participating in the subjugation of others are, in turn, the "instruments" of power.

Foucault's analysis of the Panopticon provides an account of how the mechanisms and the structures of this modern system of power actually recruited persons into collaborating in the subjugation of their own lives and in the objectification of their own bodies; of how they became "willing" participants in the disciplining of, or policing of, their own lives. These mechanisms of this modern system of power recruit persons into what Foucault refers to as the "technologies of the self, which permit individuals to effect by their own means or with the help of others a certain number of operations on their own bodies and souls, thoughts, conduct, and way of being, so as to transform themselves in order to attain a certain state of happiness, purity, wisdom, perfection, or immortality" (1988, p. 18).

The Ruse

However, this collaboration is rarely a conscious phenomenon. The workings of this power are disguised or masked because it operates in relation to certain norms that are assigned a "truth" status. This is a power that is exercised in relation to certain knowledges that construct particular truths, and is designed to bring about particular and "correct" outcomes, like a life considered to be "fulfilled," "liberated," "rational," "differentiated," "individuated," "self-possessed," "self-contained," and so on.

The descriptions for these "desired" ways of being are in fact illusionary. According to Foucault, they are all part of a ruse that disguises what is actually taking place: these dominant truths are actually specifying of persons' lives and of relationships; those correct outcomes are particular ways of being that are prescribed ways of being.

So, the practices of modern power, as detailed by Foucault, are particularly insidious and effective. They incite persons to embrace their own subjugation, to relate to their own lives through techniques of power that are molding of these lives, including their bodies and their gestures, according to certain "truths." The ways of being informed by these truths are not seen, by these persons, as the effect of power, but instead as the effect of something like fulfillment, of liberation.

Discussion

This analysis of power is difficult for many persons to entertain, for it suggests that many of the aspects of our individual modes of behavior that we assume to be an expression of our free will, or that we assume to be transgressive, are not what they might at first appear. In fact, this analysis would suggest that many of our modes of behavior reflect our collaboration in the control or the policing of our own lives, as well as the lives of others, that is, our collusion in the specification of lives according to the dominant knowledges of our culture.

In undertaking his analysis of the "technologies of power" and the "technologies of the self," Foucault was not proposing that these were the only faces of power. In fact, in relation to fields of power, he proposed the study of four technologies: technologies of production, technologies of sign systems, technologies of power, and technologies of the self (Foucault, 1988).

Although I have followed Foucault in emphasizing the techniques of a modern "positive" system of power in this paper, I believe that other analyses of power, including those that relate to Bourdieu's thoughts about the structure of social systems of power and the constitutive effects of these structures on persons' stances in life, are highly relevant in the consideration of the everyday situations that are confronted by therapists.

Other considerations of fields of power would include the extent to which some of the structures that represent the earlier system of sovereign power still exist, and the extent to which institutional in-equalities—those of a structural nature and those that relate to an inequality of opportunities—dominate our culture.

In fact, in his analysis of Bentham's Panopticon, Foucault draws attention to a structure that is at the heart of its operations. Upon considering the implications of this structure in terms of inequality, I have elsewhere suggested that, in our culture, men are more often likely to be the "instruments" of the normalizing gaze, and women more often likely to be the subject of this gaze (White, 1989). This point has also been made by other authors (e.g., Hare-Mustin, 1990).

THE DECONSTRUCTION OF
PRACTICES OF POWER

In therapy, the objectification of these familiar and taken-for-granted practices of power contributes very significantly to their deconstruction. This is achieved by engaging persons in externalizing conversations about these practices. As these practices of power are unmasked, it becomes possible for persons to take a position on them and to counter the influence of these practices in their lives and relationships.

These externalizing conversations are initiated by encouraging persons to provide an account of the effects of these practices in their lives. In these conversations, special emphasis is given to what these practices have dictated to persons about their relationship with their own self and about their relationship with others.

It is through these externalizing conversations that persons are able to:

(a) appreciate the degree to which these practices are constituting of their own lives as well as the lives of others,
(b) identify those practices of self and of relationship that might be judged as impoverishing of their lives, as well as the lives of others,
(c) acknowledge the extent to which they have been recruited into the policing of their own lives and, as well, the nature of their participation in the policing of the lives of others, and
(d) explore the nature of local, relational politics.

It is through these externalizing conversations that persons no longer experience these practices as representative of authentic ways

of being with themselves and with others. They no longer experience
being at one with these practices and begin to sense a certain alienation in relation to them. Persons are then in a position to develop
alternative and preferred practices of self and of relationship – counter-
practices. In therapy, I have participated with persons in challenging
various practices of power, including those that relate to:

(a) the technologies of the self – the subjugation of self through the
    discipline of bodies, souls, thoughts, and conduct according to
    specified ways of being (including the various operations that
    are shaping of bodies according to the gender-specific knowl-
    edges);
(b) the technologies of power – the subjugation of others through
    techniques such as isolation and surveillance, and through per-
    petual evaluation and comparison.

And I have also participated with persons in the deconstruction of
particular modes of life and thought by reviewing, with them, the
constitutive effects of the specific situation of their lives in those fields
of power that take the form of social structures. In response to this,
persons are able to challenge these effects, as well as those structures
that are considered to be inequitable.

Examples

Perhaps it would be timely to return briefly to the stories about Amy
and Robert. Amy had been recruited into certain practices of the government of the self – "technologies of the self." She had embraced these
practices as a form of self-control and as essential to the transformation of her life into an acceptable shape – one which spoke to her of
fulfillment. She had construed her participation in activities in the
subjugation of her own life as liberating activities.

Upon engaging Amy in an externalizing conversation about anorexia nervosa through the exploration of its real effects in her life,
she began to identify the various practices of self-government – of the
disciplines of the body – and the specifications for self that were embodied in anorexia nervosa. Anorexia was no longer her savior. The
ruse was exposed, and the practices of power were unmasked. Instead
of continuing to embrace these practices of the self, Amy experienced
alienation in relation to them. Anorexia nervosa no longer spoke to
her of her identity. This opened up space for Amy to enter into activities that further subverted the realities constructed by anorexia ner-

vosa, and into an exploration of alternative and preferred practices of self and of relationship.

To Robert, the unexamined and unquestioned knowledges, practices or "technologies of power," structures and conditions that provided the context for his abusive behavior, were all part of a taken-for-granted mode of life and thought that he had considered to be reflective of the natural order of things. Upon entering an externalizing conversation about these knowledges, practices, structures, and conditions, and in mapping the real effects of these upon his own life and upon the lives of others, he experienced a separation from this mode of life and thought—this no longer spoke to him of the "nature" of men's ways of being with women and children.

Then, via a unique outcome as a point of entry, Robert was able to engage in an "archeology" of, as well as the performance of, alternative and preferred practices of relationship. In addition, he began to challenge the structures and conditions that are supportive of men's abusive behavior.

KNOWLEDGE PRACTICES

The professional disciplines have been successful in the development of language practices and techniques that determine that it is those disciplines that have access to the "truth" of the world. These techniques encourage persons in the belief that the members of these disciplines have access to an objective and unbiased account of reality and of human nature.*

> What this means is that certain speakers, those with training in certain special techniques—supposedly to do with the powers of the mind to make contact with reality—are privileged to speak with authority beyond the range of their personal experience. (Parker & Shotter, 1990, p. 7)

These language practices introduce ways of speaking and of writing that are considered to be rational, neutral, and respectable, emphasizing notions of the authoritative account and the impersonal expert view. These practices disembody the perspective and the opinions of the speaker and the writer. The presentation of the knowledge of the speaker and writer is devoid of information that might give the respon-

---

*Feminist thinkers recognize these language practices as distinctly patriarchal, and seek to challenge them with an ethic of care within an emphasis on context. For example, see Carol Gilligan's *In a Different Voice* (1982).

dent or the reader information about the conditions of the production of the expert view.

These practices of speaking and writing establish accounts of knowledges that are considered to be "global and unitary" (Foucault, 1980), accounts that mask the historical struggles associated with their ascendancy, including the multiplicity of resistances to them. It is difficult for persons to challenge these global and unitary knowledges because the language practices that constitute them include built-in injunctions against questions that might be raised about their socio/political/historical contexts.

In denying respondents/readers this critical information, they experience a certain "suspension." They do not have the information necessary to determine how they might "take" the views that are expressed, and this dramatically reduces the range of possible responses available to them. Respondents/readers can either subject themselves to the expert knowledge, or they can rail against it. Dialogue over different points of view is impossible.

For the members of the professional disciplines who are operating under the apprehension that they have recourse to objective knowledge, critical reflection on their position is not an option. Thus they are able to avoid facing the moral and ethical implications of their knowledge practices.

> A description which contains no critical reflection on the position from which it is articulated can have no other principle than the interests associated with the unanalysed relation that the researcher has with this object. (Bourdieu, 1988, p. 15)

The open, vague, temporary, and changing nature of the world is rendered, by these truth discourses, closed, certain, fixed and permanent. Other ways of speaking/writing are rendered invisible or, as they are considered to be inferior, are mostly excluded. These "inferior" ways of speaking/writing are only acknowledged if accompanied by the "appropriate" deference to the warranted ways of speaking/writing.

THE DECONSTRUCTION OF
KNOWLEDGE PRACTICES

Therapists can contribute to the deconstruction of expert knowledge by considering themselves to be "co-authors" of alternative and preferred knowledges and practices, and through a concerted effort to establish a context in which the persons who seek therapy are privileged as the primary authors of these knowledges and practices. Some of the "therapeutic" practices that are informed by this perspective follow. These by no means exhaust the possibilities, and David Epston and I have discussed other such therapeutic practices elsewhere (e.g., Epston and White, 1990; White and Epston, 1990).

Therapists can undermine the idea that they have privileged access to the truth by consistently encouraging persons to assist them in the quest for understanding. This can be achieved by giving persons notice of the extent to which the therapist's participation in therapy is dependent upon feedback from persons about their experience of the therapy. It is acknowledged that the person's experiences of therapy is essential to the guidance of the therapy, as this is the only way that a therapist can know what sort of therapeutic interaction is helpful and what is not.

This can be further emphasized if therapists engage persons in some inquiry as to why certain of the ideas that emerge during the interview interest those persons more than other ideas. What is it that persons find significant or helpful about the particular perspectives, realizations, conclusions, etc.? What preferred outcomes, for persons' lives, might accompany the particular perspectives, realizations, conclusions, etc.?

Therapists can challenge the idea that they have an expert view by continually encouraging persons to evaluate the real effects of the therapy in their lives and relationships, and to determine for themselves to what extent these effects are preferred effects and to what extent they are not. The feedback that arises from this evaluation assists therapists in squarely facing the moral and ethical implications of their practices.

The therapist can call into question the idea that s/he possesses an objective and unbiased account of reality, and undermine the possibility that persons will be subject to the imposition of ideas, by encouraging persons to interview her/him about the interview. In response to this, the therapist is able to deconstruct and thus embody her/his responses (including questions, comments, thoughts, and opinions) by situating these in the context of his/her personal experiences, imagination, and intentional states. This can be described as a condition of "transparency"* in the therapeutic system, and it contributes to a context in which persons are better able to decide, for themselves, how they might take these therapist responses.

*When discussing with David Epston how I might best depict this deconstruction of the therapist responses, he suggested the term "transparency."

If the therapist is working with a reflecting team,* at the end of the session this team can join with persons in interviewing the therapist about the interview. Apart from asking questions about the particular responses of the therapist, at this time team members can be invited to explore the therapist's thoughts about the actual process of the therapy across the interview.

The therapeutic practices of deconstruction and embodiment also hold for the responses of reflecting teams. Reflecting team members can be discouraged from engaging in the time-honored structuralist and functionalist truth discourses of the psychotherapies, and encouraged to respond to those developments that are identified by family members as preferred developments or to speculate about those developments that might be preferred.** Following this, reflecting team members can interview each other about their reflections so that they might situate these in the context of their personal experience, imagination and intentional states. The options and choices available to persons is maximized through this personalizing of the knowledges of the members of the reflecting team.

The deconstruction of the responses of the members of the reflecting team can be structured around questions like: What was it that caught your attention? Why do you think this caught your attention so? Why did this strike you as so significant? How did you decide to comment on this here? What effect did you think this comment would have?† What was your intention in asking this question here?

This transparency of practice provides a challenge to the commonly accepted idea that for therapy to have its desired effects its workings need to be kept secret, the idea that if persons know what the therapist is up to then it won't work. On reviewing these practices with persons, I have learned that they often regard the embodiment of the therapist and reflecting team responses to be a highly significant factor in achieving the changes in their lives that they have valued most.

---

*For an introduction to the concept of the reflecting team, see Andersen (1987, 1991).

**As with therapist reauthoring practices, reflecting team members orient themselves to unique outcomes as one might orient oneself to mysteries. Thus, when team members make comments on unique outcomes, this is followed by questions and perceptions from within the team that are intended to engage the lived experience and imagination of family members in the unraveling of these mysteries. In this way, family members are privileged as the primary authors of alternative and preferred stories.

†This question was suggested by Stephen Madigan during his visit to Dulwich Centre through the "Down Under Family Therapy Scholarship."

CONCLUSION

Those therapeutic practices that I refer to as "deconstructive" assist in establishing, for persons, a sense of "agency." This sense is derived from the experience of escaping "passengerhood" in life and from the sense of being able play an active role in the shaping of one's own life – of possessing the capacity to influence developments in one's life according to one's purposes and to the extent of bringing about preferred outcomes. This sense of personal agency is established through the development of some awareness of the degree to which certain modes of life and thought shape our existence and through the experience of some choice in relation to the modes of life and thought that we might live by.

Those therapeutic practices that I refer to as deconstructive assist persons to separate from those modes of life and thought that they judge to be impoverishing of their own lives and of the lives of others. And they provoke in therapists and in the persons who seek therapy a curiosity in regard to those alternative versions of who these persons might be. This is not just any curiosity. It is a curiosity about how things might be otherwise, a curiosity about that which falls outside of the totalizing stories that persons have about their lives, and outside of those dominant practices of self and of relationship.

An emphasis on curiosity in therapeutic practices is by no means new, and I would refer you to Gianfranco Cecchin's (1990) recasting of neutrality. I will leave you with one of Michel Foucault's delightful contributions on this subject:

> Curiosity is a vice that has been stigmatized in turn by Christianity, by philosophy, and even by a certain conception of science. Curiosity, futility. The word, however, pleases me. To me it suggests something altogether different: it evokes "concern"; it evokes the care one takes for what exists and could exist; a readiness to find strange and singular what surrounds us; a certain relentlessness to break up our familiarities and to regard otherwise the same things; a fervor to grasp what is happening and what passes;a casualness in regard to the traditional hierarchies of the important and the essential. (1989, p. 198)

REFERENCES

Andersen, T. (1987). The reflecting team: dialogue and meta-dialogue in clinical work. *Family Process, 26*:415–428.

Andersen, T. (Ed.) (1991). *The reflecting team: Dialogues and dialogues about the dialogues*. New York: Norton.

Bourdieu, P. (1988). *Homo academicus*. Stanford, CA: Stanford University Press.

Bruner, J. (1986). *Actual minds, possible worlds*. Cambridge, MA: Harvard University Press.

Bruner, J. (1990). *Acts of meaning*. Cambridge, MA: Harvard University Press.

Burke, K. (1969). *A grammar of motives*. Berkeley: University of California Press.

Cecchin, G. (1987). Hypothesizing, circularity and neutrality revisited: An invitation to curiosity. *Family Process, 26*(4):405–413.

Derrida, J. (1981). *Positions*. Chicago: University of Chicago Press.

Epston, D., & White, M. (1990). Consulting your consultants: The documentation of alternative knowledges. *Dulwich Centre Newsletter*, 4.

Foucault, M. (1979). *Discipline and punish: The birth of the prison*. Middlesex, England: Peregrine Books.

Foucault, M. (1980). *Power/knowledge: Selected interviews and other writings*. New York: Pantheon.

Foucault, M. (1984). *The history of sexuality*. Middlesex, England: Peregrine Books.

Foucault, M. (1988). Technologies of the self. In L. Martin, H. Gutman, & P. Hutton (Eds.), *Technologies of the self*. Amherst: University of Massachusetts Press.

Foucault, M. (1989). *Foucault Live*. New York: Semiotext(e).

Geertz, C. (1986). Making experiences, authoring selves. In V. Turner, & E. Bruner (Eds.), *The anthropology of experience*. Chicago: University of Illinois Press.

Gilligan, C. (1982). *In a different voice*. Cambridge, MA: Harvard University Press.

Hare-Mustin, R. (1990). Sex, lies and headaches: The problem is power. In T. J. Goodrich (Ed.), *Women and power: Perspectives for family therapy*. New York: Norton.

Jenkins, A. (1990). *Invitations to responsibility: The therapeutic engagement of men who are violent and abusive*. Adelaide: Dulwich Centre Publications.

Kamsler, A., & Laing, L. (1990). Putting an end to secrecy: Therapy with mothers and children following disclosure of child sexual assault. In M. Durrant, & C. White (Eds.), *Ideas for therapy with sexual abuse*. Adelaide: Dulwich Centre Publications.

Parker, I., & Shotter, J. (Eds.) (1990). *Deconstructing social psychology*. London: Routledge.

Turner, V. (1980). Social drama and stories about them. *Critical Inquiry*, Autumn.

van Gennep, A. (1960). *The rites of passage*. Chicago: University of Chicago Press.

White, M. (1984). Pseudo-encopresis: From avalanche to victory, from vicious to virtuous cycles. *Family Systems Medicine, 2*(2), 150–160.

White, M. (1986). Negative explanation, restraint, and double description: A template for family therapy. *Family Process, 25*(2), 169–183.

White, M. (1988a). The process of questioning: A therapy of literary merit? *Dulwich Centre Newsletter*, Winter.

White, M. (1988b). Saying hullo again: The incorporation of the lost relationship in the resolution of grief. *Dulwich Centre Newsletter*, Spring.

White, M. (1989). The externalizing of the problem and the re-authoring of lives and relationships. *Dulwich Centre Newsletter*, Summer.

White, M., & Epston, D. (1990). *Narrative means to therapeutic ends*. New York: Norton.

3

THE COURAGE TO PROTEST:
A COMMENTARY ON
MICHAEL WHITE'S WORK

Karl Tomm

I REGARD Michael White's chapter on "Deconstruction and Therapy" as another important contribution to the psychotherapy literature. In this original paper Michael builds on and extends his previous work by refining his clinical methods and expanding his theoretical explanations. The opening section provides a superb description of his therapy in that the brief reports of four clinical situations clearly reveal a systematic pattern in his therapeutic work. The subsequent theoretical section provides a rich rationale for the current developments in his practice.

I greatly appreciate the opportunity to provide some written comments on Michael's paper. As many family therapists are aware, I have been very enthusiastic about his contributions to the field for some time. In this commentary, I will offer a second description of his work. However, it is important for the reader to bear in mind that my descriptions of Michael and his work arise from my personal views. In other words, they will not necessarily coincide with his own descriptions. Some differences are to be expected, but I hope they will be enriching. I will begin with some personal impressions of Michael because I believe some sense of him as a person deepens one's understanding of his therapy and his theory.

For me, one of the most admirable things about Michael is his courage to protest that which he considers oppressive and unfair. He always seems ready to lend his weight to challenge injustice wherever and whenever he sees it — whether it occurs at the individual level, the family level, the institutional level, the community level, or the cultural level. He readily identifies with the underprivileged, is quick to recognize inequities in power relations, and becomes energized when challenging that which is inequitable and unjust. Indeed, I would say that protesting is a major passion for him. (Michael himself has not adopted the protest metaphor to describe his work. I do so because it fits well with what I have experienced in relation to him. Perhaps one of the reasons this is so salient for me is that I have adopted somewhat of a protest life-style myself!)

What I find fascinating about Michael's protest is the extraordinary stamina that he displays in maintaining a protest. Most of us who do psychotherapy recognize the pathologizing consequences of being treated unfairly and do what we can to create the conditions for injustice to stop or at least be curtailed. But when, in some situations, we come to recognize the enormous difficulties involved and/or the personal risks entailed, we tend to back off and accept our limitations. Michael, on the other hand, tends to press on with more vigorous and more refined efforts. His capacity to persist despite the complacency of others reflects a strong determination in his commitments. It is his willingness to persevere despite intense opposition to change that demonstrates the kind of courage that commands enormous respect. He usually is not content with a simple reframe, especially when reinterpreting a situation allows an injustice to continue in disguise. Michael seeks more substantive change and he often succeeds in enabling differences that really make a difference. This is particularly true where mental pain and suffering arise from the injustices of taken-for-granted cultural practices and beliefs.

In my opinion, one of the major reasons that Michael has been so successful in the area of protest is that he has managed to develop a means of protesting that is extremely effective. His approach is to carefully direct the protest against problematic beliefs and practices rather than against the persons who hold those beliefs and enact those practices. What I am referring to, of course, is his practice of externalizing problems, or as he prefers to call it now, of participating in externalizing conversations. By introducing a clear separation between the problem and the person, he not only averts the reactionary response that inevitably results from a protest directed against a person, but also opens space for that same person to join him in the protest against the problem. And when the person (who participates in an unfair practice) begins to oppose that practice (as enacted by the self), a significant shift in power dynamics takes place. Not only is the protest channeled more precisely against the externalized problem, but a supplementary protest arises as well, that is, an injunction against allowing the self to submit to the problematic beliefs or habits. The resultant augmentation in the power of the protest makes it possible for patterns of injustice to be altered far more quickly. The shift can be likened to a move from a situation in which a victim alone is trying to stop abuse to one in which the perpetrator also takes initiative to stop it. The protest suddenly becomes dramatically more effective. Because Michael's externalizing method enables this kind of empowering shift, I see it as a major innovation in the field of psychotherapy. What is not very clear to me, though, is whether his courage to protest enabled the elaboration of his method or his method fostered his courage. Perhaps, in sound systemic fashion, it was both! In any case, I now see Michael drawing on deconstruction as a theoretical framework to further refine and extend his capacity to protest.

As many are aware, Michael has drawn heavily from Foucault in developing a protest against the use of knowledge as power. Among other things, Foucault (1979) discloses how professionals have been entitled by our culture to use their scientific knowledge to specify the personality or character of persons by diagnosing and classifying them. This can be extremely impoverishing for such persons because of the totalizing effects of such labeling and the exclusion practices that accompany the labels. I have found Michael's application of Foucault to protest certain professional practices quite inspiring. To some extent it energized my critique of the *DSM* (Tomm, 1990) and my exploration of an alternative approach to psychiatric assessment (Tomm, 1991).

What I would like to see more of in Michael's workshop presentations and in his written work is a readiness to openly and explicitly apply his critique of knowledge and power to his own use of knowledge and power during his teaching. This desire arises from my interest in the second-order perspective of observing systems. Perhaps it is unreasonable of me to expect this from him in that such a critique could undermine the effectiveness of his protest against those theories and practices that he considers pathologizing. On the other hand, I often wonder whether the receptiveness of other professionals could be enhanced if he became more open and self-reflective in this respect. I must add, however, that in his clinical work Michael is very attentive to and critical of his own power. He has always carefully monitored the effects of his influence on clients and recently even began inviting clients to interview him about his questions. In doing so, he invites them to become more aware of the influence he is having upon them. Nevertheless, this attention to his own power during therapy has not yet become an integral part of his workshop teaching, nor has a critique of his own power as a major contributor in the field become a part of his major presentations. Perhaps these are developments we shall see in the future.

What is of greater current significance to me is that Michael already offers more than an effective means to protest. He also provides a means to rebuild persons' lives. Together with David Epston (White and Epston, 1990) he has developed a method to help clients rewrite their personal stories. In his clinical interviews, Michael takes initiative to co-create new enlivening stories to replace the old oppressive ones that he externalizes for his clients to protest. In other words, he is not a passive "armchair critic"; he actively contributes to rebuilding alternative perspectives, alternative stories, alternative behavioral practices, and alternative relationship patterns. Thus, Michael does more than deconstruct; he is deeply involved in reconstruction as well.

From my point of view, Michael takes a major leadership role during his reconstruction work in therapy. He takes initiative to enable clients to set new directions in their lives. While there is seldom any concern expressed about the direction set (because it is almost always away from oppression and towards empowerment), controversy sometimes arises among processionals about the amount of initiative Michael, as therapist, takes in setting it. Michael is always very careful to base his work on the "foundation" of actual lived experiences of clients. In other words, he takes great care to determine what might be preferred outcomes for the persons he is working with. When the clients' preferred outcomes fit with his hypotheses about new therapeutic possibilities, he brings them into the conversation. Nevertheless, it is he who implicitly decides about the "fit" and which events and meanings in the lives of clients will be selected out by him to emerge as "building blocks" for a reconstruction. Indeed, a great deal of sensitivity and imagination is required to identify what could serve as an authentic unique outcome. The skill involved in this selectiveness is not trivial; it constitutes significant leadership and contributes significantly to the process of creating a new story of self (and relationship) for clients. These selective decisions are part of the leadership towards wellness that clients implicitly expect from therapists when coming for help.

In his teaching presentations, Michael's own contributions in helping clients build the new stories required to support new practices tend to be played down in favor of the stories themselves. This tendency to underemphasize his personal involvement in the reconstructive process may be a side effect of the lack of an open acknowledgment and critique of his own power. It may also be a consequence, in part, of the criticism he has encountered for sometimes coming across as "too directive" in therapy. While this criticism of his method may be valid at times, especially for less skilled professionals who try to apply his method, it obscures and devalues the importance of a therapist's active contributions to the change process. In my opinion, deliberate therapeutic initiatives are indispensable in clinical work. Hermeneutic listening, circular questioning, empathic reflection, and systemic understanding are not enough, especially when problematic patterns of injustice are entrenched.

To draw attention to Michael's active contributions in therapy, I will describe what I see as his major initiatives in the clinical situations he reports. I then will proceed to discuss the theory he presents to support his clinical practices.

COMMENTARY ON WHITE'S
CLINICAL REPORTS

I appreciate Michael's introductory remark acknowledging that his stories about therapy "are glossed." There is an elegant simplicity to these accounts while the actual conduct of therapy remains a complex, unpredictable, and irregular process. However, I experienced a strong coherence and consistency between what he describes in this paper and what I have seen him do in the sessions I have observed. In both his descriptions and in my observations of his practice there is a deliberate sequence in what he does. Indeed, I see his capacity to create such sequences as a key aspect of his therapy.

In the case of Elizabeth, Michael begins by listening to her problems and then launches into an externalizing conversation by asking her how these problems affected the lives of family members and interfered in family relationships. He extends the externalizing process by inquiring about how the problems have influenced her thoughts about herself. This opens space for a confession regarding her deeper experience of being a failure as a mother and her feelings of guilt about this. Through a careful choice of questions he guides her experience of "being a failure" to "being influenced by the view of herself as a failure." In the precision of this linguistic shift, Michael deconstructs her identity as a problematic person. The conversation lays a groundwork for a more successful protest, because in separating the problems from her identity as a person he reveals the injustice of her person being dominated by those problems.

Michael then asks Elizabeth to reflect upon whether the view of herself as a failure is acceptable to her, or whether she would feel more comfortable if she broke "free of the tyranny of this view and its associated guilt." These kinds of questions, which juxtapose two contrasting options (in this case, acceptability vs. unacceptability) and invite the client to state a preference, are obviously "loaded." They serve to mobilize and align a person's emotional responses. The questions do this by creating a bifurcation (or branching) with reference to alternative meanings and alternative directions of movement. The alternatives are usually bipolar. In this situation, Elizabeth's negative emotions become oriented toward the problems (enabling her protest against them) and her positive emotions become oriented towards breaking herself free and distancing from them. Although Michael does not speak of emotion or refer to such an emotional realignment, I see it as extremely important in providing directionality and movement in therapy. I call these kinds of questions "bifurcation questions," after Prigogine and Stengers' (1984) notion of bifurcation in his theory of dissipative structures, and see them as a means whereby a therapist co-constructs (together with the client) an enhanced awareness which could serve as a basis for therapeutic choices.

Once Michael can see that Elizabeth is separating herself conceptually from the problems and is committed to reorienting her life away from them, he introduces an interpersonal perspective by bringing forth an awareness of cultural patterns of mother-blame. In other words, the intrapersonal blame is relocated in the interpersonal domain where it is easier to visualize and oppose. He invites her to become aware of how she has been recruited into patterns of self-disqualification. In so doing, he deconstructs the practices of power that have been oppressing her. It is important to note that he brings forth the origins of recruitment (into the failure view) as located in the culture as a whole. If she attributed the source of the recruitment to her children, she might direct her negative emotions toward them as persons (which she already had done prior to coming in when she feared hating them). Thus, Michael aligns himself with her in adopting a position of protest against the externalized problems and against the practices of power that produce those problems.

Michael then begins to guide her onto a healthy path by inviting her to recognize that other women have kept their hopes alive by believing that things could be different. This is the beginning of a reconstruction process. He invites her to begin identifying times in her life when she has been able to resist the tyranny of the problem; i.e., he asks her to cite initiatives that she has taken despite the oppression of the problem. Michael is careful to inquire about whether any particular example was a positive development so that he can be confident that it represents a genuine "unique outcome" which he can then build upon for the re-storying process. Having established this, he proceeds to ask a series of "alternative landscape-of-action questions" and "landscape-of-consciousness questions" to build a network of connections among her positive actions and their meanings. This makes it possible for Elizabeth to construct a new description of herself grounded in an active protest rather than in a passive failure. Stabilization and endurance of this new self description are then stimulated by inviting her to recruit an "audience" for the reconstructed version of herself, through an awareness of other persons who can acknowledge and authenticate her new story of self. As part of this process, he also mobilizes her capacity to be an affirming audience for herself by identifying "what it was about herself that she would personally like to have in a mother." He coaches her on how this knowledge could be shared in order to recruit others, such as her children, into also appreciating her positive qualities. Michael then wisely cautions her about the possibility that the children might not immediately be enthusiastic about her change and prepares her for possible disqualification. He suggests that she decline their invitations to resume negative evaluations of herself, should these arise. Finally, he supports her in her own growing determination to sustain her new direction and in her perseverance to forge a new connection with the children.

To recapitulate Michael's major therapeutic initiatives with Elizabeth, the sequence was (a) initial deconstruction by externalizing problems, (b) bifurcation to create directional choices, (c) deconstruction of internalized past interpersonal patterns of recruitment, (d) reconstruction of a preferred view of self around unique outcomes, (e) deconstruction of anticipated future patterns of recruitment, and (f) mobilization of interpersonal support (an audience) for the preferred story.

In the case of Amy, the process again begins with externalizing conversation to deconstruct her identification with anorexia nervosa in order to begin a process of enabling a protest against the pervasive effects of anorexia in her life. More time is spent with Amy in disclosing the self-pathologizing pattern of "constantly comparing of herself to others . . . to police herself." Through his questions Michael brings forth her curiosity about patterns of interpersonal recruitment into practices of disciplining the self. This leads to further externalizing dynamics where Amy is able to recognize the cultural factors involved.

Thus, space is opened for Amy to understand "the ruse," that is, how she was deceived into believing that certain cultural attitudes about her body were in her own best interests. Unmasking such deception energizes her protest. Space is also created for her to orient her negative emotions against the "taken-for-granted practices and attitudes of anorexia." Michael then clarifies a possible choice by introducing bifurcation questions: "Is she content to submit to the problem or is she attracted to the idea of challenging it?" This bifurcation process again provides for a more precise realignment of her emotional commitments. Thus, she becomes empowered in her protest against anorexia nervosa. Michael invites her to recognize possible anti-anorectic activities, creates another bifurcation in relation to them, supports her in embracing them, and enables her to liberate herself from anorexia. Amy gradually articulates a preferred version of her life and takes steps in this direction. These steps are encouraged further by "fieldwork" regarding persons who would constitute a supportive audience for her new definition of self.

The sequence with Amy was very similar to that with Elizabeth. It entailed (a) deconstructing selective aspects of the self by externalizing anorexia, (b) deconstructing the secretive cultural ruse that supports anorexia, (c) bifurcating for redirection of emotional energy and commitments, (d) reconstructing a preferred view of self, and (e) mobilizing an audience to validate the new view. In contrast to Elizabeth, a little more work was required, on the deconstruction of attitudes and beliefs that support anorexia, before Amy was ready for an authentic commitment to redirect her life.

In the case of his work with the couple, Anne and John, Michael began by externalizing an adversarial pattern of interaction from both members of the couple. I refer to such problematic interaction patterns as "PIPs" – an acronym for Pathologizing Interpersonal Patterns (Tomm, 1991). By focusing attention on PIPs I enable myself, my clients, and my trainees to explicitly separate them from the persons who enact the patterns. In my experience, it is helpful to describe the coupling of specific behavioral components of any particular PIP and to give the pattern or its "plot" a name. Such naming, as a labeling process, pathologizes the pathologizing pattern itself, rather than the persons enacting it. Any exclusion practices that might be mobilized by this kind of negative labeling are then harnessed as resources in the protest because they are automatically directed towards the problematic pattern rather than the persons involved. In the case of John and Anne, Michael names the pattern "adversarial" and proceeds in his usual externalizing manner to explore the influence of this pattern on themselves, on their perceptions of each other, and on their relationship. Having disclosed the negative consequences of the PIP, Michael introduces a gentle confrontation, asking whether it is a pattern they prefer. Since it is not, he invites them to recognize that they had probably not invented it themselves. This provides them with a means whereby they can avoid the tendency for each of them to blame the other as initiating the pattern. This is the beginning of a process in which Michael "archaeologizes" the PIP by uncovering its remote historical origins, i.e., where it had been learned and how they had been recruited into it. This exploratory discussion opens space for a different interaction pattern to emerge during the interview itself. Michael draws attention to this different pattern and their experience of it. Consequently, it becomes possible to introduce a bifurcation with respect to leaving their relationship in the grip of the adversarial pattern or intervening to free themselves from it as they have in the interview itself. Once again, emotions are mobilized to create directionality. Michael then brings forth their resources in being able to leave the adversarial pattern behind, as they move towards the alternative they are "more attracted to." By inquiring from them what they found attractive about the alternative pattern, Michael invites them to co-create descriptions of it in his presence; in so doing, they begin reconstructing their relationship. I find it useful to conceptualize these alternative patterns as specific "HIPs" (Healing Interpersonal Patterns) or "WIPs" (Wellness Interpersonal Patterns) because it makes it easier for me to think of the kinds of questions to ask to enable a preferred reconstruction (Tomm, 1991). Michael concludes his work by asking the couple about possible historical analogs for their alternative manner of interacting, which stimulates memories of a supporting audience, that is, some friends who had previously witnessed John and Anne resolve a dispute.

The sequence with the couple was one of (a) externalizing a problematic conjoint pattern, (b) deconstructing the pattern by archaeologizing it, (c) bifurcating with a contrast of options, (d) reconstructing an alternative pattern, and (e) mobilizing support for the reconstructed pattern through a historical audience of friends.

The clinical work with Robert, who had been abusive, began a little differently. Michael first brings forth Robert's responsibility for perpetrating the abuse. He does this by opening space for Robert to recognize the "real short-term and possible long-term traumatic effects" of the abuse. It is important to recognize how we as clinicians can co-construct responsibility in others by inviting them to become more aware of the actual (though perhaps not intended) consequences of their behavior and to become more aware of whether they like those consequences or not. Having enabled the acceptance of "negative" responsibility (acknowledging unwanted consequences) in this way, Michael goes on to generate some "positive" responsibility (committing to desired consequences) to mend whatever might be mended. He then proceeds to bring forth Robert's covert knowledge about conditions, structures, and attitudes in the practices of power over others. Michael invites Robert to determine which of these attitudes he had submitted himself to and which had been dominant in shaping his relationships with others. This sets the stage for an externalizing conversation and increasing alienation from these practices of power. As Robert begins to experience a separation from the attitudes of power and control, Michael is able to guide him to identify various "unique outcomes." At this point an implicit process of bifurcation questioning aligns his emotional dynamics to set him in a direction away from problematic attitudes towards positive unique outcomes. Michael invites Robert to create some links among these unique outcomes to reconstruct his view of what being a man is all about. Identifying an uncle (known to be compassionate rather than abusive) as a possible "template" to identify with contributes to the construction of a new positive story of Robert's sense of self. I especially appreciate Michael's initiative in explicitly addressing the need for safeguards. He creates a local social structure of "escape from secrecy meetings" to minimize the possibility that Robert will slip back to abusive patterns and to maximize the possibility that Robert will continue his new direction. In other words, an actual, rather than an imaginary, audience for constructive change is created.

The steps in the therapeutic process with Robert entailed (a) co-constructing personal responsibility, (b) deconstructing the conditions for abuse, (c) deconstructing aspects of self by externalizing those conditions, (d) identifying possible unique outcomes, (e) bifurcating on alternative ways of being a man, (f) reconstructing a preferred alternative, (g) enstructuring interpersonal openness, and (h) mobilizing an actual audience to support the new direction.

In all four clinical cases, there is a basic sequence of deconstruction, bifurcation, and reconstruction. Variations do, of course, occur. Like most of us, Michael adapts his method to the specifics of each situation. Often there is movement back and forth, but the pattern is essentially the same. The externalizing process of separating self (person) from nonself (problem) is part of the deconstructive process. Archaeologizing aspects of externalized problems and disclosing patterns of unfair recruitment entail further deconstruction. The relevance of protest is obvious throughout this deconstructive work. The stance of protest is also evident in the directionality generated in the bifurcation. What is perhaps not quite so apparent, however, is that Michael's reconstruction is also grounded in protest. It is based on movement towards liberation and autonomy, which implicitly is always away from the oppression of unjust cultural practices and beliefs.

WHITE'S USE OF THE
REFLECTING TEAM

The final clinical illustration in the first section of Michael's paper describes his unique implementation of the reflecting team. When I first introduced Michael to Andersen's (1987; 1991) method of the reflecting team, he was somewhat cautious and concerned. Thus, I was pleasantly surprised when he eventually incorporated this innovation into his work and added some of his own nuances.

In Michael's version, the team members begin their reflection by highlighting their responses to what the family seemed attracted to as preferred developments in their lives and relationships. In other words, they are very selective and focus on unique outcomes. They then initiate a process of speculation about what these developments might mean and in so doing bring forward the mysterious aspects of these developments to stimulate the family's curiosity regarding previously overlooked aspects of their lived experience. The third step is for team members to ask each other about why they, as persons, found particular developments interesting. This is a way for team members to situate their contributions in their own personal experience and in so doing render their comments less mysterious and more transparent. In my experience family members greatly appreciate this personal aspect of the team's discussion, in that team members' contributions become more authentic and are less distant and professional.

After the team's reflection, the family and team trade places in the usual manner and the therapist proceeds to interview family members about the team's reflection, i.e., what they found of interest and to the point. The predominant focus is on positive developments, that is, on what new realizations and/or conclusions arose as a result of the team's comments and questions. In Michael's version of reflecting team work the therapist goes further here and asks family members for explanations to help him or her understand why they found these comments of interest. In effect, family members are invited to evaluate their responses to the team's comments more fully and explain themselves in a manner that constitutes further self-reconstruction.

Finally, the team enters the room with the family and the therapist brings the interview to a close by inviting family members and reflecting team members to interview him or her about the therapist's own questions. In this way the therapist's contributions can be situated within the context of his or her own experience, imagination, and purposes. This can be extremely valuable in disclosing the rationale behind various aspects of the therapy process, so that family members can incorporate this rationale into their understanding and in so doing contribute to greater endurance of healing and wellness patterns within the family itself. In other words, the meta-conversation about the therapeutic conversation also becomes a part of the network of internalized conversations that constitute family members and their relationships.

I find Michael's additions to the use of the reflecting team very helpful and have implemented some of them in my own work. For instance, I too encourage team members to ground their contributions in their own experience and to enter into dialogue with one another about this. However, I prefer a team process that is less structured and more open to a broad range of spontaneous responses by team members. While an affirming discussion of unique outcomes is extremely important (and is something I actively encourage), an exclusive focus on preferred developments and their meaning is rather restrictive. In my experience, the reflecting team can usefully be involved in the deconstruction and bifurcation processes as well.

When deconstructive statements are offered by team members, they are more likely to be helpful and avoid harm when they are offered in tentative terms like: "It seemed to me that...," "I wondered whether...," "My impression was...," etc. Because team members cannot observe the family's immediate responses to their comments, and, hence, cannot modify their contributions on the basis of these responses, they are best offered as provisional statements. In this way the family is left with more freedom to accept or reject the team's comments. In deciding what to say, I encourage team members to remain grounded in their intuitive emotional experiences while observing the family and to leave it to other team members to reconstruct one another's contributions to become more therapeutic if necessary. This lack of structure opens space for the unexpected and for new possibilities that may not have been touched on or even implied during the interview itself.

COMMENTARY ON
WHITE'S THEORY

Deconstruction is an excellent theoretical frame of reference to describe much of Michael's work. His definition of deconstruction as "procedures that subvert taken-for-granted realities and practices" obviously reflects his protest orientation (although it is I, not he, who is constructing it as protest). He acknowledges that he is not an academic deconstructionist. I think this is true. It is my impression that he tends to use the term "deconstruction" in a limited sense of breaking down the influence of problematic beliefs and practices by "taking them apart." I would say that as a therapist he is an applied deconstruction activist.

In order to draw attention to the familiar, taken-for-granted phenomena that need to be subverted, Michael rightly attends to the issue of describing them in ways that they become unusual so that we can estrange ourselves from them. Hence his attraction to Bourdieu (1988) in "exoticizing the domestic." Michael claims that his method of externalizing problems reflects such an exoticizing process. I agree but would suggest that his pattern of using familiar language in unfamiliar ways is a more apt focus in understanding this phenomenon. Michael has an extraordinary gift in being able to turn a common (i.e., domestic) word or phrase into something peculiar and odd (i.e., exotic). Such contributions quickly capture the attention and interest of the participants involved in a therapeutic conversation and are very refreshing, sometimes quite playful. For instance, distinguishing a soiling problem as "Sneaky Poo" or guilt feelings in a mother as "being in the grip of mother-guilt" are examples of his exoticizing use of language. Such linguistic novelty opens space for us to become more aware of certain nonconscious aspects of the familiar. Consequently, we are more likely to be in a position to make meaningful choices about what we think and how we live.

Michael describes his epistemic stance as "constitutionalist" in that "persons' lives are shaped by the meaning that they ascribe to their experience, by their situation in social structures, and by the language practices and cultural practices of self and of relationship that these lives are recruited into." His focus on the importance of re-storying persons' lives is consistent with the constitutionalist perspective. I prefer to see myself as a "bringforthist" and, as such, adopt a slightly different theoretical position. I focus on enabling persons to bring forth coherent descriptions of experience that have therapeutic potential. For the most part, however, our views are similar, in that both of us reject objectivist assumptions about the nature of knowledge and affirm social constructionist assumptions. Perhaps one difference between us lies in my tendency to place more emphasis on lived experience than on stories about that experience.

It is partly for this reason that I am less invested in the narrative metaphor than Michael. In my work, I give more priority to conversations than to stories. I regard a personal story as a concatenation of internalized conversations and find that the complexity of a full story renders it more distant from experience than a conversation that may be a component of the story. Furthermore, for me as a physician, it is going a bit too far to suggest that lives are constituted by stories and to say that "stories provide the structure of life." Such claims render our bodies passive and docile, a practice that Michael himself criticizes.

Nor am I personally attracted to the drama metaphor with its components of act, scene, agent, agency, and purpose. I guess I am too conditioned by television, movies, and theater to think of drama as "not real." This conditioning diminishes the credibility of drama, for me, as an overall model for therapy. At the same time, however, I see enormous value in a systematic development of the narrative and drama metaphors in psychotherapy. They offer heuristic frameworks, and when rigorously applied reveal new possibilities for the conduct of therapy. Furthermore, one does not have to adopt the full frame of reference of any model or method to draw upon and use certain aspects of it in one's day-to-day therapeutic work. Thus, I can still genuinely support Michael and his major collaborator, David Epston, in their continuing exploration of these metaphors.

In his paper, Michael applies the deconstruction perspective to (1) knowledges that persons live by, (2) cultural practices of self and of relationships, and (3) discursive practices of our professional culture. Thus, he organizes his discussion around (1) narrative, (2) practices of power, and (3) practices of knowledge. I will follow the same format in the remainder of my response.

Narrative

In his discussion of narrative, Michael gives primacy to the personal stories by which individuals live their lives. Not only does a person's story determine the meaning that that person gives to his or her experience, but the story also largely determines which aspects of experience the person selects out for expression. Michael emphasizes that these stories are not simply mirrored reflections of life that are post hoc; they are structures that shape actual lives and prefigure action. This is an important point. The narrative metaphor can be unduly trivialized if one conceives of a personal story as a mirror image of one's life or as something that can be made up at will, like a fairy tale. The stories that are relevant in Michael's work are stories that are authentic, in that they are lived stories.

In refining his practice of re-storying, Michael draws upon Jerome Bruner's (1986) work regarding the "dual landscapes" of action and of consciousness in personal stories. Bruner notes that the landscape of action entails (a) events, (b) sequences, (c) time, and (d) plots. The landscape of consciousness, on the other hand, is constituted by meanings or the interpretations of the characters in the story. The latter include (a) the desires of the characters, (b) their characteristics and qualities, (c) their intentions, and (d) their beliefs. Michael suggests that the elements of the landscape of consciousness coalesce into "commitments" or "life-styles," and thus become enduring aspects of a personal story.

What is relevant in this for therapy is that linkages can be forged among these various components of the dual landscapes to generate coherence and continuity in a person's personal story. This process is facilitated by the specific questions a therapist asks. In a footnote, Michael comments that his landscape of action questions are similar to what he earlier referred to as unique account questions. In other words, he now uses Bruner's landscape-of-action framework to elaborate a wider range of these questions. For instance, he differentiates past event questions into those focused on recent history and those focused on distant history. This is a useful distinction, since it brings out more events over time. In addition, Michael uses the metaphor of a physical arch, as if it were reaching over a timespan, to visualize the elements of the story being placed (like wedge-shaped stones) beside one another along an arching continuum of time in the construction of an overarching story. In other words, specific questions can be asked to bring forth aspects of distant history and placed alongside and linked to aspects of recent history, which abut current unique outcomes, immediate future possibilities, and distant future possibilities. Questions about such events may be addressed to the client, or they can be addressed to other persons who are aware of the client's life. The answers to these questions serve to contextualize unique outcomes and ground them through the creation of temporal linkages. Michael then asks landscape-of-consciousness questions, which encourage persons to look at themselves through the events disclosed in the interconnected landscape of action. Following Bruner's theoretical categories, he selects questions about desires, qualities, intentions, beliefs, and commitments. Once again, these questions may be asked of the client directly or of another person who can describe the significance of particular events upon his or her views of the client.

Michael makes the comment that "experience-of-experience questions" are often more generative in the reauthoring of lives and relationships than direct questions. I am inclined to agree in that our sense of self is generated in relation to others in the first place. His question about who would be the person least surprised about constructive initiatives (the emergence of unique outcomes) is a helpful means to identify the best person with whom one could begin a reconstruction. The syntactic structure of Michael's experience-of-experience questions ("What do you think he thinks about you?" and "What do you think I think about you?") are analogous to the "interpersonal perception questions" that were popularized by R. D. Laing (1961) some years ago. Recently I have been exploring a more experiential route to one person's experience of another person's experience. I call these "internalized other questions" (see Chapter 9 for David Epston's reflections on such questions). Briefly, they entail asking a client questions by addressing a second person (by name) within the client about the client.

Michael emphasizes that his reauthoring approach is not the same as simply "pointing out positives." I heartily concur. Re-storying is a process of historicizing unique outcomes. Clients are engaged in actively creating an awareness about how antecedents to their unique outcomes emerged and survived in the face of an "old" story that was problematic and dominant. It is a process of linking these constructive events and writing a story of successful protest.

Practice of Power

I have always been impressed with Michael's application of Foucault's (1979) analysis of power in the domain of therapy. It certainly sharpens and strengthens Michael's protest vis-à-vis injustice. My own personal interests have drawn me to Maturana (rather than Foucault) as a theoretical resource. Maturana's perspective seems less pessimistic than Foucault's; however, in many respects they are quite compatible. For instance, Maturana's (Maturana and Varela, 1980) explanation of language shows how Foucault's notion of "positive" power is, indeed, constitutive insofar as all observing, all human knowing, and all aspects of reality as we know them are constituted in language. Maturana also notes the tyrannizing effects of objectification through language. He sometimes cites this as the "original sin," referring to the story of Adam and Eve coming to "know" they were naked. A major difference from Foucault, however, is in Maturana's emphasis on "love" as a biological phenomenon that makes it possible for observing and language to emerge among humans in the first place. But that is quite another story.

Michael's initiative in drawing attention to Foucault's notion of "positive" power (as distinct from external, imposed, repressive, or "negative" power) helps unravel the self-constituting dynamics of self-observation and self-description. The effects of a person's own internalized "gaze" of "normalizing judgment" is extremely powerful in_determining one's experience of self and one's well-being. The power is positive in the sense that it proactively defines the nature of that which is being distinguished; it is not necessarily positive in the sense of being good or desired. Whether any knowledge of self as positive power (e.g., "I am blonde and average in height") is seen to be "good" or "bad" depends on an additional distinction being made on the desirability of the initial distinction about self. Thus, an awareness of positive power invites us to develop a second-order perspective of "looking at our looking" to see the nature and consequences of our seeing. This is an extremely important area that undoubtedly will be elaborated further in the future.

I regard Foucault's two forms of knowledge as power—positive constitutive power and negative repressive power—as lying on overlapping continua rather than as dichotomous. Indeed, positive power may be seen to arise developmentally from negative power. For instance, the process of colonization begins through the imposition of a foreign culture which is gradually internalized as the colonials become self-colonizing. Similarly, the process of individual socialization begins with the "imposition" of family knowledge and interaction patterns upon a child. As these become internalized there is a gradual shift, from "outer control" of the child by parents and other adults, to "inner control" as the child becomes an adult. The process is then reproduced in the next generation, as negative (outer defining) power once again becomes transformed into positive (inner defining) power. A similar phenomenon may also be seen to occur in the process of therapy. For example, the therapist implicitly exercises negative (restrictive) power in selecting preferred outcomes on the basis of their healing potential and languages them into the therapeutic conversation through questions and statements. The therapeutic languaging may be internalized by the client and eventually be woven into the fabric of his or her own new story as a form of positive (constitutive) power for wellness.

Michael's special contribution here has to do with his careful analysis of the practices of power in the intrapersonal and interpersonal relationships of clients. For instance, his initiative in drawing attention to the notion of recruitment is both liberating and empowering. An awareness of recruitment may be liberating when we become sensitive to, and turn down, invitations from others to see ourselves negatively, and empowering when we become mindful of invitations from others to see ourselves positively. Thus, recruitment can be employed in both pathologizing practices and healing practices. Given his protest orientation, Michael gives priority to disclosing the pathologizing process and points out how persons have been recruited into collaborating in the subjugation of their own lives and in the objectification of their own bodies. He introduces the notion of a "ruse" to draw attention to how the workings of this positive power is disguised and masked by virtue of the knowledge claim for some "truth" status. I use the notion of treachery rather than that of a ruse to explain how persons are incited to embrace their own subjugation.

Michael then notes how one can deconstruct such practices of power through externalizing conversations. As various practices of power are unmasked in this manner, it becomes possible to take a position of protest against them to counter their influence in one's life. Once a pathway of escape from such positive power is opened, it becomes easier to acknowledge the extent to which one has been recruited into policing one's own life and to recognize how one unwittingly participates in policing the lives of others.

Knowledge Practices

In this final section Michael focuses on how we as professionals exercise our power through our patterns of discourse. In keeping with the postmodernist tradition he critiques the modernist accounts of knowledge as "global and unitary." He points out that professionals are often privileged to speak with authority beyond the range of their personal experience. He also notes how the language practices of experts tend to disembody the personal perspective and opinions of the speaker or writer. I certainly concur but couldn't help but notice that he was writing in the third person and was becoming invisible himself. It is extremely difficult for us to escape these cultural patterns. I still can recall the struggle I had in beginning to write professional reports and academic articles in the first person — it felt improper. The positive power of "scientific" writing had possessed me to the extent that it didn't seem natural to use "I" in these contexts. Fortunately, I managed to escape that power, so that the use of "I" now feels more coherent and authentic than not using it.

In his deconstruction of knowledge practices, Michael comes quite close to responding to my concern about the lack of self-reflection in our field. He begins to apply his critique of knowledge and power to the therapy process by encouraging therapists to be more open with clients in situating their therapeutic contributions in the context of their own "personal experiences, imagination, and intentional states." This allows for two important processes to emerge at the therapist end of the therapeutic relationship, i.e., transparency of the therapist's method and techniques (as noted by David Epston) and authenticity of the therapist as a "real" person with his or her own feelings, thoughts, and desires. These complementary dynamics of increased transparency and greater personal authenticity diminish the mystique of therapy and reduce the power differential between therapist and client. This is a direction that I am trying to orient myself towards in my own work, and I am affirmed to recognize how Michael and I seem to be evolving along the same path in this respect.

REFERENCES

Andersen, T. (1987). The reflecting team: Dialogue and meta-dialogue in clinical work. *Family Process, 26*, 415–428.

Andersen, T. (Ed.) (1991). *The reflecting team: Dialogues and dialogues about the dialogues*. New York: Norton.

Bourdieu, P. (1988). *Homo academicus*. Cambridge, MA: Harvard University Press.

Bruner, J. (1986). *Actual minds, possible worlds*. Cambridge, MA: Harvard University Press.

Foucault, M. (1979). *Discipline and punish: The birth of the prison*. Middlesex, England: Peregrine Books.

Laing, R. (1961). *The self and others*. London: Tavistock.

Maturana, H., & Varela, F. (1980). *Autopoiesis and cognition: The realization of the living*. Dordrecht, Holland: Reidel.

Prigogine, I., & Stengers, I. (1984). *Order out of chaos*. Toronto: Bantam.

Tomm, K. (1991). Beginnings of a "HIPs and PIPs" approach to psychiatric assessment. *The Calgary Participator*, Spring, 21–24.

Tomm, K. (1990). A critique of the *DSM. Dulwich Centre Newsletter, 3*, 5–8.

White, M. (1991). Deconstruction and therapy. *Dulwich Centre Newsletter, 3*, 1–22.

White, M., & Epston, D. (1990). Narrative means to therapeutic ends. New York: Norton.

4

CREATIVE MISUNDERSTANDING: THERE IS NO ESCAPE FROM LANGUAGE

Steve de Shazer

WHEN I FIRST STARTED doing therapy with couples and families (around 20 years ago), the buzz word was "communication." When asked, everybody said the problem was "we don't communicate." It quickly turned out that they meant "he or she doesn't agree with me." People still say "we don't communicate" and I am afraid they are right—what they communicate when they say "we don't communicate" doesn't communicate anything at all because, as Watzlawick (Watzlawick, Beavin, and Jackson, 1967) says, "one cannot not communicate." Whenever I hear people say that they can't communicate, I am reminded of a line from social satirist Tom Lehrer: "I wish that all the people who complain about being unable to communicate would at least have the courtesy to shut up."

I realized just the other day that "conversation" has now become a similar buzz word. A couple, both professors, came to see me. When I asked, "What brings you in?" he said, "We never have conversations." She quickly disagreed. They went on and on and, as my dad would say, I had trouble getting a word in edgewise. To me, perhaps naively, what they were doing looked and sounded like a conversation. Essen-

The author wishes to thank his colleagues, Insoo Kim Berg, Larry Hopwood, Jane Kashnig, and Scott Miller, for their contributions to this essay.

tially, they were taking turns talking. It turned out that what he actually meant was that neither of them could convince the other to change his or her ideas or behaviors. Throughout the session I was puzzled by the professor's claim that they couldn't have conversations. It seemed to me – the real problem was, they couldn't communicate!

That was the obligatory opening joke, even though – like most of my jokes – it wasn't a very good one. So, let us pretend that it didn't happen.

Today, I am going to address three related "topics." The first is the words "therapeutic conversation" and what some of us may have had in mind when we read the title of this conference. Next, I will talk about the use of language in therapy, the language of problems, and in particular how the words used to describe a problem point directly to how to begin to construct a solution. Lastly, I will talk about what might be useful in viewing therapy as a conversation.

*   *   *

I have long been fascinated by certain types of puzzles, particularly mysteries that are built into the language we use. For instance, the title of this conference is "therapeutic conversations." Each of us read this in a particular way and thus it meant different things to each of us. And how each of us misunderstood this is not our fault – if there is any fault here, it belongs only to the way language works. Although I am getting ahead of myself here, I do want to point out that I deliberately used the word "misunderstand." This is because I have figured out that it is impossible to arrive at any one "true" meaning for any word, just as it is impossible to arrive at the user's (author's) true intention, even if I am the user.

One way we could misunderstand the title is to read it to mean that the conference would involve conversations about therapy. If you read it that way, then the readings of formal papers and formal presentations such as this – where I stand up here and talk while you sit there and (at least pretend to) listen – might seem at least incongruous. We would all be hard-pressed to label this a "conversation." After all, conversations generally are thought to involve two or more people taking turns talking and all of you are going to have a rather long wait for your turns to talk. So I hope that not too many people read the title this way. Of course, conversations about therapy actually do happen spontaneously at conferences: in the halls, in the bars, etc. This is actually where the action is at most conferences. But no conference can be organized on a "be spontaneous" principle of organization.

The next possible reading came to mind when I remembered what our secretary said the first time she watched a session from behind the mirror: "Shit, they aren't doing anything in there but talking!" As an astute observer, she had hit the nail on the head. This reading suggests that the conference would bring together people who think that conversations per se are therapeutic, much in the traditional way that people thought that the therapeutic relationship *per se* was the curative factor in all therapy. That is, therapy *is* conversation. This can be taken to mean that conversation is an explanation of therapy, much the same way that paradox was sometimes seen to explain therapy. Perhaps some of you hold this view and I can only hope that your expectations have been or will be met. It is not, however, a view that I share.

A third reading (or rather a third misreading) is based on the grammar of the title: The word "therapeutic" is an adjective modifying the noun "conversations." This suggests that this conference might bring together people who see doing therapy as a conversational activity; an interactional, constructivist activity: therapy described *as* conversation.

There is a big difference between "therapy *is* conversation" and "therapy *as* conversation." If therapy *is* conversation, then – by one of the rules of grammar and logic about the meaning and use of the word "is" – conversation *is* therapy. Therefore, this implies that any conversation will do. The therapist does not even need to know anything except how to have a conversation much like any conversation he or she might have in a bar.

However, if we read it to mean that therapy can be seen and described *as* a conversation, then we need to look at how this special kind of conversation fulfills therapeutic purposes and how this point of view helps us and our clients do our work together. Within this framework, our learning about therapy, our constructions of the therapeutic endeavor necessarily involve our dealing with language. There is no escape from this. This is because conversations always happen in language. (Therefore, we do not need the silly, pseudo-word "languaging.") If doing therapy is to be seen as conversational, then therapy needs to be seen as always happening in language. Thus we need to learn about how language is used in therapy. For, as the 18th century philosopher Condillac (in Derrida, 1987, p. 103) put it: "Do you want to learn the sciences with ease? Begin by learning your own language."

We cannot know with any certainty what Condillac meant by "science," but he certainly did not have the limited meaning that we now commonly have for the term. His use was probably much wider. (By the way, before we get into any unnecessary trouble, I am in no way claiming that therapy is "scientific." My position could not be further from that. In fact, I think that the traditional linkage between science and therapy is one of those ideas that has handicapped therapists, theorists, researchers, and clients alike.)

I am willing to bet that many of you are saying to yourselves that you know your own language. I am certainly tempted to make the same claim, but I am not sure that the language I think I know and the language you think you know amounts to all there is to know about our language. There are many very different ways of approaching language, three of which might help us better learn about our uses of language in therapy:

1. In traditional Western thought, language is usually viewed as somehow representing reality. This is based on the notion that there is a reality out there to be represented. Therefore, language can be studied by looking at how well it re-presents that reality. This, of course, leads to the idea that language can represent "the truth," which leads to a further idea that a science of meaning can be developed by looking behind and beneath the words — an approach usually called "structuralist" (espoused by Freud, Chomsky, and Selvini Palazzoli among others).

2. From another point of view, the Buddhists would say that language blocks our access to reality. That is, they too think there is a reality out there. So, naturally enough, this leads Buddhists to the idea of meditation which is used to turn off language, putting one in touch with reality.

3. A third view, perhaps beginning with Condillac and continuing on through Jacques Derrida (1978) is that language *is* reality. To put it in terms more familiar to therapists, this idea that our world *is* language suggests a "constructivist view," although this perspective is much wider and better built than what is typically meant in the therapy world by the term "constructivism." In brief, contemporary philosophers look at how we have ordered the world in our language and how our language (which comes before us) has ordered our world. Therefore, like Condillac, they believe that we need to study language in order to study anything at all.

* * *

You cannot solve the problem with the same kind
of thinking that has created the problem.
                                        — *Albert Einstein*

> All of the facts belong only to the problem, not
> to its solution.
> — *Ludwig Wittgenstein (Tractatus 6.4321)*

At first glance I am tempted to say that I wish I were quoting myself here rather than Einstein and Wittgenstein. The latter quote in particular even sounds like something I might say. Basically I agree with what Wittgenstein says if we are using the term "problem" in the ordinary way that we use it. That is, following John Weakland and his colleagues (e.g., Watzlawick, Weakland, and Fisch, 1974), "problem" can be defined as "more-of-the-same" of something that is not working. That being the case, doing more of something that is not working belongs only to the problem and is not part of the solution. Clearly, then, a radical distinction between problem and solution seems an useful idea. So does the idea that "facts" belong only to the problem side. This second idea implies that you do not need to know about the facts in order to get to a solution. But, it leaves the question: If "facts" belong on only one side of the distinction, what kind of "non-facts" belong on the solution side?

As I've said elsewhere (de Shazer, 1988, 1991), you need to have the idea of a solution before you can have the idea of a problem. That is, if "x" is to be seen as a "problem," then one has to be able first at least to imagine that "non-x" or the absence of "x" is possible. Otherwise, "x" would be just a fact of life to be dealt with accordingly.

So far, Wittgenstein and I have been treating the term "problem" and the concept of problem as if it were a "thing." Therefore, the term "problem" has been used as if it has a unified definition, i.e., a "pure problem." This is okay since it is the way the word is usually used, but it might be misleading.

So let's not follow the majority of theorists and become phobic about particulars and details: Instead, let's turn our attention to one specific problem:

> *Exhibitionism.* Sexual deviation in which the main sexual pleasure and gratification is derived from exposure of the genitals to a person of the opposite sex. (*ICD-9-CM*)

The dictionary definition is about the same but neither of these definitions gets at what clients talk about. That is, clients say that "flashing" is driven by a compulsion:

> a failure to resist an impulse, drive, or temptation to perform some action which is harmful to the individual or to others. The impulse may or may

not be consciously resisted, and the act may or may not be premeditated or planned. (*ICD-9-CM*)

Webster's defines "compulsion" a bit differently as "an irresistible impulse to perform some irrational act."

Over and over again I have heard about the "irresistible impulse to flash" from various clients. They say that flashing is an involuntary activity. As I've talked with them about this, they have told me that they can get the urge as many as ten times in a day. Since they say flashing is both "irresistible and involuntary," I will then ask them about how they find the time to flash 10 times per day. Well, all of them I've talked to so far say that somehow they overcome some of the urges.

So, since they can overcome the urge *sometimes*, the urge turns out not to be irresistible and flashing turns out not to be involuntary after all. This means that flashing is really voluntary since they decide to give in to the urge rather than continuing to fight it. And, of course, overcoming the urge is also voluntary since the urge turns out to be resistible.

To put this simply, it turns out that the words used to describe a "problem" automatically imply other words that point directly to how to begin constructing a solution. "Irresistible" points to "decision and choice," "involuntary" points to "voluntary," etc. When words are considered to be "facts," then the words used to talk about a "problem" belong only to the problem. But the words that these words automatically imply belong only to the solution. The "non-facts" that are not spoken about as part of the problem become the words used to talk about a solution. This line of thought is clearly not the same as the kind of thinking that created the problem.

Obviously, the involuntary/voluntary pair led to the idea of symptom prescription, making the involuntary into something voluntary. And the diagnostic manual led to the naive and mistaken idea that it was the act-of-flashing that was involuntary and, therefore, some people will get the idea that flashing was the symptom to be prescribed. But it is not quite ethical to prescribe an illegal act. Besides, the act itself is really voluntary already. Well, what about prescribing the urge since that is apparently involuntary? The same ethical difficulty applies since it may lead to an illegal act. Besides, since not overcoming the urge is only a sometimes thing, you end up prescribing more-of-the-same of something that is not working.

It turns out there is another pair of words often used in this situation: unpredictable/predictable. Flashing is usually described as something predictable and the exceptions (that is, overcoming the urge) are described as unpredictable. We've found that asking a client to predict exceptions increases the frequency of the exceptions. Having the exceptions happen more often makes them more predictable. Once a client begins to have doubts of the predictability of giving in to the urge and becomes more sure of overcoming the urge, then the urge "goes away." In this way, one-half of the pair is used to undermine the other half: Predictability (of exceptions) undermines unpredictability (about exceptions) while at the same time unpredictability (of the flashing) undermines predictability (about the flashing). This is certainly not the same line of thinking that created the problem.

This scene illustrates words at work in therapy. When studying the conversational aspects of therapy, we find that both clients and therapists use a lot of words and concepts without thinking about how these words and concepts actually work. Western languages have always been structured in terms of dichotomies or polarities: predictable/unpredictable, voluntary/involuntary, male/female, speech/writing, presence/absence, problem/solution, and so forth. In part, every term is defined and/or has meaning in terms of its opposite. One cannot refer to one term without implicitly referring to the other term. Furthermore, as Derrida (1978) points out, these opposites are not usually seen as equal and thus the second term is a fallen or corrupted version of the first term and therefore it is suppressed. The result has been the traditional privileging of good over evil, voluntary over involuntary, male over female, speech over writing, presence over absence, problem over solution. Pairs of opposites are all related in this way and the differences between each member of a pair, such as "predictable/unpredictable" or "voluntary/involuntary," are exactly the kind of difference that therapists and clients can put to work in order to make a difference.

* * *

It might seem pedantic, but I want to start talking about what may be useful in viewing therapy as a conversation by looking at the term "conversation." What do we mean by "conversation"? The dictionary suggests some meanings. In addition, since words/concepts automatically carry around their opposites – which, in part, work as sort of an automatic constraint on meaning – let's look at the "conversation/non-conversation" pair.

> *Conversation:* social intercourse; a talking together; informal or familiar talk; verbal exchange of ideas or information.

So, by looking at what conversation is not, a non-conversation turns out not to be silence but rather a non-talking *together*, an asocial or anti-social *intercourse*. It could be a nonverbal exchange of ideas or a verbal exchange of non-ideas. Or a speech, a one-way flow of ideas and information, i.e., the traditional notions about therapists' having privileged knowledge about their clients, what ails them, and how to fix them.

Therapy is not a speech, it is not a lecture, and it is not a one-way flow of ideas and information. It is some sort of exchange or interaction. By looking at what a "conversation" is not, we can have at least some ideas about what the word means and how I use it.

From the dictionary definition, we can see why some people who use the "conversation" metaphor claim to not be experts — which I hope is a false claim. Otherwise, why charge the clients?

> *Expert*, 1. very skillful; having much training and knowledge in some special field. 2. of or from an expert; as, an expert opinion.

I certainly want to retain the idea that I am some sort of expert — in the first sense of the term. I have a lot of knowledge about (a) talk about problems and how they happen, (b) talk about solutions and how they develop, and (c) how language works; moreover, as the Australian therapist Brian Cade might say, I know a lot about (d) what does not work. I also know a lot about (e) where the materials for constructing a solution come from — they come from clients. In fact, I think of clients as experts — they know a lot that I do not know. So, therapeutic conversation is a talking together between or among experts sharing and exchanging ideas and information in language.

You'll notice that I have privileged the term "therapeutic" to this point, using it only to modify "conversation" and thus to limit the scope of the topic. (This privileging of one term is a favorite trick of philosophers and theorists. There is always the hope that nobody will notice. As I work as a "therapist" by trade, my looking at language means I have to look at what the term "therapy" means.) What does the term "therapeutic" mean within the context of "therapeutic communication" or "therapy as conversation"? Let's begin by looking in the dictionary.

> *Therapeutic*, serving to cure or heal; curative; concerned in discovering and applying remedies for diseases.

Woe! This is certainly not the definition I want to *use*. Thank god that the word "therapy" and the concept of therapy — as defined in the dictionary — are not structurally determined or hard-wired together.

Instead, we can follow Wittgenstein's advice and look at the way we *use* the word to find out what it means.

The technique of looking at the implied opposites did not seem to point quickly anywhere useful or interesting, so I tried a different approach.

Under "therapy" the thesaurus lists about 40 terms, including "antidote," "cure," "medication," "medicine," "prescription," and "remedy." These words are "more of the same," in the bad sense of the phrase. "Remedy" in the dictionary pointed back to therapy, but the list for remedy in the thesaurus proved interesting because the 34th entry on that list was "solution." I could buy a definition like this:

> *Therapy*, is concerned in inventing, "discovering," and applying solutions and/or results; a mutual, cooperative, collaborative conversation between two or more experts.

That is about the way my team and I use the word.

* * *

There is nothing outside the session. When I first started using the term "conversation" in regards to doing therapy (de Shazer, 1988), all I had in mind was that the majority of time the simplest observation reveals that therapists and clients are taking turns talking together. And that's about all they do. Nothing mysterious is involved, nothing is hidden away. All I wanted to say was that therapy can be looked at as a conversation, that is, people taking turns talking together. There are no wet beds, no voices without people, no depressions. There is only *talk* about wet beds, *talk* about voices without people, *talk* about depression. There are no family systems, no family structures, no psyches: just talk about systems, structures, and psyches. When it comes to doing therapy, doing therapy is all there is and, therefore, there is nothing outside of the therapy session that can help us understand what is going on in the session. Even in our follow-up studies we are only having a conversation about results: We never *have* results, only depictions of results. As Wittgenstein says (in a different context), "You've got what you've got and that's all there is."

All I wanted to do, with my use of the term "conversation," was to point to something obvious, something that had been skillfully hidden away on the surface of things so that nobody saw it. Therapy involves the use of language. Therapy is in language and thus we need to look at the use of language in therapy. But, instead of seeing language at work, instead of seeing conversations, therapists have traditionally seen systems, structures, binds, loops, psyches, splits, dirty games, and other lamentable imaginaries. In my view, therapy is nothing but language, the client and the therapist are always using language. This, too, has been hidden away on the surface of things while therapists, influenced by their scientific frames, looked for something deep and hidden away.

I had no idea that when I started looking at doing therapy as a conversational activity it would lead me into probing contemporary philosophy (de Shazer, 1991). I did not want to do this because I was afraid that philosophy would urge me to look for something behind and beneath the dialogue. All too often philosophy gets deeply involved with "reading between the lines" and my research training and my reading of Wittgenstein taught me to avoid reading between the lines because, alas, there might be nothing there. I had long ago given up philosophy because I thought that most of it was too obscure to be of any use in the day-to-day work of therapists. About 25 years ago, when I was studying philosophy, I tried to explain Heiddegger to my father (since he had made the mistake of asking). When I finished he said, "I see. Philosophy does to men's minds what egg-beaters do to eggs." There is a lot of wisdom in that. So I more or less put philosophy aside, only lately being dragged back into it, kicking and screaming all the way. I was very reluctant, but I have learned to follow along where things lead me, so I started to read contemporary philosophy and was very surprised to find what I found.

Much of contemporary philosophy involves a critique of language and looks at the way language actually works. (It does not deal with hypothetical states and imagine the way language is supposed to work but never does.) And, as I hope I've made clear, at least some of it is immediately relevant to our doing therapy. Don't worry, I am not going to recommend that you run out and buy some books and begin reading Ludwig Wittgenstein and/or Jacques Derrida, if for no other reason then the latter is quite difficult to get through in either English or French. It is simply that I have based my remarks on the thinking I have done based on my misreading of their work.

* * *

At this point I want to continue our conversation by saying that I hope that your turn to listen and my turn to talk have finished at the same time.

Commentary

Stephen Gilligan

I AM PLEASED to have the opportunity today to comment on Steve de Shazer's work. I think of de Shazer as the Obe Wan Kanobe of psychotherapy. You probably remember the character played by Alec Guiness in the Star Wars movies — he was the kindly old warrior who taught young Luke Skywalker how to "use the force." In the first movie there is a scene where Luke and Obe Wan are trying to evade the forces led by Darth Vader. Right before they enter the bar with all the wild-looking characters, Luke and Obe Wan are stopped by a guard at a checkpoint. Since their description has been distributed, Luke is sure they will be apprehended. But Obe Wan makes the most minimal and graceful of movements to absorb the guards' attention before suggesting in a soft, hypnotic voice, "We're not the ones you're looking for." The mesmerized guide turns to some of his cronies and intones, "They're not the ones we're looking for." As he turns back Obe Wan makes another minimal entrancing gesture and says, "You can let us pass now." The guard, of course, allows them to pass. And Luke Skywalker learns an important lesson.

I think Steve de Shazer has learned the same lesson. He has a remarkable ability to use a minimum of effort to direct people into making significant changes in their life. He demonstrates a beautiful integrity in doing so and I have a great deal of admiration and respect for his work.

Having set him up with all these wonderful compliments, I'd like to spend the rest of my time criticizing him. One concern is that Steve de Shazer doesn't tell the truth! He calls his work "solution-focused," but it really has nothing to do with solutions. It seems more accurate to say that de Shazer simply works to shift attention to something else altogether, something that has little, if anything, to do with problems *or* solutions.

Take, for instance, two of his central techniques, the miracle question and identifying exceptions. In the miracle question a person is asked to imagine a world where the problem doesn't exist and then to describe what his or her life would be like. In the technique of "exceptions" people are asked to orient their attention to what happens when the problem isn't happening, and then usually directed to do more of the problem-unrelated stuff. It seems apparent in each of these techniques that clients are invited simply to attend to "what works in their life." There is very little relation to the problem and hence to a solution. So, again I wonder why this "solution-focused" term ever developed and why it continues to be used (especially when it seems that de Shazer [1991] makes points similar to mine).

Another concern of mine is de Shazer's (1991) "language about language." He espouses the constructivist view that "reality arises from consensual linguistic processes" (p. 44) and extends Wittgenstein's ideas to define therapy as a "language game" (p. 72). This approach views language not just as a string of words but as an organic contextual process that also includes nonverbal emphasis, silence and pauses, interpersonal contexts, previous learnings, and so forth. It also emphasizes "reality" as not something "out there," but as continually created by language in relationships. I find this view both powerful and empowering. At the same time questions arise.

First, is it helpful to distinguish different types of "language games" in the therapy context? I think it crucial. I would suggest that many, if not most, conversations in which we participate are decidedly nongenerative; that is, they do not actually construct or generate reality so much as reactivate previous constructions in a machine-like, predictable way. Clients complaining about the "same damn thing" happening over and over again illustrate this phenomenon, as do therapists who start an interview with answers rather than questions. I would suggest that the linguistic construction of new realities (rather than the automatic activation of past realities)—whether it be in music, marriage, therapy, poetry, or politics—is an art that requires a consciousness of aesthetic relationships (cf. Bateson, 1979). I think de Shazer demonstrates this beautifully in his actual work—he is an artist—but I fear that his writings don't adequately convey this crucial distinction.

A second question is: If "reality" arises from consensual linguistic processes, where does it arise from? Surely "reality" cannot arise from itself; it must "arise from" some "nonreal" context. One might insist that such a context is to be found "nowhere," perhaps as in Milton Erickson's hypnotic "the middle of nowhere," an inner space where new possibilities may be generated. I suggest this "middle of nowhere" as a poetic phrase to point to the domain of possibilities from which reality arises. The point here is neither trivial nor esoteric: The art of playing a "language game" (such as psychotherapy) requires a consciousness that stands with one foot in the domain of "reality" and the other in the "nonreality" domain of possibilities. The artist is a "borderline personality" who operates at the boundary between the domains, constructing and deconstructing realities, occasionally sensing Eliot's "intersection of the timeless with time." Language is the instrument, but consciousness itself is the player.

I suspect that de Shazer would find no value in distinguishing either the "nonreality" domain of possibilities or consciousness as the player of the instrument of language. My sense is that, lacking such distinctions, one increases the danger of becoming entrapped within a closed system of language where one's ideas are implicitly accepted as "true" and other epistemologies are "false." This leaves one weary and cynical, a condition I see develop in many therapists of various persuasions. In appreciating one's consciousness as more than a language game, one has the possibility of moving in and out of specific "language games" in order to invent realities that work.

Again, I appreciate watching how de Shazer does this when working with clients. He is, in the deep sense, an artist. My hope that as his writing continues to evolve it will include a similar appreciation of consciousness and the aesthetic.

REFERENCES

Derrida, J. (1978). *Writing and difference* (A. Bass, trans.). Chicago: University of Chicago Press.

Derrida, J. (1987). *The archeology of the frivolous* (J. P. Leavy, trans.). Lincoln, NE: University of Nebraska Press.

de Shazer, S. (1988). *Clues: Investigating solutions in brief therapy*. New York: Norton.

de Shazer, S. (1991). *Putting difference to work*. New York: Norton.

Watzlawick, P., Beavin, J., & Jackson, D. (1967). *Pragmatics of human communication*. New York: Norton.

Watzlawick, P., Weakland, J., & Fisch, R. (1974). *Change: Principles of problem formation and problem resolution*. New York: Norton.

Wittgenstein, L. (1961). *Tractatus logico-philosophicus* (D. F. Pears & B. F. McGuinnes, trans.). London: Routledge.

Wittgenstein, L. (1968). *Philosophical investigations* (3rd Ed.) (G. E. M. Anscombe, trans.). New York: Macmillan.

5

MICHAEL WHITE
AND STEVE DE SHAZER:
NEW DIRECTIONS IN FAMILY THERAPY

Jeff Chang
Michele Phillips

IT WAS A BUSY DAY at the adolescent mental health agency. In room 1, a therapist was meeting with 15-year-old Kyle, his father, mother, and younger brother. Lately, Kyle had been shoplifting, hanging around malls and arcades with a "bad crowd," staying out late, and coming home drunk or stoned. After careful questioning, the therapist suggested that the whole family was "under the influence" of trouble. Trouble had influenced the family to develop a story for themselves, and for Kyle in particular, that was full of despair, helplessness, anger, and frustration. She continued to question the family members about how their lives and relationships were immersed in the tale of trouble. The family agreed that this story took hold of them about 75% of the time and that if this continued Kyle would end up in jail and the parents' relationship would be fractured.

We would like to thank Karl Tomm and William Hudson O'Hanlon for their feedback on earlier versions of this paper and their personal encouragement. We would also like to thank our colleagues on the clinical team at Wood's Homes during the years 1988–1991 for providing the generative team atmosphere and unwavering support necessary for the co-creation of these ideas. This chapter is based on work presented previously at the Family Therapy Participants' Conference, Calgary, May, 1988, and the meeting of the Alberta Association for Marriage and Family Therapy, Edmonton, October, 1988.

The therapist asked: "What has been happening the other 25% of the time? What has Kyle been doing to stand up to trouble and write a new story for himself?" Kyle's parents proceeded to list examples. The therapist questioned family members about how they may have created a context for these troubles, albeit inadvertently, and they agreed that their zealous supervision of Kyle probably created a context for him to rebel even more.

To conclude the session, the therapist solemnly spoke of this being a crossroads in the family's life. They could take a stand against trouble or they could accommodate themselves to the old story. The therapist asked the family to experiment with the new story in the coming weeks to see whether they would want to continue to write it in their lives. However, she secretly believed that the experiment was academic because the family members were less blameful toward Kyle and more hopeful about standing up to trouble.

In room 2, another therapist was meeting with Teresa, also 15, and Donna, her mother, for the first time. They were fighting "like cats and dogs." Teresa had not gone to school in several weeks. Moreover, she was coming in at all hours of the night and her mother was afraid that Teresa was sexually active. After eliciting this problem description, the therapist asked Teresa and Donna what was occurring when the problems did not occur. Donna recalled that things had settled down for a stretch of about four days about two weeks earlier. Teresa had gone to school during those days, albeit for only part of the day, and the two had enjoyed pleasant conversation. Donna had even had the fleeting thought that maybe things were on the upswing. But a few days later the bottom fell out again, or so it seemed to Donna.

"What were the two of you doing," the therapist inquired, "to make these four good days happen?" They didn't know. "Well," the therapist replied, "what was different about those days?" Donna recalled that she had, for some unknown reason, felt more energetic in the morning. She had greeted Teresa with a chirpy "good morning" on each of those days. Teresa's experience of this was to believe that her mother really cared about her and was not just trying to spoil her fun and control her.

The major part of the interview was spent recounting some of the other things that each person appreciated about what the other had done. At the end of the session, the therapist did not have any novel or interesting suggestions for them. He told them that since they had been so clear about what had been helpful, they should simply do more of what works. A second session was scheduled for three weeks later, but on the way out Donna said, "I don't think we'll be needing it."

Afterwards, the two therapists ran into each other in the coffee room. In relating the stories of their interviews, they were struck by how the interview process had, in each case, brought forth solutions that their respective client families had already been enacting, albeit unknowingly. Their two interviews were miles apart stylistically, but the similarities had aroused their curiosity.

Many readers will recognize the therapeutic approaches mentioned in this account as those of Michael White and Steve de Shazer, respectively. Although this story is a fictitious one, it is symbolic of the exploration in which we have engaged individually and together over the last four years. Our attraction to these approaches and our observation of their similarities and differences led us to try and to place these two therapeutic approaches in context.*

IT'S A MATTER OF STYLE

Therapists who have seen both of these innovators at work, live or on tape, will immediately be struck, as we were, by the stylistic differences between the two approaches. We have noted a couple of stylistic distinctions.

Micro vs. Macro

One point of contrast is that White's work is "macro" while de Shazer's is "micro." White's work attends to the larger social context. For instance, in his work with couples, he will sometimes discuss the societal demands of being a "modern couple" (White, 1986b); with a young woman experiencing anorexia, he may discuss the way in which "patriarchal ideas" have influenced her life (White, 1989b). White's language has a political flavor. His description of people as being "oppressed" by problems (White, 1988) suggests that to engender change is to lead people out of their oppression. There is also a political flavor attached to his criticism of psychodiagnostic labeling. With young people experiencing schizophrenia, he "challenge[s] the subjugating effects of scientific classification" (White, 1987a). White incites clients to rebel against the oppression of the externalized problem, against problem-supporting societal beliefs, and against classification and labeling. The image suggested is one of a political revolutionary fighter.

*Recently, Kate Kowalski and Michael Durrant (1990) and Matthew Selekman (1989, 1991) have published accounts of their work reflecting the shared influence of White and de Shazer.

De Shazer maintains a "micro" focus that is pragmatic and apolitical. Family-of-origin data, gender, and the larger societal context do not enter into clinical conceptualizations. Rather than use language to incite clients and raise their consciousness, de Shazer uses presuppositional language to create the expectancy of change. To us, a Buddhist flavor is elicited (see Nunnally et al., 1986). The image suggested is that of a curious explorer searching for solutions.

Technology vs. Art

De Shazer's work has a technological flavor, while White's approach is more aesthetic. Without being dehumanizing, de Shazer's work has focused on developing maps for therapy that are teachable: "Ever since I began to do and study brief therapy in 1969, the question from observers, 'How did you decide to use that particular intervention?' has plagued me. . . . The question continues to be asked and answering it, or at least approaching an answer, is the purpose of this book" (1985, p. 3). Toward this end, de Shazer has adopted a minimalist stance, boiling therapy down to its essentials. He has pioneered the use of expert systems (de Shazer, 1988; Gingerich and de Shazer, 1991) to map some aspects of therapist decision-making. De Shazer acknowledges that this kind of map development does not account for the "art" of doing therapy.

White (1989a), on the other hand, has proposed "a therapy of literary merit." With David Epston, he has turned to the text analogy as the organizing metaphor for his work: "[The text analogy] . . . made it possible to conceive of the evolution of lives and relationships in terms of the reading and writing of texts, insofar as every new reading of a text is a new interpretation of it, and thus a different writing of it" (White and Epston, 1990, p. 9). Individuals have living relationships with their stories; this creates a richness that transcends being receptors of new information or double description.

PRECURSORS

Bateson's Influence

Bateson (1972, 1979) serves as a formative influence for both White and de Shazer. Bateson's (1972) ideas of negative explanation, restraint, and double description provide the principal theoretical map which guides White's (1986a) therapy. De Shazer (1985) used Bateson's

(1979) idea of double description to develop a metamap for conducting therapy. When the BFTC team compared multiple descriptions of the conduct of therapy, a "bonus" (i.e., an idea which is of a different class than the class of descriptions already used) developed out of the differences. This bonus provided the foundation for an early map (de Shazer, 1985) of solution-focused therapy.

Sociology and Anthropology

Other influences upon White come from anthropology (Bruner, 1986, 1990; Evans-Pritchard, 1976; Turner, 1969; van Gennup, 1960), the sociology of institutions (Foucault, 1975, 1979; Gellner, 1975; Goffman, 1961), and the women's movement (Orbach, 1978). For example, White (1986c) conceptualizes his "Ritual of Inclusion," as a ritual along the lines of Turner's (1969) description of rituals in tribal societies. Inpatient or residential treatment (Menses and Durrant, 1987; White, 1987a) are seen as rites of passage.

Critics of objectifying social practices have influenced White (Gellner, 1975; Evans-Pritchard, 1976). In their formulation, beliefs, particularly beliefs about the nature of clinical problems, are implicit. Such beliefs construct meanings through which life events are viewed and interpreted. White has identified psychodiagnostic labels, a particular expression of these implied beliefs, as a way in which scientific classification objectifies persons (Foucault, 1973). Social and spatial exclusion follows (Foucault, 1975, 1979; Stewart and Nodrick, 1990; White, 1987a). More recently, in developing the text analogy, White has depended upon the work of Jerome Bruner, a psychologist with links to anthropology, to describe how people develop narratives to create meaning for themselves. White also incorporates feminist thought into his work. In his work with clients displaying eating disorders (White, 1986c), and in marital therapy, particularly with respect to marital violence (White, 1986b), he traces how patriarchal beliefs maintain the problem.

One of de Shazer's descriptions for developing cooperation with clients comes from the sociological theory of games. To illustrate this, de Shazer (1985) describes the work of Robert Axelrod (1984). Axelrod found that in the game Prisoner's Dilemma, a cooperative strategy was ultimately the most successful. The game provided de Shazer with a model for therapists to cooperate with clients. Consistent with the macro/micro distinction we have drawn, White's roots in the social sciences address larger societal contexts, while de Shazer's use of game theory reflects an interest in small-scale, usually dyadic interaction.

The Narrative Tradition

Both de Shazer and White, in their more recent work, view therapy as a process of narrative development. As noted above, White has relied upon Foucault in discussing the objectification of persons. The objectification of persons is closely connected with the subjugation of knowledge (White and Epston, 1990). In clinical applications, a new narrative, distinct from the problem-saturated story, is co-authored to combat such subjugation of knowledge. The alternative narrative has not only a present but also a history. The historicizing of the narrative is in the service of White's goal of assisting clients to redefine their lives.

De Shazer views therapy as the development of a progressive narrative, one that justifies the conclusion that people are moving toward their goals (Gergen and Gergen, 1983, 1986). The progressive narrative is focused on the present and the future and is not historicized, since de Shazer's intent is to provide new definitions of contexts.

Deconstructivism

Recently, both de Shazer (1991) and White (this volume, Chapter 2) have acknowledged their reliance on deconstructivist philosophers, particularly Jacques Derrida (1978, 1981). Deconstruction, as defined by Anderson and Goolishian (1989, p. 11), is to:

> . . . take apart the interpretive assumptions of a system of meaning that you are examining . . . [so that] you reveal the assumptions on which the model is based. [As] these are revealed, you open up space for alternative understanding.

White deconstructs problem-saturated narratives that dominate clients' lives by introducing evidence of alternative stories. De Shazer uses Derrida's post-structuralist ideas about the co-construction of meaning as a launching point for his discussion about the nature of therapeutic conversations.

Milton Erickson's Influence

De Shazer (1975, 1978, 1979, 1980) has been heavily influenced by the work of Milton Erickson. This is particularly evident in his methods for having clients imagine problem-free futures, in communicating the inevitability of change, and in eliciting client cooperation. De Shazer has adapted Erickson's (1954) crystal ball technique, such that a standard part of the solution-focused model is to ask: "What will things be like for you and others when the problem is solved?" He notes, "Once the client has a picture of success, . . . he can spontaneously do something different so that this vision of the future . . . can become reality" (1985, p. 84).

De Shazer has been influenced by Erickson regarding the development of "fit" between therapist and clients. For instance, de Shazer (1985, 1988) assists the client to develop a "yes set" (Erickson and Rossi, 1979) by offering therapeutic compliments about what the client is already doing well.

White does not cite Milton Erickson as an influence. However, many of White's questions are similar to Erickson's trance induction procedures. For example, White uses truisms and presuppositions, as in this relative influence question: "What do you think it is about the events that you have related that tells me that you still have some influence in the life of the problem?" (White, 1989a). Many of White's questions have a confusional aspect: "Now that you are history-makers, that is, you have taken on the writing of your history from the writer of your old history, how has this history-making status changed your future from the future that has been assigned to you?" (1989b). Splitting is the hypnotic technique of using verbal juxtaposition to draw a distinction between two opposite experiences (O'Hanlon, 1987), as in this question from White: "I now have two pictures of you as a person, the old one and the new one, and I find the difference between them arresting. If you could hold these two pictures steady in your mind and compare them, what do you think you would discover about yourself?" (1987a). In fact, in referring to an old story and a new story, White is constantly using splitting to introduce multiple descriptions.

O'Hanlon and Weiner-Davis (1989) have suggested that Erickson's most important legacy is the utilization approach. Although White uses language that could be viewed as trance-inducing, he would be disinclined to utilize a problem pattern, instead inviting clients to oppose the oppression of a problem in their lives. In his early work, de Shazer (1985) developed a systematic approach to symptom utilization, in which fit was seen as a relationship between a problem pattern and a solution pattern. Thus, de Shazer's utilization orientation stands in contrast to White's against-the-problem orientation as one of the central distinctions between these approaches.*

---

*Alan Jenkins (1990), who has adapted White's approach in his work with abusive men, will ask such men whether they are "man enough" to take a stand against violence. From an Ericksonian frame, he is utilizing "patriarchy" or "macho-ness." The point is that these ideas are subject to multiple levels of analysis. Creative therapists combine models and enrich their own clinical work.

PROBLEM DEVELOPMENT AND MAINTENANCE

Problem Development

As might be expected, neither White nor de Shazer focuses much on causal explanations for specific problems. Like other constructivists, they focus on the generic processes involved in the development of clinical problems.

White's earlier ideas about etiology come from second cybernetics. Quoting Maruyama (1963), he states that problems develop when some "small and insignificant or accidental kick" triggers a process that amplifies the feedback such that the original conditions are lost. Over time the deviation is amplified, leading to the occurrence of entrenched clinical problems.

White (1984) further asserts that the search for etiological explanations leads to purposive notions that generate vicious cycles of guilt and blame, exacerbating the problem. Part of the etiology of a problem is the search for etiology. To challenge these notions, he suggests that the therapist, "after painstakingly taking a history of the problem, [announce] that s/he is sure . . . that the problem has been caused by at least one out of seven identifiable chance events [which could be] narrowed down to three or four possibilities with a further 10–15 years research . . . " (1984, p. 153).

Complementing these ideas are de Shazer's assumptions about how complaints develop. Assumption one is that "Complaints involve behavior brought about by the client's world view" (1985, p. 23). According to assumption two, "complaints are maintained by the clients' idea that what they decided to do about the original difficulty was the only right and logical thing to do" (1985, p. 25). De Shazer suggests that this "either/or thinking" restrains the search for solutions, resulting in the transformation of life problems ("one damn thing after another") into clinical problems ("the same damn thing over and over"). De Shazer suggests that virtually any course of action other than searching for the "correct" etiological explanation might lead to solution.

Problem Maintenance

White's (1986a) early description of how problems are maintained springs from Bateson's (1972) ideas of negative explanation. Rather than searching for a causal explanation for a problematic behavior, negative explanation focuses on what restrains people from taking alternative courses of action. Restraints, according to White, are of two kinds: those of redundancy and those of feedback. Restraints of redundancy are constraining beliefs and world views held by the client – essentially either/or thinking. Restraints of feedback are unhelpful circular patterns.

Using the text analogy to organize therapy gives another view of problem maintenance. Clients are immersed in dominant "problem-saturated" narratives. However, there are significant and vital aspects of their lived experience that contradict these dominant narratives (White, 1989a). Yet, these contradictions, or unique outcomes (Goffman, 1961) are not experienced by clients.

Neither White or de Shazer finds the concept of symptom functionality clinically useful. Approaches that embrace symptom functionality (e.g., Haley, 1976; Madanes, 1984; Minuchin, 1984; Selvini Palazzoli et al., 1980) would say that the problem is a solution (to another problem). This assertion has never made sense to White (1987b) who thinks "the problem is the problem" and sees people as oppressed by problems (White, 1988). De Shazer's work criticizes the belief in symptom functionality on the pragmatic grounds that it unnecessarily widens the problem definition: "the child's bed-wetting can be seen as if 'coming between the parents,' and thus an even bigger problem . . . can evolve" (1985, p. 24).

Resistance is another construct rejected by both White and de Shazer. White does not mention the word "resistance" in his published work. De Shazer pans the idea:

> Over and over I found people sent to me by other therapists (complete with the label "resistant client") to be both desperate for change and highly cooperative. . . . [The] idea that [clients] are going to resist change is at least misguided. In fact, with this kind of idea in mind, the therapist can actually generate "resistance" . . . or noncooperation, if not conflict. That is, the therapist's notions could generate a self-fulfilling prophecy with an unsuccessful outcome (1985, pp. 15–16).

THE CHANGE PROCESS

Readiness for Change

Related to the idea of resistance is the idea of readiness for change. For strategic therapists, readiness is an inherent state characterized by the clients' willingness to follow directives. De Shazer, however, eschews ideas of inherent readiness. Although his description of "visitors," "complainants," and "customers" is at times mistaken for a classification system of clients based on their motivation or readiness, he makes it clear that these labels are descriptive of the relationship between the therapist and client system. The interactional concept of "fit" between therapist and client system is much more clinically useful than the linear concepts of "motivation" or "readiness."

By contrast, White (1986a) refers to readiness as a condition that allows new ideas and descriptions to endure. White prepares the family to receive news of difference by introducing a "new code book," consisting of a cybernetic world view and novel premises about the problem, thus challenging the family's beliefs about the problem. This contributes to the endurance of new ideas in the client system.

Theory of Change

Turning to a more general discussion of the nature of change, Nunnally et al. (1986) trace BFTC's use of various metaphors for the change process. Maruyama's (1963) ideas of deviation-amplifying feedback and Wilden's (1980) ideas (derived from Bateson) about information in systems were found to be among the most useful to the BFTC team. The team's main dissatisfaction with them stemmed from their lack of attention to the role of the therapist/observer in the system; also, these metaphors were not prescriptive of therapist behavior. The "Buddhist view of change" suggests that change is constant and stability is an illusion. All kinds of change are occurring at the same time, a view consistent with both Erickson and Bateson (Nunnally et al., 1986). "Differences that make a difference" are contrasted with "differences that do not make a difference." Incorporating these ideas, Nunnally et al. summarize their view of change in this way: "Simply, satisfactory clinical change . . . is **constructed** by the therapist and the client out of various differences which are part of the constant process of change. . . . Whether a difference is part of making life more satisfactory is a matter of perception and interpretation, not fact" (p. 90). The BFTC team then turned its attention to the more pragmatic concern of the process of solution development.

Munro (1987), writing prior to White's publication of his use of the text analogy, notes that White's earlier theory of change was also based upon deviation-amplifying feedback. This is consistent with White's later explanations of change, based on Bateson's ideas of double description (White, 1986a). After preparing the family to receive news of difference, an alternative description of the problem situation is given. As family members receive the new description as "news," possibilities are opened for the family.

The emphasis on finding and highlighting alternative descriptions is continued in White's later published work (1988, 1989a; White and Epston, 1990). Identifying "unique outcomes" is necessary to the change process. Unique outcomes go unrecognized unless a context is created for their selection. "[To] pluck the new from the random requires some sort of selective machinery to account for the ongoing persistence of the new idea" (Bateson, 1979, p. 49).

The theories of change espoused by White and de Shazer are essentially the same. Yet, the operationalization of these ideas is quite different. In the next section, we will describe the procedural aspects of each approach.

PROCEDURAL DESCRIPTION

White

Following a period of joining, White obtains an account of the nature of the problem and the oppressive nature of the family's experience. Then, a "new code book" is developed (White, 1986a). This process prepares the family for the receipt of news of difference by introducing a cybernetic world view and introducing specific premises about the problem-maintaining complementarities in the family. Cybernetic questions address the relationship between the family and the world at large (e.g., "If the media successfully deceives a woman into believing she is only making a contribution when she is preoccupied with food and weight . . . how could this state of deception make it difficult for [her] to experience an entitlement to her own course in life?" [1989b, p. 69]). Complementary questions address the relationship between family members (e.g., "How does your disappearance in life invite others to make a stronger appearance in your life?" "How does your daughter's disappearance in life invite you to make a stronger appearance in her life?" [1989b, p. 72]).

Next, the problem is externalized (White, 1988). In externalization "cultural practices of objectification are utilized against cultural practices of objectification" (White, 1987a). Relative influence is then established by eliciting descriptions of the influence of the problem on the family, and of the influence of the family on the problem. Typically, the latter is more difficult, so unique outcome questions (White, 1989a) are used. These could be direct (e.g., "Can you recall an occasion when you could have given into the problem but didn't?" [1989a, p. 41]) or indirect (e.g., "What do you think it is about the events that you have related that tells me that you still have some influence in the life of the problem?" [1989a, p. 42]). Unique outcomes are historicized, and the problem-ridden narrative is deconstructed. Collapsing time may be used to trace the future course of a problem-saturated lifestyle if it were to persist. This process combats the phenomenon of accommodation by providing a stark contrast of descriptions. Next White raises a dilemma, in which he asks whether the clients wish to pursue a radical course of action in seeking to overcome the problem, as opposed to a conservative direction of further accommodating themselves to the problem. Experiments are devised for the family to decide which course to take.

When families decide upon a radical direction, White (1984) assists them in developing concrete ways to turn the tables on the problem. Change is responded to by highlighting it, sometimes through the use of awards, certificates, and other ritualized symbols (White and Epston, 1990), by the therapist expressing surprise and astonishment (White, 1985) — he may literally fall off his chair (White, 1987b) — or through the use of unique account questions and unique possibility questions (White, 1989a). The former focus on patterns formed by a multiplicity of unique outcomes (e.g., "What do you think that this achievement, as a signpost, tells me about the nature of your new direction?"), while the latter focus on the future implications of present changes ("What difference will knowing this make to your next steps?"). Prediction of relapse as a normal part of change can be introduced by the therapist to forestall a "back to square one" belief and to invite discussion of contingency plans.

Our description provides a general account of White's procedure. Of course, each case requires modifications. Externalization, for example, may not be appropriate in all cases. Cybernetic questions lend themselves well to problems with clear societal (usually gender-based) connections such as anorexia or marital conflict, but not so well to problems such as childhood fears or encopresis.

de Shazer

Solution-focused therapy generally begins with a period of joining and rapport-building. A brief description of the presenting complaint is elicited. If the client cannot construct a complaint, clients should be given compliments only and no therapeutic task. The therapist should relate to the clients as visitor (de Shazer, 1988).

If the client can construct a complaint, then the therapist searches for exceptions. In the case where the clients have experienced exceptions to the problem, it is important to elicit a description of how the complaint situation differs from the exception. If these differences can be elaborated clearly by the client, a direct prescription can be given to enact the described solution (Molnar and de Shazer, 1987). If exceptions have been experienced but the client cannot elaborate the difference between the problem situation and the exception, two courses of action can be taken. Tasks of observation (e.g., "Pay attention to what you do the next time you overcome the urge to [enact the problem]") can be used when clients perceive themselves as in control of the situation. Tasks of prediction (e.g., "Predict whether the next [time period] will have more instances of [exception to the problem]") can be used when clients perceive themselves not to be in control of events.

When the client cannot identify an exception, then the therapist's efforts are focused upon the development of hypothetical solutions ("How will you know when the problem is solved?"). If the solution description offered by the client is vague, then the Formula First-Session Task is delivered ("Between now and the next time we meet, we would like you to observe, so that you can describe to use next time, what happens in your family that you want to continue to have happen"). If the hypothetical solution is clear, then a direct prescription to enact it may be offered.

If the complaint pattern is part of a global frame, that is, an elaborate world view that provides the context not only for the problem but also for the client's life, then the frame needs to be deconstructed. Doubt is introduced when discrepancies in the logic of the frame are distinguished by the therapist and brought to the client's awareness (de Shazer, 1988).

The conduct of further sessions depends upon the clients' report on the effect of the intervention message in the previous session. When clients report behaviors and experiences that they want to continue, the therapist questions the family to clarify the appreciated changes. After this is clear to family members, the therapist focuses on expanding and maintaining these descriptions into the future (Lipchik and de Shazer, 1986).

When the family has followed a prescribed task in a straightforward way but no change is experienced, the problem may need to be redefined. If the family has not followed a prescribed task, then tasks of prediction or observation may fit better with the client system (de Shazer, 1988).

Use of Questions

Both White and de Shazer use questions to elicit, clarify, and enhance descriptions of times that the problem is not influential in clients' lives. White calls these "unique outcomes," while de Shazer calls them "exceptions." White equates unique outcomes with exceptions, noting that "the idea of exceptions produces 'exceptional persons' and that of unique outcomes produces 'unique persons'" (1989a, p. 37). We think that White has taken the term "exceptions" beyond the scope of de Shazer's intended meaning. White's intent is to co-construct new descriptions of clients, while de Shazer's intent is to introduce a new definition of a context. "Unique account" questions invite families to connect a number of unique outcomes. "Unique redescription" questions invite family members to ascribe significance to the unique outcomes and unique accounts through redescription of themselves, others, and their relationships. For example: "Do you think that the new picture of you that accompanies this new direction suits your sort of person more than the old picture did? If so, why does it suit you better?" (White, 1989a, p. 43). These new descriptions go beyond "internalizing personal agency" (Tomm, 1989) to internalize new qualities, attributes, and stories. De Shazer's questioning elicits and amplifies solution patterns in order to redefine contexts (Lipchik and de Shazer, 1986).

Hypothesizing

As we have noted above, neither White nor de Shazer finds the idea of symptoms serving functions in families very useful. Nor do they use the hypothesis-testing approach of the Milan team (Selvini Palazzoli et al., 1980). They would probably agree with O'Hanlon's (1986) views on hypothesizing:

> The Milan folks are fond of saying that one shouldn't "marry" one's hypothesis, but I'm more inclined to say one shouldn't even out go on a date with one. I think hypotheses are mere distractions at best and at worst become self (or other-) fulfilling prophesies (sic). . . . [A]ll brief therapists ought to have [couches] in their offices . . . for the therapist to use whenever he gets a hypothesis – he should lie down until it goes away! (p. 33)

RELATIONSHIP TO OTHER APPROACHES

White

Munro's (1987) description and analysis of White's work contrasted it with a number of other approaches. For instance, White's work and the Milan approach operationalize Bateson's ideas quite differently. The Milan associates introduce information through circular questioning (Fleuridas, Nelson, and Rosenthal, 1986), which draws forth differences between and among family members with respect to beliefs, behaviors, and relationships. White, by contrast, introduces information by challenging the family's problem-saturated description with a second description, de-emphasizing differences between family members. Munro suggests that White precedes *as if* there is an objective reality (i.e., the second description) which is to be preferred over other constructions of reality, while the Milan approach takes the position that there is no objective "truth." Moreover, while the Milan approach considers the effect of the observer on the system, Munro, commenting upon an earlier description of White's work, states that he does not refer to the effect of the observer on the system. She states that for these reasons the White approach is a first order cybernetic approach.

Since the publication of Munro's article in 1987, White has elaborated his approach to reflect a second cybernetic approach. First, his use of the text analogy (White, 1989a; White and Epston, 1990) suggests that he is co-authoring new stories with his clients. Secondly, White's use of questions (White, 1989a) makes it quite clear that he conceptualizes a therapist-client system. For example, the question, "What sort of journey in life do you think I am associating with this landmark?" would confirm this view. We would therefore consider White's approach, like the Milan model, to be a second cybernetic approach. In considering Sluzki's (1983) description of systemic therapies, White's approach is, like the Milan model, a world-view-based approach. This would be consistent with our view that White's therapeutic intent is to introduce redefinitions of persons.

de Shazer

In terms of related approaches, the "closest cousin" of the solution-focused approach is the MRI model (Watzlawick, Weakland, and Fisch, 1974). In fact, Munro (1987) placed de Shazer and MRI together as first order cybernetic models. Both approaches focus narrowly on interactional patterns, the problem pattern in the case of MRI, the solution pattern in the case of de Shazer. Both focus on either/or thinking as a process through which problems are maintained. Also, both have focused upon deviation-amplifying feedback as a model for describing the change process. As de Shazer states: "Only a small change is necessary" (1985, p. 16).

Solution-focused approaches differ from MRI in their emphasis on the fit between the therapist and client. For instance, in the MRI approach the therapist "sells" a reframe as reality (Munro, 1987), while a solution-focused approach would match the cooperating style of the clients and co-construct an alternative reality with them. An MRI therapist might create an ordeal or devil's pact to increase client "motivation" for change, while a solution-focused therapist would assess whether a "visitor," "complainant," or "customer" relationship exists. Because of the emphasis on fit and the role of the therapist in the system, we see de Shazer's approach as a second order cybernetic approach. The emphasis on interactional patterns suggests that, in Sluzki's (1983) conceptualization, it would be a process-oriented expression of systemic therapy. This would be consistent with a therapeutic intent to redefine contexts.

THE EVOLUTION OF CONSTRUCTIONIST/SYSTEMIC THERAPY

Real (1990) has traced the evolution of constructionist/systemic therapies. Currently these therapies are evolving from a "Batesonian, information based phase," in which the prime metaphor for therapy is creation of "news of difference," toward a "constructionist or language-based phase." This shift reflects a move from "observed" to "observing" systems (von Foerster, 1981). The central metaphor for therapy is that of a conversation.

White's work of five years ago (e.g., White, 1986a) clearly reflects the Batesonian information-based phase. Double description was the organizing principle for his work. His more recent introduction of the text analogy (White and Epston, 1990) suggests that his work, while quite similar, has evolved toward more of a language-based mode. Co-authoring a new story seems a much more collaborative description of therapy than introducing double description.

At first glance, de Shazer's (1982, 1985, 1988) work seems to have more in common with the Batesonian, information-based tradition, through its focus on disrupting patterns of either/or thinking and on interventive interviewing (Lipchik and de Shazer, 1986). A focus on co-creation of therapeutic realities appeared strongly in 1988, when de Shazer began to conceptualize "fit" differently than before. "Fit" previously referred to "the relationship between the intervention and satisfactory positive patterns" (Molnar and de Shazer, 1987, p. 350; cf. de Shazer, 1985), but evolved to refer to the relationship between therapist and the client system:

> Throughout the session, the therapist needs to be developing fit with the person or people she is interviewing. This kind of relationship . . . involves a special kind of closeness, responsiveness, or harmony. . . . Fit is a mutual process involving both therapist and the people he is conversing with during which they come to trust each other, pay close attention to each other, and accept each other's world view as valid, valuable, and meaningful. (1988, p. 90)

Although de Shazer's work tends to be seen as exception-based, the development of fit is an indispensable feature of the solution-focused model. This co-constructivist slant suggests a fit with a language-based description. More recently, de Shazer (1991) has referred to therapy as a "language game" and as a process of narrative development, clearly reflecting his shift with the rest of the field toward a language-based description.

CONCLUSION

Although theoretically very compatible, the therapeutic approaches of Michael White and Steve de Shazer are stylistically and operationally very different. The central distinctions are differences in therapeutic intent (redefining persons vs. redefining contexts) and stance toward the problem (against the problem approach vs. utilization approach). We view these approaches as alternative second cybernetic models that function to empower clients. Their focus on strengths and solutions places them at the cutting edge of a new tradition of co-constructivism in psychotherapy.

Commentary:
de Shazer & White: Vive la Différence

Steve de Shazer

CLEARLY, JEFF CHANG and Michele Phillips have done a meticulous, thorough job. My colleagues and I are quite impressed. Trying to tie together an evolving model such as ours is no easy task because, at any time, something might happen that prompts yet another shift in "style" or emphasis and thus a shift in how one reads what one reads. The authors have captured at least some of this evolution through reading the various books and papers my team and I have published between 1975 and 1991. Not only have they read widely, they have read quite well.*

I have two sorts of comments to make on this essay. The first are about the authors' view of our work and the second are about their comparison project. (I am glad to have this opportunity to look at the work of Michael White. The conference in Tulsa gave me my first opportunity to see videotapes of his work and commenting on this paper "forced" me to try to pull together my impressions.)

The author wishes to thank his colleagues Insoo Kim Berg, Larry Hopwood, and Scott Miller for their contributions to this essay.
*In this regard, I think that they under-read what I (we) have written about our "miracle question" and thus have seen our work as more "exception-based" than it actually is.

INTRODUCTION

As I see things, as a rule-of-thumb, one theoretical statement can be expressed with about 40 clinical statements/practices/skills/techniques. So there is nothing inherently impossible about having two, or three, or even many separate, highly distinct practices being seen as based on the same or very similar theoretical expressions. In fact, it is highly likely. Importantly as I see it, however, one must be able to "reason back" to theory from direct observations of practice: the two different expressions must fit.

I think it is important to note in this context that "different" means "unlike," "not the same," "not alike," such as *2 plus 2* is different from and unlike *3 plus 1*, and both are different from and unlike *2 times 2*. All three equations are similar in that they all equal four, but "similar" does not mean "the same," and the differences between them might be said to add to the richness of our description of the concept "4." Difference has nothing whatsoever to do with value judgments such as "right," "wrong," "good," "bad," "better," "worse," "inferior," "superior." Simply, distinction and difference are what allows us to prevent everything from being the same. We use words to mark distinctions and difference. Although words mean how we use them (Wittgenstein, 1968), Humpty Dumpty was dead wrong when he said "When I use a word . . . it means just what I choose it to mean—neither more nor less." "The question is," said Alice, "whether you can make words mean so many different things." And Humpty Dumpty was quite right when he continued, "The question is . . . which is to be master—that's all" (Carroll, 1972, p. 90). And Jacques Derrida (1978, 1981) is right when he says that the answer to Humpty Dumpty's question is: It is the word that is master, not its user. A word always means both more and less than we, as users, as authors, mean it to mean.

THE FAMILY THERAPY, BRIEF
THERAPY DISTINCTION

It seems to me that the sameness seen by Chang and Phillips is at least in part due to their situating both my work and White's within "family therapy." A careful look at or (mis)reading* of my works, even

---

*I am convinced that reading with any certainty that one has gotten at what the author meant is impossible. Therefore, I will use the term "misread" to suggest that my (mis)reading, like all (mis)readings, is only one of many possible interpretations of what has been written.

my early writing, will reveal that I do not and have not situated my
work within the family therapy tradition. Rather, I have all along
referred to my work as "brief therapy."*

This distinction is far from trivial. For instance, within the "family
therapy tradition" the family is usually seen as the patient, while in
the brief therapy tradition the "patient" (if that term can be used here
only for the purpose of comparison) is seen as the problem/solution
the client and therapist are working on (de Shazer, 1991).

Of course, it might be thought that this distinction inhibits or restrains me from seeing the sameness and similarities that Chang and
Phillips see. However, the first of Michael White's papers that I remember reading (White, 1986a) gave me the idea that similar developments were evolving within the family therapy tradition and I eagerly
looked forward to seeing how his work with clients resembled mine.
(Unfortunately, it turned out that I was to have a long wait.) I was
more than happy to see a certain family resemblance between his written work and mine. Subsequently, people in seminars, workshops, and
trainings asked about similarities and differences in such a way that I
began to get the idea that the differences might be more significant;
my reading of his later papers led me in the same direction. However,
I wanted to wait until I had seen his work with clients to reach any
conclusion on this.

TECHNOLOGY AND SCIENCE

In regards to the "technological" aspects of our work, I think that
"Technology vs. Art" is a muddle-making distinction and thus a dis-
traction. (As far as I know/remember, I have not used the term "science" to refer to my work nor have I used the scientific term "replica-
ble" and I do not refer to "empirical" methods. Our view is closer to
Lincoln and Guba's (1985) concept of "transferability." My point of
view is far simpler and far less "profound.")

As we watch a performer, whether it is a sax player or a center
fielder, we are watching the culmination of a long practice. That is, in
order for a performer to perform, she must master the basic techniques

*By necessity, I have been forced to publish in the family therapy journals
since there are, as yet, no equivalent brief therapy journals. This, of course,
dilutes the usefulness of the distinction between "brief therapy" and "family
therapy." The original name of our institute, Brief Family Therapy Center,
was a compromise developed by the brief therapists and the family therapists
who comprised the original group. This did not help to keep the distinction as
clear-cut as I would have liked.

and have absolute control over her horn. This is true in the classical music world and, perhaps more so, in the jazz world and it is certainly true in center field. Without a mastery of the basic skills, the "how" of performance is a mystery. To some extent, the doing of therapy and the doing of jazz and baseball are very similar. At each point along the way, the performer (therapist and/or the musician and/or center fielder) "spontaneously" decides* which of his skills are germane within the context of the endeavor. Without the basic skills, by blowing into a sax he might be lucky to produce a squak (*sic*). A therapist without basic skills? Well, I have observed many a session during which things went from bad to worse.

Empiricism and positivism (and the associated term "replicate") do not come into it at all. The primary purpose of the so-called technological side of our work is to describe the basic therapist skills of solution development with some rigor so that someone can learn them.

CONSTRUCTION, DESTRUCTION, DECONSTRUCTION

> How can I say what I know with words whose signification is multiple?
> — *Edmond Jabès (1959, p. 41)*

Elsewhere in this volume, John H. Weakland (Chapter 6) warns us about the abuse of terminology and the all too frequent resulting muddles and confusions. Chang and Phillips have pointed out that White and I (seen as "constructivists" in the way "family therapy" uses the term) both use the term "deconstruction" in our writings to refer to some aspects of our clinical work. In my view, Chang and Phillips are led astray, that is, enticed or seduced into seeing false similarities by the fact that White and I both use the term "deconstruction," although each of us uses it in a very different way.

Although there is no unified definition of "deconstruction," and one would be neither possible nor desirable, nonetheless there is a certain family resemblance among deconstructivist activities (Norris, 1982, 1983). For instance, Elizabeth Grosz (1990) in her feminist study of Jacques Lacan describes "deconstruction" as involving "a very careful, patient reading of the text," involving looking at a text "from a point

---

*These "spontaneous decisions" an observer might see as illustrations of "rule-following"—hence our work with expert systems.

of view sympathetic to the text's concerns and its logic; and at the same time, reading it from the point of view of what is left out, foreclosed, or unarticulated by it but is necessary for its functioning." Thus, this mode of "reading a text from both inside and outside its terms, i.e., from its margins, must remain ambivalently an act of love and respect, and of self-assertion and critical distancing" (Grosz, 1990, p. 190).

The unit of analysis here is author and text and reader; if we carry over the framework of this activity into the therapy world, the unit of analysis is client(s) and therapist and the conversation they have together about the client's concerns. These approaches attempt to use the structure of a construction (including what is left out, foreclosed, etc.) to open up the construction itself, thus allowing space for new meanings to develop.

As I see it, this is reflected in our use of the client's own language and logic (rather than ours) to put any difference that is noticed to work in such a way that difference opens up the possibility of new meanings, behaviors, etc., developing.

While White acknowledges that his use of the term "deconstruction" is not synonymous with the academic definition, what he seems to be talking about is a radical, critical dismantling or undoing of the clients' construction of reality. Academically, this seems closer to a Heideggerian "*destrukion*" (Gasche, 1986, p. 111), a destruction of a construction *from the outside*. This seems to be reflected in White's use of what the authors call his political "code book" as a tool for challenging the family's beliefs. Although the term "deconstruction" may seem preferable within the context of "family therapy's" use of the term "constructivism," the term "destruction" is a perfectly useful, long accepted, and highly respected name for this kind of activity.

DIFFERENCE

Now to my central point: I disagree with the authors' assertion that "the theories of change espoused by White and de Shazer are essentially the same"* (p. 105). As a context in which to make clear the differences between what I see as radically distinct theories of change, I want to describe and exhibit the radical distinction between White's concept of "unique outcomes" and our concept of "exceptions" and the

---

*Or, as an alternative, White's practice is severely disjunct from his theory and/or his theory is disjunct from his practice.

related or consequent radical distinction between "anti-problem" and "solution."

First, I disagree with White's (1986b) statement that the term/concepts "unique outcomes" and "exceptions" are the same, are in fact interchangeable, and thus that "unique outcomes" produce "unique" persons while "exceptions" produce "exceptional" ones. The word "unique" suggests that it is a one-time event and misses the point and the word "outcome" means an end point: Exceptions are times or, better, depictions of times when the complaint is absent; the term "exceptions" always has a plural form. Exceptions to the rule of the complaint are always seen as repeatable to the point where "the exception becomes the new rule," an idea missed entirely by the term "unique outcome" which implies nonrepeatability (since an "outcome" is usually defined as an end or a result). (Furthermore, a point of rhetoric: Although I realize that White is using a trope, a figure of speech, nonetheless: Concepts cannot produce people.)

Second, I also disagree with the authors' idea that "unique outcomes" are used to redefine persons while situations are redefined via "exceptions." As far as I can see, when people are talking about the situations (contexts) they are in, then talking about that situation also involves the people in that situation. One must be careful not to abstract the people from the context or the context from the people.

As I see it, our concept of exceptions is broader than that: "Exceptions" are seen by us as signs and/or signals and/or indications and/or behavior(s) and/or thinking and/or talk that indicate that *a solution has already begun*! That is, neither is the context reified nor are the people abstracted from the situation.

So far, my comments have been based on what has been written about "exceptions" and "unique outcomes." Now I want to relate practice to theory to practice.

Based on the videotape White showed in Tulsa (which I assume was meant to illustrate current practice/theory as were the videotapes I showed there), I find it surprising and interesting that White seems to use "unique outcomes" as a tool in the battle against the power of anorexia. As I see it, what the authors call White's political "code book" is what establishes the equation "unique outcomes" equals "anti-anorexia." This sets up "pro-anorexia vs. anti-anorexia," which leaves the focus precisely on "anorexia." That is, the "anorexia" is still the focal point of life and thus "anorexia" has lost none of its "power to oppress." In fact, it now has two ways to "oppress the victim" (including the whole family), i.e., "pro-" and "anti-" ways. His behavior during the session indicates that he thinks that he has a better way: He introduces his "code book," his cybernetic/political jargon, his world view; in short, his language is used rather than the client's language. (Another point of difference between the two practices and theories which I think is far from trivial [see above].)

Thus my view, my misreading of Michael White's practice, agrees with Munro's and disagrees with the authors': White's practice strongly suggests that he does indeed believe in an objective reality. Using his "code book," he is going to teach clients a better way (or ways) to deal with that reality. He confirms for them that anorexia is powerful and it needs continued "anti" practices to keep it in its place, i.e., under control. It is not a "both/and" practice but an "either/or" practice: Something is *either* "pro-anorexia" *or* it is "anti-anorexia."

Thus, going from theory to practice to theory confirms for me that there are crucial differences between White's concept of "unique outcomes" and our concept of "exceptions" as reflected in his practice. These differences are even more salient than I had previously believed. White draws a "pro-problem"/"anti-problem (unique outcomes)" distinction, while I draw a "problem"/"solution (exception)" distinction. It is clear to me now that his "anti," his concept of "unique outcomes" is on the "problem" side of my distinction. His clinical practice of constructing the historical predictability of the "unique outcome" undermines its *uniqueness* and emphasizes the *outcome* or the end of a long process. The "unique outcome" is now just as historical as the problem of which it becomes just one part. Since the "unique outcome" is constructed as a historically predictable event, then it is just as causally determined as the rest of the problem, rather than the turning point that I had thought he was describing. As such, it leaves the concept of "anorexia" intact.

Thus Michael White's view is a very traditional one. It is, in fact, similar to the traditional view of alcoholism that states that, even though a person has not had a drink in 20 years, he is, nonetheless, an alcoholic. Reasonably enough, this point of view leads to the development of a parallel "anti-anorexia league,"* which was much discussed (in Tulsa) by White's co-author David Epston. That is, externalizing the problem and the unique outcome, objectifies and reifies them: In practice, "anorexia" exists as a real thing.

In contrast, as I see it, "exceptions" point to the start of a new

---

*This of course means that we can look forward to the development of some new ACOA, "adult children of anorexics." And then, of course, any nonstandard treatment that works will be dismissed because the patient was not a "real anorexic."

life without the problem, i.e., with *neither* "pro-anorexia" *nor* "anti-anorexia." Thus, once exceptions have been depicted, we will begin to refer to the problem as "it" and situate it in the past. Therefore, I want to continue to draw a radical distinction between "unique outcomes" and "exceptions," which I think are vastly different concepts and part of a vastly different theory of change.

White's concept of "solution" is a classical one in which the solution is intimately connected to, dependent upon, and determined by the "problem" (both "pro" and "anti" forces). Beginning in 1982, and, I hope, with increasing clarity since then (de Shazer, 1985, 1988, 1991), we have been drawing a radical distinction between "problem" and "solution," describing what is only a nominal relationship between the two concepts.

In terms of therapeutic outcome, White's approach may well work: I don't doubt that. The "anti-anorexia" may replace the "pro-anorexia" and thus the client may well be satisfied. As I see it, it is okay that "anti-anorexia" becomes a beneficial symptom substitution as long as clients do not complain about it and are satisfied. They will probably forget about it after some time.

CONCLUSION

I want to thank Jeff Chang, Michele Phillips, Michael White, and the organizers of the Tulsa conference for giving me this opportunity to clarify my thinking about the similarities and differences between White's approach and mine. The differences between them might be said to add to the richness of our description of the concept "therapy." Now it is time to see if these differences can be put to work in some useful way.

Now I have a way to respond when I am asked by workshop participants to compare and contrast my work with that of Michael White's. (My usual response over the years has been "I cannot do it because I have never seen him work."*) Now that I have seen videotapes of his work and have misread this paper, I can at least begin to respond to these requests for comparison.

"Unique outcomes" and "exceptions" are vastly different concepts. They lead to, follow from, and are related to vastly different clinical practices and theories of change. "Unique outcomes" are used in prac-

---

*I do not know what his response has been to the request for comparison. I would not base a comparison just on written works.

tice as part of the war against the problem, while "exceptions" are used as proof that the solution has already begun.

Thus I am impressed more by the differences than I am by any similarities. In fact, the differences substantiate and reaffirm my thesis that the two approaches are members of different families (problem focused/solution focused), different traditions (family therapy/brief therapy), and are not "theoretically compatible" at all! Metaphorically, the relationship between the two theories, models, and practices is similar to the relationship between apples and pineapples. That is, the term "apples" in the names of these two very different fruits implies and suggests a similarity that is nonexistent.

Commentary: The Histories of the Present

Michael White

I WAS RATHER HESITANT about putting together a response to the Jeff Chang and Michele Phillip's chapter, and wound up leaving this task to the last minute. This hesitation wasn't to do with what Jeff and Michele had written. In fact I really admire their piece. Apart from anything else, it reflects uncommonly good scholarship. To review, in the space of one chapter, Steve de Shazer's work as well as my own, and to include an account of the development of our current ideas and practices as well as a comparison of these, is no small task. To do so, and to demonstrate an understanding of some of the more subtle nuances of the respective approaches is indeed a significant achievement.

My hesitation related more to questions that I had about what sort of response from me might contribute further to the discussion. These questions related to several factors. First, what sort of commentary on Jeff and Michele's comparison would be likely to advance the discussion? Their piece was thorough, and I agreed with many of their conclusions – at least those that pertained to my work (although the speculation that ideas from hypnotherapy may have played a significant role in the development of my work does not strike a chord).

Second, I experienced some degree of trepidation about the idea of comparing my work with Steve's if this required me to generate some characterizations of his work. I had, in a 1988 publication, commented on what I assumed to be similarities in our respective ideas of exceptions and unique outcomes, even suggesting that the terms were interchangeable. Subsequently, Steve strongly repudiated this. In hindsight I realize that I drew this comparison without having developed anything like a reasonable familiarity with his work, and regard this repudiation to be correct — although I do not agree with the terms of it. While I do appreciate the generosity suggested in Steve's position on "(mis)reading," I am sure that a distinction can be drawn between informed (mis)reading and misinformed (mis)reading. I had assumed a familiarity with his work that I didn't have, and for this I owe him an apology.

The third factor that figured in my hesitation over this response relates to Steve's essay on the piece by Jeff and Michele, which he sent to me some time ago. Steve's account of my work, or, as he would probably prefer, his (mis)reading of my work, rendered it mostly unrecognizable to me. Despite the fact that this is an account of my work that is obviously shared in a particular community of persons, comprising Steve de Shazer, Insoo Kim Berg, Larry Hopwood, Jane Kashnig and Scott Miller, it was not "experience-near" enough for me (or experience-near enough for another community of persons) to enter into some dialogue over and to learn from.

Given this, and considering that I have only a passing acquaintance (but hopefully now a better informed one) with Steve's work, I eventually decided that I might best contribute to the discussion by elaborating more on particular aspects of my own work. However, before I proceed to do this, I would like to make just a few comments on what I perceive to be a couple of Steve de Shazer's general but important contributions to this field.

In my view, Steve de Shazer has played a key role in challenging the pathologizing and deficit-based thinking and practices that have so saturated the culture of psychotherapy. It is not possible to overestimate this contribution when one considers the fact that the invention of psychopathology is probably the most central and significant achievement of the culture of psychotherapy. He has directly challenged not only this invention, but also the very subjugating practices that are associated with it. And he goes further than this. He also eschews the structuralist and the functionalist traditions of thought that made possible, in the first place, the construction of the psychopathologies, the disorders, and the dysfunctions. Although it entirely depends on one's definition of "political," I can't help but observe a political aspect of this achievement.

Another contribution relates to the extent to which he has been prepared to spell out the actual practices – the very skills that are necessary for therapists to develop – of brief therapy, and I think that he has rendered it one of the most accessible and user-friendly competence-based approaches available today. He has complemented this by standing against obfuscation in the domain of theory and ideas, and for rigor in thought. I don't know if this would fit with Steve's definition of an exception in the field of psychotherapy, but it does fit with my definition of one.

I am not suggesting that these are Steve's only contributions, or that these overshadow other contributions, but they spring most immediately to mind when thinking about his work. He has undoubtedly been a central player in the "mega-trend" that Bill O'Hanlon has referred to.

A DISTINCTION

If these reflections on the more general contribution of Steve's work are reasonably well founded, then I do believe that my work can, to an extent, be aligned with his. This reflection enables me to entertain the idea that we might share some common purposes, and it might further explain why others have, on occasion, made the assumption that we are kindred spirits.

However, in moving away from the level of generalities, and upon developing a more informed acquaintance with the specifics of Steve's work, I have reached the conclusion that his apples/pineapples analogy is probably correct – the differences in our respective ideas and practices are far more evident and significant than the similarities. In fact, on closer examination, the differences appeared so numerous that, in attempting to draw out those that might be relevant to this current discussion, I hardly knew where to start.

After thinking this over some, I decided to concentrate here on the distinction that is to be drawn around the matter of "history." Since Steve's position on history is quite apparent in his essay, I will not attempt to represent it here. Instead I will endeavour to draw out, more completely, my interest in the "histories of the present" – in the history of the dominant present, and in the histories of the alternative present/s. Since I have a very particular appreciation of the histories of the present, it will be necessary for me to provide a context for this discussion.

My interest in the histories of the present is situated in the context of a tradition of thought that I will refer to here, for the want of a better word, as "constitutionalism," and is considerably inspired by the work of Michel Foucault and other "critical theorists." Many of the practices of therapy that accompany this constitutionalist perspective I regard to be forms of "deconstructive method."

But before proceeding to further explore these thoughts, first a rider or two. I am not drawing out this distinction around different appreciations of history in order to argue the relative merits of Steve's and my own respective contributions. Also, in concentrating on this distinction with regard to history, I am not taking a position against a future orientation – in fact, I believe that a future orientation features very strongly in my work. I do not wish to wind up in a debate with others around what I regard to be totalizations of my work – "it is all historical." I have never been prepared to offer, to others, these sorts of totalizations, and haven't been able to relate to any totalizations of my work that have been presented to me through the interpretations of others.

CONSTITUTIONALISM

Constitutionalism brings with it the proposition that, upon entering into life in the social world, persons become engaged in particular modes of life and thought – or, according to Foucault, particular practices of power and knowledges about life that have achieved or been granted a truth status. According to this perspective, these practices and knowledges are not radically invented – the individual person does not simply "dream them up." These practices and knowledges have been negotiated over time within contexts of communities of persons and institutions that comprise culture. This social formation of communities and institutions compose relations of forces that, in engaging in various practices of power, determine which ideas, of all those possible, are acceptable – they determine what is to count as legitimate knowledge.

It is not my intention to more fully articulate these processes here, nor the intimate relationship of knowledge and power, which I have discussed elsewhere. However, I will emphasize a central proposition of this constitutionalist perspective: these modes of life and thought are actually shaping or constituting of persons' lives and of their relationships; persons' lives are made up according to these knowledges and practices, which are in fact specifying of life. For all persons living in specific cultures, these dominant modes of life and thought come to reflect the truth about human nature, about authenticity, and about identity. So these dominant modes of life and thought represent the history of a person's existence in this world.

The constitutionalist perspective that I am arguing for refutes foundationalist assumptions of objectivity, essentialism and representationalism. It proposes that an objective knowledge of the world is not possible, that knowledges are actually generated in particular discursive fields. It proposes that all essentialist notions, including those about human nature, are ruses that disguise what is really taking place, that essentialist notions are paradoxical in that they provide descriptions that are specifying of life; that these notions obscure the operations of power. And the constitutionalist perspective proposes that the descriptions that we have of life are not representations or reflections of life as lived, but are directly constitutive of life; that these descriptions do not correspond with the world, but have real effects in the shaping of life.

How does this constitutionalist perspective position us in relation to the familiar ideas and practices of our worlds? Let's review a notion that has become a taken-for-granted fact in the discipline of psychology. When studying psychology in graduate and postgraduate programs, many students are taught that Maslow's hierarchy of needs provides an objective and a universal or global truth about the nature of persons. The discussion of this hierarchy is usually accompanied by some account of what persons would be if they had the opportunity to become essentially who they really were—that is, the opportunity to be self-actualizing—and by a description of what their lives would look like under these circumstances. From a constitutionalist perspective, this hierarchy of needs is not considered to be some objective and universal truth, or to identify who we essentially are, but is viewed as a cultural production that is specifying of a highly individual version of personhood, one which is relatively unique to contemporary Western culture.

And the descriptions of life that accompany this hierarchy are not considered to be representations of life under circumstances in which persons are free to be truly who they really are, but descriptions that are specifying of life—descriptions that have real effects in terms of the constitution of life. What are some examples of the real effects of descriptions of life of this sort? With the sort of conceptions of personhood and techniques of self that accompany schemes like Maslow's hierarchy, is it at all surprising that so many psychotherapeutic practices are organized around the notions of differentiation, individuation and self-fulfillment, and are carried out on an isolated stage? With the accounts of life that are associated with such highly individual conceptions of personhood, is it all surprising that resolving grief in psychotherapeutic contexts so often has to do with assisting persons to reach the point of accepting the loss and getting on with a life that is bereft of the lost loved one?

How might we proceed to deconstruct established truths, to render them visible as ideas and practices that are actually constitutive of our lives? One approach to this that seems relatively effective is to visit alternative cultures. Over the past 18 months I have been consulting to an Aboriginal health service in the setting-up of a counseling service by Aboriginal persons for Aboriginal persons that is relevant to the urban Aboriginal culture. It would be very difficult to do this work and not draw powerful distinctions around different knowledges and practices in different cultures, and to experience the strangeness of many of the taken-for-granted modes of life and thought in one's own culture.

How would the presentation of a rival hierarchy of needs contribute to the deconstruction of various truths about personhood that have been legitimized in one's own culture? And how would this contribute to establishing a degree of awareness of the constitutive effects of these truths? Consider these questions in relation to the following observations. From the various Aboriginal informants that I have had the opportunity to interview over the past 18 months, I have discovered a very different hierarchy of needs – a hierarchy with solidarity, affiliation, and spirituality at the pinnacle. With the conception of personhood and the techniques of self that accompany this hierarchy, is it at all surprising that the traditional healing processes in the Aboriginal community are communal? With accounts of life that are associated with this definition of what it means to be a person in Aboriginal community, is it at all surprising to find practices of grief that emphasize the development of skills in conjuring up or hallucinating (my ethnocentric description, not theirs) the lost loved ones back into their lives in a way that is generally enriching, and particularly supportive of them during times of stress or in the face of adversity?

In being non-foundationalist, the constitutionalist perspective that is being argued for here does not provide us with any basis for determining which of these two cultural perspectives on personhood is the more correct version – in fact, this is not a question that will be considered relevant or answerable. However, what will be obvious from a constitutionalist perspective is that the power relations of certain communities of persons and institutions have determined that one of these perspectives on personhood, the first, will be privileged over the other and granted a truth status. The other version has been systematically disqualified and rendered virtually invisible. It could be said that one group's (mis)reading (to borrow a term from Steve de Shazer) is not accepted, and is therefore denied the social space required for its acknowledgment and authentication. This lack of balance might be addressed, at least to an extent, and a degree of reciprocity instated, through actions that are of a "social-justice" nature.

DECONSTRUCTION IN PRACTICE

In that some of the practices of therapy that are informed by a constitutionalist perspective encourage persons to "situate" or "embody" their experience within the modes of life and thought of the dominant present, they can be considered to be practices of deconstruction. Let's take an example.

Some young women and young men, having embraced the idea of "liberation" as a means of becoming authentically who they really are, seek therapy because, despite their best efforts to live out this idea, they continue to experience personal discomfort or a sense of disquiet. Very often these young persons interpret this discomfort as a reflection of some inadequacy or lack of courage that needs to be resolved. In order to assist such young persons to "situate" or "embody" their experience within the modes of life and thought of the dominant present, the therapist might suggest that the following questions be explored:

- What practices of life and ways of thinking stand behind this word liberation?
- What sort of operations on your life, on your body, and on your soul does this way of living and this way of thinking require you to engage in?
- What are the real effects of these ways of thinking and living? How do these ways of thinking and living shape your life, including your relationships with others?
- If you were to step further into this particular way of being, how would this further shape your life? What other real effects would you witness?
- From which other positions might you evaluate these effects? From these positions, which of these effects are preferred, and which of these effects are not preferred?
- At what point in history did the idea of liberation emerge? To what use has this idea been put? What has this idea made possible, and what has been its limitations?

- What are the specific processes by which you were recruited into the practices of life and ways of thinking that are associated with this idea of liberation?
- By what processes has the notion of liberation, in providing the grounds for an authentic way of life, been privileged over other notions, which provide different claims about such grounds?

Let's take another example. Consider the experience of those persons who have been diagnosed with schizophrenia. Very often these persons subject themselves to extraordinary pressure in their efforts to achieve a sense of moral worth. So often, they attempt to achieve this by entering their lives into the dominant present of this culture — a present that is constituted by those modes of life and thought that specify self-possession, self-containment, autonomy, independence and so on (the antithesis of many of the experiences of these persons). To assist these persons to situate or to embody their efforts within the expectations and the practices of these modes of life and thought deconstructs these truths about what constitutes a person as someone of worth. This deconstruction undermines their sense of failure, and frees them to engage in the exploration and identification of other ways of life and of thinking that do not require such extreme acts of self-torture in order to establish this sense of worth.

A therapy of exploration that is informed by questions of the sort referred to here does serve to emphasize the history of the dominant present in a very particular way. This therapy encourages persons, at least in part, to:

(a) deconstruct those truths that have been granted an objective status by bringing forth the modes of life and thought that they imply,
(b) expose the paradox that is associated with all essentialist notions,
(c) explore the specifics of the ways of life and thought that accompany these notions,
(d) develop an awareness of, evaluate, and monitor the real effects of particular ways of being and ways of thinking in the constitution of one's life,
(e) confront the moral and ethical responsibilities associated with living their life in the way that they do,
(f) locate particular modes of life and thought within the structures and processes that have provided for their legitimation and for the exclusion of other modes of life and thought,

(g) enter into some exploration of alternative modes of life and of thought.

It is important that such questions are also applied to the truths that therapists introduce into the therapeutic context. This confronts therapists with the moral and ethical responsibility for the real effects of their interaction with those persons who seek help. It rules out the option of therapists' justifying certain outcomes on the basis of foundationalist premises – "this distress has to do with the process of adjusting to the way that things should be in this family," "this pain is a necessary part of getting to the roots of the problem," and so on.

Contrary to a number of critiques of many of the post-modern developments in thought, those developments that I refer to as constitutionalist do not introduce forms of relativism that might suggest that "one description of reality is as good as any other," or that "experiences are only traumatic because reality is described in that way." Relativism of the first sort is only something that might be arrived at from a foundationalist perspective, and relativism of the second sort is only something that might be arrived at through some form of "radical constructivist" or "nominalist" perspective.

THE HISTORY OF
THE DOMINANT PRESENT

I have proposed that externalizing conversations have a part to play in the deconstruction of the modes of life and thought that are constituting of persons' lives. To encourage persons to define or to reflect on the relationship that they have with their problems opens the possibility for them to experience a separation or alienation from the taken-for-granted modes of life and of thought that are associated with the problem. In this way, these modes of life and thought are rendered strange, and they no longer speak to persons of the truth of their identity – of their nature. In Chapter 2 of this book, I have likened this process to Bourdieu's proposal for the "exoticizing of the domestic." Thus, I believe that these externalizing conversations assist persons to situate their experience in the history of the dominant present.

I have also proposed that the processes that are associated with this exoticizing of the domestic raise, for persons, the mantle of choice. Persons are more free to explore other modes of life and thought into which they might enter their lives, and to evaluate the real effects of these. And, as well, these processes also encourage persons to assume the moral and ethical responsibilities of such choices.

I have tried to draw these ideas together with the narrative meta-phor. If it is the case that narrative provides the structure for life, then it is reasonable to conclude that the study of narrative could provide us with some of the intimate particularities of how lives are inserted into particular modes of life and thought.

I believe that those externalizing conversations which have the effect of bringing forth the private stories that persons have about their lives, and that contribute to the deconstruction of those modes of life and thought that frame these stories, are transformative. This is nowhere more apparent than in the therapy of those persons who have been abused and who have been recruited into highly negative truths about their identities, into practices of self that are neglectful and abusive, and into practices of relationship that are isolating of them. Through these externalizing conversations, persons experience alienation from these truths, are able to name the dominant plot to which they have been subject (torture, exploitation, abuse, etc.), and begin to challenge the impoverishing practices of self and practices of relationship.

As this work proceeds, persons become better aware of and more able to honor their history of resistance to these modes of life and thought. This is a particular version of resistance—not one that is to be erased, worked through, or defined as a form of cooperation. But this is another story, and leads me to a discussion of the histories of the alternative present/s.

HISTORIES OF THE
ALTERNATIVE PRESENT/S

There is much to say about the histories of the alternative present/s, and I will only say a little of it here. I have argued that what I refer to as unique outcomes are gateways to these other histories, and thus to alternative versions or stories of persons' lives. And I have done my best to provide some examples of how unique outcomes might be constituted as such.

In that these alternative histories provide for a re-storying of life, they are of critical importance in this work. When we take seriously the narrative metaphor, we conclude that it is not contradictions or exceptions that persons live by, that provide a structure for life, but stories—and that it is the performance of alternative stories that is transformative of persons' lives. It follows that these alternative stories are, to an extent, accompanied by alternative modes of life and of thought, the real effects of which can be reviewed and explored.

I would like to make three further points about the ideas associated with this work. First, I do not have an investment in "unique outcome" as a name for a contradiction of the sort to which I have referred, and thus am not prepared to defend the term. It was a description that I borrowed from Erving Goffman, whose work I have admired greatly. There are many other candidate descriptions, including "distinction," that could be appropriate—and perhaps it would be better to refer to actual "sites," using descriptions like "tension," "breach," "disjunction," and so on.

The second point that I would like to make is that I believe that the alternative stories that are generated/resurrected in this work are not "radically" invented "out of the blue," so to speak. These stories do not stand apart from the world's cultures, or from the facts of the persons' life as it has been lived. To encourage a person to orient him/herself to the mystery associated with a contradiction can trigger the construction of sequences of events though time that lend a sense of coherence to the persons' life. This construction is work that takes place on the inside of culture and on the inside of personal and community history.

The third point relates to the employment of imagination in this work—it bears closer study. The identification of contradiction with mystery is provocative of imagination, and the use of particular languages of therapy, often picturesque, is evocative of powerful images. At times, in special circumstances, these images can extend the known limits of culture. Elsewhere (see Wood, 1991), in following the ideas of Gaston Bachelard, I have speculated that these powerful images "trigger reverberations" that reach back, in history, to certain events or experiences that "resonate" in some way with the image—many experiences of the past, that would not be remembered under ordinary experiences, "light up" and contribute to alternative story lines.

COMMENT

Recently, in the professional literature, some advocates of the foundationalist perspective have loudly criticized post-modern developments in thought, arguing that they deprive therapists of a value position and thus deny them a basis for action. I do hope that I have argued well enough here that this is not the case. Those developments in thought that I refer to here as constitutionalist emphasize the extent to which the acknowledgment of a value position is inescapable, and the extent to which therapists are required to squarely face and accept the moral and ethical responsibility for the real effects of their interactions with others. And, as well, this constitutionalist position confronts therapists with demands for action in relation to their value position.

I would like to briefly address just two aspects of the value position that is implied in the forgoing discussion – commitment and solidarity. The first of these, commitment, has had particularly bad press in the past couple of decades. Some have considered commitment to be a contradiction to professionalism. Others have interpreted it as a problem to be worked through. Still others have considered it to be the outcome of blurred boundaries between work and life in general.

But I like the word, and when I am thinking about it I am thinking about it in a very particular sense. When I am thinking of commitment, I am not associating it with zeal; I am not evoking commitment in the name of ideology or of some political program; I am not relating it to a vision of some utopian society, some totalizing scheme – all of which I think we should be deeply suspicious of. Instead, I am thinking of a commitment to action against the abuses of power: against neglect, against cruelty, against injustice, and against the subjugation of the alternative knowledges. I am thinking about a commitment to action that is for reciprocity. I am thinking about a commitment to action that does not have to be justified on some privileged ground, but a commitment to action that is based on the actual accounts that persons have of their predicaments and their distress.

And what of solidarity? I am thinking of a solidarity that is constructed by therapists who refuse to draw a sharp distinction between their lives and the lives of others, who refuse to marginalize those persons who seek help; by therapists who are prepared to constantly confront the fact that if faced with circumstances such that provide the context of the troubles of others, they just might not be doing nearly as well themselves.

REFERENCES

Anderson, H., & Goolishian, H. A. (1989). Dialogic rather than interventionist: An interview by L. Winderman. *Family Therapy News.* November/December.

Axelrod, R. (1984). *The evolution of cooperation.* New York: Basic Books.

Bateson, G. (1972). *Steps to an ecology of mind.* New York: Ballantine.

Bateson, G. (1979). *Mind and nature: A necessary unity.* New York: Bantam.

Bruner, J. (1986). *Actual minds, possible worlds.* Cambridge, MA: Harvard University Press.

Bruner, J. (1990). *Acts of meaning.* Cambridge, MA: Harvard University Press.

Carroll, L. (1972). *Alice's adventures in wonderland and through the looking-glass.* London: Tavistock.

Derrida, J. (1978). *Writing and difference* (A. Bass, trans.). Chicago: University of Chicago Press.

Derrida, J. (1981). *Positions* (A. Bass, trans.). Chicago: University of Chicago Press.

de Shazer, S. (1975). The confusion technique. *Family Therapy, 2*(1), 23–30.

de Shazer, S. (1978). Brief hypnotherapy of two sexual dysfunctions: The crystal ball technique. *American Journal of Clinical Hypnosis, 20*(3), 203–208.

de Shazer, S. (1979). On transforming symptoms: An approach to an Erickson procedure. *American Journal of Clinical Hypnosis, 22,* 17–28.

de Shazer, S. (1980). Brief family therapy. A metaphorical task. *Journal of Marital and Family Therapy, 6*(4), 471–476.

de Shazer, S. (1982). *Patterns of brief family therapy: An ecosystemic approach.* New York: Guilford.

de Shazer, S. (1985). *Keys to solution in brief therapy.* New York: Norton.

de Shazer, S. (1988). *Clues: Investigating solutions in brief therapy.* New York: Norton.

de Shazer, S. (1991). *Putting difference to work.* New York: Norton.

Erickson, M. H. (1954). Pseudo-orientation in time as a hypnotherapeutic procedure. *Journal of Clinical and Experiential Hypnosis, 2,* 261–283.

Erickson, M. H., & Rossi, E. (1979). *Hypnotherapy: An exploratory casebook.* New York: Irvington.

Evans-Pritchard, E. (1976). *Witchcraft, oracles, and magic among the Azande.* Oxford: Clarenden Press.

Fleuridas, C., Nelson, T. S., & Rosenthal, D. M. (1986). The evolution of circular questions: Training family therapists. *Journal of Marital and Family Therapy, 12*(2), 113–127.

Foucault, M. (1975). *The birth of the clinic: An archaeology of medical perception.* New York: Random House.

Foucault, M. (1979). *Discipline and punish: The birth of the prison.* London: Peregine.

Gasche, R. (1986). *The tain of the mirror: Derrida and the philosophy of reflection.* Cambridge, MA: Harvard University Press.

Gellner, E. (1975). *Legitimization of belief.* Cambridge, MA: Cambridge University Press.

Gergen, K. J., & Gergen, M. J. (1983). Narratives of the self. In T. R. Sabin & K. E. Scheibe (eds.), *Studies in social identity.* New York: Praeger.

Gergen, K. J., & Gergen, M. J. (1986). Narrative form and the construction of psychological science. In T. R. Sabin (ed.), *Narrative psychology: The storied nature of human conduct*. New York: Praeger.

Gingerich, W. J., & de Shazer, S. (1991). The BRIEFER project: Using expert systems as theory construction tools. *Family Process, 30*(2), 241–250.

Goffman, E. (1961). *Asylums*. New York: Doubleday.

Grosz, E. (1990). *Jacques Lacan: A feminist introduction*. London: Routledge.

Haley, J. (1976). *Problem-solving therapy*. San Francisco: Jossey-Bass.

Jabès, E. (1959). *Je bâtis ma demeure: Poèmes, 1943–1957*. Paris: Galimard. Translation cited in Derrida, J. (1978). *Writing and difference* (trans. A. Bass). Chicago: University of Chicago Press.

Jenkins, A. (1990). *Invitation to responsibility*. Adelaide: Dulwich Centre Publications.

Kowalski, K., & Durrant, M. (1990). Overcoming the effects of sexual abuse: Developing a self-perception of competence. In M. Durrant & C. White (eds.), *Ideas for therapy with sexual abuse*. Adelaide: Dulwich Centre Publications.

Lincoln, Y. S., & Guba, E. G. (1985). *Naturalistic inquiry*. Beverly Hills: Sage.

Lipchik, E., & de Shazer, S. (1986). The purposeful interview. *Journal of Strategic and Systemic Therapies, 5*(1/2), 88–99.

Madanes, C. (1984). *Beyond the one way mirror*. San Francisco: Jossey-Bass.

Maruyama, M. (1963). The second cybernetics: Deviation-amplifying mutual causative process. *American Scientist, 51*, 164–179.

Menses, G., & Durrant, M. (1987). Contextual residential care. *Journal of Strategic and Systemic Therapies, 6*(2), 3–15.

Minuchin, S. (1984). *The family kaleidoscope*. Cambridge, MA: Harvard University Press.

Molnar, A., & de Shazer, S. (1987). Solution-focused therapy: Toward the identification of therapeutic tasks. *Journal of Marital and Family Therapy, 13*(4), 349–358.

Munro, C. (1987). White and the cybernetic therapies: News of difference. *Australian and New Zealand Journal of Family Therapy, 8*(4), 183–192.

Norris, C. (1982). *Deconstruction: Theory and practice*. London: Routledge.

Norris, C. (1983). *The deconstructive turn: Essays in the rhetoric of philosophy*. London: Methuen.

Nunnally, E., de Shazer, S., Lipchik, E., & Berg, I. (1986). A study of change: Therapeutic theory in process. In D. Efron (ed.), *Journeys: Expansion of the strategic-systemic therapies*. New York: Brunner/Mazel.

O'Hanlon, W. H. (1986). Fragments for a therapeutic autobiography. In D. Efron (ed.), *Journeys: Expansion of the strategic-systemic therapies*. New York: Brunner/Mazel.

O'Hanlon, W. H. (1987). *Taproots: Underlying principles of Milton Erickson's therapy and hypnosis*. New York: Norton.

O'Hanlon, W. H., & Weiner-Davis, M. (1989). *In search of solutions: A new direction in psychotherapy*. New York: Norton.

Orbach, S. (1978). *Fat is a feminist issue*. London: Hamlyn.

Real, T. (1990). The therapeutic use of self in constructionist/systemic therapy. *Family Process, 29*, 255–272.

Selekman, M. D. (1989). Taming chemical monsters: Cybernetic-systemic therapy with adolescent substance abusers. *Journal of Strategic and Systemic Therapies, 8*(2), 5–10.

Selekman, M. D. (1991). The solution-oriented parenting group: A treatment alternative that works. *Journal of Strategic and Systemic Therapies, 10*(1), 37–50.

Selvini Palazzoli, M., Boscolo, L., Cecchin, G., & Prata, G. (1980). Hypothesizing, circularity and neutrality: Three guidelines for the conductor of the session. *Family Process, 19*, 3–12.

Sluzki, C. (1983). Process, structure, and world views: Toward an integrated view of systemic models in family therapy. *Family Process, 22*, 469–476.

Stewart, B., & Nodrick, B. (1990). The learning disabled lifestyle: From reification to liberation. *Guidance and Counselling, 5*(3), 54–72.

Tomm, K. (1989). Externalizing the problem and internalizing personal agency. *Journal of Strategic and Systemic Therapies, 8*(1), 54–59.

Turner, V. (1969). *The ritual process.* Ithaca, NY: Cornell University Press.

Van Gennup, A. (1960). *Rites of passage.* Chicago: University of Chicago Press.

Von Foerster, H. (1981). *Observing systems.* Seaside, CA: Intersystems Publications.

Watzlawick, P., Weakland, J., & Fisch, R. (1974). *Change: Principles of problem formulation and problem resolution.* New York: Norton.

White, M. (1983). Anorexia nervosa: A transgenerational system perspective. *Family Process, 22*(3), 255–273.

White, M. (1984). Pseudo-encopresis: From avalanche to victory, from vicious to virtuous cycles. *Family Systems Medicine, 2*(2), 150–160.

White, M. (1985). Fear busting and monster taming: An approach to the fears of young children. *Dulwich Centre Review.*

White, M. (1986a). Negative explanation, restraint, and double description: A template for family therapy. *Family Process, 25*(2), 169–183.

White, M. (1986b). The conjoint therapy of men who are violent and the women with whom they live. *Dulwich Centre Newsletter*, Spring.

White, M. (1986c). Ritual of inclusion: An approach to extreme uncontrolled behavior in children and young adolescents. *Dulwich Centre Review.*

White, M. (1987a). Family therapy and schizophrenia: Addressing the 'in-the-corner' lifestyle. *Dulwich Centre Newsletter*, Spring.

White, M. (1987b, November). *Recent developments in systemic therapy.* Conference sponsored by the Family Therapy Program, Faculty of Medicine, University of Calgary.

White, M. (1988). The externalizing of the problem and the reauthoring of lives and relationships. *Dulwich Centre Newsletter*, Summer.

White, M. (1989a). The process of questioning: A therapy of literary merit? In *Selected papers* (pp. 37–46). Adelaide: Dulwich Centre Publications.

White, M. (1989b). Anorexia nervosa: A cybernetic perspective. In *Selected papers* (pp. 65–76). Adelaide: Dulwich Centre Publications.

White, M., & Epston, D. (1990). *Narrative means to therapeutic ends.* New York: Norton.

Wilden, A. (1980). *System and structure (2nd ed.).* London: Tavistock.

Wittgenstein, L. (1968). *Philosophical investigations* (G. E. M. Anscombe, trans.) (3rd Ed.). New York: Macmillan.

Wood, A. (1991). Outside expert knowledge: An interview with Michael White. *Australian and New Zealand Journal of Family Therapy, 12*, 207–214.

6

CONVERSATION—BUT WHAT KIND?

John H. Weakland

WHEN GREGORY BATESON—one of my chief mentors—got up to give a talk, you never knew what he might talk about. There was, of course, a title set in advance, but Gregory would always talk about whatever he was pondering when the actual time to speak arrived. Recalling this as I began to prepare for this conference, I must say that I felt rather envious of his freedom, which I, raised to be rather disciplined and obedient, have never possessed. This was all the more so because I was quite uncertain *how* to be obedient—what I could say that would be relevant to the announced theme of this conference. Indeed, this was not much clarified for me after I had done some reading, or rereading, of a number of recent papers that professed to discuss this topic. And finally, having seen the titles of a number of papers to be given at this conference, I am wondering how *they* will relate to its announced theme—or if some of my colleagues have learned from Bateson better than I did.

As you will soon hear in more detail, my eventual response to this difficulty involves two phases. First—in line with my own approach to therapy—let's get the problem stated as clearly as possible. What is my difficulty in thinking and talking about "Therapeutic Conversation"? Then, rather than attempting to get "clear on the concept" globally, let me approach this more modestly. I hope to do this by discussing how the approach of my colleagues and myself at the Brief Therapy Center looks from a conversational viewpoint.

THE USE AND ABUSE OF
TERMINOLOGY IN OUR FIELD

I think that clarity is desirable in communication between colleagues—even though I also believe that vagueness or ambiguity are valuable at times in speaking to our clients. More specifically, I propose that before we go much further in getting on the therapeutic conversation bandwagon, we ought to define what we are talking about as clearly as possible—and I think it should be evident from my introductory remarks that I do not believe we have yet done so.

I stress this concern for a broad as well as a specific reason. We work in a field which in large part arose out of studies of human communication and which has quite properly continued to emphasize its importance—not only matters of general content, but also the particulars of wording and labeling. In addition, our field has also been actively concerned to note and point out the potential dangers of labeling in the psychiatric field in general—that labels can have serious and lasting consequences. Yet despite this, it appears that our own field has displayed—and continues to display—considerable abuse of terminology.

One form of such abuse is especially pertinent here. In the course of developing the new field of family therapy, naturally it was necessary to produce—to invent or import—new terms to refer to new observations or ideas. Bateson (1941) long ago warned that until we are sure we know what we are talking about, this should be done provisionally, even to the extent of making up "non-word" terms as reminders of our ignorance or uncertainty. And we all have seen the ease with which concepts of the unobservable, such as "the id" or psychiatric diagnostic categories, can take on a life and power of their own, becoming more "real" than observed behavior (cf. Rosenhan, 1973). Yet something very similar has occurred repeatedly in our field. Terms that originally were useful tools—markers that helped direct our attention toward something to be noted and considered, or that served as counterweights to conventional concepts that appeared unhelpful—as the "system" concept helped to focus on interaction in contrast to individuals in isolation—have over and over become reified, even deified, into clichés that obscure observation and effective action at least as much as promote it, often also leading to fruitless controversies.

Examples are easy to adduce. "System" is one; "power" is another. "Communication" itself has largely changed from a useful pointer toward an important focus of investigation to a vague catch-all, even spreading to many clients who say "We don't communicate" and be-

lieve they have stated a problem clearly. "Homeostasis" has moved
from Don Jackson's (1957) original proposal that psychiatrists should
be more aware that change in an individual patient may lead to
changes and difficulties in the behavior of other family members, to a
view that even if positive change occurs there is some active force
working to reverse this.

I will restrain myself from lamenting about the abuses and trouble
"double bind" and "paradox" have given rise to, except to mention the
request "Give me a paradox for this case" often heard at workshops.
Instead let us go on to perhaps the worst examples of all: "family" and
"family therapy." I do not deny that our use of "family" terminology
has had some quite practical advantages for the field. It certainly
seems to refer to something familiar, important, and concrete, and
these features have no doubt been helpful in carving out a territory of
our own in the crowded and competitive world of psychotherapy practice, teaching, and writing. Even at this level, however, there are corre-
sponding drawbacks. There have been numerous but inconclusive efforts to specify just what we mean by the apparently specific term
"family," and as de Shazer (1991) has pointed out, there seems to be
even less consensus or clarity on what "family therapy" is. More important, though, I believe our heavy investment in these concrete terms
instead of more general ones functions to limit severely both our vision
of the nature of our work and our potential for its practical application.
That is, in my view our field is most basically concerned with an interactional, rather than individual-centered, view of human behavior in
general, which includes any behaviors which may be labeled as "a
problem."

Our continued emphasis on the term "family" has, in my view, contributed to restricting our vision and the scope of our work in three
respects, at increasing levels of generality. First, it has led to an emphasis on routinely seeing whole families conjointly, even when this is
difficult to arrange and may not be either necessary or the most efficient procedure. Second, it promotes acceptance of our field of practice
as a limited (and often subsidiary) realm within psychiatry, rather
than as proposing a new paradigm that should apply to all of psychiatry except for clearly organic difficulties. Third, it obstructs the application of our views to problem behaviors in all sorts and sizes of systems involving human interaction beyond the family.

A second source of difficulty lies in our tendency to become awed
and carried away by sweeping, grand abstract terms, often imported
from other fields, which sound wonderfully scientific, like "epistemology" or "autopoiesis"; perhaps even "second-order cybernetics" should
be included here.

While these terms are polar to those of the first group in being general and theoretical concepts rather than appearing concrete and specific, they pose the same basic danger: that we will use either overly concrete or overly general terms too freely — that is, not as tools of thinking, but instead of thinking. Instead of making the effort to define clearly what we mean by our terms, and just how we see them as relevant to understanding and resolving the kind of problems we deal with daily, we are tempted to assume all this is evident.

There are of course important reasons why we are repeatedly in danger of falling into terminological traps. Almost all of us are active practitioners in a field that is often obscure and difficult and involves heavy personal responsibilities. All this magnifies the general human desire for simplicity and certainty, weighing heavily on us all and especially on students and the less experienced in the field. Concrete terms, unexamined critically, at least appear to provide some certainty. Meanwhile, on the other hand, for the experienced and especially the "experts" among us, using general terms of high theoretical sweep proposes, whether accurately or not, that we are concerned with and comprehend large and profound matters — and may help our reputation and competitive position within our field. But perhaps the existence of these dangerous pressures is a prime reason to maintain awareness of the power of terminology and the importance of care in its use.

"THERAPEUTIC CONVERSATION"

Obviously, I hope that we can avoid falling into difficulties like those discussed above with the term "therapeutic conversation", and that we be as clear and explicit as possible about what we mean by this term so that we can avoid turning this too into a cliché or catchword that appears to explain while actually obscuring the subject. I especially hope so because I believe this term does point to important matters, as I will specify later.

But I am not too confident. It seems to me that in this general area we are already both using words, including "conversation," rather freely, as if no definition is necessary. In addition, we appear to be inventing new terms, such as "languaging," rather casually, as if ordinary English is — for unspecified reasons — inadequate for our work.

I certainly do not propose that I can here resolve all the potential problems I foresee. I would be greatly surprised if this conference should reach a consensus on the meaning of "therapeutic conversation." I would consider it a considerable achievement if any of us were to make his or her own usage and meaning clear. I only hope to make some contribution to this cause, in two ways: First, by outlining some things that to me seem essential elements in making our use of important terms as clear as possible, and second, by examining my own approach to treatment from a "therapeutic conversation" viewpoint.

I would suggest that three things are important in making clear our use of such a general term as "therapeutic conversation." First is to attempt to state explicitly our meaning and usage – the conceptual content – of these words and of their combination. This is perhaps belaboring the obvious, yet it seems often neglected. Less obviously, meaning may be clarified by giving attention to the context in which such a term is utilized. There are two ways in which this may be done. One is to make as explicit as possible the purpose or end that introduction of a new term is supposed to serve. What is the value of the new conceptual focus; what, implicitly at least, does the term propose is important to the field but has been neglected or overlooked? This matter often receives some attention – though equally often it deserves more.

The final element, I believe, presents the greatest risk of being neglected or left only to implication rather than explicit discussion: What, in proposing a new term, are we trying to get *away* from, in theory, in practice, or both? I acknowledge that this probably seems especially important to me because it so closely parallels a major focus of the Brief Therapy Center's theoretical and practical approach. Our main focus is on what are our clients doing – their attempted solutions – that needs to be discarded so that their problems will not continue to exist. But also, I have already cited one fundamental example of the importance of such a viewpoint in our field: an emphasis on interaction as the basic source or context of behavior – even when we talk of families or systems somewhat concretely – is a move to get away from the idea of behavior as a property of separate individuals.

Since I place such emphasis on this matter, let me briefly consider "therapeutic conversation" from this angle. I perceive two such "negative" – "away from" is probably better – emphases in the use of this term. First, the term "conversation" appears to imply an attempt to move away from the medical and especially the accompanying "pathology" conceptions that are still the basis, in fact the absolute foundation, for most of the psychiatric field. I am heartily in agreement with this proposed direction of motion, and am only concerned that we are not going for enough; I view our own work at MRI as very consistent with this. I also feel, however, that "therapeutic" tends to bring the medical model back in. Some other term – though at this point I do not know which – would be more consistent. Second, "conversation" apparently is being used, though less clearly, to propose an avoidance of "hierarchy," any position of the therapist as "expert," even of any intentional influencing of client behavior by the therapist. Although the one word "conversation" seems used to convey both implications, and the notions of "pathology" and "doctor knows best" are closely joined in the medical model, I still see the two implications as separate and different in the case of "conversation," and I am not in agreement with the second one.

These views can best be clarified further by describing the approach of our Center, and viewing it in relation to the "therapeutic conversation" concept.

MRI BRIEF THERAPY

The basic conceptual model underlying our work is very simple, though carrying it out in practice can be complex and demanding. We view "problems" as consisting of undesired or undesirable behaviors that have persisted in the face of attempts to alter them, of sufficient duration and importance that a client finally comes to a therapist for help in changing or ending the behavior in question. We see the persistence of such problem behaviors as depending primarily — and ironically — on the ways people have been trying to change them, their "attempted solutions." That is, most simply, the client is "stuck" in attempts to resolve a problem by means that do not work. This fruitless struggle may escalate and spread, and the client is blocked from getting on with his or her life. Correspondingly, we see the primary task of the therapist as introduction of these attempted solutions, either by replacing them with new and different behaviors, or less often, by reevaluation of the original behaviors of concern as "no significant problem."

Our practice is correspondingly simple in outline, though seldom in detail. Our first aim is to find out, in terms of observable behavior, what the problem is that brings a client to treatment, together with who is the client and who the identified patient, since often they are not the same person. We want to know "*Who* is doing *what* that is seen as a problem, *who* sees this behavior as a problem, and *how* is it seen to constitute a problem?" Note that in addition to the behavioral focus, all of the crucial points are explicitly matters of interpretation, not of "reality." We begin to inquire about these points (though of course not all at once) by asking direct questions. Also, of course, guided by the client's responses, we try to frame and word these questions so as to get clear and specific information. We then inquire similarly about what the client's attempted solutions have been, and what observable behavior would be a first sign of progress toward resolving the primary complaint. After this, we begin to present suggestions about a different way to view the problem and new and different action to take in relation to it (while these may be called "assignments" they are still only suggestions, since we have no power to enforce them), and to note the client's responses to these. If all goes well, the treatment — actually, "consultation" would be a more accurate term — concludes with a mutual acknowledgment that the complaint has been sufficiently resolved so that no further work together is needed, and the client can again get on with life in terms of his or her own aims and resources.

Webster's Seventh New Collegiate Dictionary defines "conversation" as an "oral exchange of sentiments, observations, opinions, ideas." Our treatment certainly qualifies as conversation within this broad standard. It does not matter that the contributions to the exchange by therapist and client may not be equal in amount or may differ in kind (e.g., questions and answers), or that the therapist may give deliberate thought to the framing and wording of what he or she says — this may also occur in everyday conversations, as when one party wants to present some point convincingly, or just to make himself as clear as possible to the other. So to us our therapy is conversational — and often rather informal in style. If others have a different or more restricted meaning in mind when using this term, let them state that meaning.

Even though we often speak of "therapy" or "psychotherapy," by old habit and to use terms familiar to clients, we really no longer would seriously subscribe to the term "therapeutic." As mentioned earlier, this term is too closely tied to the medical idea of "mental illness," with its concept of specific "pathology" on the one hand, and "normality" on the other, with the implication that there is some one right way — but where is any consensus? — for an individual or a family to think and act. Instead, our thought and practice are now essentially complaint-based, as described above.

We also, however, see our work as very strategic. This is not in the military sense, since we view treatment as a cooperative endeavor, not an adversarial one. But the broader dictionary definition refers to strategy as "a careful plan or method," which certainly proposes forethought, judgment, and deliberate choices of one's actions.

All these in turn imply some knowledge, some expertise, on the part of the therapist. And why not? Why should any client consult and pay a therapist if these are lacking? Somewhat similarly, we think the therapist inevitably will have – and indeed needs to have – somewhat different views from the client, especially about the problem situation. The client has sought help because his or her views have proven inadequate or inappropriate to resolve the problem. If the therapist has identical views, things will continue as before. Fortunately, this is almost an impossibility. Not only are they different individuals, but also their positions are different; the client lives the problem, the therapist only, however empathically, hears about it. This difference in position probably is the greatest asset of the therapist in helping the patient – though some therapists seem bent on trying to negate it. Perhaps they should recall that, for all his humanism and concern about power, Bateson stressed the value of "binocular vision"; certainly difference in position promotes this.

Strategy involves deliberate choice of action, and particularly deliberate influence. Our position on this is simple to state: Just as one cannot *not* communicate, one cannot *not* influence. Influence is inherent in all human interaction. We are bound to influence our clients, and they are bound to influence us. The only choice is between doing so without reflection, or even with attempted denial, and doing so deliberately and responsibly. Clients come seeking change which they could not achieve on their own; expertise in influencing them to change usefully seems to us the essence of the therapist's job. Therefore, we give much thought – guided, of course, by what a client does and says – to almost every aspect of treatment: To whom we will see in any given session, to the timing of sessions, to what suggestions we will offer as to new thoughts and actions, to responses we make to clients' reports of progress or difficulties encountered, and especially not just to the content of what we say, but to how we will phrase it. This strategic emphasis, however, does not mean that we propose or favor any arrangement in which a therapist has all the power, knowledge, control and activity, while the patient is just a passive object of therapeutic actions – if indeed this were possible, which is very doubtful. Indeed, any strong imbalance of this sort increasingly appears as unhelpful even in the treatment of strictly medical illness – and for both the physician and the patient. Similar considerations apply in the case of "objective" psychiatric diagnosis of "mental illness," which I have already expressed our concern to avoid. But the answer to or remedy for the dangers of such positions is not to leap toward some opposite pole of similarity between therapist and client, while misinterpreting this as "equality." We do not see this attempt as feasible, nor as in the client's best interest.

Instead, we see therapy as a joint enterprise in which the parties have quite different parts to play, yet with much complementarity, and a certain sort of equality. As already noted, each party necessarily influences the other, and any difference in "power" may not be great. The client needs the therapist's expertise and help, but the therapist needs his fee and the client is the customer—"hierarchy" cuts both ways. The case is similar even for "expertise." In our approach, the client defines the problem, even though the therapist may take a considerable part in clarifying just what behavior is involved and in focusing on what is most important to the client but initially expressed in a vague or confused manner. That is, the client is the expert on and basic determiner of the *ends* of treatment. The therapist is the expert on the *means* of achieving these ends. (On the pragmatic basis of experience, the therapist may also have some expertise about the incompatibility of certain desired ends, or of certain means and ends [Cade, 1991; Fisch, Weakland, and Segal, 1982]—that is, valuable knowledge of "what won't work".) In such a situation, to be strategic does not mean to be exploitative; it means to be competent, like a skilled technician, at the job one is hired to do.

To close, one broad consideration which I believe underlines all the preceding discussion: An announcement of this conference spoke of its focus on "therapeutic conversation" as a move toward an "approach not based on a general theory of psychopathology." I have emphasized this further in stressing that our own approach is complaint rather than pathology based. Why is this so important and difficult a task? I believe that we still have not adequately recognized the enormous influence on the whole psychiatric field of the fact that historically this field arose out of attempts to deal with extreme forms of deviant and difficult behavior. This included, somewhat secondarily, attempts to comprehend such behavior—or more accurately, to label it as "pathology"—that is, as non-behavior, unconnected with ordinary human action, and often as incomprehensible to boot.

Not only are we the inheritors of this tradition, which is still alive and well, but its circumstances of origin are still being replicated. Until recently, and still to a considerable degree, psychiatrists got their first real experience with hospitalized patients. Thus, teaching, thought and practice have correspondingly, and with little reflection, been based on the premise that the most severe disorders are the "real thing." Then lesser and more everyday problems come to be viewed as milder versions of the same sort of thing. One is reminded of Bateson's view that medical practice has been unduly influenced by the fact that the first patient of every medical student is a cadaver, not a person. Understandably, but I think very unfortunately, this has led to lasting and pervasive emphases on pathology and mental illness; on the patient as incompetent, fragile or both; and on the therapist as the authority not just on the means but also the ends of treatment—involuntary treatment occurring as a very important aspect of this.

In spite of the fact that the family therapy movement arose out of work—but it was *exploratory* work—with severe problems such as schizophrenia and extreme delinquent behavior, we have partially escaped the pathology conceptualization through our focus on interaction and behavior, together with our extensive involvement in working with everyday problems from this standpoint. Our work has given more attention to the pragmatic—and basically scientific—questions of *what* observably happens, and *how* it happens, in human behavior, and less to moral labeling of "bad vs. good" or implicitly moral labeling of "sick vs. well". I hope that we may continue this orientation, and go further. Could we rebuild our whole viewing of problems so as to look up from the commonplace examples toward the extreme ones, and to connect them, rather than the reverse? It would make a profound difference.

Commentary

Steve de Shazer

I CAN ONLY SAY that, as usual, I agree with (at least almost) everything John H. Weakland said in this chapter. Both what he says and how he says it have long been an influence on me. As usual, he squarely hits the nail on the head and does not use even one stroke more than is absolutely necessary. We all need to respect words as much as he does. Thus, there is no need for me to provide an exegesis.* I, therefore, will only echo his words for sake of emphasizing a point I wish to amplify.

Having had a lot of experience with such stuff, having been victimized by terminological abuse, Weakland cautions us against thinking we know what a term means – specifically "therapeutic conversations" – when the meaning is, or better, the meanings are indeed far from clear. He further cautions us against reification and deification of the term "therapeutic conversations," reminding us that even useful words/concepts, like "system" or "double bind," often or even usually end up obscuring what they were meant to clarify.

Looking at therapy as a conversation can be useful because it helps to keep the therapist and client in the same picture, thus helping us to focus on the interaction. The danger Weakland points out is that it is all together too easy to slip from this descriptive mode into an explana-

---

*An exegesis might imply that I think you had difficulty reading something that is clearly written.

tory mode. Once this happens, once the "therapeutic conversation" is seen as *the* curative factor in therapy or an explanation of therapy, then it will at least obscure our picture and blind us to what else is going on that might be worthy of note.

John Weakland says all this and more. But the main thing is the warning, the cautionary note about the abuse of terminology and the rigidification of concepts. As I see it, this process is probably inevitable and, therefore, we need to keep alert and on guard against any hardening of concepts into blinders. We need to encourage John Weakland to continue to keep us on our terminological toes.

REFERENCES

Bateson, G. (1941). Experiments in thinking about observed ethnological material. *Philosophy of Science 8*, 1. (Reprinted in *Steps to an Ecology of Mind*. New York: Ballantine Books, 1972)

Cade, B. (1991). Interview with Bill Hiebert. *AAMFT Family Therapy News, 22*, 3.

de Shazer, S. (1991). *Putting difference to work*. New York: Norton.

Fisch, R., Weakland, J. H., and Segal, L. (1982). *The tactics of change: Doing therapy briefly*. San Francisco: Jossey-Bass.

Jackson, D. D. (1957). The question of family homeostasis. *Psychiatric Quarterly Supplement 31*, Part 1, 79–90.

Rosenhan, D. L. (1973). On being sane in insane places. *Science 179*, 250–258.

7

PRO-CONSTRUCTED REALITIES

Michele Weiner-Davis

I AM VERY EXCITED to be a part of this conference and honored to be in such good company. Illinois, my home state, recently passed a licensing law requiring social workers to pass a clinical exam. Last week I went to Chicago to face this three-hour exam designed to assess the level of my clinical knowledge and skills. Situations commonly faced by therapists were depicted and, via multiple choice, I was asked to decide upon the most appropriate course of action.

On the surface, one would assume that after 14 years of practice I would have no trouble answering these questions, particularly since a portion of them pertained to family therapy. However, prior to my going to take the exam, I tried my hand at a practice test and failed miserably. You see, I've forgotten how to do "real therapy." I'm not sure I know what to call what I do with my clients anymore, and I must admit that makes me a bit uneasy. That's why I'm excited to be here. Maybe I'll leave this conference with a name or a label for what my clients and I are doing. If not, at least I'll take comfort in the fact that I spent this weekend with approximately 350 people who could understand how I might have failed that exam last week. Perhaps they too have forgotten how to do "real therapy."

If I'm not doing real therapy these days, what *am* I doing? I start with the premise that people come to therapy to change. When they walk through my door, their ideas about what has been troubling them

149

are tentative. As people begin to describe the problematic situations in their lives or tell their troublesome stories, I begin to channel the conversation in such a way that new, more useful stories emerge. These new stories then free clients to think and act in more productive ways.

This description of the therapy process is my current story about how people change. It differs dramatically from my past stories about therapeutic change. This paper describes the unfolding of my new story of therapy and events along the way that have contributed to it. In other words, it is a depiction of how I forgot to do real therapy.

The question of what therapists say and do during the session to help clients obtain new perspectives has been of interest to me for some time. In 1983, Steve de Shazer, Wally Gingerich and I spent countless hours researching how therapists elicit from their clients what we then called "change talk." "Change talk," we decided, is what happens when clients discuss:

a. Positive changes in the problematic situation:
   During a second session a mother might report, "My son has been more cooperative for the past week." Or, a father might say, "My wife has been more consistent with our son lately."
b. Exceptions to the problem:
   A wife might say, "Although I was tempted to respond to his cutting remark, I decided to go for a walk instead and that made me feel good."
c. Changes in how the problem is perceived:
   "The kids still bicker, but it doesn't seem to bother me as much. I guess I realized that brothers and sisters just fight sometimes and that's okay."

After defining the category "change talk," we developed additional codes that focused on the verbal content of what both therapist and client said. Next we coded transcripts of actual sessions. Once we identified the specific instances where clients discussed change, by working backwards we could then identify the therapist behaviors immediately preceding them. We were able to decipher what we were doing during the course of the session that led clients to report differences in their actions or the way they perceived their situations.

One finding that was of particular interest to us was that if therapists actively attempt to elicit change talk from clients, it more than quadruples the likelihood that clients will discuss change in the following speaking turn. For instance, clients who wish to be less tense and anxious seldom spontaneously discuss what helps them to feel relaxed. However, when asked about exceptions to the problem, the trademark of this approach—e.g., "Tell me what's different about the times you feel more relaxed? What do you do differently to make that happen?"— most clients can and do describe how they achieve relaxation. When the client is asked to elaborate further, change talk comes to predominate in the conversation.

As we became more knowledgeable about which particular questions led to our clients' discussing change, we began to ask these questions sooner and more frequently throughout the session. As a result, we noticed that our clients engaged in change talk at earlier junctures in the session and reached their goals more readily (Gingerich, de Shazer, & Weiner-Davis, 1988).

Recognizing that clients were able to describe positive changes in behavior or perception earlier in the session required a major shift in my thinking about therapy. Until that point, I believed that clients continued talking about problems during the session because:

a. no positive changes had yet occurred;
b. positive changes had occurred, but were not yet noticed; or
c. the clients were not ready to shift into change talk, i.e., they needed to talk about the problem longer.

It is evident from the above explanations that I assumed continued talk about problems was due to factors pertaining solely to my clients. I failed to understand the very simple fact that part of the reason my clients weren't talking about changes was because I wasn't asking the right questions. I became intrigued with the possibility that the difference between clients' saying the same old thing in the same old way and their talking about themselves in new ways appeared to be partially contingent upon my choice of questions. I began to wonder about additional ways to access reports of change.

At approximately the same time I observed something interesting about first sessions: I noticed that people would frequently comment on changes they made in between the phone call for an initial appointment and the time of the first session. However, when they alluded to these changes, they attached little significance to them, since they considered the changes to be flukes. It was my contention, though, that the kinds of changes clients initiated prior to the first session were precisely what they needed to do more of to solve their problem.

As I discussed this with my colleagues, they also recalled clients who reported such improvements. We agreed that there is a distinct advantage in highlighting changes clients initiate without the help of the therapist as a way of giving credit to clients. Clearly, attributing improvements to our clients' efforts builds self-confidence to resolve future difficulties. Furthermore, the solutions clients discover on their own are already within their repertoire of behaviors and, therefore, more likely to be repeated.

I suggested that since clients think of pretreatment changes as flukes, perhaps most pretreatment changes go unreported in therapy. Curious about the actual prevalence of pretreatment change, we developed a method to systematically elicit this potentially useful information by developing several questions. We intentionally worded the questions in a suggestive manner in order to increase the likelihood of our clients' reporting changes.

1. Many times people notice in between the time they make the appointment for therapy and the first session that things already seem different. What have you noticed about your situation?
2. (If yes to #1) Do these changes relate to the reason you came for therapy?
3. (If yes to #2) Are these the kinds of changes you would like to continue to have happen? (Weiner-Davis, de Shazer, & Gingerich, 1987)

Clients were asked the questions immediately after the initial intake information was gathered and immediately preceding the beginning of the session. Our results? Approximately two-thirds of the clients surveyed had initiated pretreatment changes and offered concrete examples of new behavior.

An unexpected effect of doing this research was that it altered the usual way I conducted the first session. Once clients described concrete examples of pretreatment changes in response to the research questions, it seemed inappropriate to then begin the session by asking, "So, what do you want to change?" Instead, a more useful question following the reports of pretreatment change became, "What do you need to do to keep these changes going?" or, "In order to feel relatively certain that the problem is completely solved, are additional changes necessary or do you simply need more time to assure yourself that these changes will stick?" By asking follow-up questions such as these, I demonstrated my belief that these changes were not simply flukes and helped people develop a plan to maintain the changes.

Imagine, for a moment, how odd it must seem to a client to be responding to the question, "What do you need to do to keep these changes going?" within the first few minutes of the initial encounter with a therapist. Most clients have different expectations about therapy. This surprise beginning to the session frequently influences clients to reevaluate their assumptions about the problem and their problem-solving strengths. Even if the conversation shifts to the presenting problem, which it usually does at some later point, the problem can be evaluated in a new light. The discussion of pretreatment change provides a useful context for exploring what remains of the difficulty.

A question I am frequently asked as I travel around the country doing workshops is, "If you focus on change early in the session, don't clients feel misunderstood?" It has been my observations that some people definitely want to discuss their view of and feelings about the presenting problem in great detail, particularly if they are veteran clients. In that case, more time is spent asking questions about and responding to their concerns about the problem. I allow my clients to teach me what will work for them. However, most people are quite willing to discuss what they have been doing right even if, by so doing, they forfeit the opportunity to elaborate on the problem.

This observation surprised me initially because my old therapy story included the idea that people need to vent or elaborate on the problem, at least for a period of time. I believed that therapy cannot proceed until the client feels that therapist completely understands the problem. Sometimes this is true, but the emphasis here is on *sometimes*. Other times, clients seem quite content to follow my lead toward solutions.

Why all this emphasis on directing clients' attention to change talk as early as possible? There are several reasons. Many years ago I attended a workshop by one of Bill O'Hanlon's co-authors, Jim Wilk. During the workshop he made a comment which I, at the time, thought was a joke. He said that the way in which clients formulate the nature of their difficulty can be best characterized by the expression, "Let me say so I know what I think." He was suggesting that once clients talk about their problems in particular ways during therapy sessions, vivid images become indelibly imprinted in their minds.

Now I understand what Jim Wilk was saying, and realize he wasn't joking. Mark Snyder (1984) demonstrated this phenomenon in an interesting study. Subjects were told that they were part of an investigation of how people get to know each other by asking questions about a person's likes and dislikes. They were instructed to find out about particular personality characteristics that were outlined on a card. Some participants were asked to assess whether a particular person was an extrovert (outgoing, sociable, confident, and so on), while others were asked to assess whether a particular person was an introvert (shy, timid, reserved, and so on). Participants then chose 12 questions that they believed would best help them make these determinations.

Snyder found that subjects chose to ask leading questions that confirmed rather than disconfirmed their hypotheses. In other words, to test the hypothesis that the people they were trying to get to know were extroverted, participants chose questions that solicited evidence of extroversion, such as, "What would you do if you wanted to liven things up at a party?" "In what situations are you most talkative?" and "What is it about these situations that makes you want to talk?" Similarly, to test the hypothesis that the people were introverted, participants chose questions that solicited evidence of introversion, such as, "In what situations do you wish you could be more outgoing?" "Tell me about some time you felt left out of some social group," and "How did you handle these feelings?"

Participants were then asked to rate the interviewee on a 1 to 10 scale measuring introversion or extroversion. The people who were asked and responded to the introverted questions were rated as introverts and the people who were asked and responded to the extroverted questions were rated as extroverts by the participants.

But the plot thickens. When the people being rated were asked to rate themselves after having been asked either set of questions, those who were asked introverted questions rated themselves as introverts and those who were asked extroverted questions rated themselves as extroverts.

Two additional studies in this area are also intriguing. One study by Fazio, Effrein, and Falender (1981) indicated that the impact of self-evaluation based on the conversation during the interview extended beyond the time of the interview. Subjects who rated themselves as extroverts behaved in an extroverted manner even after the experiment was over. Another study by Swann, Giuliano, and Wegner (1982) suggested that even when people are aware that the questions are leading, they are likely to ignore this fact and assume that their behavior warranted being asked those particular questions.

What are the implications of these studies for those of us interested in the impact of language and therapeutic conversations? There are several. The first has to do with the choices therapists make with regard to the content of the session. If we ask about the problem, clients cooperate by talking about the problem and the picture of pathology comes into focus. Then the problem needs to be eliminated, reduced, reframed, and so on. If, however, when clients talk about a problem, reporting, "We had an argument last night," rather than explore all the sordid details of the argument, we listen and wait for the next opportunity to redirect the conversation back to their problem-solving strengths, asking, "Well, how did you resolve it?" a very different picture is painted during the session. Further, even if clients can't immediately describe how they resolved the argument, the fact that the therapist asked, "Well, how did you resolve it?" conveys the therapist's expectation that the problem was resolved and that they have the necessary problem-solving skills. When used consistently throughout the session, questions that focus on clients' problem-solving skills send powerful messages about the clients' abilities to change, regardless of their specific response to the questions.

The other implication of the introvert-extrovert research for those of us interested in the impact of language pertains to the power of suggestive questioning. All questions contain within them assumptions or presuppositions. Each time we ask our clients a question, we are requesting information, but we are also telling them something about us. Simply posing the question, "What's different about the times the two of you get along?" tells a couple that you believe there are times they get along. Phrasing the question, "Are there times the two of you get along?" sends a different message and might yield a very different response.

Recently, Jay McKeel and I completed a study, as yet unpublished, in which we investigated whether clients confirm the expectations communicated through therapists' leading questions. We were interested in whether varying the wording of questions does, in fact, yield different client responses. To test this, we asked clients about their experiences with pretreatment change. Unlike the previous study, where our wording of questions suggested that pretreatment change was likely, we included both a neutral question and one suggesting that pretreatment change was unlikely.

For example, in this project one-third of the clients were asked question A:

"Many times in between the call for therapy and the first appointment, things already seem different. What have you noticed about your situation?"

One-third were asked question B (neutral question):

"Since the time of the call for an appointment and now, would you say your situation has stayed the same, gotten better, or gotten worse?"

One-third were asked question C (sameness):

"Since the time of the call for an appointment and now, has your situation stayed the same?"

We found that, when we suggested that change was likely (question A), approximately 67% of the clients reported pretreatment changes. When we asked the neutral question, 41% of the clients reported changes. When we asked clients whether their situation had remained the same, approximately 67% stated that their situation remained the same and only 28% reported pretreatment changes. Additionally, clients offered therapists concrete evidence of changes or sameness, depending on their responses.

What does this tell us? The obvious lesson is that it is not enough to pay attention merely to what we say, we must be mindful of how we word it. We need to be aware of the subtle and not-so-subtle suggestions we are sending to our clients through our questions. We should be asking ourselves: Is the embedded message in this question the one I really want to be sending my client? Is it possible to phrase this question in some other way that would better demonstrate my belief that change is inevitable? For example one could ask, "What good things have you been doing for yourself this week?" rather than, "Have you done anything good for yourself this week?" The reason is that, according to our findings, two-thirds of our clients will confirm our expectations. Since we cannot avoid leading, the question becomes, "Where shall we lead our clients?"

I believe that it is the therapist's responsibility to channel the conversation toward change talk as early and as much as possible. It is my clinical impression that, by identifying the difference between times when the problem occurs and problem-free times, approximately two-thirds of my clients find solutions to the problems they bring to therapy. Helping people rediscover solutions by focusing on what they have done that works is, in my opinion, the least invasive or intrusive intervention possible. When problem-solving skills rather than problems are the topic of conversation, problems don't become reified— they simply dissolve.

However, eliciting information about exceptions, while useful for most people, doesn't work for everybody. When it doesn't work, it becomes necessary to discuss problems and utilize questions that ask clients to think about their difficulties from different perspectives. Asking a worn-out wife how she might respond differently to her husband if his so-called "spiteful and angry" behavior was really due to his hurt feelings is one such example. Undoubtedly, different views of the problem suggest different solutions.

The question being raised here, however, is, "If it is even *sometimes* possible to help dissolve a problem frame rather than see the problem from a different angle, why not start there?" Perhaps after hearing about and seeing my strong emphasis on exceptions and solutions, one might get the impression that I have a problem-avoidance personality disorder. One might suppose that I drive my clients' negative feelings underground by administering a mild electric shock every time the conversation veers from solutions. Certainly, this is not the case. Those familiar with this approach know that my clients cry and express pain, anger, disappointment, and fears, just as they might in any other therapist's office. And I respond with compassion.

We all know that the map is not the territory, that clients' descriptions of their problems are not their problems and that my therapy story is not the total picture of how I do therapy. Clients' stories are incomplete pictures that emphasize certain meaningful aspects of their experiences. Similarly, today I have chosen to emphasize the therapist's role in initiating change talk during the session, because this has been an extremely useful way for me to think about doing therapy. Furthermore, it is my hope that the views I presented today will stimulate further conversation about the change process. So, can we talk?

Commentary

William Hudson O'Hanlon

I WAS AMUSED BY Michele's story about no longer knowing how to do "real therapy." It seems to me that the aim of this conference is, in part, to redefine what "real therapy" means. David Epston regularly invites clients who have successfully resolved their concerns in therapy to record on paper, videotape, or audiotape their story of wrestling with and overcoming their problems. When I told David that many clinicians in the U.S. would have great concerns about this practice, because, even though the clients are free to refuse to make such a record, the mere existence of the record could be seen as a threat to confidentiality. David replied that he could understand the historical importance of protecting clients' confidentiality at all costs if one is using traditional psychotherapy models. In those practices, clients often appear sick and the information that emerges could be shameful if disclosed. In this approach to therapy, he said, clients appear as heroes in their own lives. They usually want their heroism to be publicly acknowledged and celebrated.

Real therapy, in my view, is concerned with supporting and empowering people to help show that they are or can become the heroes of their own lives and stories. Michele had trouble with that exam because the kinds of knowledge and practices that are current have little of this flavor to them. They are concerned with discovering the nature

158

and origins of problems, identifying the underlying pathologies or functions of problems, in order to treat them.

Michele used an analogy at another presentation at this conference that I think summarizes the position she takes in the paper quite well. She said that the conversation in the session is like her use of a word processing program on her computer. When she types the initial draft of a paper or a letter, it is not saved in any fixed form at first. She can edit, add, delete or otherwise change things on the screen. Nothing gets firmed up until it gets saved to disk. She said this was a good analogy for clients' views and feelings. Before they come into the session and during the session, they are like the words on the computer monitor screen. They are changeable. The session helps edit them into a solvable form and a form that gives hope and possibility for change. I would extend the analogy a bit as well. Even after the words are stored in a fairly fixed form, they can be recalled and changed again. The talk in therapy is just that. We bring up to the conversational screen clients' ideas about their situation and we help edit and channel them in direction that leads away from blame, invalidation, and the closing-down of possibilities, and towards empowerment, validation, and possibilities. This is what Jim Wilk and I were getting at in our book, *Shifting Contexts* (O'Hanlon and Wilk, 1987), in which we wrote at length about this notion of "Let me hear what I say so I can see what I think."

My final reaction to this paper is that it is totally obvious. And as some wag said once, to help a person realize the obvious is a great and honorable and very difficult thing in this life. Thanks to Michele for helping us realize the obvious once again.

REFERENCES

Fazio, R. H., Effrein, E. A., & Falender, V. J. (1981). Self-perceptions following social interactions. *Journal of Personality and Social Psychology, 41*(2): 232–242.

Gingerich, W., de Shazer, S., & Weiner-Davis, M. (1988). Constructing change: A research view of interviewing. In E. Lipchik (Ed.), *Interviewing* (pp. 21–32). Rockville, MD: Aspen.

O'Hanlon, B., & Wilk, J. (1987). *Shifting contexts: The generation of effective psychotherapy*. New York: Guilford.

Snyder, M. (1984). When belief creates reality. *Advances in Experimental Social Psychology, 18*, 247–300.

Swann, W. B., Jr., Giuliano, T., & Wegner, D. M. (1982). Where leading questions can lead: The power of conjecture in social interaction. *Journal of Personality and Social Psychology, 42*(6), 1025–1035.

Weiner-Davis, M., de Shazer, S., & Gingerich, W. (1987). Constructing the therapeutic solution by building on pretreatment change – An exploratory study. *Journal of Marital and Family Therapy, 13*(4), 359–363.

8

INTERNALIZING DISCOURSES VERSUS EXTERNALIZING DISCOURSES

David Epston

SEVERAL WEEKS AGO, I was visiting with my good friend, Michael White, in Adelaide. During our work together, he was interviewed by a psychologist for a study of therapists working in the area of male violence. The interviewer's questioning assisted Michael in reviewing his career and those ideas that were influential in the development of his unique practice. I was invited to join them as a spectator. Near the end of the interview, the psychologist turned to me and offered an invitation I couldn't refuse: "David, if you were to ask Michael one question and one question only, what would it be?" I was quite flummoxed, as this question intruded into my reflections. Still, I decided to reduce my million and one questions of Michael to the following: "Michael, if you hadn't invented that 'talk' we refer to as an externalizing discourse, where do you think your work would be today?" Michael's reply was immediate and conclusive. "Nowhere!"

That one question had been on my mind even prior to receiving the invitation to address this conference. My answer, had I been asked, would also have been "Nowhere!" I had written something to this effect in 1989.

> If I were to restrict myself to only one aspect of White's work that I have taken over, it would be that of "externalizing the problem." This is summarized by his maxim: "The person isn't the problem; the problem is

161

the problem." This provided a rationale and a practice to position myself in
therapy, that is, to be on everyone's side at the same time and to act with
commitment and compassion against the "problem," whatever the problem
might be. It freed me from the constraints of some of the prevailing practices that I found distanced me from the family and reduced my fervor.
(p. 26)

I had always been interested in the problematizing of the notion of
the "problem." I credit the Mental Research Institute for pioneering
this undertaking and it seems very appropriate that John Weakland
is here to represent it. According to one of Karl Tomm's (1989) many
aphoristic summaries: For MRI, "the problem is the attempted solution"; for the Milan associates, "The problem is the solution." The Milan associates have ironicized the idea of problem, with an unsurpassed
mastery. In my reading of the literature, both MRI's and the Milan
associates' revisionings of the idea of the "problem" were radical departures from the taken-for-granted and by now sedimented and buried-
over practices relating to the construction of the "problem."

Such practices were the methodologies of what Foucault (1980) refers to as "regimes of truth," so-called regimes in which power and
knowledge were inextricably linked. Those practices had come to be
warranted as special forms of procedure leading to a "truth" and accordingly were considered inviolate. Those professions whose prestige
and privileges were founded on those "regimes of truth" had arrogated
to themselves the warrant of establishing the "lawful" and "universal"
truth.

My preference is to conceive of "truth" as a fiction that has been
constructed in line with truth-making procedures into a "fact." Latour
and Woolgar (1979), in their ethnography of the construction of a scientific "fact" in a prestigious research laboratory, conclude:

> Scientific activity is not "about nature." It is a fierce fight to construct
> reality. The laboratory is the workplace and the set of productive forces,
> which makes construction possible. Every time a statement stabilizes, it is
> reintroduced into the laboratory and it is used to increase the difference
> between statements. The cost of challenging the reified statement is impos-
> sibly high. Reality is secreted. (p. 240)

The professional histories of how they gained access to these truth-
making methodologies, of how they superseded the "untrue," and
how they won hegemonic or partial authority over rival claimants to
truthfulness, were written as if they were history-taking rather than

history-making. No matter what reading you wish to give Foucault (1979) and his critiques of the extant histories of professional practices and his rival historical method (the "genealogical"), we can no longer be so innocent.

But let me go back to my story. In the late 1970s, freshly qualified, I returned to New Zealand from studying in England and at The Family Institute in Wales. I started working in psychiatry and soon found myself responsible for the supervision of a young social work graduate working in a psychiatric hospital ward. His idealism was as yet undimmed and he found himself distressed, without quite knowing why, when he witnessed those practices referred to as "grand rounds." He was currently researching his masters thesis, so we decided upon our own informal research project. We constructed notions of kinds of "talk": solution talk and problem talk. We hoped these terms would have the capacity to distinguish one kind of talk from the other. Any conversation inquiring of the "problem" was deemed problem talk and any conversation concerned with a solution was regarded as solution talk.

You might have thought such a distinction would not have been fine-grained enough to separate one kind of talk from another. In fact, the forms of talk were determined by the arrival of the tea trolley punctually at 10 a.m., exactly one hour after the grand round had been called to order. You may wonder how a tea trolley could punctuate a grand round, which must be considered as an exemplar of positivist practices. You guessed it; from 9 a.m. to 10 a.m., there was nothing but talk relating to the "problem." The tea trolley's arrival precipitated an embarrassed, "Well, what do we do now?" The next two minutes or so were a frenzy of banalities, which seemed to be recycled from one week to the next, a bit like an old threadbare shirt that had fit someone or other sometime or other. Each of the more senior people made the selfsame suggestions. The discussion was concluded when the most senior person settled the matter with, "Well, why don't we just keep a watchful eye on it?" This was immediately met with agreement and relief. However, this pensive moment dissolved spontaneously in a flurry of activity, with everyone foresaking the grand round for the allure of the tea trolley. All this problem talk can sure make a professional person thirsty!

It is interesting to note that Ben Furman and Tapani Ahola, freewheeling brief therapy practitioners in Helsinki, Finland, appropriated solution talk for the title of their recently published book: *Solution Talk: Hosting Therapeutic Conversations* (1992). They define the conduct of such a talk:

In our search for alternative ways of talking about problems we have been
drawn to the traditions of family and brief therapy. Over the years we
have gradually found a number of useful ideas for conducting therapeutic
conversations and consultations which we will refer to in this book as
"solution talk." This way of working is characterized both by an atmosphere of openness and by what could be characterized as a constructive
way of talking. This conversational style is achieved by thinking positively
and by focusing on subjects that foster hope, such as resources, progress,
and the future. (p. xxiv)

Allow me to review a recent article by Howard Waitzkin entitled "A
Critical Theory of Medical Discourse: Ideology, Social Control, and
the Processing of Social Context in Medical Encounter." I don't think
anyone would be surprised by the conclusions of discourse-analytic
studies. And Waitzkin, at the same time, punctures any nonmedical
practitioner's pretensions or smugness by adding, "Similar patterns
may appear in encounters with clients and members of other 'helping'
professions" (p. 223). I feel certain that they do.

What does Waitzkin find when what professionals really "say" is
scrutinized, rather that what they say about what they say? According to him, the "talk" is disengaged and uncritical of social context. In
fact, unwittingly, "medical encounters tend to convey ideologic messages supportive of the current social order and these encounters have
repercussions for social control . . . " (p. 223). He goes on to say: "The
technical structure of the medical encounter . . . masks a deeper structure that may have little to do with the conscious thoughts of professionals about what they are saying and doing" (p. 227). He also argues
on the basis of his earlier research that the "traditional format of prob-
lem-diagnosis-plan" is used "as an organizing framework" of medical
encounters.

What is a medically proper diagnosis and what effect does that
have on what is said, recorded, and thought? Mischler (1984) reveals
that medical language encourages the saying of some things and the
leaving unsaid of others.

If thought is enacted through talk, what would happen if a person
were to live their life medically? To research such a question by, say,
rearing a person in such a way as to exclude him/her from all other
discourses would be an ethical outrage. I wouldn't have even been able
to formulate such a prospect if I hadn't met the Medical Model Man
on the 27th day of February, 1990, in my office in a very modest
suburb of Auckland, New Zealand. As I was to learn as we got talking,
his life so far had been a kind of "natural" experiment. But I don't
want to get ahead of myself.

It was early in my work year. I was just back from my summer holidays. At such times, my preference is to meet with calm, considered people. I don't have anything in particular in mind, just so long as people aren't too alarming. That was the frame of mind I was in when Rob and Sandy entered my office. Both were in their mid-to-late thirties. Rob extended his hand to me. I responded in kind and nominated myself: "Hi! I'm David." His reply disconcerted me, to say the least: "Hi! I'm the Medical Model Man." Before I could say anything, Sandy fiercely announced her presence with a tirade: "There he goes again. I have had enough of this. This has been going on now for six months. The moment this interview is finished, I'm leaving and I won't be back for a week. He's already spent $20,000 on psychiatrists. And what did he end up with but ECT. The rest of the time I had to nurse him, with him crying four, five hours a day." She then looked at me with a cool intensity and warned, "You had better watch out or he'll try to out-doctor you!" I thought this might be an out and said, "He can't. I'm a social worker. Do you think you've gone to the wrong professional?" Rob was quick to reassure me that he had been referred to me by two psychiatrists in another country and that settled the matter for him.

Rob seemed as eager to get on with the consultation as Sandy was to have a holiday from Rob. They had just repatriated themselves after being overseas for less than a year. Six months of this period Rob had spent in bed with depression, alternating between crying and reading psychiatric texts in preparation for his next psychiatric consultation. Talking to him was like talking to a history of psychiatric nosology: melancholia, neurasthenia, and more current terms like anhedonia. It seemed that Rob had become depressed during what he described as "a brutal time." The job that had been promised him turned out to be in a company on the brink of financial collapse, and their first pregnancy was stillborn.

The following was a letter I sent to them summarizing our meeting together:

Dear Rob and Sandy:

I enjoyed meeting you both very much. Rob, for a depressed person, you make very good company. In the company of Sandy and myself, you were far more a "person" than a "patient." Sandy, I certainly experienced Rob as you did during the seven years of your anti-depressive relationship. You said that you had regraded him, refusing to see him as fragile, requiring medical intervention, but instead saw him "as a strong human being," as you put it. You both agreed that your relationship was 95% anti-

depressing then. And Rob, you were able to appreciate Sandy's appreciation of you. You said, "Sandy was proud of me." Sandy, you also enjoyed
Rob's lively sense of humor, his creativity, and his decency. Here, I gather
you were alluding to his sense of justice and fairness and in your words:
"his goodness." You also considered that Rob has "perspective . . .
he can tell chalk from cheese."

However, your trip to America was "a brutal time." The business enterprise you joined was on the brink of financial collapse. And the birth of
your first born was stilled. Sandy, you responded to this unexpected tragedy with all your feelings. When it was your turn, Rob, you "medical modelized" your feelings and turned yourself into a case study.

From what you told me, Rob, you had been trained in the family you
came from that any distress should be put to bed with a few Valium for
good measure. I wish I had asked you the following questions:

"Do you think your doctor father was providing the best for you when
he prescribed Valium instead of sympathy?"

"Do you think your father wanted you to grow up to be a Medical Model
Man?"

"Did your father treat himself to the same treatment?"

"Did your father treat your mother to the same treatment?"

"What do you think he would have thought if he knew you arranged
some ECT for yourself after he had died?"

"Did you think your father, by treating you rather than talking to you,
was preparing you for a medical career?"

"Do you think he was disappointed when you only got a MBA?"

"Did you feel a failure, even though you topped your class?"

"Did you think that if you couldn't be a good doctor, at least you could
have a great patienthood, one in which you could out-doctor doctors?"

"What sense do you make of your patronage of psychiatry?"

"Do you feel indebted to psychiatrists?"

"How did you convince them to ECT you?"

"What do you think they thought about a person who supported ques-
tionable psychiatric practices more than they did?"

"Do you think they realize that you were a living Medical Model Man?"

Ever since you "medical modelized" yourself and your feelings, you have
been bed-ridden and a "good patient": passive and devoted to psychiatric
nosology, which must have given you some satisfaction. Still your medical
modelizing is starting to hurt. It seemed that you were getting "sick" of
your depression, even though it has become your preoccupation and, as
you put it, "my hobby." Depression, according to you, is "my raison d'être
. . . my reason for living" but it seemed to me that you were beginning
to question whether you wanted to be an "object" of your medicalization
anymore. You have found that depression now has taken priority over all
other pursuits, including your relationship. Your medical modelization has
tried to recruit Sandy into nursing you, but Sandy, you gave me the undeniable impression that you had had your fill of that.

Rob, you said that depression had taken over 100% of your life. Sandy, you said that depression had taken over 100% of your relationship.

Sandy, I wish I had had the wit to have asked you a few questions:

"Do you think that Rob's depression is good for your relationship?"

"Why have you decided not to go along with the medical modelization of Rob's life and the life of your relationship?"

"Do you get the impression that Rob is more attracted to the medical model than to you?"

"How far has depression come between you?"

"How far do you think it will go, if the weight of your relationship is not pitted against it?"

"What is Rob's depression doing to your love and respect for him?"

"Is Rob's depression reducing your intimacy with him and do you feel constrained to act towards him more like a nurse than an intimate partner?"

"Is nursing Rob's depression an attractive undertaking for you?"

"Rob, do you have any wish to take your life back from depression or is being a doctor to yourself more appealing?"

Last week I met a woman whose life had been "medicalized" recently. Following that experience, she had a dream which might interest you. She dreamt that she was paralyzed on an operating table, helpless and speechless. She looked up to see what she described as "technical looks" on her doctors' faces. Then, and only then, did she discover to her horror what they were doing. They were taking her heart out. And that reminds me of a quote from Michel Foucault, the French philosopher and historian of medical, psychiatric and penal ideas. In *The Birth of The Clinic* (1973) he writes: "In relation to that which he is suffering from, the patient is only an external fact; the medical reading must take him into account only to place him in parentheses."

Rob, it struck me that you have put your "heart" in parentheses and medical modelized it. It may be preferable, if you are to pursue a medical modelizing course in life, that you consult cardiologists rather than psychiatrists. You could conceivably have your heart removed and replaced with some technology that won't respond to grief and disappointment. All that will be required is another micro-processor.

"Rob, is it time to critically scrutinize whether you wish to continue medical modelizing your life?"

"Do you think it would interest you to set aside depression for a while and undertake an archaeology of the seven years of anti-depression in your relationship?"

"Don't you think that would be worth digging up?"

The questions you might ask yourself are:

"How do we keep depression at bay?"

"How did Rob specialize in being a person rather than a patient?"

"Sandy, how did Rob make you respect and love him before depression first turned you into his nurse and then estranged you from him?"

"Rob, do you think you might bring your studiousness to bear on the mess depression is making of your life and relationship?"

"How did the tragedy of a stillbirth separate you rather than bring you together?"

Yours in anti-depression
David

Just before the end of our meeting, I informed Rob and Sandy that Margaret Newmark and Chris Beels would be joining me the week of their next appointment. I added that Chris had formerly been a professor of psychiatry at Columbia University in New York. Sandy vehemently opposed my proposal that they join us, alleging that Rob would out-professor the professor. Rob grinned and looked rueful. He said, "I'd love to meet him but I don't feel depressed now." I tried to save the day by saying, "Don't worry about it . . . fake it and they won't know the difference."

Rob rang me soon after he received the letter. He informed me that Sandy had retired to a beach cottage for a rest from depression. However, he avowed his desire to become a "person." In the meantime, he had found a job three days after our meeting and had bought a new car. Sandy had arrived home the night before our next meeting and telephoned me in a state of alarm. She warned me that Rob was going to kill himself. "How can you tell?" I inquired. She said that he was yelling and shouting. "At whom?" I asked. "His father and mother!" she replied. "Has he ever done this before?" She said, "Never!" "Sandy, I think he's becoming a 'person.' What do you think?" The tone of her voice dropped in hushed reflection. "You're right . . . sorry about disturbing you . . . I'm looking forward to seeing you tomorrow." "Can't wait to catch up with you both."

At the beginning of our second meeting, Rob presented me with a 13-page document, which began:

So how do I begin to record my feelings about my life and my seemingly uninterrupted battle with what's been variously labeled as "depression," "affective disorder," "arrhythmic cyclothymia," "melancholia," etc. These terms trip off my tongue/pen with such ease and perverse pride—it's as if they represent some kind of accreditation. Certainly they take precedence over my ability or desire to define myself in human qualities. Frankly, I feel devoid of any human qualities. I'm a medical case, not a human being. I no longer relate to the world as a person or character.

We were to meet five more times, during which Rob constituted himself as a "person" and his depression subsided. Probably the most important event was when Rob met with his male friends and told them that he had lied to them about his physician father. His father had not been a great man but rather a "drunk."

I rang Rob to ask his permission to tell you (at this conference) about our meetings. He asked if he could address you:

Dear David and Colleagues:

I address this letter to you, primarily, David. But I also invite you to verbally share it with your professional colleagues. Why? Because I think it motivating for you all to realize the importance and usefulness of your collective work. Specifically, as a result of six or seven one-hour sessions over the last 15 months (with a seven-month hiatus over the spring-summer of 1990–91), I have been freed from the doubts and limitations imposed by the well-intentioned "medical model." Such bondage existed for at least twenty years on and off . . . thankfully much more of the latter than the former.

As I once said to you, David, the medical school of mental diagnosis and treatment has several shortcomings. It turns acute conditions into chronic problems. It is problem-oriented, not solution-driven. It therefore uses drug therapy to treat weakness, not human insight to lever a person's strengths. You introduced me to the later approach. Thanks! Its pharmacological prescriptions become junk-mail subscriptions. Getting away from "them" is like trying to convince American Express you don't want your card renewed . . . and so on.

I'd appreciate you keeping my name anonymous but I find it appropriate that I acknowledge your help in this slightly formal way.

Yours sincerely,
Rob

This leads me to review what Michael White (1990a) has referred to in his earlier publications as "the externalization of the problem," which some would relegate to the realm of technique, tactic, or strategy. As Karl Tomm (1989) has said, "To do so would certainly be both naive and limiting." It is my purpose, in what is to follow, to locate externalizing in the realm of discourse. White (1990b) has proposed the notion of "counter-discourse." Elsewhere I have argued for externalizing in relation to a problem as "countercultural." I am now wondering if externalizing problem discourse (Madigan, 1992) qualifies as what M. A. K. Halliday (1978), the noted sociolinguist, has described as an "anti-language."

I should first like to acquaint you with the notion of *discourse* and those discourses, in particular, that frame problems. Secondly, I would argue that discourse is always situated in a cultural and historical content. Thirdly, discursive practices relating to problems have very real effects on how the problem is experienced by the parties to it — whether the problem is experienced as a state of being or as an influence on one's life and relationships. It is also critical whether the "problem" speaks to and of the person and his/her identity or whether the person speaks of and to the "problem." The latter refers to the matter of "position" in discourse and I would like to refer to that as the "grammar of experience."

Lowe (1991) makes the point that:

> ... one way of characterizing postmodern experience would be to describe it as being *discourse-sensitive*. Discourse has become a central concept, not only in postmodern thought, but in the general sphere of contemporary social and cultural theory. The term can be confusing because of its varying usages, in different fields, but there appear to be two related usages. ... In the first, discourse refers to the process of conversation. ... The postmodern repudiation of a representational view of language suggests that meanings are not given or "found" through conversation, but are progressively made or fashioned through conversation itself. ... The second use of discourse relates to a broader and more overtly political form of analysis which began in the 1970's, generated by reaction against aspects of the prevailing intellectual movement of structuralism. ... Poststructural theory tended to displace attention from language to discourse. Discourse *historicises* and *politicises* the study of language use through emphasizing the historical specificity of what is said and what remains unsaid. It is this sense of discourse which is most typically associated with postmodernism and particularly the work of Foucault ... (pp. 44–45).

For Foucault, the familiar objects of the social world, whether they be disease, death, madness, sexuality, etc., are not "things" set apart from and independent of the discourse. They are realized only in and through discursive practices which surround the objects in question. He argues that discourse is not a narrow set of linguistic practices but is composed of a whole assemblage of activities, events, objects, settings, and epistemological precepts. Discourse and practice walk hand in hand and my inquiry concerns itself with those practices linked to a distinction I want to draw between externalizing and internalizing discourses.

Foucault, along with others, traced the rise of Western medicine. I would add an internalizing problem discourse, emphasizing the power and influence of clinical and experimental pathology in its development. He cites Morgagni's (1761) treatise *De sedibus and causis in morborum* as transitional to the notion that one can pinpoint the site of death and mortality within human anatomy, writing, "From the point of view of death, disease has a land, a mappable territory" (1973, p. 17). In other words, disease was internalized within the living bodies of individuals. Anatomy superceded pathology in the late 18th century and came to monopolize clinical medicine in the 19th century. Here anatomical space became causal space, the home of both death and disease. This was followed by the body being regarded as the repository of human qualities. Mind, intelligence, madness, and a myriad of human qualities were regarded to be located in living bodies. This is a superficial version of a history of the siting of human problems. Karl Tomm (1990) brings us up-to-date in regard to the *DSM-III-R*, probably the most significant contemporary text:

> The authors seemed oblivious to the theoretical significance of their individualistic presuppositions. There was no mention of another point of view. They simply ignored the body of knowledge based on an alternative assumption, namely that human behavior, the mind, and its disorders, may be more fundamentally grounded in social phenomena than individual phenomena. (p. 6)

I believe that the same historical developments relating to the siting of problems could be traced for other disciplines, e.g., psychology, but I do not have the space to survey them here.

So what are the effects of positioning oneself differently in relation to a "problem" and construing it as *external* rather than *internal*? I propose the following effects: Persons/couples/families are more likely to become *agents* rather than *patients*. They do not appear dulled and stupified as patients often do; rather, they are creative, enlivened, enthusiastic, and can call upon problem-solving capabilities that are surprising even to them. However, their surprise, in my experience, is quickly overtaken by delight. They are more likely to enter into various development/identity projects as "persons" in relationship to themselves and others. They seem to take more pride in themselves and their relationships and never degrade themselves to that condition, described by Goffman (1961), of "utter shamelessness" (p. 121). These were "patients" who had been entered into and entered themselves into what he referred to as "psychiatric stories" or "sad tales." An externalizing discourse seems to position people so that they have access to other culturally available storylines. Here the characters they play are often heroic ones or what Goffman (1961) refers to as "success stories." Foucault (1979) commented on the significance of the "case" and the "case history" in general:

The turning of real lives into writing is no longer a procedure of heroization. It functions as a procedure of objectification and subjection. The carefully collated life of mental patients or delinquents belongs . . . to a certain politics of the function of writing. (p. 192)

If persons fade away or are absorbed into descriptions of their problems that are foundational to an internalizing discourse, in an externalizing discourse they seem to emerge and come to life as protagonists in their life stories, which can now admit of a life lived forwards rather than a one transfixed in various versions of chronicity. People speak of and to their problems, thereby becoming speaking subjects. When people are rendered into problematic descriptions of themselves, they seek authorities vested with "disciplinary" power/knowledge to speak of them and for them. Problems then can speak of a person's identity — but who speaks the "truth" of the problem? No wonder so many patients have to "lie" to tell their "truth."

I connect the distinction between externalizing and internalizing discourses with Goffman's (1974) "primary frameworks." The first he calls natural, in which events are seen as the result of unguided, unmotivated, and purely physical processes. The second he calls social, in which human agency, will, motivation, and purpose are embedded. The same set of events can be interpreted, he contends, in either framework. Both may incorporate concepts of causation, though with an entirely different meaning.

WOLFGANG SPEAKS

Wolfgang was a man in his mid-thirties. He confessed to me that he was killing himself slowly, such was his despair. He had been advised to manage his kidney disease through careful attention to diet, no smoking, and drinking in moderation, all of which he was doing to excess. I learned that at 15, Wolfgang had had a mild stroke which resolved itself, leaving him with virtually unnoticeable traces around his mouth and eyes. After the stroke and rehabilitation, he had never discussed his concerns with anyone, even his wife, from whom he had recently separated after seven years of marriage. In fact, he had married her because of her physical attractiveness. He thought that when he was in her company all eyes would be on her. He described himself as "paranoid" and found himself unable to go out in public, except after dark or under certain circumstances. Making arrangements to meet together was very difficult, as he insisted on entering my premises unseen. At the end of the second session we externalized "self-depreciation," and within the next two months he stopped smoking and drinking and maintained a sensible diet. He had also become actively involved in training for public speaking, engaged in a number of social activities (including lunch dates with his former enemies), and confided in a friend about his stroke. During the fourth session, Wolfgang commented:

> I can recognize self-depreciation now. Before it was my way of life. I am catching myself doing self-depreciation – the chatterbox. I now see it from a distance. It's not so close to me. I used to accept whatever I heard most of the time and I even agreed with it. The sentences are now the same but they are from a distance. I've known it for most of my life – this chatterbox. It can be so powerful. I have to be careful. But now I have weapons. My most important weapon is I know that it's not true. My growing self-esteem is also a weapon. I can be aware that it can take me over . . . the way I look at myself. It's not vanished . . . it's not gone away. Before I took it to be like an illness in my body. Now it's out there and it wants to come back. It wants to return to the position of dominance it once had over me.

NATALIE SPEAKS

I met Natalie, who was almost ten at the time, along with her parents, Sally and Mike, and her older sister, Jane, age 11. She had what they described as an intractable soiling problem that had defeated eight interventions – four medical, three psychiatric attempts, including a hospitalization, and family therapy. They informed me that it had now been declared a lifelong problem for young Natalie. However, Natalie would retire to her room every night, crying both in pain and despair. Her mother could bear this no longer and had tried to kill herself. She survived and starting working night shifts as a nurse to save her sanity. However, Natalie would leave notes on her pillow which she would discover on her return home. "Mum, what's wrong with me? My tummy feels all squishy and watery. My knee feels like it has been cut in half. I can't work properly and I just feel sick all over. PLEASE HELP ME." So, despite all the help they had received, they felt obliged to attempt yet another therapy, even though they felt hopeless about it.

The following is the summary of our first meeting:

> Dear Sally, Mike, Jane and Natalie:
>
> It didn't take me long to understand what a mess Sneaky Poo was making of Natalie's life in particular, but you all in general. Sneaky Poo

has kept Natalie at a five-year-old level, made her have to hang around toilets instead of friends, and, in fact, stopped her from visiting friends. It has even stopped her from swimming in pools. Sneaky Poo has started to stink her life up so that no one will have anything to do with her because of the smell. But what was most tragic was that it has caused her to switch off her mother and father 50% of the time. This means that Sneaky Poo has deprived her of 50% of the learning she might have learned from the two people who care about her most. Sally, no wonder you feel that "I can't get through to her." It must be very depressing to lose 50% of your daughter. Jane, Sneaky Poo has been getting through to you, too, by embarrassing you and making you reluctant to have friends round to stay.

I got pretty depressed myself, thinking what a mess Sneaky Poo was making of Natalie's life; what a mess Sneaky Poo was making of her mother's and father's lives and their relationship; what a mess Sneaky Poo was making of Jane and Natalie's sisterhood; what a mess Sneaky Poo was making of this family in general. However, my depression lifted when I realized, at long last, that Natalie was starting to clean up her life. Natalie, you mustn't have allowed Sneaky Poo to grow you down anymore. Look what you went and did.

Last year, Sneaky Poo made your poo sneak three times a week. This year, you have started out-sneaking your poo more and more and it only snuck out on you once a week. More importantly, Natalie, you have stopped Sneaky Poo from messing up your school, even though there probably still is the smell of it around. When I asked you, Natalie, what your tactics were, you had this to say. "I work out when I usually go to the toilet and round that time, I usually put my mind on my stomach feelings. I start feeling a soreness in my stomach." Natalie, you are getting a few clues. The more clues you get, the less sneaky poo will be. For some time, Sneaky Poo must have thought you were clueless. When I asked you how you were able to do this, you told me you were more mature. I wish I had asked you how you were able to mature yourself when Sneaky Poo was trying to keep you a five-year-old. By the way, I thought that Sneaky Poo was pretty mean to keep you young and undergrown. You said that on the inside you were smiling and that you didn't feel sorry for Sneaky Poo, as you no longer wanted to be its playmate. I wish I had asked if there were any other ways you were growing up.

When I asked you, Natalie, whether you wanted to out-sneak Sneaky Poo, that seemed a good idea to you. I guess you must be sick and tired of a messed up life and want to clean it up. So we came up with a lot of ideas to get back at Sneaky Poo and the mess it has made of your life, your mum's life, your dad's life, your sister's life, your mum and dad's relationship with each other.*

---

*The approach I detailed was akin to that described by White (1989), but employing the metaphor of "detective work/clues," etc.

We met a month later and Natalie announced that she had not done any "detective work"; she had just stopped soiling once and for all. Three months later, we met for a review. The following is extracted from that interview.

DE: Before, were you scared of Sneaky Poo?

N: Sort of . . . because it was ruining my life. And I didn't have much control, I didn't think I could do it.

DE: What made you, on that particular day – the 12th day of February – what made you understand or realize you had heaps of control? Is there anything, in particular, that happened on that day . . . or is there anything anyone said? Did you have a dream or a vision or anything?

N: I was reading these books. There's a series of Value Books. There's one about Helen Keller . . . about determination. And she was blind and she learned. At first, she was determined to be a nasty, horrible person. And then Ann Sullivan started writing words on her hand and it made her understand her thoughts.

DE: When did you read that book?

N: I got them about two years ago. I got a whole series.

DE: So why now – on the 12th day of February – did it have an effect?

N: When I came to you, I realized what was in the book, what it meant.

DE: What the book meant? How's that?

N: Most of the other people just thought I was another patient . . .

DE: What did I think of you?

N: You were more interested in my problem . . . you were like Ann Sullivan. You kept asking me questions.

DE: Did those other people who thought you were a patient, didn't they ask you questions about yourself?

N: They just asked how it had been. I went to them every six months.

DE: Did you think I treated you more like a person than a patient?

N: Yah . . .

DE: How do you see it as different? Say I wanted to teach a person not to talk to a young person as a patient but as a person, how would you do that?

N: You'd just understand and have faith.

DE: Did you think I had faith in you?

N: Yah . . .

DE: How could you tell? I know I did, but I didn't say, "I've got faith in you." Or at least I didn't say it out loud. How did you know I believed in you? How could you tell?

N: The sort of questions you were asking . . .

DE: Do you have any regrets about out-witting Sneaky Poo?

N: Not that I can think of.

DE: No way you would want to go back and have a friendship with Sneaky Poo? Do you think there are any tricks you used or any talking to yourself you did that you could tell the other kids? Any pearls of wisdom?

N: I just understood things more.

DE: What did you understand?

N: Before I didn't know Sneaky Poo was bad or anything.

DE: You didn't! You thought it was a friend? That must be a big difference. So did Sneaky Poo talk you into thinking that it was your friend rather than your enemy?

N: Yes.

DE: Well, it's pretty hard to go against your friend. So that is what maybe is at the heart of your success. How do you figure Sneaky Poo was able to trick you into thinking it should be your play-mate?

N: It was sort of telling my mind, because sometimes my mum and dad smacked me for soiling and things. It sort of said in its own special way that they were blaming me. And it was good to have a problem like that.

DE: Do you feel sort of angry that Sneaky Poo lied to you like that?

N: Yah.

DE: Was there something I said or asked you that helped you undo this . . . and helped you figure out the trick?

N: You kept calling him Sneaky Poo instead of the other name and that helped me to understand that he was in the wrong.

DE: Did you think that you were in the wrong?

N: Yes.

DE: Oh, I see. That's sad because if you thought you were to blame that might have weakened your determination. Did you think that when you got free of the idea that it was your fault and it was really Sneaky Poo's fault, you could determine your determination against it?

N: Yes . . . I could have done it all without anybody else. I just had to have faith in myself and believe that I could do things.

I would like to end my address by paying my respects to Sergej P., who was known almost to the very end of his life as the "Wolf Man," the psychoanalytic name granted him by Sigmund Freud. His given name became anonymous, as the interpretation of one of his dreams became foundational to psychoanalytic theory and practice. Still, after 60 + years of analysis he refused to accept a psychoanalytic ban to talk only to duly appointed interviewers. Karin Oberholzer (1982) persisted.

> "It seems that I want you to write something after all," the Wolf-man said once. "But it must not be published until after my death. You must understand, I cannot do otherwise." (p. 7)

Sergej P. is remarkable on two accounts: surely, he is the longest follow-up study in the history of psychotherapy (60 + years) and secondly, his interviews with Oberholzer stand as the first time the "other" speaks back as a person rather than as a case study. And just listen to some of what the "other" says when he is asked:

> OBERHOLZER: When you read the "History of an Infantile Neurosis" for the first time, what did you think?
>
> WOLF-MAN: I didn't think much about it.
>
> O: Did you believe at the time that everything Freud had written in the text was correct?
>
> W: I didn't think about it. That was because of the transference.
>
> O: And today?
>
> W: There is that dream business. I never thought much of dream interpretation, you know?
>
> O: Why not?
>
> W: In my story, what was explained by the dreams? Nothing, as far as I can see. Freud traces everything back to the primal scene which he derives from the dream. But that scene does not occur in the dream. When he interprets the white wolves as nightshirts or something like that, for example, linen sheets or clothes, that's somehow far-fetched, I think. That scene in the dream where the windows open and so on and the wolves are sitting there, and his interpretation, I don't know, those things are miles apart. It's terribly far-fetched. (p. 35)

By Sergej rehabilitating himself in his dying days, perhaps, he ends what his therapy began: the professional monologue of internalizing discourse.

Commentary

William Hudson O'Hanlon

HOW ABOUT INTERNALIZING *and* externalizing discourses? David implies that internalizing discourses are, of necessity, oppressive and always lead to some power-mongering therapy "expert" foisting his/her TRUTH upon people with whom s/he works. I stand opposed to blaming, invalidation, discouraging, oppressive, and physically harmful interventions, talk, and other activities, whether they emanate from clients or therapists (or from anyone else, for that matter). I do not always externalize, however.

Externalizing, the way David and his colleagues practice it, avoids the unhelpful practices of blaming the person (i.e., implying or asserting that s/he has bad or pathological intentions or traits) and of confusing the person's identity with some of her or his actions or experiences ("obsessive-compulsive" or "schizophrenic"), but there are other ways of avoiding these practices. To assert, as David does in his paper, that his and Michael White's work would be "nowhere" without having developed externalizing is a bit of an exaggeration. Both of them are bright, creative, caring, and articulate fellows. Without externalizing they would be somewhere helpful, I trust, just not where they are today.

I consider externalizing interventions (discourses) to be, in part, an invitation from the therapist to clients to develop a different relationship to their concerns or their troubles. The invitation goes something

178

like this: "I invite you to consider that you are not your problem(s). [Or alternately, I invite you to consider that your son, daughter, wife, husband, father, mother, etc., is not the problem.] You [or you and they] have successfully done something other than the problem or not identified yourself with the problem at times in the past. I invite you to notice and tell me about those times when you have opposed or resisted being identified with the problem or letting 'it' control your actions, experience or relationships. From there, I invite you to reconsider your previous conclusions about who you [they] are, who you [they] can be and what you [they] can do."

Externalizing was a means for David, Michael White, and others to find an alternative to (or, in their usual prison/oppression metaphorical frame, to escape from) the traditions of blame and discouragement so rampant in traditional psychiatric and psychotherapeutic practices and discourses, but it is not the *only* route. To identify the means as the end is a mistake akin to what my dog used to do sometimes when I would point things out to him—he would look at my finger rather than whatever I was pointing to.

In sum, internalizing discourses are not equivalent to oppressive, discouraging, pathologizing discourses, as David would have us believe. There are internalizing discourses which empower, are collaborative, and lead away from an identification with the problem. I would retitle David's paper "Oppressive Discourses Versus Empowering Discourses." I think that is what his finger is pointing to.

REFERENCES

Epston, D. (1989). A reflection. In D. Epston, *Collected papers*. Adelaide: Dulwich Centre Publications.

Foucault, M. (1973). *The birth of the clinic: An archaeology of medical perception*. London: Tavistock.

Foucault, M. (1979). *Discipline and punishment: The birth of the prison*. New York: Vintage Books.

Foucault, M. (1980). *Power/knowledge: Selected interviews and other writings*. New York: Pantheon Books.

Furman, B., & Ahola, T. (1992). *Solution talk: Hosting therapeutic conversations*. New York: Norton.

Goffman, B. (1961). *Asylums: Essays in the social situation of mental patients and other inmates*. New York: Doubleday.

Goffman, E. (1974). *Frame analysis*. Harmondsworth, Middlesex: Penguin.

Halliday, M. A. K. (1978). Antilanguages. In M. A. K. Halliday, *Language as social semiotic: The social interpretation of language and meaning*. London: Arnold.

Latour, B., & Woolgar, S. (1979). *Laboratory life: The social construction of scientific facts*. Beverly Hills, CA: Sage.

Lowe, R. (1991). Postmodern themes and therapeutic practices: Notes towards the definition of 'Family therapy: Part 2.' *Dulwich Centre Newsletter*. No. 3, 41–52.

Madigan, S. (1992). *The application of Michel Foucault's philosophy in the problem externalizing discourse of Michael White*. Unpublished manuscript.

Mischler, E. G. (1984). *The discourse of medicine: Dialectics of medical interviews*. Norwood, NJ: Ablex.

Oberholzer, K. (1982). *The wolf-man: Sixty years later (Conversations with Freud's patient)*. London: Routledge and Kegan Paul.

Tomm, K. (1989). Workshop notes. University of Calgary, Alberta.

Tomm, K. (1990). A critique of the DSM. *Dulwich Centre Newsletter*, 5–8.

Waitzkin, H. (1989). A critical theory of medical discourse: Ideology, social control, and the processing of social context in medical encounters. *Journal of Health and Social Behavior, 30*, 220–239.

White, M. (1989). Pseudo-encopresis: From avalanche to victory, from vicious to virtuous cycles. In M. White, *Selected Papers*. Adelaide: Dulwich Centre Publications.

White, M. (1990a). Externalizing the problem. In M. White & D. Epston, *Narrative means to therapeutic ends*. New York: W. W. Norton.

White, M. (1990b). Personal conversation. Adelaide.

Part II

CLINICAL
APPLICATIONS

9

INTERNALIZED OTHER QUESTIONING
WITH COUPLES:
THE NEW ZEALAND VERSION

David Epston

I DEVISED A PRACTICE around 1985 which I then referred to as a cross-referential questioning. This practice of questioning owes a great deal to Michael White's (1989) innovations relating to both the purposes and methods of questioning in therapy. In particular, I am indebted to his "hypotheses regarding the couple's prescription for the therapist and the outcome if the therapist inadvertently conforms to the couple's prescription" (White, 1984). From discussions with Karl Tomm from between 1989–91, I have taken his designation of "internalized other questioning" to describe this practice, although he has certainly elaborated what I refer to as cross-referential questioning to many other therapeutic contexts.

This format of questioning was invented to disrupt those warring couples who construed couple counseling as a venue to contest their differences. These couples seemed to lack any conception of themselves bound together, for better or for worse, in a relationship. It seems that without a "relationship," they can only act out of individual interest and contest their differences within one or more domains, each of which allocates certain practices and specified roles for the

This paper owes a great deal to the editing of Carole Samworth.

participants. In addition, each domain assigns the therapist/counselor both a role and specified functions. These domains of practice are (1) the juridical, (2) the ecclesiastical/moral, and (3) the politics of reality. These prototypes are derived from cultural institutions and have rather obvious analogues in the courtroom, ecclesiastical courts of the Inquisition, and the psychiatric/neurological interview.

Those practices and stances modeled on the courtroom are usually pale reflections of tactics of attack/defend, counter-attack/counter-defence, and discredit/discredit. In this domain, the therapist is required to adjudicate the competing claims submitted to him or her and find parties innocent or guilty or to establish that neither has a case to hear or establish that no ruling can be made. Should either party to a relationship have recourse to this model, he or she will work hard preparing a "case" and gathering supporting evidence to undermine the anticipated counterclaims. A partnership soon dissolves into prosecuting and defense attorneys.

Those practices modeled on the ecclesiastical court or Inquisition also position the partners in opposition to each other. The only difference between the court of law and the ecclesiastical court is that the "case" is argued not on the issue of lawfulness, but rather on the morality of innocence versus sinfulness. Here the therapist is positioned to adjudicate the competing claims in order to find between innocence and sinfulness. The sinful party in the dispute is assigned penance and the innocent party is morally elevated.

Those couples who have been organizing their differences according to the psychiatric/neurological interview assume not only a "world" that is objectively present but also one to which one can have direct and persistent access. Furthermore, it is taken for granted that others experience the "world" in an identical fashion. So what happens when persons responding to the same "world" experience and/or describe it in disparate or contradictory ways? The solution is to question the adequacy of the methods through which the "world" is being experienced and/or reported on by the other. One then calls into question the mental capabilities of the other by either critiquing his or her method of observation or by attributing pathology. The partner in the couple who assumes the role of the psychiatrist/neurologist claims a privileged and uncontestable view of the world. Accordingly, any counterclaims or counterexperiences must be due to specious or inadequate perception or an underlying pathology. In such a situation, you have either a reluctant or recalcitrant "patient" who won't comply with prescriptions or two pseudo-scientific opinions at odds with each other.

Here the therapist is positioned as the consulting expert in the field in order to add greater weight to their junior colleague's prescriptions for his/her "patient" partner.

I have found that if I don't do something to the contrary very quickly, many of my meetings with couples rapidly assume the shape of the courtroom, ecclesiastical court, or psychiatric/neurological interview, with me being recruited very unwillingly into one of the above-mentioned roles. Such couples often become both perplexed and vexed if I decline to participate accordingly. With an interest both in avoiding these recruitments and in disrupting the couple's familiar relationship tactics, I have devised a format of questioning that allows me to decline these roles and permits each partner to experience something of the other's experience.

I have found it necessary to add both a *prologue* and *apology* prior to embarking on what was then referred to as "cross-referential" questioning. The prologue goes something like this:

> If you aren't a "one in a million" couple with a problem, I believe I can safely predict that you both have been asking each other a lot of questions and that those questions have not relieved the situation in any appreciable way or brought you closer to a mutually satisfying solution. My guess is that, if anything, you have found the situation deteriorating right before your eyes. I can safely predict, too, that you have been asking yourselves a lot of questions and those questions have not brought relief or a mutually satisfactory answer. I base these conclusions on the fact that you are here. Am I right in thinking that all your questions have not so far provided an agreeable answer?
>
> In that case, this leads me to a conviction that it would be folly for me to ask you the questions that you have asked either of the other or of yourselves. So I propose that I ask you questions that it is very unlikely you have asked each other or yourself. If you had, I would guess that you wouldn't be here today. And if by any chance I slip up and ask you a question already asked, please draw my attention to this so I won't waste your time by asking a question that has already been tried and found fruitless. I give you full credit for having tried your questions and, given the state your relationship is in, it would be unwise for us to employ the selfsame questions that have not stopped your relationship from being brought to its knees. Do I have your agreement to depart from the divorcing direction these questions are leading you to and to experiment with some questions that conceivably could lead to a reunion in your relationship?

The apology is very necessary to prepare the respondents for the difficulty in first construing the questions and then answering them.

For that reason, they are forewarned as to how they might experience these questions.

> As these questions are very likely questions that you have never thought of before or never asked yourselves before, I need to warn you of their difficulties and to seek your permission to pursue a course that may cause you discomfort. You might not have quick or ready answers. If you had either a quick or ready answer, I would distrust your seriousness, as these questions will require you to think what you never or rarely thought before. You can expect to take awhile to get the gist of these questions, but you will if you persist. And I think I can guarantee you that it will take a minute or two or even more to think up the answers. In fact, the longer the better. So I apologize to you now for their difficulty. You may be stretched in ways you have never been stretched before. Do I have your permission to go ahead with this questioning process?

After having received the couple's permission to proceed, I ask: "Who would like to go first?" I request that the person who goes second listen to his or her partner's answers. I make it clear that they both will be subjected to the same line of questioning, after which both will be provided with equal opportunity to inform the other to what degree (or how close) their partner came to understanding their experience.

Assume that I am interviewing a hypothetical couple, Jack and Jill, whose relationship has been deteriorating over the last 10 years. Jill has offered to go first, so I direct my questions to Jill:

> Jill, what do you think Jack would say if I asked him the following question: "Jack, how do you account for the deterioration in your relationship over the past 10 years?"

In very adversarial and other-blaming couples, the form of this question seems to have the effect of taking the vindictiveness out of the answer. Essentially, Jill is invited by the question to render Jack's complaints about her, even though the question is directed at their "relationship." In this instance, it is very likely that Jack will be restrained from reacting by jumping to his defense. Instead he may seem spellbound and curious as to how Jill will represent his complaints (or, in fact, blame herself). Even if Jill's answer is self-condemning (e.g., "Jill isn't giving me enough love."), I then ask a further question of Jill: "Jack, what effect has this 'lovelessness' had on your relationship?" If Jill should find this question hard to answer, I would assist her with some questions to introduce some ways of assessing the impact on their relationship of this externalized version of the complaint, condemnation, or accusation: "Do you think a loveless direction is good or bad (healthy or unhealthy, adds to or takes away from, increases or decreases) the share value of your relationship?"

With some practice (and it is surprising how rapidly people can respond to these questions if the interviewer is comfortable with them), the interviewer can delete the preamble and merely direct his or her gaze at Jill and inquire: "Jack, you have come up with three theories for the shape your relationship is in. There must be more than that! Are there any little reasons you think are too small to mention out of embarrassment or any big reasons you think are so big you are reluctant to mention them out of fear?"

As the nature of the questions leads respondents (especially men) to reflect in unusual ways, the answers come slowly, cautiously, and are carefully couched. The listener is extremely attentive. Since their complaints are being heard, the partners seem willing and curious to hear each other out without interruption. There is little need to defend against one's own allegations. Even if the mood at the beginning of the session is extremely combative, this is soon replaced by a contemplative ambience, with each person digging deep into his or her experience of the other.

On the single occasion that one party couldn't answer the questions (a couple who had been married 27 years), the interview was called to a halt and questions were asked of the unknown wife. "Judy, were you aware that, even though you have been married for 27 years, Dick doesn't know anything about you? Is this a surprise to you?" She replied that it wasn't at all. "Judy, what effect does this knowledge that Dick doesn't know anything about you have on your relationship to your 'relationship'?" Judy then went on to say that she had known this all along but she needed to hear it and that she was ending the relationship right there and then. I then asked Dick: "If it is now Judy's intention to end this relationship, when did you think it would end?" Dick thoughtfully said that he thought it would have lasted for another 20 years.

The answers are then cross-referenced. "Jack, Jill thought that you would explain the downfall of your relationship by way of an 'I'm all right and you're all wrong' patterning. How close is her representation of your experience to your actual experience of how your relationship is declining?" An ambience of thoughtfulness, curiosity, and a degree of generosity is usually sustained throughout the interview.

I respond by "marrying up" the different versions of the story of their relationship at the end of our first meeting. This brings the story of their relationship up-to-date, customarily concluding in some sort of dilemma for the future of their relationship.

An example of a letter to a middle-aged couple summarizing the information derived from this format of questioning follows:

Dear Terry and Gloria:

From what you told me yesterday, your relationship has come to something of a cross-roads. Gloria, from your point of view, you were "blackmailed" into the marriage in the first place; Terry, you must have wondered what hit you when Gloria, soon after you married, became dismayed and was called "depressed." My guess is that at that time you both would have found it very difficult to understand what was happening to you, especially as it was quite contrary to the images you had of what your married lives would be like. Gloria, without wishing to discount your suffering, those events in your life could now be considered *teachings*. Your tuition was a long and grueling ordeal, but look what you have made of yourself. When I asked you to tell me about yesterday's person, you described that person as lacking in assertion, "not knowing what I wanted and how to get it," "totally revolving around the needs of others," so much so that you became an other-sensitive person at the same time as being insensitive to yourself. This led you into what they called "depression" and you thought the way out was a chemical life-style. So weaning yourself off that was just one more struggle that had to be overcome. One of your most important learnings was that you had "grit" and that was there for me to see.

At the same time, Terry, you became Gloria's nurse and looked after and cared for her the more she became dismayed. There was a price you paid for this and that is the neglect of your own pursuits. You cared for, supported, and promoted Gloria into self-discovery, so much so, in fact, that yesterday's person has almost been eclipsed by today's person. I wouldn't be surprised, Terry, if you were wondering if you didn't do too good a job. You have been so successful at promoting Gloria that you may have fallen behind her. As you put it, "She's hard to keep up to. . . . I'm being left behind. . . . I'm still back doing the same old job. . . . I feel stuck."

Terry, I wonder if you aren't feeling dismayed in the sense that things haven't worked out at all in the way you might have thought they would. In addition to all this, it would have been inevitable that you both would have been required by the departure of your children to turn and face each other again without them in the way. All couples need to, if they are going to last the distance, go through a period of review and reevaluation. I got the impression that that was exactly where your relationship is, with each of you wondering whether you want to do the next half of the marathon together or on your own or with someone else? I can see, too, that you, Terry, have also started to feel the pinch and have started taking some initiatives on your own, firstly joining a men's group and coming here to couple counseling. Both of these ventures are quite new for you.

You tell me that your relationship is imperiled and that if left to its own devices, according to you, Gloria, will go on to the rocks in six months or so and, according to you, Terry, could survive for a few more years. You could let your relationship drift and find out whose estimate is closer to the mark. On the other hand, you could, if you desired it, take your relationship out of the water and survey it. It may require a refit if you wish to sail in deep waters. If you do so, will you restore it to the fashion of the '60s or bring it up-to-date by the appropriate modifications.

I await your decisions on behalf of your relationship and I cannot conceal my curiosity as to what you will make of it or by continuing of a divorcing course, break up on the rocks. However, despite my appreciation of the dangers to your relationship, I found it very easy to like and respect both of you as persons.

Yours sincerely,
David

Such an account entails a "double externalization," as it externalizes both the problem(s) the partners are experiencing *and* the relationship itself. This paves the way for a trialogue between, say, Gloria, Terry, and their relationship, replacing Gloria versus Terry. The latter only allows for the establishment of guilt, sinfulness, or pathology. The process of therapy from here on can now become a meta-commentary on the direction of their relationship as it heads for the metaphorical rocks or, by their determining a new direction for it, gets out of danger or departs from the problem(s). This is achieved by the deployment of some newfound or recovered relationship tactics or the reorganization of their relationship according to some other "recipe," "design," or "plan."

Such paradigmatic questions can inquire about anything but always invite the respondent to answer from his or her experience of the other's experience. This has the effect of undermining those cultural practices that affirm an objective reality. It seems to me that when a problem is understood in terms of an objective reality, most couples immediately seek recourse in practices that are detrimental to their relationship. The problem-solving practices derived from the analogues of the courtroom, ecclesiastical court, and psychiatric/neurological examination tend to divide partners rather than reunite them. It is hoped that the practices described in these pages can serve to offer a remedy to this less than useful way to conduct a relationship and the prescriptions for the therapist that follow from it.

Commentary: Systems of Understanding, Practices of Relationship, and Practices of Self

Michael White

HAVE YOU MET couples whose relationships seem dominated by interactions that are of an adversarial nature?* Have some of these couples been so locked into these interactions that they couldn't extricate themselves long enough to allow space for you, the therapist, to comment on their situation? And, when meeting with these couples, have you ever experienced the very real risk that you might get caught up in these interactions, or overwhelmed by them in some way? If your response to these questions is in the affirmative, chances are that you have, from time to time in therapy sessions, experienced yourself:

(a) entering into unwanted roles; for example, the "adjudicator" or the "magistrate,"
(b) going comatose,
(c) wondering whether you might be hypoglycemic,
(d) starting to clock-watch,

*Although this essay primarily addresses work with couples whose relationships are dominated by adversarial interactions, and when there does not appear to be a significant imbalance in these relationships with regard to power, the practices of David Epston's "internalized other questioning" do render power imbalances more explicit and provide one avenue for redressing such imbalances.

(e) wishing that there was a real therapist in the room who might intervene and save the situation, or

(f) trying to figure out how on earth you got into the therapy business in the first place.

Very few therapists would consider these sort of outcomes of their interaction with these couples to be desirable. And I doubt very much that such outcomes are ever considered desirable to the couples who feel so locked into adversarial interactions. If therapists are recruited into and contribute to the patterns of interaction that dominate the relationships of these couples, or if they find themselves overwhelmed, frustration and despair will be experienced by all parties.

What sort of analysis of such predicaments might save therapists and couples from this fate? How could such an analysis assist therapists to engage with couples in a manner that might bring about preferred real effects for all parties to the interaction? How might this analysis contribute to the desire that these couples have to interact with each other around possibilities in their relationships, rather than around the "settled certainties" that have so paralyzed them?

Here, I will briefly review one approach to the analysis of these predicaments. This approach will focus attention on the extent to which the interactions that so dominate the relationships of these couples are constituted or shaped by particular systems of understanding, practices of relationship, and practices of self.

SYSTEMS OF UNDERSTANDING AND PRACTICES OF RELATIONSHIP

Do you have a sense that there is something entirely predictable about how things go in these adversarial relationships, and about how these couples explain their predicament? Has it occurred to you that relationships that are characterized by these adversarial interactions are not uncommon in the world at large? Have you noticed strong parallels in the relationships of these couples, and in the relationships of persons whom you know outside of the therapeutic context—perhaps even in the relationships of some distant relatives? Have you ever had the suspicion that these adversarial interactions are common enough to be represented as institutionalized practices of relationship?

If your response to these questions is in the affirmative, might it be reasonable for you to assume that each couple who feels locked into these interactions did not totally dream up or invent these ways of being together? And would it also be reasonable for you to assume that there could be common systems of understanding and relationship practices that relate to these scenarios, and that these might be of a cultural nature? If so, would it really seem all that farfetched to assume that these systems of understanding and practices of relationship may actually be constitutive or shaping of these relationships?

Do these considerations have you searching for ways of describing and naming the systems of understanding and the relationship practices that constitute such adversarial interactions? And do these considerations have you thinking about ways of engaging these couples in other systems of understanding and relationship practices that do not constitute such adversarial interactions: systems of understanding that initiate alternative explanation of events, and practices of relationship that are not so polarizing and paralyzing?

PRACTICES OF SELF

Have you found that partners whose relationship is dominated by adversarial interactions seem to find it almost impossible to step into each other's experience even for a second? Have you ever observed that partners who are locked into such interactions are in pursuit of an individuality that denies relationship? Have you had the thought that these couples conflate differentiation and separation, and juxtapose individuation and connection? Have you sensed that the version of individuality that is performed under these circumstances is one that distances and isolates partners from each other, and that this is a form of individuality that is somewhat familiar?

If your response to these questions is in the affirmative, might you consider it fair to assume that there are some cultural practices of the self at work here that reinforce a particular version of individuality and that discriminate against other versions of individuality? And might it be reasonable to assume that these practices of self mitigate against the possibility of partners' "stepping into" each other's experience?

Certainly, approaches to the constitution of the self that conflate individuality and separation are pervasive in this culture. One example of this is the extent to which the isolated or detached individualities dominate accounts of developmental processes (consider, just for a moment, the part that the isolating individualities play in the structuring of adolescent stage of development). Indeed, so pervasive is this dominant approach to the self that it is constantly being reproduced in "new clothing." For example, consider the patriarchal reproduction of this practice that is performed by a dominant form of the men's movement in North America, which emphasizes differentiation through separation from women.

Are you stirred by such considerations to assist couples to challenge the practices of the isolated individualities and to explore, in the constitution of the self, alternative individualities—individualities that are not conflated with separation, individualities that are not cancelling of connection? The alternative individualities that I am referring to here are those that are in league with affiliation, individualities that are derived through a collaboration between persons in the identification, articulation, and acknowledgment of aspects of each other's preferred identity—including desires, preferences, qualities, purposes, values, goals, commitments, and so on.* Relationship is not a contradiction to these alternative individualities; connection does not subtract from them, but contributes to them.

INTERNALIZED OTHER QUESTIONING

David provides an important contribution to the breaking of the impasse or the predicament referred to at the outset of this essay. He does this by first describing and naming the systems of understanding and the relationship practices that constitute adversarial interactions in couple relationships and that often recruit therapists into particular roles that contribute further to frustration and to despair.

He names these systems of understanding the "juridical," the "ecclesiastical/moral," and the "politics of reality," and typifies their associated practices of relationship. Once these practices are named and described, therapists will find it easier to know how to avoid participating in these highly institutionalized and culture-specific forms of interaction.

David then introduces a prologue that explicitly disrupts these systems of understanding and the performance of their associated relationship practices. This prologue makes it possible, often for the very first time, for couples to step back from their institutionalized ways of being with each other, and to experience a degree of alienation from these ways of being. This is an important first step in encouraging

---

*I have no doubt whatsoever that women have traditionally been better at performing the practices associated with the affiliative individualities, whereas men have traditionally been better at performing the practices associated with the isolated individualities.

couples to draw a distinction between their relationship, on the one hand, and what they experience about their interaction that is so problematic to them, on the other.

The apology that follows the introduction opens space for persons to experience alternative systems of understanding and relationship practices. The discomfort that couples might expect to experience as they depart from habitual interactions is acknowledged, and is associated with new possibilities.

Following this, David proceeds to introduce a system of questioning – "internalized other questioning" – which not only effectively disrupts the institutionalized systems of understanding and relationship practices as named and described by David, but also those practices of self that constitute the isolating individualities. These questions require that each partner enter into an experience of the other partner's experience of him or her. In response to these questions, an atmosphere of thoughtfulness, generosity and curiosity is established.

I believe that the cross-referencing of the answers to these questions provides an important opportunity for the evolution of other individualities – those that are affiliative rather than isolating. This is particularly the case if these questions evolve in the direction of reflecting on events in the relationship to determine what these might say about the preferences, desires, qualities, wants, goals, values, beliefs, and so on, of the internalized other. The discussion that is initiated by the cross-referencing of the answers to these questions makes it possible for partners to experience a mutual contribution to the identification, articulation and acknowledgment of these aspects of the "self." For these couples, individuation and connection are no longer juxtaposed, differentiation and separation are no longer conflated.

COMMENT

When David first introduced me to the practices associated with his internalized other questioning, I did not find these at all difficult to enter into – they seemed almost familiar. For some time I had been exploring what I have referred to as "experience-of-experience" questions, such as, "What do you think these difficulties have talked your partner into about you?" But David's internalized other questions do more than strike a familiar chord – to interview each partner's internalized other in this way is something else, a distinct development in this work.

In collaboration with some couples who have felt locked into the institutionalized interactions that David describes and names in his paper, I have been experimenting with prologues, apologies, and internalized other questions. In this process, I have been recasting experience of experience questions and coming up with "internalized other" versions of these like:

> (*addressing Jill*) "Jack, what has this conflict been talking you into about Jill, and about your relationship?"

We have all been enjoying the outcome of these questions. So why don't you, and the couples who meet with you, give them a try?

REFERENCES

White, M. (1984). Marital therapy—Practical approaches to long-standing problems. *Australian and New Zealand Journal of Family Therapy, 5,* 27–43.

White, M. (1989). The process of questioning: A therapy of literary merit? In M. White, *Selected papers.* Adelaide: Dulwich Centre Publications.

10

BRINGING FORTH THE RESTRAINING INFLUENCE OF PATTERN IN COUPLES THERAPY

Jeffrey L. Zimmerman
Victoria C. Dickerson

THIS CHAPTER IS organized by first situating our particular therapy approach in the theory which informs it. This is followed by a description of our work with couples and a partial transcript of a session, which we hope will illustrate the conversational process that takes place in our work. Finally, we discuss some of the ways we think the work could proceed and what we see as valuable about the process.

The influences on our work include social constructionism, second-order cybernetics/negative explanation, the notion of narrative, and the ideas of Michael White. Since these ideas overlap, we could start in any place, but we will begin by discussing narrative and then look at the meta-model that informs this approach.

Narrative (Bruner, 1986, 1990) is a way of describing our lives. We cannot know ourselves or describe ourselves in the totality of our experience. We can, however, describe ourselves in terms of particular events located in our experience and strung together as a "story." Usually one story becomes "dominant" and is the way we think about ourselves. This story "constitutes" us as persons and shapes our lives. Dominant stories for people in therapy are problem stories or stories that are problem-saturated. The implication is that there are other possible stories available to us made up of events we have been less likely to attend to or have not noticed. In terms of negative explanation, we are "restrained" from seeing those events by the dominant story.

Negative explanation (Bateson, 1972; White, 1986a) is an understanding of events as occurring "instead of," rather than "because of,"
other events occurring. The focus is on restraints, rather than on
causes. Certain events in our lives carry an "inevitability" with which
we continue to notice those events; we are thus restrained from the
possibility of noticing other things about ourselves or our relationships. Restraints can be located in several aspects of our experience,
including social or familial discourse, personal stories we might have
about ourselves, and patterns of behaviors or beliefs. Dominant stories – as problem-saturated stories – tend to close people off from other
possibilities, and continue to shape what is currently occurring.

Our work is also informed by a cybernetic metaphor in that we
emphasize the reciprocal patterns that influence a couple's relationship. These patterns connect the socially constructed practices that
each member of the couple exhibits, as well as the meaning systems
that influence these practices. However, the description of pattern
is not "discovered" or "found" by the therapist (Hoffman, 1985), but
co-created or co-constructed by the therapist and the client. This is
clearly a second-order view in that we cannot separate the influence of
those who are observing from what is observed. It is a social constructionist view in that the meanings which influence the couple *and* the
therapist are considered. It is through social discourse and through
conversation that reality is created. Constructions of pattern in this
therapy model take into account the meaning system of the couple as
it is affected by both social discourse and the couple's experience, as
well as how they are restrained by this meaning system from preferable stories.

A constructionist perspective might lead to the following questions:

1. What meanings about relationships influence each member of
   the couple and in what ways?
2. What experiences and discourses affected these meanings?
3. What can I (the therapist) construct with my clients to bring
   forth these meanings (and consequential practices) to help people
   separate from them?
4. How can I (the therapist) help the spouses notice and draw from
   some of their other meanings and experiences in order to make
   the changes they desire?

A constructionist perspective allows for the use of any analogy. We
have found the text analogy, or the narrative model, to be very useful
in describing meaning systems. For couples, reciprocal patterns (be-

haviors and beliefs) can support a disempowering or pathologizing description or story about each person and the relationship. Using a narrative approach, a restorying process can be facilitated by the therapist, who brings forth alternative stories (descriptions) by helping people attend to other aspects of their lived experience.

We have also found some of the specific techniques that Michael White (1989; White and Epston, 1990) has written about to be very useful in helping construct a context for restorying. These include the objectification of problems, *not* persons or families; externalizing conversations; relative influence questioning; and using "unique outcomes" (exceptions to the problem description) as entry points to a new story. Externalization of "the problem" can mean externalizing specific habits which support certain patterns, the pattern itself, aspects of one's discourse about self or relationships, and cultural specifications, e.g., patriarchy, dominant gender attitudes, which might be influencing persons or relationships. Once couples begin to separate from the problem, their alternative experiences can be more readily brought forth in a way that they become engaged in a new story. Further questions (White, 1988) can be used to invite clients to develop this new story.

Influenced by these constructions, we have developed an approach to working with couples. In brief, when a couple comes in with certain problems, these problems are mapped out, with careful attention paid to constructing a reciprocal pattern that supports the problem. The therapist then helps the partners discover unique outcomes to the problem/pattern so that they can begin to develop new stories about themselves and their relationship. This is an empowering process for the couple because the new stories are generated from the couple's own ideas and experience, with a message that supports the ideas. Couples may have to be helped to resist the influence of disempowering cultural specifications, such as patriarchy and gender, or other idea systems that dictate what is right or wrong for people. In this way they can begin to write their own specifications for themselves. A dual process of deconstructing old meanings (through attention to family of origin and cultural discourses) and reconstruction of meanings that fit more for each person becomes a model for the process of therapy.

WORKING WITH COUPLES

We begin our conversations with couples by focusing on who they are, separate from the problems affecting their relationship. We do this by asking about other contexts they find themselves in (work, play, etc.). We invite them to ask about us – a way of indicating the kind of nonhierarchical process we employ.

We then suggest that couples usually come to tell us a story that has a problem in it and we ask to hear each member's version separately – one talks, while the other and the therapist listen. We believe it is important to make space for each member to share as much of his/her experience of the problem as possible. Some people, especially those under the influence of highly specifying dominant stories, require a great deal of work to co-create a description that fits their experience but separates them from the problem.

We have found it useful to begin the process by constructing a reciprocal pattern that seems to be dominating the couple's relationship. Often we end up constructing a pattern that is some variation on the *pursue-withdraw* description. We are aware that other therapists and researchers (Gottman, 1991; Markman, 1991) see this as a common pattern in which couples in conflict find themselves – perhaps a pattern that is an effect of problems that divide members of a couple, with each responding in ways typical of their gender. Nevertheless, this is often an excellent starting point: to begin an escape from a pattern that is defined as the problem. (Of course, there are many other possible patterns and their descriptions.)

We see these patterns as forming a support system for what is becoming the dominant story of the relationship, a problem story that overshadows the more positive story the couple once held about the relationship. We see the reciprocal responses which make up the pattern as inviting each other rather than causing each other. Each member notices the patterned response of the other and thus does not notice other interactions or responses when they occur. The dominant problem story gets bigger and the couple's relationship, as originally developed, gets smaller.

When each member of the couple describes the problem, he/she often describes it as something the other member does. For example, the wife might protest that her husband is never available to her; he just won't stand up and fight; he's gone a lot, comes home late, finds other things to interest him, and has begun to withdraw more and more. As she launches on her complaint, the therapist focuses on the specific behavior, *withdrawal*, as the habit that the wife is finding problematic. By asking the question, "What effect does this have on you?" the therapist begins to construct a pattern.

The therapist can then elicit the problem as described by the husband. Usually the husband will agree that he withdraws. However, he protests that it is because she doesn't give him any space. He says that she is always nagging at him; she says he never does anything right; she can always find something she wants to be different. The *pursuing* of him often escalates into screaming. As a result, he spends as little time as possible in her company. While the wife agrees that she spends a good deal of time *pursuing*, she sees her husband's behavior as causal in the sequence. In this example, the wife's *pursuing* invites the husband's *withdrawal*, as his *withdrawal* invites her *pursuing*. By using the notion of invitation (White's term) rather than causation, the therapist begins to deconstruct the problem as being the *pattern* rather than the other *person*. This pattern can be described as supporting a type of relationship, e.g., *overly distant*, which has captured the two of them. The pattern can then be externalized and contrasted to the kind of relationship the couple prefers.

Relative influence questioning is the next process the therapist employs. The therapist first wants to know how the problem has influence over the persons, their lives, and their relationships. The questions are explored with each member of the couple individually, with the other present. In this manner, each end of the reciprocal pattern begins to be externalized for the person it is affecting. We find it useful to focus in two ways: First, we look at specific behavior habits, e.g., the husband reading the paper immediately when he comes home rather than talking. Second, we examine how the problem is affecting the person's life – his/her happiness, closeness, attitudes to self and other, conclusions about the relationship, etc. We think this helps the spouses begin to notice the habitual responses they currently are not noticing and to see what effects their participation in the problem is having on their lives. Proceeding in this manner also allows us to develop a wide field in which "unique outcomes" – outcomes not predicted by the problem story – can be noticed by the therapist.

To return to the "generic" example we have been using, after externalizing *withdrawal* (for the husband) and *pursuit* (for the wife) in the specific and general ways we have just discussed, we go back over each person's description and look for times and ways each person has escaped his/her end of the pattern, even if in small ways or for a brief time. The focus can be on present or past times in the relationship or on future pictures of more preferred relationship patterns. These unique outcomes serve as entry points to alternative stories about the person and the relationship. A woman recently told one of the authors that she was able to counter some of the effects of *anger* (not acting pleasantly) by remembering her interest in developing a long-term family life. Her husband told how he escaped *withdrawal* and acted in a more "loving" manner, remembering that he wanted someone to grow old with—the *withdrawal* responses didn't fit into his picture of how he wanted to act with that person. Both were quite surprised to hear they had similar goals.

Eventually the therapist can make the link between these "individual" habits. This is done so the couple can begin to see a pattern, and may be done by asking each partner if they can see how the problem that influences them "invites" the behavior of the other partner. Again, the therapist searches for "unique outcomes," when *pursuing* and *withdrawal* were not in charge and the couple managed to relate in a different way. Perhaps the wife had been overcome by *pursuing* and the husband had declined the invitation to *withdraw*, or the husband had given in to *withdrawal* and the wife had escaped the invitation to *pursue*. When this has occurred, questions can be asked to help them notice that, when the pattern is escaped, they can experience something different—perhaps they can even manage to enjoy each other's company or team up and solve problems.

Usually by the end of the first session the therapist manages to elicit from the couple two descriptions of their relationship. The dominant story, an *overly distant lifestyle*, is one which is problem-saturated, as it is supported by the interrelationship between pursuit and withdrawal. The other description involves an alternative story where the spouses relate to each other in a different way, separate from *pursuit* and *withdrawal*. This description is just as grounded in experience as is the problem-saturated or dominant story. Under the guidance of the new story, other experiences (past, present, future possibilities) will be selected out by the couple, which will further develop the new story.

Wherever one begins the work, one is deconstructing the problem. Deconstruction helps clients to begin to reevaluate what were previously thought to be truths about themselves and their relationship. Deconstruction helps to situate the meaning people give to their experience in the experiential context in which this meaning evolved. This may involve past or present familial, social, or cultural experiences, as well as the experience created when the marital relationship was being affected by problems originally seen as inherent in the persons or the relationship itself.

As the process of deconstruction proceeds, questions can be asked which invite each person to notice how a certain habit of relating developed in his or her family of origin. How, for example, was this habit a friend in helping them escape or handle a difficult family issue in the past, even though it is now haunting them in their current relationship? For example, a man may have developed a habit of shutting things out to close off abuse he got from his father. This habit was helpful to him in the original context, but now operates automatically and prevents him from being able to hang in there and stay connected with his wife. Locating original habits and beliefs in this manner offers an acceptable contextualization of the problem. This results in people feeling less blame, and highlights for them the difference between their current relationship and the original relationship context in which the habits and beliefs arose.

Efforts are also made to locate certain habits and beliefs in a context of gender specifications (Neal and Slobodnik, 1990). This serves to further deconstruct the problem. Women are often trained to have certain ideas, e.g., being for others and not for themselves, and are more comfortable affiliating under stress and discussing their affective experience. Men are often trained in patriarchal power tactics, e.g., aggression and stonewalling, and are disinclined to discuss things in an emotional way. They also see their opinions as truths and tend to try to fix/protect rather than listen; under stress they prefer to be alone. These habits are normalized and attributed to gender training. Each partner is then asked whether these habits suit them and their relationship. It is also suggested that certain ways of relating will always be more comfortable for one than for the other. One can readily see the influence of gender training on the sample pattern *withdrawal* and *pursuing*. We like to engage couples in a great deal of discussion around these issues.

When couples come for further sessions, we recommend that the therapist look for unique outcomes, even if the couple prefers to bring up a problem or an interaction dominated by the problem. Often the therapist can comment that it would be more helpful if they would catch the therapist up regarding steps taken since last time before discussing new problems. This will help orient the therapy in the direction of noticing small steps away from the problem and toward a new story. In our experience, it is more useful to talk to each member of the couple individually about the steps he/she has taken without directly asking the other. If the partner volunteers, he/she can be included. If not, it is best to let each person talk about his/her individual steps, because each is more apt to notice what he/she is doing before the partner does. Responding to each person's steps not only develops a new picture and a new direction but shifts the picture the partner has of the other. If the problem is chronic, the beginning steps might be small and alluded to vaguely. With problems somewhat less chronic, the steps can be dramatic.

After a thorough discussion of the new responses, attention may be focused on a problem, if the couple is interested in doing so. In cases where very little change has occurred, we might look carefully at what stops each partner from making the steps. When couples begin to take steps away from a particular problem pattern, often they turn their attention to long-standing ideas that affect the relationship. For example, a couple may move from *pursuing* and *withdrawal* to beliefs of the *frightening aspects of closeness*. This too can be externalized, and unique outcomes can be elicited. The therapist can begin to help the spouses embrace beliefs more suited to the kind of persons and relationships they prefer. Often, without much help from the therapist, examples of these problem discourses "tumble out" once the couple has become separated from the dominating pattern. In this manner, therapy becomes a parallel process of deconstructing or unpacking meanings and reconstructing or restorying new meanings. We prefer to emphasize the latter process, if possible. Some situations are so problem-saturated, however, that more efforts to deconstruct must be undertaken before much restorying can occur.

A CASE EXAMPLE

We would like to illustrate the above description via a transcript of a consultation session with a couple. The interview demonstrates how a reciprocal pattern is created. As you will see, some persistence was required to accomplish this with the couple (more than is usually the case). We would like to invite you to imagine what discourses are operating here, and we will share our ideas with you after a presentation of parts of the interview.

The couple was being seen by a therapist who had attended some of our supervision and training groups. The therapist was frustrated in her efforts to describe a pattern which would allow the wife to see the effects on her of a problem (*anxiety*) which had significant effects on her husband's life – a pattern in which the wife participated, thus *inadvertently* supporting the problem.

> THERAPIST: Well, Joanne had told me just a little bit about some of her work with you and told me she had been seeing you about a year. In that year, she had seen you fight some problems. She told me that recently there had been quite an important turning point. I was really excited to hear that after a year of fighting these problems . . .

ROBERT: Still fighting them myself. Susan's doing fine. It's a combination of health, because of my Dad being ill, Mom being ill. But I'm not sure that's the reason.

THERAPIST: I'll tell you what would help me – if I could hear from both of you about what the problem is right now. You know more about where it is today. That would help a lot.

ROBERT: Okay, I think for me . . . Susan is doing everything humanly possible, as my wife, to encourage me to do anything that makes sense, that she can do. There's just not much more she can do except do handstands – that's a "little joke." I can't praise her for . . . I'm not trying to be melodramatic.

THERAPIST: So you feel supported by her?

ROBERT: Yeah, almost too much.

THERAPIST: Too much?

ROBERT: I wouldn't say too much. I think maybe I am being, not trying to be, melodramatic. I think that she does . . . I guess, I say that because maybe I do not feel good about it myself.

THERAPIST: That you don't want her taking care of you in a way – that way . . .

ROBERT: I don't think men do like that.

THERAPIST: Yeah, yeah, you understand that it is really well meant, and really nice, that she is willing to do that.

ROBERT: I feel guilty because I am not like I should be, you know, mentally or physically.

THERAPIST: So you think it would be good for her if she took care of herself more and you less?

ROBERT: Yeah, I told her she should go to the doctor for her annual checkup.

(A short discussion follows about why she does things and his ways of encouraging her to do things.)

THERAPIST: And you feel guilty . . . you insinuated that . . .

ROBERT: Sure. I feel guilty because I should be more responsible for . . . I keep on saying that . . . I have not been able to accomplish it . . . but . . . I don't know if she is trying to do the . . . uh, I'm repeating myself. Her task is to make me do things to feel better about myself.

THERAPIST: She tries to make you do things to make you feel better about yourself?

ROBERT: I don't ask her to make dinner, because it is ridiculous; she doesn't understand that. She worked all day. She doesn't have to make dinner for me anyway; then she is insulted because I don't have any. There's no point if I have eaten something for lunch. It's enough. I am not that hungry, so I think that she is the type of person trying to please not only myself but trying to please my son and daughter.

THERAPIST: So this habit she has of pleasing others and being more for others . . . she has a really big habit of, as you see it, being for others.

ROBERT: I think she is a giving person . . . nothing wrong with that as long as she takes care of herself.

THERAPIST: As long as she takes care of self—if she is for others *and* for self. It's okay, but if it leans . . .

ROBERT: I think it leans towards . . . let's see, I am trying to think . . . it leans toward me too much, maybe.

THERAPIST: To you. I get the picture. Let me ask you, Robert, about this one point. When this habit overtakes her and pushes her more towards you than toward herself, when it leans that way . . .

ROBERT: (*Interrupting*) I don't know . . . you can put the words together . . . I don't think . . . I think she does things . . . I don't think she, you know, I want to put it in a better perspective. I think she does things for herself. (*Turns to Susan*) Maybe you can answer better than I can.

THERAPIST: I want to get a picture of what you see, then I am going to talk to her, get her picture.

ROBERT: The only thing I know is that a certain amount of time doing for herself, but she . . . I still think she probably gives more than I do.

THERAPIST: More to you than you give to her.

ROBERT: Yeah, by a long shot.

THERAPIST: It's out of balance. When she's taking care of you or pleasing you or being for you, what effect does that have on you?

ROBERT: You know, I told her: Why are you being so nice? I am not saying it is wrong, but sometimes I can't, uh . . . uh, understand her reasons.

THERAPIST: So, one of the effects you suggest is that guilt attacks you? Does that happen when. . . . Is that part of what happens?

(A short discussion about guilt and anxiety follows. However, the therapist is most interested in bringing forth the real effects of the problem in his life.)

THERAPIST: So what happens when guilt affects you, what happens to you when guilt affects you? Do you get anxious? Do you get mobilized, immobilized?

ROBERT: Sometimes I do.

THERAPIST: Which?

ROBERT: Well, I get, I get, I become immobilized.

THERAPIST: Immobilized?

ROBERT: Yeah.

(A long discussion about guilt, anxiety, and immobilization follows. As you can see from the portions you have read, getting a description that Robert will hold onto is difficult. However, the immobilization habit finally becomes one end of the reciprocal pattern. Then Susan's description is elicited and developed.)

THERAPIST: *(To Susan)* Do you have a percentage – like what percent are you oriented to Robert and the kids and what percent to yourself, roughly?

SUSAN: I am not good at math *(hesitantly)*.

ROBERT: 99%. I was teasing.

THERAPIST: Is it 50-50? 40-60?

SUSAN: I probably do for myself – 40%.

THERAPIST: And 60% for them. And you see that at times guilt starts to hang around Robert – you started to say that. How do you see guilt affecting Robert?

SUSAN: Well, I know . . . I mean, he . . . he always, I guess, he tries to compensate because he's not doing anything. Then, like, he will tell me: You don't have to cook dinner. That's the main thing – cook dinner.

THERAPIST: You mean he discourages you from doing some of those taking care of things.

SUSAN: Cooking dinner or doing . . . you know.

THERAPIST: Cooking dinner.

SUSAN: He says, "You're too tired," or "Don't do it." Maybe I want to eat, you know, but like, last night we were supposed to go grocery shopping. I ended going myself. Robert didn't feel like going. That sort of upset me.

ROBERT: You didn't tell me it upset you.

SUSAN: When I got home at 2:30–3:00, he was in his robe, not dressed, and I said: "Why are you not dressed?" He said, "Oh, I don't feel good. Here's the list of what I have." Some of it was my daughter's list because she has to have some stuff from the market. I think Robert realized I was a little upset with him. So when I got home from the market he was dressed. So I felt that he needed to get out a little bit besides being in the house – that's why I wanted him to come with me to the market. He didn't.

THERAPIST: So is that an example of what Robert and I talked about as an immobilization kind of thing or immobilization habit?

SUSAN: And on the weekends, I say, let's do this or that, you know. "No, I don't feel like . . . I feel weak today. I can't go." Well, what do you do? So I go out and do what I have to do and come back. You know. I'm not going . . . I work all week . . . and I don't want to wait home all day.

THERAPIST: You don't want to wait around. Don't wait around – that's good. Would it make sense to you if I said that sometimes *immobilization* invites the other person to *take care* of him, so that if *immobilization* takes over one person, it is an invitation for the other to *take care* of him, to do things for him? Does that make sense to you?

SUSAN: Yeah, it probably happens like that.

THERAPIST: Yeah, yeah, so you can see how that might work that way. Inevitably, *immobilization* moves in on one person. It invites other persons to try to get them going, do things. Given what happened, it's almost inevitable that process would occur. Does that make sense to you? Have you been caught up in that a bit?

(Discussion follows about patterns and the relationship between "taking care of habit" and "immobilization." Given the time needed for the reflecting team and the difficulty of creating a pattern that fit their experience, the therapist, instead of asking more externalizing questions, went on to look for some unique outcomes.)

THERAPIST: Has this been helpful to you so far?

COUPLE'S THERAPIST: Very helpful.

THERAPIST: Okay, so you can work with that pattern stuff?

COUPLE'S THERAPIST: Umhm.

THERAPIST: All right. Good. 'Cause what I know is breaking patterns sometimes is really helpful in escaping problems. Given that I'm really curious about . . . your therapist told me there had been this recent turning point and that you've been escaping *immobilization* somewhat, that you're moving in that direction.

ROBERT: Well, it's like hot and cold, like running water.

THERAPIST: That's how everybody escapes certain habits, Robert. Nobody goes like this (*therapist gestures up*). They go like this (*gesturing up and down*). You've been more like that!

ROBERT: Yeah.

THERAPIST: Yeah, but that's how everybody ... *immobilization* is a powerful thing. You can't just ... uh ... throw it in the garbage and turn around and walk away. You take a couple of little steps away from it and then it attacks back.

ROBERT: Yeah. I don't have agoraphobia?

THERAPIST: No, no, I didn't think you did.

ROBERT: No, but people do have, can have ...

THERAPIST: Well, that's an example of ...

ROBERT: I think what it is, it's a combination of not feeling good about yourself. Maybe you have a medical problem, maybe you don't.

THERAPIST: Right.

ROBERT: All those things and then, uh ... I still think a person, um ... who really feels good about himself sometimes can overcome his problems.

THERAPIST: Well, it takes feeling really good about yourself to escape *immobilization*. *Immobilization* is a powerful thing. And, as you know, for example, you haven't let *immobilization* turn you into an agoraphobic. Uh, that's what ... how'd you manage that?

ROBERT: I just don't think I ... I never had a fear of going outside.

THERAPIST: Yeah, but *immobilization* can reduce someone to that. You've just pointed that out. And you're quite right. So how have you been able to not let *immobilization* turn you into an agoraphobic? I'm really curious about that.

ROBERT: I don't know. I think I like people, I think it's just a ... I don't know ... I don't have an answer. I think that when I was younger, I might. I don't know. I had a period of not going to school, maybe, a fear of not doing well. But I don't think ...

THERAPIST: No, no, no.

ROBERT: Being successful at school.

THERAPIST: That's different. So what I'm curious about is ... I think you're quite right when you said a minute ago that, um, you have to have enough self-esteem, you know, to not let *immobilization* turn you into an agoraphobic. So what is it about yourself that you're able to notice? Let me ask it this way ...

ROBERT: Yeah, yeah, I'm not going to answer it.

THERAPIST: What do you think it tells me about you? When I see you haven't let *immobilization* turn you into an agoraphobic. What do you think that tells me about you?

ROBERT: I don't know. Could you ... are you saying that in a scientific way, or are you saying it in a personal way? How are ...

THERAPIST: Personal way. What do you think it tells me about you as a person? What strength do you think I can notice when I see you haven't let *immobilization* turn you. . . ?

ROBERT: I don't know.

THERAPIST: You don't know. Well, what do you think? (*Turning to Susan*) What strengths do you that Robert has to not let *immobilization* turn him into an agoraphobic? Strengths in himself?

SUSAN: Well, I think he likes to be around people.

THERAPIST: Liking of others.

SUSAN: Yeah.

THERAPIST: His likability. He is pretty likable. I like him.

SUSAN: He'll just . . . I mean, if we go out he'll talk to anybody.

THERAPIST: Oh, okay!

ROBERT: Not quite anybody.

THERAPIST: He's comfortable; he's likable; he engages people.

SUSAN: Yeah.

(Further discussion follows of Robert's verbal and relationship skills. As you can see, a different picture was emerging of Robert and his ability to handle immobilization. The therapist took a risk when he asked Susan a redescription question about Robert. If the conflict is high we do not recommend asking one spouse about the other early on. The focus then shifts to Susan.)

THERAPIST: How have you begun to push aside some of those *taking care of habits*? I mean . . . or is that difficult?

SUSAN: No, no, I've done it (*starts to cry*) . . . a . . .

THERAPIST: Long time. Yeah, it must be really hard.

ROBERT: You've never said that to me. True confessions.

SUSAN: Well, I don't know, it seems like I have a lot of load on my shoulders, and . . .

THERAPIST: Yeah, I bet it does.

SUSAN: And Robert hasn't, you know, I mean it's not 50-50.

THERAPIST: Right. So you're anxious to resign from that load on your shoulders.

SUSAN: Oh yeah.

THERAPIST: Like . . . like what might you imagine doing or not doing, when that load is gone?

SUSAN: Okay, well, probably have more time for myself.

(Susan has been separated enough from the taking care of habit to acknowledge its effects on her. Discussion of some of her interests follows.)

SUSAN: Well, my girlfriend is in . . . uh, uh . . . a chorus group at the College of Notre Dame, and . . . uh . . . I might do that. I have sung before.

THERAPIST: That would be neat.

ROBERT: You're getting information I never heard.

SUSAN: (*Animated*) Well, she asked me to come, but I have always declined. So, before . . .

THERAPIST: Well, what do you think would happen if you accepted that invitation and broke the pattern, you know . . . that we talked about. What do you think might happen?

SUSAN: Uh . . . (*pausing*)

THERAPIST: Do you think it would be good or bad?

SUSAN: Yeah, I think it would be fine.

(Discussion follows about the difficulty of being the first one to break the pattern.)

THERAPIST: All right, yeah. Well, I really . . . uh, and somehow, somehow you must have taken a little . . . somehow can you see how I might imagine that you might have taken a little tiny step, because Robert has moved a little off his mark? You might have taken a little tiny step and not be aware of . . .

SUSAN: Yeah, and I'm not aware of it.

(The therapist continues to ask questions to open space for them to notice a step she has made.)

THERAPIST: Yeah, all right. Can I ask you to think about what the possibilities . . . you know, think about that a little.

SUSAN: All I know is that Robert was calling me at work, and I finally said: "You can't call me anymore!"

THERAPIST: There's a step. There you go. Good for you.

ROBERT: She didn't want to do that.

THERAPIST: Good for you . . .

SUSAN: I did that . . .

THERAPIST: (*Reaching out for Susan*) That's an important step. A good step.

SUSAN: I told him before . . . I don't know . . . he didn't listen.

THERAPIST: But you kind of . . . you . . .

SUSAN: I put my foot down.

(The therapist then called for the reflecting team.)

So, what ideas do you have about the makeup of the discourse in which these spouses situate themselves? We will share some of ours, but only Robert and Susan could tell us which ones fit their experience.

One area of focus might be a gender-influenced discourse. For Robert, this might mean a discourse on "rightness." In his case, however, the effect of this discourse would be in promoting self-torture supported by guilt and anxiety, rather than aggressively asserting his ideas to others, as many men seem to do. For Susan, this might be to "take care of or be for others rather than herself," with guilt prescribed at any deviation from this, no matter how overwhelmed she might become. We actually began this process, but we would develop it further by bringing forth messages about her adequacy as a woman and the need to keep a man by behaving in accordance with this discourse.

With Robert, we might move to discourses related to evaluation and adequacy, and how this affects his attitudes in relationship to himself and to Susan. We might also explore how it creates tremendous pressure toward handling situations, bringing up harsh specifications for performance. We suspect some similar discourse with Susan, although based on this interview, there did not seem much space to enter into it. Our fantasy moves us to consider the influence of this discourse on Susan outside of the family interactions in terms of achievement, social life, etc.

DISCUSSION

When working in this manner, our experience is that each member of the couple begins taking steps in a new direction, while at the same time sharing more of their relationship "beliefs" with the therapist. What begins as a concrete focus on behavioral patterns becomes a focus on aspects of relationship discourse that have been around a long time. As we stated, these ideas seem to "tumble out." We believe this is largely due to the blame-free context created by working within this model. When we use descriptions that are not foreign to people's experience and empower instead of pathologize, resistance does not occur. Constructing beliefs about relationships and oneself or identifying habitual responses (behaviors, ideas) also provides an efficient and effective way for working with "family of origin" issues. Noticing the influence of this discourse on the present and not adopting structural or functional notions about the individuals' roles in the family of origin provide a context for efficient separation from these ideas and rapid development of people's own pictures of themselves.

Seeing these patterns and the relationship discourse which supports them as restraints is an example of using negative explanation (as discussed in the introduction). From this viewpoint, persons affected by any discourse would simply not see other possibilities of behavior or believing. One common effect of socially constructed discourse in our culture is for men to believe they have power over women and for women to believe they must give up themselves for men. For example, White (1986b) points out that the idea "women are the property of men" influences men to think they have the right to do whatever they wish; it is a belief that restrains men so that they would not consider or see the need for negotiation. In this view, patriarchy is a discourse which affects a large enough portion of the population that its influence is dominant. This construction leads to a situation where power is experienced; another experience is not available given the restraint of the construction. When separated from the influence of the construction, men can begin to appreciate the experience of women and question whether holding onto patriarchal ideas suits them. With respect to the larger theoretical picture, more careful attention to negative explanation thus allows one to retain a cybernetic metaphor (which does not involve circular causality or positive explanation) and still account for the issue of power—despite recent criticisms such as by Dell [1989] and Fish [1990]. In the work we do, we find it helpful to engage the clients in discussions about the effects of societal discourse in their lives (which helps separate them from the discourse to see other possibilities) and then question them about their own preferences regarding differential amounts of power. Our experience is, when approached this way, the answer is usually "We don't prefer such an arrangement."

You can see how, once separated from the restraining influence of certain habits, evidence for alternative stories and ideas for Robert and Susan began to emerge. We could fantasize about this and see Robert's obvious pleasure and self-satisfaction when he realized he was able to set limits on *immobilization.* An emerging description of likability, sociability, humor and intelligence seem to result in interpersonal adequacy. What is the history of this? Does it fit in his intentions for himself in his life? Susan's desire to pursue a direction of singing also provides an entry point to new stories, as well as her ability to put her foot down with Robert and protect her own space. What do these things tell us about her that we wouldn't have otherwise known? What questions might you have?

Questions such as these engage the clients in a collaborative process with the therapist in becoming writers of their own new story. The questions are (hopefully) evocative of the clients' experiences—ones which have not fit into the old dominant narrative. The meanings the clients provide in response could begin to form a new story, one which is more preferred by them. Through new meaning given to the past and present, as well as its greater fit with their own intentions and values, clients begin to document details unique and more preferred by them as persons and as a couple.

CONCLUSION

This therapeutic approach allows couples to separate from the reciprocal patterns and ideas in which they have situated themselves and which act as restraints toward their making changes which would better fit their preferred story. Creating a context for reauthoring, through asking questions about aspects of experience which do not fit into the problem story, seems a useful and empowering way to think about therapy with couples.

We hope that this chapter has been interesting for you and appreciate your consideration of these ideas. We are interested in what was helpful to you and what was not. Our work is constantly evolving, so we expect to expand our understanding. Your feedback is welcome.

Commentary

Janet Adams-Westcott

WHEN PARTNERS present for relationship therapy, problems are most often described in a highly charged emotional context characterized by accusations of blame and deficiency. Zimmerman and Dickerson describe a way of working with couples that helps each partner escape such disempowering descriptions and take steps toward participating in the kind of relationship they prefer. The approach creates a receiving context for change by minimizing blame and maximizing each partner's experience of personal agency. This commentary highlights three key aspects of the work that facilitate this process.

RESTRAINT AND RELATIVE INFLUENCE

The couples I have worked with in therapy have found our conversations about restraints to be particularly useful. This approach begins by helping partners identify the reciprocal patterns of interaction and narratives about self and relationships that maintain the problem by restraining the perception of alternatives. Externalizing these restraints decreases depreciation of self or the other by separating the problem from the person. Cooperation among the partners is facilitated when the problem is redescribed as the restraint.

The authors construct the experience of agency by asking questions that orient the partners to think in terms of influence rather than causation. They invite each person to consider how he or she is influenced by and responds to the partner's behavior. The experience of choice emerges as each person begins to perceive the other's behavior as an invitation to participate in the problem that can either be accepted or turned down.

PROBLEM FOCUS VS.
SOLUTION ORIENTATION

The authors contribute a practical perspective to the conversation among therapists about the balance between problem talk and solution talk. In this approach, the balance between deconstructing the problem and reconstructing new meanings is guided by the particular situation each couple presents.

Much of the therapeutic conversation using this way of working with couples involves a reevaluation of each person's narratives about him/herself, the partner, and relationships. One can begin the process of intervention by inviting an examination of these beliefs in situations where conflict is low and partners are able to collaborate. The conversation can quickly move from discussion of problems to consideration of solutions.

Unfortunately, most couples present for therapy after conflict has escalated to high levels. In such situations, the authors create a context for cooperation by externalizing a series of problems. In relationships characterized by high levels of distress or the presence of chronic symptoms, intervention often begins by deconstructing these experiences. This opens space for partners to begin to notice their participation in problematic patterns of interaction. Externalizing these reciprocal invitations diminishes blame and enhances agency. This opens space for partners to begin to collaborate and consider restraints at the level of discourse.

Though early sessions focus on deconstructing the problem, a solution orientation is maintained by questions that examine the influence that each partner has on the problem. Subsequent sessions begin with a solution focus. Each partner is asked to catch the therapist up with steps they have taken before introducing any new problems. When viewed through a lens of competence and success, partners perceive any "new" problems as much more manageable.

USING THE PREFERRED STORY TO
CONSTRUCT NEW MEANINGS

Blame is minimized and agency is maximized by techniques that juxtapose the problem story with the partners' preferred story about how they want to be as people and in relationships. The authors describe therapy as a dual process of deconstructing old meanings and co-constructing new meanings that "fit" each partner and their relationship.

The people that I have worked with have found the notion of "fit" to be particularly freeing. The authors ask questions to help each partner consider the context where the restraint evolved. In doing so, they often discover that the particular narrative or pattern of interaction was useful in the past but is problematic in the current relationship. Each partner is then invited to consider his/her preferred story and to take small steps toward interacting with the other and embracing beliefs that "fit" with how he/she wants to be.

Inviting couples to reevaluate their interactions and narratives brings forth the experience of personal agency. The authors minimize the potential for blame by encouraging each partner to take steps independent of the other. Notions of personal deficiency are dissolved by constructing restraints as ways of thinking and interacting that "fit" in the past, are problematic in the present, and limit the possibilities for the future.

REFERENCES

Bateson, G. (1972). *Steps to an ecology of the mind*. New York: Ballantine Books.

Bruner, J. (1986). *Actual minds, possible worlds*. Cambridge: Harvard University Press.

Bruner, J. (1990). *Acts of meaning*. Cambridge: Harvard University Press.

Dell, P. (1989). Violence and the systemic view: The problem of power. *Family Process, 28*, 1–14.

Fish, V. (1990). Introducing causality and power into family therapy theory: A correction to the systemic paradigm. *Journal of Marital and Family Therapy, 16*, 21–37.

Gottman, J. M. (1991). Predicting the longitudinal course of marriages. *Journal of Marital and Family Therapy, 17*, 3–7.

Hoffman, L. (1985). Beyond power and control: Toward a "second-order" family systems therapy. *Family Systems Medicine, 3*, 381–396.

Markman, H. (1991). *How to help couples fight to save their marriage*. A plenary given at the American Association for Marriage and Family Therapy Conference. Dallas, Texas.

Neal, J., & Slobodnik, A. (1991). Reclaiming men's experience in couples therapy. In M. Bograd (ed.), *Feminist approaches to men in therapy*. New York: Harrington Park Press.

White, M. (1986a). Anorexia nervosa: A cybernetic perspective. In J. Harkaway (ed.), *Eating disorders*. Maryland: Aspen. Also in M. White, *Selected Paper*, 67–75.

White, M. (1986b). The conjoint therapy of men who are violent and the women with whom they live. *Dulwich Centre Newsletter*, Spring, 1986. Also in *Selected Papers*, 101–105.

White, M. (1988). The process of questioning: A therapy of literary merit? *Dulwich Centre Newsletter*, Winter. Also in *Selected Papers*, 37–46.

White, M. (1989). *Selected Papers*. Adelaide, Australia: Dulwich Centre Publications.

White, M., & Epston, D. (1990). *Narrative means to therapeutic ends*. New York: Norton.

11

QUESTIONS ABOUT QUESTIONS: SITUATING THE THERAPIST'S CURIOSITY IN FRONT OF THE FAMILY

Stephen Patrick Madigan

> The stupidity of people comes from having an answer for everything. The wisdom of the novel comes from having a question for everything. The novelist teaches the reader to comprehend he world as a question. There is wisdom and tolerance in that attitude.
>
> *Milan Kundera*

A CERTAIN THERAPEUTIC adventure began one night in a pub with my colleagues. I puzzled aloud over how to make public for families in therapy the excitement of our team's private conversations behind the mirror, conversations that wove together debate, deconstruction, politics, family therapy theory, personal musings, and metaphor. For some reason these discussions lost their verve when held in the presence of clients. Our reflecting teams served up weightless political speeches filled with superlatives like "I was *so* impressed" or "I am *so*

I would like to thank the following members of my team for the support, curiosity, and creativity that they contributed to the writing of this paper: Arlene Gordon, Jim Rudes, Dawn Shelton, and Kate Warner. I would also like to thank David Epston and Cheryl and Michael White for their continuing enthusiasm and support, and Charles Waldegrave and Kiwi Tamasese for helping me stretch my view of cultural restraints.

totally amazed." Our team breaks during the session, although fascinating for the therapists involved, were somehow losing the family in
the process. I spoke to other colleagues who shared my concern,
though none of us bothered to discuss this phenomenon with any clients. Through these conversations I began to experience a certain
discomfort with our "closed network" of conversations regarding clients, who had been so openly sharing the story of their lives. The
private space behind the mirror began to feel like a private viewing
box for public "gazing rituals." I wondered if I could find a way to
translate and situate my experience of myself, the team, and our clients to the clients.

Then two questions were asked: First, what would happen if another
therapist (or supervisor/consultant) began interviewing therapists
about their observing process of a family *while that family was present*? Second, if we considered ourselves co-authors in the evolving
therapeutic narrative, how was it that the restraints of the therapist
were never questioned publicly? These questions stimulated others: If
the team pursued these questions in practice, how would the therapist/
client narrative change? How would the therapy team discourse be
influenced? What would be the real effects if all discursive practices
were open for public discussion within the therapeutic context? Was
it possible to question the conversational, cultural, and theoretical
restraints of the therapist in front of the family? If so what new
"frames and galleries" (Keeney, 1990) would be created? Could all
questions be viewed as contributing to change within the problem-
saturated story line (White and Epston, 1990)?

In the next section the theoretical underpinnings of these questions
are explored.

DISCURSIVE PRACTICES
ABOUT PRACTICES:
THE STORY OF THE THEORY

To ask questions about therapists' questions serves to highlight their
discursive practices, that is, the ways in which people actively produce
social and psychological realities (Davies and Harre, 1990). This process of questioning questions usually takes place through the forums
of supervision, training, case consultation, workshop presentation,
and other forms of professional discourse. Professionals invited to attend these forums of discussion may attend out of duty, interest, debate, or fiscal remuneration. These forums of inquiry have created a

structure for family therapists to exchange theoretical and practice information.

According to some family therapists (Andersen, 1987; Anderson and Goolishian, 1988, 1990; White and Epston, 1990), a therapeutic conversation co-evolves between those persons talking, questioning, and listening to descriptions about the problem. Specifically, all individuals involved with the talk about the case, behind or in front of the mirror, silent or verbal, are viewed as participating in the evolution of the case story (Andersen, 1987). It is within this context that clients and therapists co-author a new text about the problem (Bruner, 1986; Gergen and Gergen, 1984; Howard, 1991; Keeney, 1983; Maranhao, 1986; Tyler, 1987; Tyler and Tyler, 1990).

Within the process of co-authoring, the new cultural, contextual, and theoretical restraints of therapist and client are viewed to "cohabitate," evolving over multiple reflexive recursions (Tomm, 1987, 1989). It is through the reflexive process of mutual shaping and influencing that people's ideas come together to formulate the plot of the new story (Keeney, 1990; White and Epston, 1990).

Bateson (1979) observed that the basic unit of survival is neither the person nor the community, but the ecosystem that holds the two together. Bateson suggested that any organism that seeks to destroy its environment will engage in an action of destroying itself. This suggests that when one thinks in terms of either/or logic one sets up conditions that place in opposition those entities that are actually part of the same system. It is only when one considers a both/and logic that relationships can be considered not in terms of opposition, but rather in terms of difference. Western society, as evidenced by the recent environmental and moral hangover of the Gulf War, may soon come to realize the importance of recognizing the other-in-self and self-in-other as essential.

Derrida (1981) writes that the subject can never be set apart from the multiple others who are its very essence. Therapist and client articulate a conversation through the culturally structured context of the therapeutic interview. The emphasis of inquiry is not on family members' talking while therapists sit back, posturing and observing a strategy of one up or down. Instead, intrigue rests on the discursive practices of families and therapists talking together.

White and Epston (1990) write that a therapist's questions act to open space for alternative client explanations thought to be previously restrained. Questions act to recruit, liberate, and circulate alternative knowledges and preferred acts of meaning (White and Epston, 1990).

But at the same time, since all narratives are necessarily restrained (Ricoeur, 1983), the linguistic structure of the question itself can also act to oppress and obstruct the search for other novel solutions. For example, the question a therapist chooses to make public may place an emphasis on other questions *not* asked (Tyler, 1987, 1990). The question asked by the therapist is bound by its own set of cultural, contextual, and theoretical restraints (White, 1986). Such restraints are also contained within the therapist's speech act and in the structure of speech itself. A therapist's questions therefore provide the listener with a textual narrative regarding the therapist's work, which includes narratives involving his or her wider personal, political, and professional beliefs.

Since every utterance and question asked during a therapeutic interview can be defined in the class of speech acts, all are said to be restrained. Tulio Maranhao (1986) claims that every system of knowledge involves a system of power and rhetoric. This would include the knowledge systems that inform a therapist's questions. Questions can be viewed as culturally pervasive linguistic ideas and involve a rhetoric of expression. These ideas are maintained and supported through a variety of levels of public and private ownership and "feed" both the self and the society (Foucault, 1980; Parker, 1989). Hence all expression of therapist language, as well as the practices and techniques of these expressions (Foucault, 1971, 1980, 1982, 1984), are attempts to rhetorically persuade the listener of something that is based on the therapist's culturally based knowledge system. Questions are then never viewed as *rhetorically liberated*, but rather as evidence of what kind of rhetoric the speaker is choosing to bring forth and for what purpose. We can therefore not act outside the class of rhetorical speech acts.

Family therapy narratives that argue for practice postures of noninstrumentality and simple curiosity, and that claim apolitical sanctuary through being "value free," suddenly take a step back into the world of modernity. Likewise all therapists, even those who address their work as noninstrumental or neutral, inevitably experience a myriad of restraints through language and the practice of speech acts. In addition, therapists must also consider the dominant restraints of gender (Diamond and Quinby, 1988; Hare-Mustin and Maracek, 1989; Harstock, 1990), culture (Tyler, 1987, 1990; Waldegrave, 1990), race (Waldegrave, 1990), and theoretical position (Rose, 1989). Even as I write this text, and as you the reader read it, these restraints are in operation.

Munro's (1987) suggestion that "the net effects of all restraints is to narrow the client's set of responses drastically" (p. 183) parallels a similar process of restraint that the therapist and therapist team must not only endure but also somehow recognize as inherent in their "selves." To generate a family therapy discourse that invites and makes public an inquiry into both the therapist and client narrative restraints thus appears necessary. Such a discourse would provide a meeting place of critical inquiry for all involved in the co-authoring process. For example, conversation within a reflecting team might reference the experiences of both clients *and* therapists. Thus, questions asked of clients to counter dominant cultural stories of themselves as persons and open up new domains of inquiry (White, 1988), might be similarly asked of the therapist in the presence of the clients. To ask therapists these questions without clients present allows only one side of the therapeutic production of co-authoring to be considered at one time. Hence the structure of the therapeutic process from which most therapy is practiced cuts the client off from multiple "other" descriptions, possibilities, and alternative stories regarding a therapist's discursive practices. However, the intricacies of the client's story are viewed as part of the public domain. It appears, then, that a possible wealth of substitute therapist storylines are not voiced.

It is within this "one-sided" structure of therapy that we keep ourselves therapeutically strapped to practice "models" of contemporary therapy. And although some family therapists (Andersen, 1987; Anderson and Goolishian, 1988, 1990; Hoffman, 1990) advocate the move from systemic to narrative ways of thinking, their practice of therapy remains primarily focused on the authoring voice of the client. Therapeutic curiosity that directs itself only to narrative accounts of client restraints, without publicizing and recognizing therapist restraints, continues to perpetuate modern myths of expert knowledge. Although one might argue that clients are the senior authors of the new and evolving story, the therapist and therapist's team are at the very least second authors, where all authors are viewed as linguistically restrained.

If we are to render meaningful the ideas of narrative (Bruner, 1986; Gergen and Gergen, 1984; Gergen and Davies, 1985; White and Epston, 1990), rhetoric (Maranhao, 1986; Rorty, 1990), deconstruction (Derrida, 1976, 1981), restraint (Bateson, 1979; White and Epston, 1990), and the subjugating effects of knowledge as power (Anderson and Goolishian, 1988; Foucault, 1971, 1980) within the therapeutic context, then we must find ways to address these ideas within the practice of therapy. Freedom to question the "constituted experience" (White and Epston, 1990) of both therapist or client would enable recognition of the social, cultural, and political restraints that all speakers in the therapeutic context are influencing and are influenced by.

In the next section a description of therapeutic practice created within the context of the Nova University family therapy doctoral program will be discussed. The practice recruits ideas from certain interpretations of postmodernism, narrative, rhetoric, feminism, anthropology, literary criticism, and the therapeutic work practice of Michael White, David Epston, and Charles Waldegrave.

THERAPY PRACTICE

With the above theoretical ideas as a foundation, a frame of therapeutic practice has slowly taken shape. Supervision, training, and therapy are viewed as part of the same discourse, and not to be separated. We have dropped the either/or distinction between private professional talk and public client talk. As we merged these arenas, a more complete distinction (Flemmons, 1991) emerged. The therapy of co-authoring the therapeutic narrative from a both/and perspective encourages the public viewing of all discourse pertinent to the joint work of therapists and clients. Within this discursive structure the power practices of supervisor and therapist as experts are challenged and the multiplicity of ideas and difference encouraged.

The therapist engaged in the actual interviewing of the client I call the "performative therapist" (PT). The PT was so named after playing with thoughts on performance and meaning from Edward Bruner (1986), Clifford Geertz (1973), and Victor Turner (1986). Personal conversations with David Epston, Michael White, and Brad Keeney regarding their most recent works were also influential. Performance in this context suggests that it is through various performative acts, such as language, song, dance, etc., that we co-create a context complete with norms, restraints, and rituals. While the PT and the client construct the story, another therapist (or supervisor, consultant, trainee), called the "listening therapist" (LT), is situated in the therapy room and carefully listens to the PT's questions/statements. The history of the LT's position and name comes from my many wonderful walks and talks with Tom Andersen in Norway on the importance of listening. In addition to the client(s), PT, and LT, a reflecting team sits behind a one-way mirror.

The therapy starts out with the PT talking with the family while trying to set a "sense" of the talk about the problem. After a period of time, the PT seeks questioning about the questions they have privileged thus far in the interview. There is an understanding that all questions asked are among a multitude of others not asked. Some of these questions the PT is cognizant of, others he/she is restrained from knowing. The LT asks questions about the PT's questions, and the family is invited to listen in on this dialogue between therapists. These questions are attempts to situate the PT in the curiosity of his/her own questions. This conversational interlude is not viewed as a strategic prearranged one-down maneuver; nor is it considered a "model" of co-therapy. All LT questions are asked with the intent of "opening space" for the PT. These questions about questions act to broadcast and bring forth for the PT news of difference through the circulation and resurrection of alternative knowledges. Questions about questions may also create for the client a "meaningful noise" (Keeney, 1983), whereby a multiplicity of other possible meanings, descriptions, and questions are made public. The clients listening in have actually assumed the LT position and are soon invited by the PT to offer reflections on the PT-LT conversation.

A few examples of questions that the LT asks of the PT may be helpful. An LT might ask:

> I observed that you asked Mum a question regarding who reacts most when Johnny "acts up." Were there other questions that came to mind at this juncture that you could have asked but didn't?
> How is it that this was the direction you decided to go as opposed to the others you also considered?
> If you had asked these other questions, how might you see the family differently?
> How do you think they might see you differently?
> What does this tell you about yourself that is important for us to know?
> What has this family taught you about yourself that you might find helpful in your work with other families?
> At this point in the interview what would you consider your most important question and why?

This LT/PT dialogue usually takes five or six minutes, and the therapists may disagree with one another during their conversation. The PT concludes the talk by turning back to the clients for their reflections.

Towards the end of the session, the clients, PT, and LT change position with the reflecting team behind the mirror. The reflecting team now discusses the conversational events that have transpired thus far in the session, including the PT-LT dialogue. Then everyone involved with the session returns or remains in the interview room to reflect on the team's reflections. The client, PT, and LT are invited to comment on any reflections they have, whether interesting, agitating, or curious. All questions and reflections are viewed as contributing to the therapeutic story and to the telling of the speaker's own story and restraints. At the session's conclusion, a meeting time for the next session is arranged. Throughout the following week(s) the therapists do not enter into conversation regarding the clients without the clients' being present.*

Although interested in reflecting team ideas, many therapists often complain that their working contexts are restrained by time, financial considerations, or the unavailability of other therapists. The practice of questioning therapist questions can be structured to accommodate most of these conditions. For example, an agency supervisor may sit in on a staff member's case in the position of the LT. The next session the supervisor would invite the staff member to be the LT. In private practice a therapist could offer to set up an LT-PT exchange with other colleagues in the community or office, or with a student in training at the local university. Other possibilities include asking government social workers, teachers, and doctors working with the same case to sit in on the session and participate within this unique format. This process of questioning acts not to further structures of 'surveillance," but rather to open space for dialogue and difference.

Case Talk

Anne Wilson, a sole parent of two teenagers, Martha, 16, and Season, 13, called the clinic to discuss her younger daughter's recent failing school grades. An appointment for the mother and daughters was set up and assigned to our team. Two linguistic themes between the PT and the family emerged in the session. The first was the discomfort Season was experiencing with her new (as she explained) "bad student"/"bad attitude" career that seem to be sneaking up on her and taking over her life. The second theme that the PT punctuated was Anne's recruitment into the cultural position of "mother blaming." Anne explained that the recent school "crisis" had occurred because she had been working too much in her career as a film teacher, and also cited her sole parent status as a possible contributing factor. A discussion around both narratives ensued. Thirty minutes into the session the PT invited the family to listen in on the LT's questions regarding the PT's questions/responses. The following is an excerpt of this discussion:

> PT (talking to the family): As I explained to you earlier, I'm now going to have a discussion with Sue (the LT) and she is going to

*It may be important to note that this practice of therapy has also been performed without the participation of the reflecting team and proved helpful to all participants involved in the session.

ask me some questions about the questions I have asked you
here tonight. So I invite you to listen in and if you find anything
interesting to please comment.

SEASON: Oh, this should be fun, you get to be on the hot seat now!

PT: Hot seat?

SEASON: Well, not really hot seat, but you know . . . we get to kind
of hear about you.

PT: Any ideas on what you think Sue might ask me?

SEASON: No not really. But, I don't know, it's just kinda neat.

PT: Yeah, I think it could be kinda neat as well.

LT: I'm interested in your framing of Anne's experience as "mother-
blaming." Where did you come up with this idea?

PT: Well, we see lots of sole parents here in the clinic and it seems
to me that the majority are women. I think that in our country
there is this cultural myth that if a child is not brought up in the
"proper way," meaning with two parents together in the same
home, then the chances are that the kids are going to have problems. In my experience of working here and other places, this has
not been the case. Secondly, there is another tradition that has
built up over time that suggests that if a child has a problem of
some kind it can always be directly related to poor mothering,
and I think a lot of women get caught into this kind of oppressive
thinking about themselves. I think these kind of cultural messages do violence to mothers, children, and fathers.

LT: How come you prefer to describe Anne as a sole parent rather
than a single parent?

PT: Well, I got this idea from the family therapists working in New
Zealand and Australia. Biologically, it is not possible for one
person to have a child (laughter) . . . so even though one parent
may be the main person raising the children, the other absent
parent never completely disappears. I also think that our society
often too easily explains away a child's or family's difficulties
with the fact that there is only one parent living in the home. So
the word single parent often conjures up "bad" or "unhealthy"
images about a family that quite simply are not fair or correct
and that certainly do not promote health. I think when we jump
to conclusions like this we help support myths of what a "proper"
family must look like and do not respect the unique experience of
each separate family that we meet with.

LT: Have you ever experienced this kind of "mother/single parent-
blaming" yourself given that you, too, are a sole parent?

PT: Well yes, my child is presently home with a sitter and I sometimes feel very awkward about this, so I guess I was really feeling on a personal level what Anne was saying about feeling so guilty and responsible. But you know talking tonight with Anne and Martha and Season has helped me get a little clearer on this. I guess up until now I wasn't aware of how pervasive the idea of mother-blaming can be.

LT: In saying this what other questions about this family might come to mind that you could have asked but didn't?

PT: Well, I guess it might be important to check out Anne's struggle with Martha and Season. I wonder if, in not doing this, I merely shifted the blame from Mom to the kids, and that's not good either. I don't think that there has to be a good person and a bad person, but just a place to talk openly. I guess I would also want to question those times when no one is feeling guilty or self-blaming. I might also question how in the future mother-blaming techniques might stand in the way of Anne's experiencing Season's successful escapes from the bad attitude.

LT: If you were to consider these new questions, how might you see yourself seeing this family differently?

PT: Well, I suppose I could be more aware of how these three have worked out a way of being together that they consider helpful and that works.

SEASON (to mother): I just want to say something. Like what happened, Mom, isn't your fault.

MARTHA: Yeah, like when you and I were always yelling that time about a year ago, like we worked it out and everything is fine.

SEASON: Just look at Joanie's family next door—I mean, there's two parents and their kids are like taking drugs and sleeping in cars and all kinds of stuff and we're not.

MARTHA: Look Mom, I talked to Season and she knows she's got this bad attitude and she feels lousy about flunking . . .

SEASON: Yeah, and you shouldn't have to worry about my schoolwork, and I'm starting to take time after to school to do it.

MARTHA: Yeah, she started last night. . . . I saw her and was like blown away.

Anne and the children returned to the clinic three weeks later for their second session to report on their many recent victories over the once oppressive mother-blaming story. Anne said she felt a "renewed sense of confidence" not only in herself but also with her children. Anne then went on to explain that Season had had an "almost total escape" from her bad attitude both at home and at school over the three weeks.

DISCUSSION

Keeney (1983) writes that "therapy is a process of weaving stories between therapist and client systems together" (p. 195). This sounds simple enough, but what has proven most difficult to practice in this therapeutic approach is the act of taking the conversational focus off the client and concentrating it on both clients and therapists. Even though most therapists/supervisors/consultants working with our team are versed in the text analogy, the theory of narrative, and the ideas of second-order cybernetics, the client somehow remains the primary focus. Despite our theoretical insights, the language of "modern models" continues to sneak up on the team to ring forth and echo familiar chants that either the therapist is somehow not involved, influenced, or influencing of the therapeutic production, or the therapist is making a nice, slick maneuver to make the client see things differently. The team has realized that, beyond the rhetoric of viewing ourselves as co-authors in therapy, we must also view our selves in the contexts that we shape and are shaped by. Hence the acts of supervision, training, reflecting teams, and consultation must also be framed in light of the restraints that are ever constituting in the context of therapeutic language practices.

Within our process of situating therapist questions in the presence of the family, the particular position a trainee, consultant, or supervisor takes as a team member is less important than the act of questioning *all* talk brought forth in the session. The process of questioning questions advocates diversity in all therapist positions, including those of the supervisor and consultant. This can be likened to the game of "musical chairs," but in this particular language game no one ever loses his/her chair. For instance, a supervisor may take the PT position with one set of clients and a student in training may take the position of the LT. For the next set of clients, they may reverse their positions. In this way all therapists' discursive practices can be questioned, all therapists have a chance to experience the view from all positions, and all therapists may view themselves as participating and co-authoring in the process of therapy. In addition, team members have voiced a renewed sense of egalitarianism, which they had not found in working in more traditional supervision/training "models." This is not to suggest that respect has been lost for those therapists/

supervisors/consultants who have trained and worked longer. In our case a deep sense of respect has developed among the team and the clients we work with, through a recognition that all persons involved in the therapy are working hard to coproduce new sets of stories for everyone involved.

Richard Rorty (1990) suggests that, as we move from habit to inquiry, the acquisition of "attitudes towards new truth-value candidates" (p. 94) are introduced. These truth-value candidates act as alternative beliefs that can be woven into the fabric of the reweaving process of reauthoring. The process of questioning, questioning questions, and reflecting on these questions acts to "recontextualize" the therapeutic context. The more widespread the options for change entertained by therapists and clients, the more the new story can evolve.

The family therapy stories currently emerging in the literature seem to be "hitchhiking" on those ideas which have influenced change in the fields of anthropology, ethnography, literary criticism, architecture, philosophy, feminism, and social psychology. This may be a sign that there is currently a move away from systems thinking and towards narrative thinking. Apart from the therapeutic practices of Michael White and David Epston, this shift has occurred primarily in theoretical discussion and debate. While this is important to the creation of new stories in any field, it is necessary that family therapy go one step further. We must create new means of therapy practice which adhere to those new ideas we privilege in our theory. This will support the consideration and deconstruction of all present language acts and practices of the therapeutic context, which include supervision, training, consultation, workshops, and conventions. The above discussion regarding the practice of situating all therapist discursive practices in the presence of the family is one therapeutic posture that attempts to translate theory into practice.

Commentary

David Epston

THIS PAPER INTRODUCES the novel and curious practice of "questioning the questions" the so-called "performative therapist" has directed to family members. Undoubtedly, parallel practices are commonplace in case supervision, but there the dialogue is in the absence of the family members; this difference makes all the difference. In situating the therapist's questions, family members are not only privy to the PT/LT dialogue but also party to it. This is of the same order of distinction as the difference between the activities of the remote, hidden, one-way screen teams issuing oracular pronouncements and the two-way reflecting teams. Situating the therapist's questions is very much in line with "constructivist inquiry" (Guba, 1990) and parallels other developments within family therapy proper, such as Andersen's (1987) "reflecting teams," Anderson, Goolishian, and Winderman's (1986) conversational ideas, and the various practices Michael White describes in Chapter 2 as providing a condition of "transparency" in the therapeutic system. Making your work transparent allows more discretion in formulating personal responses to therapist responses.

It is reassuring to me that constructivism is being translated from "grand theory" to workperson-like practices. Although constructivism was introduced into family therapy in the early 1970s by Paul Watzlawick and his colleagues at the M.R.I., it was not until Sept./Oct. 1988 that *The Family Therapy Networker* announced: THE CON-

STRUCTIVISTS ARE COMING, along with 10 pages of "Constructivism Applied" ("Questions as Interventions" by Karl Tomm and John
Lannamann; "Constructing Solutions" by Steve de Shazer and Insoo
Berg; and "The Reflecting Team" by Judy Davidson et al.). Despite
this bold statement, constructivism has remained the property of the
philosopher class of family therapy and has thus become an endan-
gered species of potential practice. You can't help but sympathize with
the frustrations and concerns of such family therapy veterans as Sal
Minuchin and Frank Pittman, both wise men and very able practitioners. Both find much to rail at, revile, and ridicule. For example,
Pittman (1992) writes:

> Postmodernism entered family therapy in the form of constructivism, es-
> pousing that reality is in the eye of the beholder, and that it doesn't matter
> what people do, only what story they tell about it. What a breakthrough!
> People don't have to change what they do! They can just use different
> words instead! Constructivism is fun intellectual masturbation, until we
> notice that the world that constructivism is defining away is a cruel, un-
> safe, unfair place that hurts real people. (p. 58)

Has constructivism lost some of the momentum that the *Networker*
heralded and failed us by burying itself under the weight of philosophical speculation and at times becoming just plain silly? Gergen (1991),
referring to social scientific research, warns of such hazards:

> Are we to dismantle the scientific apparatus, declaring all attempts at
> 'objective', 'authoritative', knowledge to be fatuous? Are we to conclude
> that because we are locked into our subjectivities we cannot even be certain
> that there is a 'world out there', or that we are truly communicating with
> other persons? Is there nothing left but to reflect on our own subjectivities,
> and then to reflect upon the reflection in an infinitude of self-reflexive
> iterations? These are dolorous conclusions, indeed, and one would scarcely
> wish to pursue lines of thought for which these are the inevitable conclu-
> sions. However, the consequences of obliterating the subject-object dichot-
> omy largely depend on how we understand or interpret the problem. (p. 77)

In fact, Gergen (1991) proposes the possibility, according to his
social constructionist view, that "new vistas of research are opened for
exploration" (p. 77). By the same token, if family therapy were to
rescue constructivism from the philosophers, I could foresee similar
"new vistas" in front of us. But perhaps we have to go beyond ourselves, since family therapy can, in no way, be considered to be in the

vanguard of constructivist practice. I refer the field to the extensive work of Egon Guba and Yvonna Lincoln (1989; Lincoln and Guba, 1985) in attempting to establish criteria for qualitative research that can substitute for the rigor criteria (reliability, validity, and objectivity) of quantitative, positivist research. I recommend in particular Lincoln's (1990) article: "The Making of a Constructivist: A Remembrance of Transformations Past." In a review of her views, she argues "that we desperately need new models of knowledge and knowledge accumulation" (p. 84).

I consider "situating the therapist's questions" as a promising venture in this direction. The questions of the LT of the PT are intended to provoke a curiosity in all concerned as to how the questions asked and the questions unasked might be situated in the PT's autobiography, anthology of clinical stories, "expert" or "local" knowledges, or perhaps, the admission of sheer, educated guessing. This can have the effect of deconstructing the therapist's knowledge – unmasking practices and no longer privileging them as specific to professional contexts, e.g., training, supervision, case consultation. This practice then admits of many "knowledges" rather than isolating knowing as an activity conducted by those credentialed in the psychological/mental health discourses. The foundations and contexts of these questions are made "transparent." This can lead to a questioning of "truth" itself and the grounds/methodologies by which it is constituted and legitimated. The questions themselves can no longer be considered neutral, innocent steps to the "truth," but instead thought of reflexively, a turning back of one's questions upon oneself. Such practices are already being entered into the program of more formal research itself. The researcher Steir (1991) writes: "As inquirers and researchers, we create world through the questions that we ask coupled by what we and others regard as reasonable responses to our questions . . . we as researchers construct that which we claim to 'find'" (p. 1).

Another potential effect of situating is the pulling apart of "knowledge" and "power" and the subsequent de-privileging of "expert" knowledge. Professional practices confer power on professionals in much the way Foucault (1980) theorizes about power/knowledge; these practices motivate professionals recurrently to take up the position of power/ knowledge. If the client-person cannot resist his/her complementary positioning by having access to alternative discourse or practices, then the relationship will reproduce these power arrangements. Situating would seem to me to seek remediation for the disparity between "knowing" professionals and the disinterested knowledge they seek through detached, disengaged "objectivity," on the one hand, and an interested knowledge, co-created by the compassionate participation of all concerned parties, on the other.

The paper leaves me with considerable curiosity, which I have tried to frame in questions addressed to Stephen and his colleagues:

1. How difficult is it for PTs to situate their questions at the outset? Are their replies somewhat stereotyped at first?
2. What difference does situating make to their subsequent family therapy practice?
3. How do family members respond to viewing/listening to the dialogue between the PT and LT? What are their reports of their experience of listening to/seeing this dialogue as performed?
4. The questions of the LT as detailed here are somewhat limited. How does the LT refresh his/her questions? How does the PT steer clear of reiterating his/her responses?
5. What is the experience of the therapists/team undertaking such an inquiry as an integral part of their work with families? Does the team become more collaborative,, more humble, and does their work together become "curiouser and curiouser"?
6. Do the family members become "curiouser and curiouser" or do they find such departures tiring, intrusive, or irrelevant?
7. Do the PT and LT find their dialogue fatiguing or exhilarating?
8. To what extent do family members actively enter the PT/LT dialogue as they become more familiar with it?

REFERENCES

Andersen, T. (1987). The reflecting team: Dialogue and meta-dialogue in clinical work. *Family Process, 26*, 415–428.

Anderson, H., & Goolishian, H. (1988). Human systems as linguistic systems: Preliminary and evolving ideas about the implications for clinical theory. *Family Process, 27*, 4: 371–393.

Anderson, H., & Goolishian, H. (1990). Understanding the therapeutic process: From individuals and families to systems in language. In F. Kaslow (Ed.). *Voices in family psychology 1*. Beverly Hills, CA: Sage.

Anderson, H., Goolishian, H., & Winderman, L. (1986). Human systems as linguistic systems: Preliminary and evolving ideas about the implications for clinical theory. *Family Process, 27*, 371–393.

Bateson, G. (1979). *Mind and nature: A necessary unity*. New York: Dutton.

Bruner, E. (1986). Ethnography as narrative. In V. Turner & E. Bruner (Eds.), *The anthropology of experience*. Chicago: University of Illinois Press.

Davies, B., & Harre, R. (1990). Positioning: Conversation and the production of selves. *Journal for the Theory of Social Behaviour, 20, 1*: 43–63.

Derrida, J. (1976). *Of grammatology*. Baltimore: John Hopkins University Press.

Derrida, J. (1981). *Positions*. Chicago: University of Chicago Press.

Diamond, I., & Quinby, L. (1988). *Feminism and Foucault: Reflections on resistance*. Boston: Northeastern University Press.

Flemmons, D. (1991). *Completing distinctions: Interweaving the ideas of Gregory Bateson and Taoism into a unique approach to therapy*. Boston: Shambhala Press.

Foucault, M. (1971). Nietzche, genealogy, history. In D. Bouchard (Ed.), *Language, counter-memory practice: Selected essays and interviews*. Ithaca: Cornell University Press, 1977.

Foucault, M. (1980). *Power/knowledge. Selected Interviews and writings*. New York: Pantheon.

Foucault, M. (1982). The subject and power. In H. Dreyfus & P. Rabinow (Eds.), *Michel Foucault: Beyond structuralism and hermeneutics*. Chicago: University of Chicago Press.

Foucault, M. (1984). Space, knowledge and power. In H. Dreyfus & P. Rabinow (Eds.), *The Foucault reader*. New York: Pantheon.

Geertz, C. (1973). *The interpretation of cultures*. New York: Basic Books.

Gergen, K. J. (1991). Toward reflexive methodologies. In F. Steir (Ed.), *Reflexivity and research*. London: Sage.

Gergen, K. J., & Davies, K. E. (1985). *The social construction of the person*. New York: Springer-Verlag.

Gergen, M. M., & Gergen, K. J. (1984). The social construction of narrative accounts. In K. J. Gergen & M. M. Gergen (Eds.), *Historical social psychology*. Hillsdale, NJ: Lawrence Erlbaum Associates.

Guba, E. G. (1990). (Ed.). *The paradigm dialogue*. Newbury Park, CA: Sage.

Guba, E. G., & Lincoln, Y. S. (1989). *Fourth generation evolution*. Newbury Park, CA: Sage.

Hare-Mustin, R., & Maracek, J. (1989). Thinking about postmodernism and gender theory. *American Psychologist, 44*, 10: 1333–1334.

Harstock, S. (1990). Foucault in power: A theory for women? In Nicholson (Ed.), *Feminism/postmodernism*. London: Routledge.

Hoffman, L. (1990). Constructing realities: An art of lenses. *Family Process,* *29,* 1–12.

Howard, G. (1991). Culture tales: A narrative approach to thinking, cross-cultural psychology, and psychotherapy. *American Psychologist, 46,* 3: 187–197.

Keeney, B. (1983). *Aesthetics of change.* New York: Guilford.

Keeney, B. (1990). *Improvisational therapy.* St. Paul, MN: Systemic Therapy Press.

Lincoln, Y. (1990). The making of a constructivist. In E. G. Guba (Ed.), *The paradigm dialogue.* Newbury Park, CA: Sage.

Lincoln, Y. S., & Guba, E. G. (1985). *Naturalistic inquiry.* Beverly Hills, CA: Sage.

Maranhao, T. (1986). *Therapeutic discourse and socratic dialogue.* Madison, WI: University of Wisconsin Press.

Munro, C. (1987). White and the cybernetic therapies: News of differences. *Australian and New Zealand Journal of Family Therapy, 8,* (4), 183–192.

Parker, I. (1989). Discourse and power. In K. Gergen & J. Shotter (Eds.), *Texts of identity.* London: Sage Publications.

Pittman, F. (1992). It's not my fault. *Family Therapy Networker,* January/ February.

Ricoeur, P. (1983). *Time and narrative, Vol. 1.* Chicago: University of Chicago Press.

Rorty, R. (1990). *Objectivity, relativism, and truth, Vol. 1.* Cambridge, England: Cambridge University Press.

Rose, N. (1989). Individualizing psychology. In K. Gergen & J. Shotter (Eds.), *Texts of identity.* London: Sage Publications.

Steir, F. (1991). Introduction to F. Steir (Ed.), *Reflexivity and research.* London: Sage.

Tomm, K. (1987). Interventive interviewing: Part II, Reflexive questioning as a means to enable self healing. *Family Process, 27,* 167–84.

Tomm, K. (1989). Externalizing problems and internalizing personal agency. *Journal of Strategic and Systemic Therapies, 8,* (1).

Turner, V. (1986). Dewey, Dilthey and drama: An essay in the anthropology of experience. In V. Turner & E. Bruner (Eds.), *The anthropology of experience.* Chicago: University of Illinois Press.

Tyler, M. G., & Tyler, S. A. (1990). The sorcerer's apprentice; the discourse of training in family therapy. In B. Keeney, B. Nolan, & W. Madsen (Eds.), *The systemic therapist.* St. Paul, MN: Systemic Therapy Press.

Tyler, S. A. (1987). *The unspeakable: Discourse, dialogue, and rhetoric in the postmodern world.* Madison, WI: University of Wisconsin Press.

Tyler, S. A. (1990). Eye of newt, toe of frog: Post-modernism and the context of theory in family therapy. In B. Keeney, B. Nolan, & W. Madsen (Eds.), *The systemic therapist.* St. Paul, MN: Systemic Therapy Press.

Waldegrave, C. (1990). Just therapy. *Dulwich Centre Newsletter, 1,* 5–46.

White, M. (1986). Negative explanation, restraint, and double description: A template for family therapy. *Family Process, 25,* (2), 169–183.

White, M. (1988, Winter). The process of questioning: A therapy of literary merit? *Dulwich Centre Newsletter.*

White, M., & Epston, D. (1990). *Narrative means to therapeutic ends.* New York: Norton.

12

THERAPEUTIC RITUALS:
PASSAGES INTO NEW IDENTITIES

Stephen Gilligan

NOT TOO LONG AGO, my father died. Resting and reading in the afternoon, he was felled by a massive heart attack. Upon hearing the news several hours later, I burst into a torrent of tears followed by wave after wave of overwhelming emotions and images. Emotional riptides carried me over great distances, bringing to the surface a multitude of feelings, images, memories, and conversations.

Luckily, this journey was navigated within a special context. For three days, family and friends gathered for the ritual process of honoring my dad and saying good-bye to him. With his body as a focal point, ceremonies were performed—a large wake where people gave moving testimonies, a funeral mass, a party, and the burial.

In retrospect, this process was a conversation of the deepest sort, a conversation that brought forth in me (and presumably others) a significant new self-identity. Immersed in the multi-level, multi-participant, multi-modal conversation, yet buoyed by the support of friends and the ritual structures, I found myself saying good-bye to an old self-identity and allowing a new one to be born.

Such crises are inescapable in each of our lives, cutting to the core of our basic identities and demanding the creation of new ones. These

This chapter is dedicated to the memory of my father, John Gilligan, Jr. I am proud to be his son.

crises may be planned or expected—as in a birth or a marriage, a retirement or a graduation—or they may be quite sudden and shocking—as in a rape, the loss of a child, a brutal assault, or a major illness. Regardless, they all provoke a challenge to redefine one's world in significant ways.

When these challenges are successfully navigated, people grow stronger, more confident, and perhaps a bit wiser. Unsuccessful attempts may leave one stranded on an isolated island of despair, subsisting on the bitter fruit of depression, guilt, fear, and shame. Such a diet gives rise to strange and undesirable behaviors, from self-abuse via food, drugs, or sex to self-focus on weaknesses, failures, and doubts. A life of quiet or not-so-quiet desperation develops, with the greatest passion devoted to self-devaluing acts.

When individuals become mired in these struggles, they sometimes see a therapist with the hope of changing things. Our challenge, of course, is to help them. Our cultural histories are rich with traditions for doing this, for such problems existed (and were solved) long before the advent of modern psychotherapy.

This chapter explores how one such tradition, that of healing rituals, may be used in psychotherapy. Some basic distinctions regarding rituals are first outlined. A four-step model for using rituals is then developed. These four steps include (1) suggesting a ritual as a possible solution, (2) planning the ritual, (3) enacting the ritual, and (4) postritual activities. A case history illustrates each step.

WHAT ARE RITUALS?

Rituals are perhaps the oldest form of therapy.* Virtually every culture has developed rituals for major social-psychological functions. *Transitional rituals* such as baptisms or brisses, weddings and funerals have been used as bridges from one stage of life into another—at birth, graduations, promotions, rites of passage into adulthood, marriages, retirements, deaths and so on. *Continuity rituals* such as anniversaries and holidays affirm and regenerate the values and identity of a system. *Healing rituals* provide recovery from trauma and

*My understanding of rituals has been helped by many authors, especially van der Hart (1983) and Turner (1969). Others include Campbell (1984), Haley (1984), Imber-Black, Roberts and Whiting (1989), Jung (1954), Madanes (1990), and Selvini Palazzoli, Boscolo, Cecchin, and Prata (1978). My biggest influence, however, is Milton Erickson (1980a, 1980b) and his contributions to working with "the unconscious" with an awareness of social context.

reincorporation of the dissociated person into the social-psychological community. And *atonement rituals* provide vehicles for apology and redress of damages done.

In the present view, a ritual may be regarded as an intense, experiential-symbolic structure that recreates or transforms identity. It is intense in that participants develop heightened absorption that excludes all other frames of reference. It is experiential in that analytical and other "one-step removed" processes are depotentiated, leaving participants deeply immersed in primary processes, such as bodily feelings, inner imagery, and automatic (spontaneous) process. It is symbolic in that the thoughts, feelings, and behaviors stand for other meanings. (For example, the flag placed on the funeral coffin stands for the deceased's contribution to his or her country; the marriage ring stands for a sacred union.) And lastly, rituals perform meaning at the meta level of identity; they affirm or transform in a deep cultural language a person's place in a community. In other words, they constitute a meta-conversation between individual(s) and community.

Rituals are more than ceremonies and distinct from behavioral tasks. A ceremony becomes a ritual only when participants become fully immersed in nonrational, archaic language; until then, it is merely a traditional behavior sequence having little therapeutic value. (For example, as a child growing up in an Irish Catholic family, I most definitely did not enter ritual space during the nightly ceremony in which the entire family knelt down through five decades of the rosary!)

Similar characteristics separate rituals from behavioral tasks. Rituals involve a *predetermined behavioral sequence*, such that little cognitive decision-making is needed during its enactment. *No meta-commentary* (such as self-talk or evaluations) is permitted, such that no part of the system is split off in an "outside observer" role, thus allowing holistic properties of the system to be expressed (see Bateson and Bateson, 1987). *Special symbols* mark ritual space: the place where it occurs, the clothes worn, the words expressed, the behaviors enacted, and the artifact used all indicate a special, unique situation. *Pre- and post-phases* are used as inductions into and exits out of ritual space. *Binding commitments* are secured to promote commitment and heighten the drama and significance of the event.

Rituals occur simultaneously and equally in private and public realities. The inner world is amplified and reorganized, as in a hypnotherapeutic trance (Gilligan, 1987). At the same time, outer behaviors signifying crucial relationship changes are performed and witnessed by significant others in the social community. The simultaneity of inner and outer changes makes rituals especially powerful and relevant to psychotherapy.

In fact, this feature of rituals is what led me to become interested in them. I had been working a great deal with clients recovering from sexual abuse. The hypnotic tradition (with its orientation to "going inside," relaxing and just letting things happen, and "going deeper") proved markedly unsettling to a number of these individuals, especially when there were parallels to the traumatic event(s). Cognitive talk also seemed inappropriate, especially in its inability to encompass the emotional intensity and dissociative nature of many of the processes. The question thus arose as to what method might make room for what clients were bringing into the conversation while supporting them in reclaiming their connections to themselves and to the rest of the community. Ritual was one of the emerging answers.

Of course not all rituals are therapeutic. In fact, many symptoms presented by therapy clients may be expressions of dysfunctional rituals in which individuals recreate a negative self-identity characterized by self-abuse and helplessness. For example, sexual abuse may be viewed as a traumatic ritual in which a person's biological and psychological boundaries are invaded and desolated. This triggers an automatic and immediate "break in belonging" with the rest of the world, engendering a sort of negative trance characterized by hypnotic phenomena such as time distortion, body dissociation, regression, amnesia, and so forth (Gilligan, 1988). This dissociated state can last indefinitely (years and even generations), leading to *a disidentification with the rest of the world and a misidentification of the self as "being" the traumatic event*. This misidentification includes a constellation of distinctions – e.g., "my body is to be abused," "I have no boundaries," "My own needs are non-existent" – that elicits further self-abusive behaviors (involving food, drugs, relationships, etc.).

Viewing such traumatic processes in ritual terms suggests possible therapeutic interventions. Following Erickson's (1980a, 1980b) principle of utilization, the problematic pattern may be used as the solution pattern. That is, if a person's complaint can be framed in terms of a recurrent ritual, then another ritual may be used as a solution. The remainder of the chapter describes how this might be done in a four-step method.

The method usually takes four to six weeks, and can be done with individuals, couples, families, or groups. It assumes that certain long-standing, somatically-based complaints may be advantageously described as symptoms of a negative self-identity generated from inva-

Table 1
Suggesting a Ritual as a Possible Solution

1. Identify repetitive symptom: chronic body symptoms, low cognitive insight, nonrational expression.
2. If needed, use hypnotic methods (ideomotor questions, art work, trance work) to identify emotional trauma or developmental challenge underlying symptom.
3. Frame symptom positively as incomplete attempt at developmental change or healing process.
4. Elicit full experiential cooperation and motivation to perform ritual.

sive traumatic experiences.* It works to experientially activate and externalize the verbal, visual, and kinesthetic symbols of such "identity events" so that a person may perform a ritual act of casting away the "old identity" and taking on a new one.

The model further assumes that conversations involving "identity shifts" cannot occur within normal analytical processes, since such processes generally function to conserve one's existing frame of reference. Thus, the therapist uses hypnotic or similar processes to develop a conversation that utilizes a more experiential-symbolic emotional language. (This use of a different, more archaic language can be found in many traditional rituals, such as religious ceremonies.) The use of hypnosis occurs within the tradition pioneered by Milton Erickson, featuring a cooperative relationship organized around client values, styles, and resources (see Gilligan, 1987).

STEP 1: FRAME SYMPTOM IN
RITUAL TERMS

Table 1 lists the components of the first step. The therapist first elicits a description of the symptom the client wishes to change. This description should include both a specific behavioral sequence and any inner experiences occurring during the sequence. For example, Joseph was a 32-year-old computer scientist who sought relief from "an uncontrollable facial grimace" that occurred especially in the presence of his

---

*I don't assume this is true, but rather practically useful; that is, it suggests one way of solving the stated problem. Other ways can and should be considered. The proof is in the pudding.

superiors at work. In a typical instance, Joseph would go to present his research at an in-house meeting and find himself tremendously anxious and self-conscious as his face contracted into frightened grimaces when he began his presentation. Usually this severely compromised his presentation, to the point where his projects were not being supported and his job advancement retarded. Joseph further reported that he usually sank into the gloom of depression each time the pattern occurred; he added that depression was experienced by many people in his family.

Joseph also related that he was the second of three boys in his family. He described his father as a "brilliant inventor" who was "extremely brutal" with his sons. Joseph emphasized that he had little contact at present with his family (they lived 3,000 miles away) and that he wished to move on with his life without them. He specifically requested hypnosis for symptom relief of his facial grimaces.

The complaint of facial grimaces had several characteristics suggestive of a ritual intervention. Specifically, it was (a) long-standing, (b) somatically focused, and (c) nonrational and noncognitively-based. In the domain of hypnosis, which is an intimate cousin to rituals, these are characteristics of trance phenomena. In other words, such symptoms may be viewed as the spontaneous occurrence of a "negative trance," a sort of ritual enactment of some traumatic experience.

Of course, not all such symptoms are best resolved via rituals. Many can be handled by simpler and less time-consuming procedures. (In fact, I usually try such procedures before considering rituals.) To determine the appropriateness of a ritual, a next step is to explore whether the symptom is strongly connected to some emotional trauma or developmental challenge. With Joseph, I initially took his complaint at face value—that is, as simply an undesired behavioral expression that might be modified via some straightforward hypnotic processes. I therefore guided Joseph into a hypnotic trance with a general hypnotic induction centered around suggestions of relaxation and ideomotor finger signaling (Gilligan, 1987).

Joseph initially seemed to develop a comfortable trance state, but then suddenly the unexpected occurred. Joseph rapidly dissociated into what appeared a terribly unpleasant state: His body and breathing froze and his face blanched and grimaced. Completely unresponsive to my requests for a verbal report, he seemed to be tailspinning into some otherworldly nightmare. Further suggestions to reorient were also unsuccessful, so I tried to simply join him in his state, saying with soft intensity something like the following:

Joseph, I don't know where you are. Joseph, I don't know why you had to go there. But I do know that *you are also here with me*. I do know that *you can hear me* and listen to me. Joseph, I don't how far away you had to go. I don't know if you need to go even further away in order to comfortably listen to me. But I do know you can hear me and respond to me in ways that are appropriate and helpful for you.

Using this sort of talk I was able to develop a link with Joseph. Over the next 10 minutes I extended this connection to include holding his hand and developing finger signals to communicate with his unconscious mind.

Gradually he reoriented, but upon opening his eyes he froze again in wide-eyed terror, apparently "seeing" someone or something in front of him. I asked if it was his father he saw and his head nodded. Taking hold of his hand and encouraging him to breathe, I gently coached him to expand his attentional field to include me on his right side and to hallucinate a friend on his left side. Gathering strength from these additional relationships, he shouted at his "father" to "get the hell away." The terrifying image receded and Joseph collapsed in a paroxysm of tears. To reorient him, I walked him around my office for a while. When we sat back down I sought to ease the seriousness by asking him in a soft humorous tone what he thought of his "standard hypnotic experience." We chuckled a bit, then rode the release to a serious but more relaxed connection. I suggested that perhaps his unconscious mind had decided it was time to say good-bye to some relationship and that this might be the meaning of his recurrent symptom. He was curious about this hypothesis, so we used ideomotor finger signals to ask his unconscious mind (a) whether his symptom of facial grimaces was connected to experiences with his father, (b) whether the preceding hypnotic dissociation was connected to some past emotional event with his father, and (c) whether it was time to say good-bye to that abusive relationship.

His yes finger signaled to each of these questions, as it did to the inquiry of whether a specific memory had been accessed. It turned out that the remembered event occurred when Joseph was six years old. On Christmas morning he had received a toy train. Later that day he and his brother were playing with it in the basement. Joseph somehow broke the train and its tiny ball bearings scattered across the basement floor. His brother ran and reported the incident to his father, who came roaring downstairs to unleash a brutal physical assault on Joseph. The boy spent the rest of the day in the basement trying to

pick up every last ball bearing while his father periodically returned to
beat him again.

This event became the symbolic representation of the "old self" under the influence of his abusive father. (In rituals, as in hypnosis and
any form of artistic expression, it is very important to deal with concrete symbols—i.e., specific stories rather than general identities. This
event is not seen as the original or singular "cause" of present experience, but rather as a representation of a relationship around which
one's identity is organized. Working with more general descriptions
such as "wounded child" or "low self-esteem" does not seem to provide
the requisite experiential ground needed for a ritual act to be effective.)

Joseph was extremely impressed by the responses generated by his
unconscious. He voiced an interest in doing something to change his
relationship to the memory and inquired about how this might be
done. I introduced the possibility of performing a ritual, suggesting
that sometimes terribly invasive experiences lead people to self-
identify with voices, images, and behaviors that really belong to someone else. It was further noted how such a self-misidentification could
give rise to various uncontrollable expressions, such as Joseph's gri-
macing and depression. Healing rituals were described as processes
wherein one first *externalized* (through letters, paintings, and other
experiential processes) these voices, images, and body feelings, then
planned and enacted a ritual to once and for all say good-bye to the
external influences and hello to one's own voice, images, and feelings.
A few simple examples were offered to emphasize how rituals were
co-created by therapist and client, with the therapist providing expertise on structures and the client generating the specific materials,
making the decisions and enacting the ritual. It was also noted that
individuals really needed to sense that the time was right to do the
ritual, for it required their full commitment and participation. To
stress this point, Joseph was asked to take the next week to decide
whether to commit to such a process. He returned the following week
and said he was definitely interested in doing the ritual. (If a full
commitment is not possible, the therapist should abandon the possibility of a ritual and explore other interventions.)

The above description indicates the importance of connecting the
complaint to an emotional trauma or developmental challenge, framing the symptom as an incomplete or unsuccessful attempt to change
one's identity in relation to the event or challenge, and then suggesting
a therapeutic ritual as an effective means of transforming one's identity and dissolving the symptom. The success of the ritual requires
the client's full motivation and participation.

The case also illustrates how the connection of the symptom with a trauma must occur experientially. An intellectual hypothesis that symptom X is connected to event Y is wholly inadequate, for it leaves the therapeutic conversation at a cognitive level. (To reiterate, it is precisely in those cases where cognitive understanding is of little or no value that rituals may be especially indicated.) The language of ritual operates at a more primary, experiential level, much like symptoms and hypnotic phenomena (Gilligan, 1988). Thus, the therapist should make use of such language to lead into the possibility of a ritual.

There are, of course, other methods for conducting this experiential inquiry. With some clients I suggest that they develop a light "centering" trance, contemplate the question, "What is this (symptomatic) experience connected to?" and then use crayons or paints on art paper to let their "unconscious mind" express a response. This can be done in the office with me or at home during the week. In the latter case, therapists should insure that clients have adequate resources – for example, the presence of a friend or a physical symbol (see Dolan, 1991) – to stay centered if the process brings to mind difficult material.

Another possibility is to use other hypnotic explorations – for example, general "searches" for relevant material (Gilligan, 1987; Lankton and Lankton, 1983) or ideomotor questions. Whatever the method used, the therapist seeks to frame a chronic symptom over which the client feels no control as an "identity event" that may be transformed via ritual.

STEP 2: PLANNING THE RITUAL

This second step typically takes three to six weeks. As Table 2 indicates, it involves generating and externalizing the experiential symbols of both the old and new selves and then evolving a ritual that allows the transition from the former to the latter. Time and care are taken to insure that this process is generated, guided, and ratified each step of the way by the client's inner self ("the unconscious") rather than by his or her normal, intellectual process.

The first two parts of the planning are usually done concurrently. First, the verbal conversations that the person has internalized are experientially activated and externalized in physical form. This is often done via letter writing. In the case of Joseph, I suggested (and he ratified via finger signals) that he take 40 minutes each day to write two letters. Following the more structured approaches inherent in ritual, we decided upon a specific time of day (8 p.m.) and place (his

Table 2
Planning the Ritual

1. Have client select/generate/elaborate physical symbols of old self-identity (letters, photographs, art work, jewelry, etc.).
2. Have client select/generate/elaborate physical symbols of new identity (same as above, but perhaps including living symbol such as plant or pet).
3. Identify basic ritual act (burning, burying, declarations, etc.).
4. Plan actual ritual (where, with whom, when, what specific actions).
5. Have client emotionally/spiritually prepare (prayer, meditation, fasting, diary writing, etc.) for ritual.

study) to write these letters. After a brief centering process, he would spend 20 minutes writing a first letter to someone involved in the "old self" event of the broken train. On different nights, this person was (six-year-old) Joseph, his brother, his father, and his mother. The letter was to describe what happened, how he felt then, how the event had influenced his subsequent self-image, and what he wanted to do about it now. The second letter (also 20 minutes) was to his "future self" and specified the life he was interested in living and differences in his behavior. (Sometimes in this letter a person finds it more helpful to write as his future self back to the present self or to a childhood, younger self.)

Before this task is carried out, hypnotic questioning is used to insure that it is appropriate and that sufficient resources are available. Often, some modifications are needed — e.g., a person or other resource may need to be present with the client while he writes the letters (Dolan, 1991). Hypnotic questioning is also used in the next session to determine whether any more letters need to be written. The therapist might read the letters to insure the client is centered and connected to the process. (For example, I discontinued the ritual process with a client who wrote letters to his younger self in a nasty, caustic manner, sensing that it was premature to develop a healing ritual.) These ongoing "checks" are part of the ongoing collaborative process between therapist and client(s) that shapes and modifies the ritual.

The next externalization process involves images. As in the letter writing, it is suggested that the client take 40 minutes daily (over a week or so) to paint, draw (with color), collage, or otherwise visually display first the "old self" event and then some version of the "new self." Clients concerned about any lack of artistic talent ("I can't draw") are encouraged to just let happen whatever happens, from actual depictions to just intense colors. They are encouraged to let these expressions come from their own inner selves while focusing on the questions, "What did the traumatic event look or feel like?" (for the first drawing) and "What will things look or feel like after the symptom (or problem) is resolved?" Again, the therapist takes steps to check (a) that the process is appropriate, (b) that sufficient resources are available, (c) that the person is emotionally connected and centered in the process, and (d) whether any further work needs to be done after the person returns in the next session with the externalized images.

The client is then asked to select physical symbols of the new and old selves during the following week. Self-hypnosis, meditation, and open curiosity might be used in this process. The person need not cognitively understand or explain why he selected a symbol. Examples of "old self" symbols include the baby clothes knitted by a woman who had lost her baby daughter; the photograph another woman found of the uncle who sexually molested her; and the toy train (resembling the old train) that Joseph bought. Examples of the "new self" symbols include Japanese bonsai trees purchased by the woman grieving her daughter; African shields and spears chosen by the sexually abused woman; and a ring selected by Joseph. Again, the therapist works to insure that each of these selections is appropriate and complete.

The client has now concrete, physical, external symbols of the old and new self. The next step is to select the basic ritual acts for saying good-bye to the old self and welcoming the new self. The therapist might outline "menu selections'—e.g., burning or burying—and then support clients (e.g., via hypnotic process) in making their own choice. Hypnosis helped Joseph to generate the ritual acts of (a) dumping ball bearings of a toy train over actual train tracks and then (b) crossing the tracks to "the other side" to declare his new self. These choices were ratified by his ideomotor finger signals.

The next session involves planning the details of where, when, how, and with whom the ritual will occur. Each should be considered carefully, and all discussions should be ratified in some significant way by the person. With Joseph, the plan was to go to the train tracks a mile or so from my office. He would bring the train along with the letters and drawings. The "saying good-bye" part of the ritual would involve reading aloud the "old self" letters and showing the pictures before dumping the toy train's ball bearings over the train tracks as a way of declaring his letting go of these symbols. He would then cross the tracks and do several ceremonial declarations of the new self.

The issue of who else to include is especially important since, to reiterate, a ritual takes place at the intersection between two worlds: the public and private, or the inner and outer. Persons performing a ritual act are not only reorganizing their inner world but also declaring to others a new social self. Witnesses not only observe a person's declarations but also participate in and validate the creation of a new social and psychological identity. This extraordinary complementarity is a major reason for the effectiveness of healing rituals.

With Joseph, this issue proved to be painful. After much deliberation he decided that he didn't feel sufficiently close to anyone to invite them to participate. (Developing friendships and community became a major focus of his post-ritual activities.) He asked me to participate, and I reiterated that I would, though primarily in the role of the "ritual specialist" guiding the process and providing minimal coaching if needed. He also accepted my suggestion to consider communicating the effects of the ritual to family members (all of whom lived 3,000 miles away).

As a last preparation step, the client is asked to take the week before the ritual to orient inwardly and emotionally prepare for the event. Depending on a person's practices and values, this might include solitary walks, diary writing, self-hypnosis or mediation, light fasting, prayer, etc. This is a crucial step in most traditional rituals (as well as other important performances), since it shifts attention away from normal "business as usual" process toward a more dramatically heightened inner focus.

STEP 3: ENACTING THE RITUAL

As Table 3 illustrates, the performance of the ritual has three parts: the pre-ritual induction that develops the liminal consciousness of ritual space (Turner, 1969); the ritual itself; and the post-ritual process that incorporates a person back into the normal social space. The pre-ritual induction is similar to a hypnotic induction, involving the use of attentional narrowing, repetition and rhythm, and symbolic activities that shift the person into a heightened state of experiential-symbolic

Table 3
Enact the Ritual

1. Pre-ritual induction
2. The ritual itself
3. Post-ritual processes: celebration, vacation, outings, etc.

consciousness (Gilligan, 1987). This may involve convocational speeches, chants, prayers, inward meditations, ceremonial acts, etc. The induced mood is generally serious and intense, with a sense that something very important is about to happen.

In the case of Joseph, he arrived at my office on the appointed day, bringing with him his ritual symbols (the letters, drawings, train, etc.). In a soft and focused conversation we reviewed all that had happened over the past month and he reaffirmed his commitment to performing the ritual. We drove in separate cars to the ritual site (the railroad crossroads), got out, and marked out the ritual space with rocks and sticks. Joseph faced the tracks, laid out the ritual symbols of the old self, oriented inwardly for several minutes, then turned to me and indicated his readiness.

When I nodded solemnly for him to "go for it," he again closed his eyes to deepen his involvement. When he opened them several minutes later, he appeared intensely focused and in an emotionally heightened, altered state of consciousness. Fighting back tears, he visualized all around him the members of his family. His strong but vulnerable voice cracked with emotion as he greeted each person and declared his purpose in summoning them to the event. He picked up the "old self" letters and read them one by one, declaring after each that he was finished with those words and then proceeded to tear up the letter. His emotions appeared ready to overwhelm him periodically but each time he paused to compose and center himself before continuing. (Some clients may benefit from some gentle support and encouragement during such times.)

He next displayed each "old self" drawing, describing what had happened, how he felt then, how his identity had been influenced, and how he was ready now to let go of this self-image. He would then rip up the images and place the torn tatters into a box (that was later burned). A variety of emotions—grief, anger, sadness—surged through him during this process.

The final "good-bye" process involved the toy train. He had removed its bottom to expose the ball bearings, which were now held in place by a single piece of tape. As he focused his attention on the train in his hand, he lapsed into convulsive sobs. After a minute or so, I moved in, whispered for him to breathe and allow the feelings to just "move through," and gently encouraged him to continue. This helped him to center and refocus his attention on the ritual task. Looking at this imagined family, he declared that the time had come for him to move on. He recounted the "train incident" in slow, emotional measures, then announced that he was ready to reclaim that event for his own development. In ceremonial declaration he held the toy train over the train tracks, removed the tape, and let the ball bearings pour out all over the tracks. (I had not appreciated until then how small these ballbearings are, or how many of them there are in a toy train.) Many emotions were also released, but Joseph seemed to grow in strength and stature as they did. Finally he turned to me and said he was ready to "move on."

With Joseph in the lead, we walked over the crossroads. He then performed the "new self" ritual by reading the letters written to his future self, showing the drawings, and ceremoniously donning the ring he had selected to symbolize his new commitment. This part of the ritual seemed much easier for him, as if he was guided by some new-found strength and spirit.

One final piece of the ritual remained. Joseph had decided during self-hypnotic explorations several weeks earlier to send the toy train back East to his brother (who had "turned him in"), along with a letter. In this poignant letter, Joseph mentioned the horrible childhood they had shared, and how it had apparently made both of them depressed and unhappy during their adult lives. (His brother struggled under the clinical diagnosis of depression.) Joseph expressed his commitment to free himself from such unhappiness, and then recounted the train incident from childhood. He described the ritual process in which he had been immersed over the previous six weeks, and noted that during his self-explorations he had developed the strong sense that he should send the train to his brother after the ritual, for he was finished with it. He confessed that he was not entirely sure why this was important or what his brother should do with it (he suggested donating it to charity), but felt strongly that he was finished with it and that it should be given to his brother. (At several points during the weeks of ritual preparation, Joseph confirmed to me through ideomotor signaling that this was indeed a proper course of action.) He concluded the letter by stating that he loved his brother deeply and that he wanted their relationship to deepen and grow stronger.

Joseph placed this letter along with the train in a package he had addressed to his brother. We drove in our respective cars to the post office, and he went in and mailed it. Upon returning he reported that during the ritual an incredible weight that "had been there for so long I was no longer aware it was there" had lifted and dissolved. He looked and sounded remarkably calm, centered, and confident. I complimented him on the incredible courage and commitment he had shown during the ritual (and throughout the entire preparation process) and told him he had done a great job.

He had arranged (at my suggestion) to take the rest of the day off, so I encouraged him to go home to relax and savor his achievements. I also suggested that he use letter writing anytime over the next couple of weeks that he felt any "old voices" revisiting him, since it was a good way to externalize and let go of occasional residual processes that were "looking to leave and go back to where they belong." (Many clients find this process very helpful.) I also reminded him that he could review any of the "new self" letters, images, or symbols that he was taking home with him, especially anytime he needed to recenter himself. (Most clients leave behind—indeed, burn, bury, or otherwise trash—the "old self" symbols and find a special place at home for the "new self" symbols.)

STEP 4: REINCORPORATING SELF INTO COMMUNITY

Planning and performing a therapeutic ritual is an especially intense process. Participants withdraw from everyday life—emotionally, psychologically and behaviorally—for a prolonged time and become deeply immersed in alternate, inner realities. It is therefore crucial that the person be reincorporated back into the social community following a ritual. Any further "inner work" explorations are generally curtailed and attention oriented to practical challenges and responsibilities, such as friends, jobs, families, social skills, etc. Therapy ends after another session or two, unless short-term concrete goals are negotiated. Rituals generally work as an "all or none" phenomenon, with transformation occurring during the ritual act itself. Thus, additional "inner" work on the issue is often counterproductive.

When Joseph returned the following week, he looked great. He said that after the ritual he celebrated by going shopping for a new wardrobe. He felt alive and "open," and proudly reported making a presentation at work without any grimaces. (He reported feeling very aware of the new ring on his finger during the presentation.) He felt confident

Table 4
Reincorporating Self into Community

1. Give structure for expressing remnants of old identity (letters, physical activities, simple exercises).
2. Develop structures for expressing new identity (social activities, new symbol, imaginal guides, new clothes/artifacts, new relationship with unconscious, etc.).

about continuing these new behaviors, and we mutually agreed after a little further talk that the therapeutic goals had been achieved and so we could stop meeting.

About a year later, Joseph called me on the phone. He reported a continuing absence of facial grimaces and requested some hypnosis to help him in his new hobby of kick-boxing. We spent several sessions on this project, during which time he reported having a great time at his job.

DISCUSSION

The case of Joseph illustrates how rituals may be powerful mediums for therapeutic change. They allow the transformation of identity and the dissolution of undesired symptoms. Rituals are decidedly nonrational events in which individuals tap into deep inner resources and engage in profound experiential-symbolic conversations. Most important, they empower individuals to externalize self-negating images, voices, and behaviors and rediscover and claim their own voices, visions, and bodies.

While the case example involved an individual, rituals may also be used with couples, families, and groups. They may be helpful with many different types of complaints. I have used rituals with individuals, couples, or families dealing with sexual abuse (e.g., incest or rape), and also with groups of incest survivors. Divorce ceremonies (with one or both people) including friends and family can be helpful. Purification and atonement rituals may work in cases of infidelity. Rituals marking deaths (including abortions) have been profoundly moving. Other rituals may be co-created for rite of passage, eating disorders, substance abuse, and leaving abusive communities (e.g., cults, ritual abuse).

In each of these cases, the therapist respects and empowers the inner uniqueness and intelligence of clients so that the actual symbols and acts of the ritual emanate from them, not from the therapist. The therapist acts as a "ritual specialist" who provides possible structures, supports clients in staying in relationship with their primary processes and witnesses and occasionally guides the process. When client and therapist are both fully participating and contributing, each in his or her own way, the ritual can indeed be a therapeutic event.

Commentary

_____

Stephen P. Madigan

WHEN I WAS growing up Irish Catholic in Toronto, Canada, there came a time, around my seventh birthday, when I was to receive my First Holy Communion. For weeks prior to the big event fifty of us neighborhood kids studied, prayed, and prepared ourselves to receive "God in the flesh." As the day grew closer, I remember the building excitement among my parents, neighbors, and teachers. I recall growing nervous with feelings of responsibility, my first little suit (purchased with great reverance to Holy Communion fashion particulars), and the general feeling that something very significant was about to happen.

Finally the day came and among the pomp and incense this wee heathen was instantly transformed into a participant member of the church. I was given holy instructions regarding my new persona from the parish priest, along with kisses from the neighbors and presents from my parents. I remember going home, where I was the guest of honor at a party. During the first few weeks following the communion I was so proud going to church as a bona fide member I remember kneeling with my father at St. Rose of Lima's marble communion railing and feeling very changed, grown-up, and—dare I say—holy.

I can think of two specific reasons why the ritual of my First Holy Communion stands out for me. The first is that I have partaken in so few rituals able to promote life change or offer much meaningful significance. However, the communion ritual was able to "suture" me into a profound and ongoing ritual space. Rituals such as weddings, funerals, birthdays, participation on a national sports team, trips overseas, and my yearly transformation into a diehard hockey fan during the NHL playoffs – although wonderful in the moment – have never perturbed a pronounced reality shift or personal transformation in me as the holy ritual once did.

The second reason relates to my recognition of the power and influence that my First Holy Communion ritual (along with other "holy" rites of passage through time) have had in my life (my family, like Steve Gilligan's, used to say the rosary every evening until I was about 12, and although I agree with Steve that the actual saying of the rosary did not constitute a ritual space, it was a powerfully insurgent narrative technique). What else explains why it has taken me all of these years to break free of Catholicism? Unfortunately, there seemed many varied rites, rituals, and "ritual specialists" that assisted my weaving into the fabric of Catholic experience. There also seemed a dire lack of alternative rituals and ritual specialists to help me move away from church culture.

Stephen Gilligan's chapter brings to print his unique use and understanding of rituals within the practice and context of therapy. He suggests that common to every culture is the practice and acknowledgment of rituals. Rituals worldwide are viewed as sacred in their performance and meaning; they punctuate specific temporal events and often involve a repetitive consistency of historical actions and practice. He comments that rituals are designed to express certain rites of redefinition of personhood and understanding. This redefinition is constitutive in both the internal and external definition of the person.

Gilligan outlines a four-step model for therapy, lasting four to six weeks. His method of therapy brings together a deft knowledge of hypnotherapy and an appreciation of healing rituals. This juxtaposition is highlighted in a footnote where he acknowledges both Milton Erickson and anthropologist Victor Turner as contributing to his work (I thought I also heard the voices of Clifford Geertz, Barbara Myerhoff, and Stephen Tyler).

I found Gilligan's description of the "basic distinctions regarding rituals" in the first part of the paper to be both succinct and helpful. In addition, it was clear from the start that he was *not* practicing rituals from a structuralist position, which would advocate and situate all ritual work within the scientistic/psychological hydraulic metaphor – the common therapeutic belief that it is helpful to the healing process for a client to release the "pressure" of one's pain through reliving (over and over!) the traumatic events of one's history. Further to this structuralist deconstruction, Gilligan makes the astute observation that "conversations involving identity shifts cannot occur within normal analytical processes, since such processes generally function to conserve one's existing frame of reference."

As an alternative, Gilligan began his practice of rituals by thinking in terms of "ritual space." He made this shift by acknowledging the hypnotherapeutic tradition of "going inside" to be "markedly unsettling" and often "paralleling" the experience of individuals who had experienced traumatic events. In other words, Gilligan found that in itself a therapist's hypnotherapeutic performance could further perpetrate the client's story of trauma. This permutation in Gilligan's rhetorical position is testament to his clinical posture, which seems to advocate that "one size *does not* fit all." More therapists might consider Gilligan's ethical practice of therapeutic flexibility.

Gilligan's four-step ritual healing method acts to externalize what he calls a person's "misidentification of the self." In addition, the four separate phases of the method externalize the person's "disidentification with the rest of the world." Gilligan identifies the recursion between the inner and outer dialogues of misidentification and disidentification as "*being* the traumatic event." His means of externalization is through the client artistically expressing the voice of misidentification and disidentification. Gilligan's use of *artistic externalization* through letter writing, photography, painting, etc., seeks to express both the voice of the client's "old self" and the more preferred voice of the "new self" or "future self." I believe he is suggesting that the externalized conversation (through both oral and artistic experience) that ensues between the old and the new can encourage a narrative uncertainty of the old through the resurrection and promotion of the person's new life story of a preferred future identity. Through this method he encourages people to consider their lives as ever-changing experiences in a sea of alternative possibilities along a temporal landscape.

For Gilligan, the ritual is considered successful only when the new identification of the person's self is no longer an identity spoiled and guided by the traumatic event; the old self is transformed into an identity of resolution and empowerment. I really enjoyed Gilligan's careful emphasis on checking and rechecking with the client that the process is appropriate, that sufficient processes are available, that the person is emotionally connected and centered in the process, and if necessary, that any further work be done after the person returns in the next session with the externalized images. Too often a therapist's excitement regarding a healing ritual's possibilities for change places him/her "ahead" of the client. When a therapist begins to leave the client behind, it can only act to plasticize and suburbanize the sacred nature of the client's ritual space (here I am using the word *sacred* within a Batesonian frame rather than a Christian one).

Gilligan's four-step method creates a liminal space for the performance of alternative artistic externalizations of internalized misidentifications and disidentifications. Through the method's careful reconstruction of the trauma, an alternative dialogical space is created. To assist in grounding clients' ritual experience even further, Gilligan asks them to enlist an audience to be witness to their change. This public and private dialogue promotes and supports a common discourse of the new and future self. Gilligan quite rightly acknowledges that "this extraordinary complementarity is a major reason for the effectiveness of healing rituals."

Gilligan appears to utilize many components of healing rituals common to many cultures across many traditions, including those of my Holy Communion ritual. His work with rituals also draws from his extensive experience with hypnosis and includes shades of the narrative metaphor. My only questions regarding his therapeutic work involve his views of its limitations, i.e., in what situations and with whom, and for what reasons, he would not use healing rituals. He does suggest that one client did not seem ready, but was it necessary for him to drop the practice of ritual altogether? I would have been interested in Gilligan's perceptions of which specific problem identities he views as not warranting or benefiting from a healing ritual. I would also have enjoyed more discussion on how his use of healing rituals and acknowledgment of ritual space have influenced him personally and in which future directions he feels they may take him professionally.

It appears to me that the use of therapeutic ritual through the therapist-client co-creation of ritual space is of importance to both parties. For therapists working with Gilligan's method, I see numerous opportunities to open space for the creation of new discursive practices. For the person coming into therapy, especially if his/her experience of ritual in everyday life has been as limiting as my own, Gilligan provides a context for expressing and creating a rewarding ritual space and for rewriting the traumatized self. Perhaps with Stephen's assistance I might now bury my scapulars!

REFERENCES

Bateson, G., & Bateson, M. C. (1987). *Angels fear: Towards an epistemology of the sacred.* New York: Macmillan.

Campbell, J. (1984). *The way of the animal powers.* London: Times Books.

Dolan, Y. M. (1991). *Resolving sexual abuse: Solution-focused therapy and Ericksonian hypnosis for adult survivors.* New York: W. W. Norton.

Erickson, M. H. (1980a). *The nature of hypnosis and suggestion: Collected papers of M. Erickson, Vol. 1.* (Edited by E. L. Rossi). New York: Irvington.

Erickson, M. H. (1980b). *Innovative hypnotherapy: The collected papers of M. Erickson, Vol. IV.* (Edited by E. L. Rossi). New York: Irvington.

Gilligan, S. (1987). *Therapeutic trances: The cooperation principle in Ericksonian hypnotherapy.* New York: Brunner/Mazel.

Gilligan, S. (1988). Symptom phenomena as trance phenomena. In J. Zeig & S. Lankton (Eds.), *Developing Ericksonian therapy: State of the art.* New York: Brunner/Mazel.

Haley, J. (1984). *Ordeal therapy.* San Francisco: Jossey-Bass.

Imber-Black, E., Roberts, J., & Whiting, R. (1989). *Rituals in families and family therapy.* New York: Norton.

Jung, C. (1954). *Symbols of transformation.* Princeton, NJ: Princeton Univ. Press.

Lankton, S., and Lankton, C. (1983). *The answer within: A framework for Ericksonian hypnotherapy.* New York: Brunner/Mazel.

Madanes, C. (1990). *Sex, love, and violence: Strategies for transformation.* New York: W. W. Norton.

Selvini Palazzoli, M., Boscolo, L., Cecchin, G. F., and Prata, G. (1978). *Paradox and counterparadox.* New York: Jason Aaronson.

Turner, V. (1969). *The ritual process: Structure and anti-structure.* Chicago: Aldine Publishing.

van der Hart, O. (1983). *Rituals in psychotherapy: Transition and continuity.* New York: Irvington.

13

ESCAPING VICTIM LIFE STORIES AND CO–CONSTRUCTING PERSONAL AGENCY

Janet Adams-Westcott
Thomas A. Dafforn
Patricia Sterne

TRAUMATIC EVENTS can disrupt or shatter one's sense of being an agent who actively influences the direction of one's life. Persons who have experienced trauma often perceive themselves as having few choices and little power to influence their situation. They engage in internalized conversations that replicate the traumatizing events to which they have been subjected. These inner dialogues have the effect of (a) disqualifying their experiences, (b) limiting their ability to take a reflexive perspective and consider alternative explanations or actions, and (c) inviting their participation in pathologizing interpersonal patterns that maintain a sense of powerlessness. They are likely to make sense out of their experiences of trauma and subsequent victimization by adopting an oppressive story about themselves and their relationships.

This chapter considers the use of therapeutic conversation to help persons who have experienced trauma (a) externalize disqualifying self

We gratefully acknowledge the contributions of our many colleagues who privileged us with conversations about therapeutic conversations. We are especially thankful to participants at the Tulsa conference who enriched our understanding and practice by voicing their own experiences and reflections.

Most of all, we are thankful to Lynda for teaching us about agency. We applaud the courage and fortitude she demonstrated in her journey.

stories, (b) develop a reflexive perspective, and (c) take charge of directing their lives through the performance of more empowering narratives. The story of Lynda will be told to illustrate the co-construction of personal agency within the context of narrative psychotherapy.

A STORY ABOUT THERAPY

Lynda was the second of two children born to college educated parents. Her father was a mental health professional and her mother worked as an office manager.

When Lynda was five years old, her father began behaving bizarrely and was placed in an inpatient psychiatric facility. He kept insisting that the problem was physical, not psychological, and pleaded to be transferred to a medical unit. His physicians assured Lynda's mother that the problem was emotional. Her mother followed their advice and decided that he should remain in the psychiatric unit. Shortly following this decision, he died suddenly. Results of an autopsy revealed that his symptoms resulted from a rare neurological disorder that had not been diagnosed.

Following her father's death, Lynda clung to her mother "like an appendage" and experienced terror when separated from her. She remembers being extremely sensitive to her mother's sadness. Other people said that she "loved her mother too much."

When Lynda was seven, her mother married a man who worked as an architect. He built a house for the family similar to Jeremy Bentham's Panoptican. Developed as an architectural model of social control, the Panoptican had a courtyard in the center that allowed direct observation into all living or work spaces (Foucault, 1980; White and Epston, 1990). Lynda's room was designed so that she never had any privacy in relationship to the courtyard. Her stepfather organized her room with an arrangement of windows and doors so that she was unable to hide in her closet or bathroom.

When Lynda arrived home from school, her mother would still be at work. Her stepfather would leave work early and masturbate while watching Lynda from the courtyard. She remembers trying to hide under her bed to avoid his gaze. Then he began to touch her and direct her to touch him. This physical contact continued until she was 12. At that time, she began telling him "no" when he tried to fondle her. When she would refuse his advances he would tell her that she was worthless and would never measure up or make it in life. He quit touching her but continued to watch her.

Lynda remembers being afraid to tell her mother about the abuse, not because of what her stepfather might do, but because she worried about what it would do to her mother. Her mother first took her to a psychiatrist when she was in elementary school. The psychiatrist never asked her if she was being abused and she never told him.

School became a safe haven where Lynda could excel. Though she did well academically, she was shy and socially isolated. She wanted to be close to people but had difficulty participating socially. During high school, Lynda began using drugs and engaging in sexual activity as a way to be with someone. She would attach herself to one young man at a time. Her social contacts were limited to "getting high" with his friends. Lynda decided to stop using drugs after almost failing her first semester of college. She returned to therapy and was placed on anti-depressant medication.

She worked with a professor who recognized her potential and encouraged her to attend graduate school. She was accepted into a prestigious doctoral program in a different state. When Lynda began the program she experienced a sense of constant observation and evaluation from her professors. She compared herself unfavorably to her classmates and became convinced that the school had made a mistake by accepting her. Depression and hopelessness overtook her and she tried to take her life. It was during a three-month hospitalization that Lynda finally disclosed her experiences of emotional and sexual victimization by her stepfather.

When we first met Lynda she was new to our community. She had returned to graduate school in a technical field that required limited social interaction. She was living with a young man she met while working on a school project. Her social interactions were limited to her partner and his work-related acquaintances. She seldom left their apartment. When she ventured out she felt that people around her were watching her and making negative evaluations.

NARRATIVE PSYCHOTHERAPY

Our understanding of Lynda's experience was based on a narrative approach to psychotherapy. A therapist influenced by narrative ideas is interested in the dominant story adopted to organize and explain experiences. This approach assumes that problems develop when people perform oppressive stories about themselves and their relationships.

The narrative therapist would intervene by: (a) helping Lynda access her resources and use them to challenge this oppressive story, and (b) working with Lynda to co-create a different story that includes a future with many more alternatives than were possible in her traumatic past. A therapist influenced by a narrative model would not assume special knowledge or embrace techniques designed to help Lynda conform to a model for normative behavior, nor would he or she be interested in predictions about prognosis. Instead, the therapist would be interested in helping Lynda access her own unique knowledge and develop her own expertise. This expertise would include past and present exceptions to the problem story. The narrative therapist would be especially curious about Lynda's ideas about directing her life in the future.

Self Stories

Individual psychology models assume that what we call "personality" and "self" represent the "true essence" of the person. Narrative psychotherapy is influenced by postmodern writers who have taken issue with this essentialist understanding of "self." They argue that what we call the "self" is a socially generated phenomenon that occurs in language (Anderson and Goolishian, 1990; Gergen, 1991; Rose, 1989; Sampson, 1989). A person's sense of self emerges when interpersonal conversations are internalized as inner conversations (Tomm, 1989b, 1991). These conversations are then organized into stories that we use to understand our experiences (White and Epston, 1990).

The dominant stories we perform evolve from a variety of sources. Our lived experiences make the most important contribution to our sense of self. These include our experience of our behavior as well as our experience of other people's experience of us (White, 1988d; White and Epston, 1990). Narratives outside of our experience also contribute to the self stories we perform. Parry (1991) has described how we can be influenced by stories about who we are that were developed by family members prior to our birth. Dominant cultural discourses about personhood, gender, and relationships also shape our narratives about self (Hare-Mustin, 1991; White and Epston, 1989, 1990).

The dominant stories we perform about self create a "perceptual lens" through which subsequent life events are interpreted. We notice information that fits with the dominant story about our lives and relationships. Experiences that are not consistent with our self story are not selected out as meaningful (Gergen, 1991; Parry, 1991; White, 1988a).

Dominant stories can be empowering and generative or disempowering and oppressive. People experience personal agency when they internalize conversations about themselves that reflect the richness of their lived experience. Such stories allow them to consider a variety of possible explanations for events and choose viable solutions to the challenges of living. Problems develop when people internalize conversations that restrain them to a narrow description of self. These stories are experienced as oppressive because they limit the perception of available choices (Tomm, 1989b, 1991).

Disempowering stories are maintained by restraints that prevent people from noticing exceptions to their constrained descriptions of self (White, 1986). Among these restraints are the beliefs and expectations that are internalized about self and relationships. People are also restrained by participation in repetitive and pathologizing interpersonal patterns. Over time, people influenced by such restraints may develop a view of self that is "problem-saturated" (White, 1988a). As the person's description of self becomes increasingly narrower, so does his/her experience of available choices.

The Impact of Trauma on Self Stories

The experience of trauma has the potential to profoundly affect one's story about self (Adams-Westcott and Isenbart, 1990; Durrant and Kowalski, 1990; Kamsler, 1990). The circumstances of traumatic events seldom permit the experience of personal agency. People subjected to such events perceive themselves as controlled by some external force or person. They believe that they have little ability to affect their circumstances. When this experience of helplessness and powerlessness becomes part of the conversations that are internalized about self, people begin to experience less and less agency in circumstances outside of the traumatic event. Gilligan (1991) has noted that persons who have experienced trauma often engage in disempowering inner dialogues that resemble the traumatizing conversations to which they have been subjected. Over time, they may begin to experience themselves as more under the influence of others and less influential in their own lives. They are likely to adopt a victim life story and participate in interactions with others that reinforce this description of self.

Internalizing a view of self as helpless and powerless is *not* an inevitable outcome of traumatic experiences (Browne and Finkelhor, 1986). Whether or not a person adopts a victim life story depends on the meaning that is ascribed to the traumatizing events (Durrant, 1987; Durrant and Kowalski, 1990). In the area of sexual abuse, reports indicate that the long-term adjustment of children who have been victimized is influenced by the availability of a supportive adult who provides protection from further exploitation. If the child believes that the person who was abusive has a problem and is responsible, he or she may not develop difficulties as a consequence of the experience of abuse.

The self stories that are internalized following the experience of trauma often include a disqualification of the person and his or her experiences. Durrant and Kowalski (1990) describe how persons victimized by sexual assault develop stories about self as helpless and incompetent. These stories create an "abuse dominated lens" which only allows the person to notice information that reinforces a view of self as powerless. The person is blind to those aspects of his or her lived experience that contradict this disempowering story. They fail to notice or ascribe meaning to those lived experiences where they behaved in a competent manner or where others treated them as a person of worth. They may participate in interpersonal patterns that have the effect of isolating them from the experiences of other people and the experiences that other people have of them.

Access to alternative knowledge derived from their own experiences may be limited by inner dialogues that disqualify their own experience. These disqualifying inner conversations can contribute to self-pathologizing behaviors that invite further disqualification from others. When other people interact with them in a respectful rather than a disqualifying manner, the internalized dialogues discount these experiences.

Personal agency can be further impaired by psychiatric diagnoses. By locating a mental disorder inside the person and predicting certain prognostic limitations, a "psychiatric story" can reinforce the idea that the person is unable to meaningfully impact his/her situation. The experience of powerlessness can be replicated when the person assumes a one-down position in relationship to the therapist's expertise. Durrant and Kowalski (1990) argue that therapies that require persons who have experienced trauma to recount the details of these events may be experienced by the person as abusive. Abreactive techniques that require the person to "relive" traumatic events can replicate the experience of powerlessness and, hence, have the potential to reinforce disempowering stories about self. They acknowledge that people can be helped by talking about what happened to them in a supportive environment, but believe that each person should decide for him or herself whether such a discussion would be experienced as helpful or oppressive.

The Impact of Trauma on Lynda's Self Story

Lynda developed a story about herself that replicated the traumatic events and conversations. She described herself as a mental patient. She believed that there was something wrong with her that couldn't be changed. She wasn't sure whether her problem was primarily biological or primarily psychological.

Sometimes she thought that she was being punished by an outside force. She thought that she deserved this punishment because she could have stopped her stepfather from abusing her by refusing his advances when she was younger.

Lynda believed that normal people did not have struggles in life. She expected that she should be able to automatically cope with life's challenges. She interpreted any hint of struggle as more evidence that she was not normal.

She recognized her intelligence but viewed herself as a social misfit. She wanted to participate in social interactions but believed that if she did others would know that something was wrong with her. When she did interact with others she experienced herself as one-dimensional, as "a cardboard person."

Lynda internalized her stepfather's story that she could never "measure up" or make it in life. Her view of the future was bleak, as she believed that she had little ability to change her situation. She interpreted her participation in therapy as evidence of this view of herself.

REFLECTION AND THERAPEUTIC CONVERSATION

Disqualifying self stories are challenged by therapeutic conversations that invite the experience of agency. Agency evolves as people separate from oppressive stories and take a reflecting position with themselves (Tomm, 1989a). The resulting conceptual space allows people to reexamine the stories about their lives and relationships (Tomm, 1989b, 1991). They gain access to alternative knowledges that differ from the dominant story. The process of reflection also creates the opportunity for people to access self-knowledge and to give voice to their own experiences. As they reflect on the perceptions and assumptions that make up their story, they begin to know what *they* think, often for the first time (Andersen, 1991). The information provided by these alternative knowledges contributes to a new understanding of their experiences. More empowering stories emerge from the dialogues that are opened up by these new understandings.

Externalizing Disqualifying Self Stories

Persons who have experienced trauma perceive those in authority as the only legitimate sources of knowledge. Many of the people we have worked with attempt to understand their experience by seeking out explanations provided by experts who publish popular literature. We often begin our conversations using language they have adopted from these writings. Disqualifying inner dialogues are externalized as particular "instructions/messages/tapes/scripts" that the person received growing up. Pathologizing interpersonal patterns are externalized as "survival behaviors," that is, coping strategies that were useful in the past but do not work in the present (Dolan, 1991).

Conversations that externalize the problem help people begin to understand their experiences within a context of oppression. This account is elaborated by questions that trace the evolution of disqualifying beliefs and interpersonal patterns. This process of juxtaposing the person's experiences across time invites reflection. People begin to realize how their lives have become increasingly more restricted as the traumatizing inner dialogues have become more influential. Many people find it helpful to represent this "map" concretely through written narratives, flow charts, paths, collages, or review of photographs. This process sets the stage for people to describe their experiences and discover alternative self-knowledges that contradict dominant stories of incompetence and unworthiness.

Lynda's work, for example, required an understanding of computers, so the interaction between disqualifying beliefs and behaviors was plotted using a flowchart (see Figure 1). Her experience of constant evaluation was externalized and described as "the committee." She chose this label because she often experienced herself as in the center of an arena, with people holding clipboards watching her from the stands. They evaluated her every move to see if it measured up to certain criteria or specifications for normality.

Her previous therapy experiences taught Lynda a number of self-care activities that created the opportunity for reflection. When she engaged in these activities (e.g., regular exercise, visual imagery, and positive self-talk), she would experience brief periods of respite from "the committee."

Lynda stopped caring for herself when her schedule got hectic or when she was influenced by the belief that "normal people" don't need to participate in such activities. She would then become sensitive to the negative reactions of others, especially those in positions of authority. She would personalize other people's reactions and assume that she was not measuring up to their expectations. This would increase her hypervigilance to other people's responses. She would self-monitor her own behavior to try to meet their expectations. As a result, she would "turn Lynda off" and "become a cardboard person." Every interaction was then a failed test of her self-worth. Lynda would feel hope-

FIGURE 1: *Lynda's Flowchart*

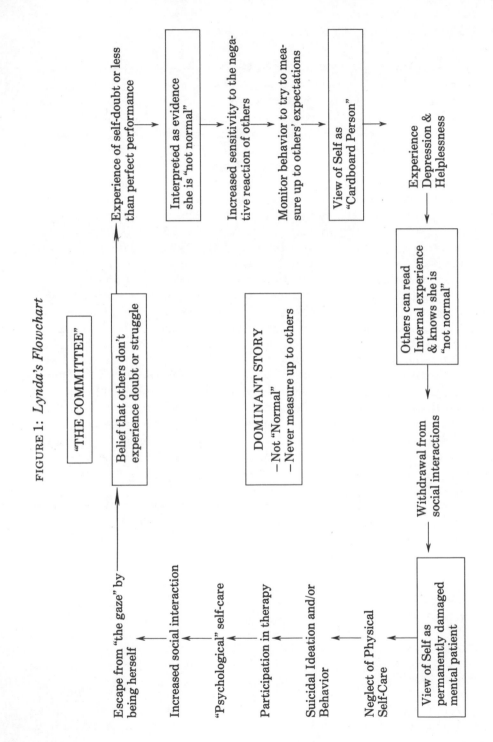

266

less about the future and give serious consideration to ending her life. She would withdraw from others, who she believed were watching her and knew she was crazy because they could see exactly what she was experiencing. Over time, she would quit taking care of herself physically, quit eating, and quit getting out of bed.

Internalizing Stories of Competence

As people begin to escape a view of the problem as resulting from some personal defect, and develop an understanding of the problem as the inevitable outcome of a history of oppression, they begin to reflect on their experience and understand examples of competence in terms of a "heroic struggle." Within the context of this new understanding, the person begins to notice examples of competence in the past and present (White, 1988a, 1988c).

Lynda was invited to notice her competency through questions such as:

- What was it about her that allowed her to take care of herself at age 12 and say "no" to her stepfather?
- How had she managed to keep depression and the effects of her history of abuse from robbing her of her intelligence?
- How had she managed to make a comeback from depression and complete her education?
- How had she been able to overcome shyness and develop a relationship with her significant other?

By reflecting on such questions, people begin to recognize exceptions to the problem as examples of protest that had been disqualified in the past. This new reading of events promotes the experience of agency.

Alternative Knowledges

The ability to take a reflexive perspective is facilitated when people gain access to knowledges derived from a variety of sources. The new story emerges from the dialogue generated by reflecting on these multiple views.

Information from other people's experiences provides an important challenge to the restraints that prevent access to self-knowledge. Persons who have experienced trauma tend to be isolated from other people's experiences. As a consequence, they often assume that others "measure up" to certain standards and that they do not. Opportunities to understand others' experiences are often experienced as liberating when people with histories of trauma discover that few people meet or exceed such standards. In the context of therapy, participation in therapy groups and comments by reflecting team members serve as important sources of alternative knowledges. An appreciation of multiple views emerges when the person becomes aware of the experiences of people outside of the therapy context who do not support the dominant story of disqualification.

Lynda began to challenge "the committee" by experimenting with participation in various groups. First, she began to experiment with social interaction by volunteering at a social service agency. Next, she began to participate in a therapy group for adults molested as children. She married her significant other, finished her degree, and obtained a job with a major company. She joined Toastmasters and learned to speak up and share her ideas with others.

A person's experience of others who refuse to participate in the disqualifying story provides another source of alternative knowledge of "self." People gain access to a new view of self when the therapist asks questions that locate someone in their past who appreciated their unique qualities, recognized their competence, and treated them as persons of worth. Current relationships provide a second source of alternative viewpoints. The person can also be assisted in developing more validating relationships with other people.

Lynda's relationship with her significant other and with the professor she worked with in undergraduate school were important avenues to such alternative views of self. These ideas were explored by asking such questions as:

- What qualities did her significant other recognize in her that "the committee" had blinded her to?
- Were there other people in her life who recognized similar qualities?
- What was it about her that convinced her college professor that she should go to graduate school?

Individuals' sense of agency is further extended by inquiring about their relationship with themselves, a notion generally quite foreign to persons who have experienced trauma. Individuals may be asked about how they will treat themselves differently given their growing recognition of their competence and worth (White, 1988b). Self-acceptance is further enhanced by emphasizing exceptions to the oppressive dominant story (White, 1988c, 1988d). People are asked about those times in their past when they were able to stand apart from the story of disqualification and recognize their competence. They are then asked to consider what qualities led them to accomplish this and how they can use these qualities to assist them in the present and future.

The notion of developing a different relationship with herself seemed to be particularly important in helping Lynda escape the gaze of "the committee." The committee became less influential in her life during those times when she engaged in self-care activities she learned from self-help books and during her previous participation in therapy. Lynda had an interest in human development, so her knowledge of theory in this area was used to challenge the disqualifying view of herself as permanently damaged. This knowledge suggested that the "developmental delay" that resulted from trauma could be remediated. She explored this idea and decided to engage in activities that would help a latency-age child achieve a sense of mastery and nurturance. She quickly shifted from these activities to choosing activities that would help a young woman feel nurtured and competent.

A particular turning point in Lynda's work occurred when she was asked questions about how it might have been different for that latency age child if she had an adult like Lynda to guide her. She was asked to take the perspective of herself at seven and consider:

- How would her future have been different if, during her latency years, she would have had herself as a parent?
- What would that seven-year-old have appreciated about her as a parent?
- Would the child have trust in her ability to protect her from further abuse? What about her would help the child know this?
- What qualities would that seven-year-old appreciate about her as a person?
- How would her awareness of the experience of this seven-year-old make a difference in how she pictured herself? What difference would it make in how she treated herself?

Relapse and the Development of Agency

White (1988c) argues that relapses are inevitable during times of transition and stress, given that the dominant story remains part of the person's lived experience. Relapses can be storied in a manner consistent with the dominant story of disqualification, or they can be storied in a manner that punctuates the person's evolving agency. To punctuate the person's growing competence, time can be collapsed backward to consider how similar events were handled in the past. This process of reflection invites the person to understand relapses as opportunities to develop a better understanding of ways to challenge the restraints that contribute to disempowering stories.

Lynda experienced certain specifications for recovery that had the effect of placing her under the gaze of "the committee." Among these specifications was the idea that she shouldn't have to care for herself. She challenged this idea by developing prompts to remind herself about the importance of self-care, including weekly messages to herself on her computer at work. The idea that "normal people never struggle or experience self-doubt" was externalized. This idea invited Lynda to lose sight of her progress and appreciation for the many small steps she had taken to achieve it. She described her experience as climbing up a series of never ending steps. A picture was drawn depicting this image and she was asked to collapse time backward and consider her progression from the time she was hospitalized to present. This helped her regain a perspective on the many positive changes she had made. Time was collapsed forward to help her establish expectations that fit her much better than those suggested by specifications for recovery.

Recently, Lynda returned for a therapy session following the birth of her first child. She began the session by discussing the experience of filling out the application form which asked her to identify the problem for which she was seeking assistance. She explained that she saw herself as a normal person requesting help adjusting to a normal developmental transition. She explained that she never thinks of herself as a mental patient. She sees herself as a "creative and competent professional woman who is in charge of her life." She is still uncomfortable initiating social contacts, but she doesn't let her discomfort stop her.

Occasionally she compares herself to others. When she catches herself making such comparisons she reminds herself that doing so is like comparing apples and oranges. She is attracted to the notion of "fit." Today she compares herself to herself.

She finally has some resolution to the question about whether or not her difficulties were primarily biological or primarily psychological. Lynda believes that she experienced problems because she developed a certain way of thinking that helped her survive given her experiences as a child. Thinking about the problem as something outside of herself helped her understand that the abuse wasn't her fault and provided her with hope that she could change her situation. Learning to reflect back on her experiences by comparing herself to herself provided her with the ability to do so.

CONCLUSION

This chapter has considered the use of therapeutic conversation to help persons who have experienced childhood trauma escape victim life stories and discover that they can make a difference in their own lives. The people we have worked with begin to approach life from a stance of curiosity. They come to appreciate multiple views and to privilege both their own experience and the experiences of others. They escape the influence of their traumatic past and become more influenced by the possibilities they see for the future.

Commentary

Jill Freedman
Gene Combs

IN TEACHING A narrative approach to psychotherapy we are regularly asked, often skeptically, whether and how these ideas apply in the areas of trauma and sexual abuse. We are delighted to see such a thorough description of using this approach with people who have experienced severe or prolonged trauma for two reasons: both because it is such an important area of work and because so many people do have questions about the application of a narrative approach in this arena.

At the actual workshop presentation, especially as we watched the videotapes, we were impressed with the exquisite care the authors take to establish rapport and to go at the clients' pace. What was crystal clear in the videotapes was the care, gentleness, patience, and strong—yet not dependency-inducing—contact that underlies the application of all the techniques that Adams-Westcott, Dafforn, and Sterne describe in their paper. This matter of establishing a context of safety and security without fostering undue dependency is an important and delicate one, and the authors handle it exquisitely in the examples we have seen of their practice. By coupling this with their steadfast belief in people's ability to achieve personal agency, they illustrate a therapeutic position that, even for people who don't have the authors' command of specific techniques, is effective in countering the legacy of trauma.

The authors' description of how interpersonal conversations (which include, in our view, words *and* actions) can be internalized as extremely limiting and critical self-narratives is noteworthy. It makes clear how *externalizing* these problematic "instructions/messages/ tapes/scripts" is an important part of the therapy. Such externalization fosters dissociation from problematic stories while allowing people to maintain a sense of their integrity and wholeness as persons. Practiced within the context of security and safety that they establish so well, this kind of externalization opens space for reflection on alternative meanings for past experiences.

We are particularly interested in the idea the authors put forth that "whether or not a person adopts a victim life story depends on the meaning that is ascribed to the traumatizing events." We are reminded of a couple we saw in marital therapy. The wife had been raped some months before therapy began. The husband brought this up and talked about his feelings of fear, helplessness, and inadequacy in its wake. The wife, on the other hand, said that although she certainly wished it had never happened, she felt that she had moved beyond it. In asking questions to discover how she had accomplished this we found that she now remembered the incident with an awareness of the strength and resourcefulness she demonstrated in surviving it.

Although we agree with the cited opinion of Durrant and Kowalski that requiring people to relive or recount traumatic events can be experienced as being abusive and disempowering, we believe that inviting people to think about past events in *different* ways can have the opposite effect. We often ask people questions focusing on their agency in surviving. We find that such questions can be helpful for people who have suffered severe and prolonged abuse, as well as those who have survived acute trauma.

The questions we use for this purpose have the greatest impact when considered through a lens of self-appreciation, so we ask them only after clients have already begun the process of externalizing disqualifying self stories and developing a reflexive perspective, as part of the process of taking charge of their lives through developing more empowering narratives. First we ask questions that invite people to look at past traumatic events from outside of those events, appreciating themselves for surviving and for how they survived without reexperiencing the trauma. This is accomplished by using a different perspective—seeing through the eyes of someone who loves them or watching as though this had happened to a friend.

Once people begin to view traumatic events from the outside they are free to perform new meanings on the events. The narrative can begin to change from one of powerlessness to one of empowerment in survival. This new meaning can be amplified by questions that invite the expression and experience of appreciation.

One can then proceed to develop new stories of self-appreciation, competence, and hope in the ways described by the authors. We especially applaud their steadfast belief in people's abilities to achieve personal agency, regardless of their personal histories. This belief not only brings forth an optimal atmosphere for therapy but also guides the questions and nonverbal interactions. We thank Adams-Westcott, Dafforn, and Sterne for extending this belief into the conversation.

REFERENCES

Adams-Westcott, J., & Isenbart, D. (1990). Using rituals to empower family members who have experienced child sexual abuse. In M. Durrant & C. White (Eds.), *Ideas for therapy with sexual abuse* (pp. 37-64). Adelaide, Australia: Dulwich Centre Publications.

Anderson, H., & Goolishian, H. (1990, November). *Changing thoughts on self, agency, questions, narrative and therapy.* Paper presented at the Reflecting Process, Reflecting Teams Conference, Salzburg, Austria.

Andersen, T. (1991, May). *Relationship, language and pre-understanding in the reflecting process.* Paper presented at Narrative and Psychotherapy: New Directions in Theory and Practice for the 21st Century, Houston, TX.

Browne, A., & Finkelhor, D. (1986). Impact of child sexual abuse: A review of research. *Psychological Bulletin, 99,* 66-77.

Dolan, Y. (1991). *Resolving sexual abuse: Solution-focused therapy and Ericksonian hypnosis for adult survivors.* New York: Norton.

Durrant, M. (1987). Therapy with young people who have been victims of sexual assault. *Family Therapy Case Studies, 2*(1), 57-63.

Durrant, M., & Kowalski, K. (1990). Overcoming the effects of sexual abuse: Developing a self-perception of competence. In M. Durrant & C. White (Eds.), *Ideas for therapy with sexual abuse* (pp. 65-110). Adelaide, Australia: Dulwich Centre Publications.

Foucault, M. (1980). *Power/knowledge: Selected interviews and other writings 1972-1977.* New York: Pantheon.

Gergen, K. (1991). *The saturated self: Dilemmas of identity in contemporary life.* New York: Basic.

Gilligan, S. (1991, March). *Healing trauma survivors: An Ericksonian approach.* Paper presented at the Family Therapy Networker Conference, Washington, DC.

Hare-Mustin, R. (1991, May). *Discourses in the mirrored room: A feminist postmodern view of psychotherapy.* Paper presented at Narrative & Psychotherapy: New Directions in Theory and Practice for the 21st Century, Houston, TX.

Kamsler, A. (1990). Her-story in the making: Therapy with women who were sexually abused in childhood. In M. Durrant & C. White (Eds.), *Ideas for therapy with sexual abuse* (pp. 9-36). Adelaide, Australia: Dulwich Centre Publications.

Parry, A. (1991). A universe of stories. *Family Process, 30,* 37-54.

Rose, N. (1989). Individualizing psychology. In J. Shotter & K. Gergen (Eds.), *Texts of identity* (pp. 119-132). Newbury Park, CA: Sage.

Sampson, E. (1989). The deconstruction of the self. In J. Shotter & K. Gergen (Eds.), *Texts of Identity* (pp. 1-19). Newbury Park, CA: Sage.

Tomm, K. (1989a). Externalizing the problem and internalizing personal agency. *Journal of Strategic and Systemic Therapies, 8,* 54-59.

Tomm, K. (1989b, October). *Pips, tips & slips: A heuristic alternative to the DSM-III.* Presentation at the meeting of the American Association of Marriage and Family Therapy, San Francisco, CA.

Tomm, K. (1991, June). *Reflexive questioning revisited.* Paper presented at the Therapeutic Conversations conference, Tulsa, OK.

White, M. (1986). Negative explanation, restraint, and double description: A template for family therapy. *Family Process, 25*, 168–184.

White, M. (1988a, Summer). The externalizing of the problem. *Dulwich Centre Newsletter*.

White, M. (1988b, Winter). The process of questioning: A therapy of literary merit. *Dulwich Centre Newsletter*, 8–14.

White, M. (1988c, October). *The process of therapy*. Institute conducted at the meeting of the American Association of Marriage and Family Therapy, New Orleans, LA.

White, M. (1988d, Spring). Saying hullo again: The incorporation of the lost relationship in the resolution of grief. *Dulwich Centre Newsletter*, 7–11.

White, M., & Epston, D. (1989, October). *Challenging stereotyping and opening space for alternatives*. Institute presented at the meeting of the American Association for Marriage and Family Therapy, San Francisco, CA.

White, M., & Epston, D. (1990). *Narrative means to therapeutic ends*. New York: Norton.

14

IF YOU REALLY KNEW ME: AN EXPLORATION OF THERAPEUTIC CONCERNS IN COLLABORATING WITH THE "DAMAGED" SELF

Reese Price

IN WRITING THIS paper I am thinking of many people who have sat across from me in my office over the years: people who have been sadistically tortured or sexually abused throughout their childhood by parents who are still represented internally and continue to have a profound influence on their daily social functioning. This paper represents an attempt to map some of the inherent difficulties in generating new possibilities in contexts of abuse and blatant impingement upon the child's attempts to generate a sense of personal autonomy and value.

I would like to begin by focusing on the issue of language. Consider, for example, the word "depression." Is it a word that references something that has an independent status in the world, or is it a constructed representation held in place by consensual agreement in a "language game"? In other words, are linguistic realities constructed, or are they referential to a reality that we are describing? The question represents a hotly debated topic in current philosophy of language and is now emerging as a topic of debate in our field as well.

The movement from the notion that language stands referential to an independent reality to a position that problems and their causes are constructions is tremendously important. It creates a focus on looking at what people are doing rather than being stuck in the morass of what they are.

Examine the following three statements.

1. "You are a depressive."
2. "You are under the influence of a depression."
3. "You are doing depression."

The first statement represents an objectifying of a person into a thing. It gives rise to classificatory schemes such as *DSM-III-R* and to the notion that there is an entity in the world referenced by the word "depression." This viewpoint leads to statements such as "You have an x," where "x" can denote anything from a personality disorder to an unresolved oedipal complex. It is unclear, however, whether this viewpoint can contribute in a meaningful way to collaborating with an individual around the theme of change. How, for example, do you change a depression? Psychiatry's answer increasingly seems to be: medicate it as an organic abnormality – a biologically based something.

The second statement is central to Michael White's (1988) notion of externalization. The therapist operates within the world view that you are dealing with a something, i.e., a depression. The exploration is then turned towards how this something is influencing this person's life and how he/she can empower him/herself relative to it. Questions about how one's life is being "recruited into this lifestyle" become central to engaging with the client. Alternate versions of how the person could be are explored and solidified en route to a new, more empowering story line. What one believes about the reality status of depression is bypassed, as the emphasis is on the person adopting a new, empowered sense of him/herself relative to the influence of "depression."

The third statement represents the notion that a depression is something that one does. It represents a process of engagement, both with oneself and with one's social environment, that can be languaged in a variety of ways. The central question for exploration is, "How do you do depression?" (O'Hanlon, 1990). Within this exploration there emerges the possibility of doing something different. There is, of course, a variation on this theme underlying the solution-oriented work of Steve de Shazer, where the question becomes, "What's happening when the individual isn't doing depression?" The focus becomes the amplification of those times when behaving depressively is not occurring.

The last two positions create the possibility of an actor who has the power to do something different relative to depression or in relation to how he does or doesn't do depression. It is within such therapeutic conversations that authoring a new story line or generating new possibilities and/or solutions can emerge most readily. There is, therefore, an emphasis on the person as actor, as a generative agent who possesses the capacity to change and empower himself or herself in life.

But what about those individuals whose sense of "authorship" has been undermined or fragmented to such an extent that there is an internally derived sense of another wrestling with one for control of the pen? Or what of those who are so under the influence of shame and guilt that the only "difference that makes a difference" is to sacrifice themselves for the interests of the other person? Or what if there is an inability to register or integrate "unique outcomes" in relationship to presenting difficulties such as self-hatred, shame, and a continued inability to generate self-valuing meanings in life? These and other questions come to mind as regards the clients I would like to focus on for the balance of this paper. They represent individuals who grew up in a matrix of double-binding, no-win situations where their experience of themselves is fundamentally discounted. Such discounting is not concerned with the truth or falsity — if there be such criteria — of a person's self-definition, but rather negates that person as the source of such a definition. In other words, while rejection amounts to the message, "You are wrong," disconfirmation says, in effect, "You do not exist" (Watzlawick, Beavin, and Jackson, 1967, p. 6).

What becomes of the capacity to generate a sense of self in relationship to such discounting? How are we to generate therapeutic conversations that will allow a new sense of authorship or self-generation to emerge in such contexts? The capacity to generate a viable sense of self has four fundamental components:

1. *Generativity*, a capacity to create meaning and orientation toward goals;
2. *Autonomy*, a capacity to stand authentically as a separate and distinct self;
3. *Self-valuation*, a capacity to ascribe positive attributes to oneself with attendant feelings of deservedness to succeed;
4. *Self-support*, an internalized capacity to nurture and soothe oneself in relationship to negative affect or experience or in relationship to goals.

Within the matrix of abuse and neglect, each of these components faces serious restraints on their development. The abuse is usually either denied as real, or the child is accused of causing it. Thus, the child is either mad ("crazy") or bad. For example, a client who was sexually abused by her father was beaten for lying when she told her mother; another was slapped across the face for being a "little whore." In such families it is understandably difficult for children to value themselves and to feel they deserve to take initiative in a meaningful way. Rather, they are forced to collude in distorting and/or denying reality in the service of the abusive family's need to maintain a facade of social propriety. It is not uncommon for such children to struggle with the fact that their parents play respected roles in the community while being abusive in private.

The compartmentalization of one's internal representations of significant others is often used to deal with the hostile and/or abusive realities in such families. The family colludes by labeling the perpetrator "good," and the abuse or neglect is either denied or defended as justifiable. In either case, the child is bad and at fault. The child's only out is to deal with this betrayal either by dissociating and developing amnesia for the experience or by using a process of splitting off from painful experiences in order to deny that the abuser is bad. This strategy exacts a high price, however, because the "goodness" of the abuser becomes a direct function of the perceived "badness" of the child. These children are often left with tremendous internally directed anger and "vicious internal voices" (Clarkson, 1988), or they compensate for their powerlessness by identifying with those who have abused them (Miller, 1983).

The other mechanism central to the functioning of these families is the concept of double binds (Watzlawick, Beavin, and Jackson, 1967). Such binds need not occur in a context of physical or sexual abuse, but in such situations they have the most damaging effect on the developing self. For example, after being sexually abused by her stepfather, one little girl was beaten when she tried to tell her mother and then was required by the mother to buy the stepfather underwear for his birthday. Another child, who witnessed her father beating her mother, interposed herself between them in response to a nonverbal plea from the mother and because she feared the mother would be killed. Instead, the child was beaten. Her reward was an admonishment from mother not to make her father so angry in the future. On other occasions, this same child was hit by the mother she tried to save. Finally, a third child was beaten by her mother when she tried to individuate; when she regressed in the face of such an attack, she was attacked by her father for being a "lazy, good-for-nothing bitch." The outcome of such untenable double binds is a no-win situation for the child, who internalizes an increasing sense of inadequacy and helplessness.

The other crucial dynamic in these families is the need to deny trauma in order to protect the image of the abusive parent as good (Clarkson, 1988; Miller, 1983). For example, in the context of hypnotically induced age regression, a client fantasized that her mother did not desert her at age five, leaving her in the hands of abusive grandparents. In a fetal position she intoned, "My mommy is not leaving! My mommy is a good mommy!" She repeated these words, eyes tightly shut, as the denial of what was happening deepened. Breaking that fantasy by repeating to her. "Your mommy is leaving; you are a good girl, and your mommy is leaving," lead her into the agony of the abandoned child's depression. The suicidal depression that she worked through in subsequent weeks pointed to both the power of and need for such tactics on the child's part, as a desperate attempt to maintain an image of the parent as a person who is capable of loving and caring about the child.

Children often deal with the unbearable reality of neglectful or abusive parents by maintaining an idealized image of the parents even if the cost is to deny reality and/or to label themselves as bad. The resulting compartmentalization of reality-based perceptions into good and bad by using denial and/or autogenically-based defenses is used by children to lessen their fear of or rage at their parent(s) (Masterson, 1981). Children also collude with these social/contextual factors in a desperate attempt to adapt to the incongruent social realities inherent in their family in an attempt to protect the possibility of being loved. For, "If I am the bad one, then I can change or do something that will make a difference in your treatment of and love for me."

The child becomes locked into an interactional matrix (Figure 1) that predicates the child's badness. The general form of this matrix can be found in the work of object relations theorists such as Masterson (1976, 1981). Masterson's model is based on the notion that social circumstances leave the child unable to formulate a coherent sense of self and other. He suggests that the mother rewards regressive, dependent behavior and withdraws libidinal supplies when the child makes attempts to individuate. This results in a rewarding object relations unit, "RORU," that is split off from a withdrawing object relations unit, "WORU" (Masterson, 1981). These split object representations in turn resonate with split self-representations: the compliant, nonindividuated, regressed self versus the self that is fundamentally bad if the child tries to be autonomous. In this model, the child attempts to deny the reality of the WORU and to elicit the RORU through regressive and non-autonomous behaviors.

FIGURE 1: *The Matrix*

GOOD OTHER		BAD OTHER
1. Social facade (faked)	D I	1. Exploitive/impinging
2. Wish, fantasy (imagined)	S	2. Abusive/criticial

3. Alternating ego state (Parent represents dissociative disorder)	S O C	A. Explosive/impulsive
		  B. Premeditated/compulsive
		  C. Premeditated/sadistic

4. Dependent upon compliant non-individuation (Masterson's RORU)	I A T	3. Withdrawing/undercutting (Masterson's WORU)

— DENIAL/DISSOCIATION —

GOOD SELF		BAD SELF
Non-individuated Compliant Perceives in "right way" Nongenerative, or if generative, no ownership Self-sacrificing An extension of the needs of the other	O N / D E N I A L	You misperceived You are causal in what happened You are always too much or too little You should feel shame/guilt Autonomy, personal agency labeled as "bad"

The matrix illustrated in Figure 1 serves as a template for "more of the same" in social interactions as an internalized complementarity between abuser and abused, exploiter and victim is continually enacted. This is held in place by the denial and/or dissociation demanded of the child in such families. It denigrates the ability to integrate one's perception of current social circumstances or to formulate either an alternative reality or a sense of sufficient generativity, autonomy, or value necessary to making a difference in one's current circumstances.

The danger at this point is the entification of the individual into a "borderline disorder" – a something – rather than focusing on the process of engagement that this matrix represents. This is something a child *does*, not a something the child *becomes*. It is my belief that in reacting against the objectification inherent in the latter, we are in danger of rejecting the benefits of understanding how one does this particular way of structuring social perceptions. There is a tremendous tyranny in this matrix, which generalizes into a perceptual set influencing the individual's social interaction throughout a lifetime, as well as his or her ability to form any viable sense of self-generativity, value, or "authorship."

I agree with the rejection of "borderline personality" as a definable something or as a doing that reduces a person to a *DSM-III-R* diagnostic cell. However, there is "a process of doing" that biases one's social perceptions. This bias transfers and colors the individual's ability to interact successfully both with the world at large and in a self-valuing manner with him/herself. It is a process of constructing compartmentalized internal representations of self and others in order to deal with the realities of abuse, neglect, and incongruence on the part of the child's primary caretakers.

Several difficulties emerge as a result. I would like to examine two of them: (1) internalization of the impinging and/or abusive "bad other," and (2) development of a sense of the "bad self," with an attendant sense of shame.

The notions that one's sense of self emerges due to internalized interpersonal conversations (Epston, Chapter 9) and that disqualifying inner dialogue can arise in contexts of abuse are important. My own experience is that there is a continuum of internalization of the abusive other that influences both social perception and resultant behaviors. For example, one can engage in an inner dialogue of self-disqualification, or experience disqualification via an internalized "other." The direct experience of the internalized other as a dissociated part-self which has more or less taken on a life of its own can be a frightening reality, as illustrated by the following cases.

Leslie developed night terrors accompanied by panic attacks. A deep trance was induced in which she revealed that her terror stemmed from a belief that something was lurking under her bed. Using imagery, she and her therapist crawled under her bed and discovered a werewolf, which was dragged to the light. This part-self, which was capable of direct communication, felt it could kill the client and survive with impunity. When it and client's conscious self realized that their survival was intertwined, the client's fear of homicide at night disappeared as a treatment issue. Later this dangerous figure transformed into another internal representation of Leslie's father.

Eighteen-year-old Tina came to therapy for various concerns, including sadomasochistic behavior. She actively sought abusive males with whom to engage in sadistic sexual scenarios and indicated that only in being brutalized by them could she find relief from internal agitation and self-hatred. Exploration revealed that the agitation was tied to an inner voice that was unremitting in its attacks on her. In two-chair work, the voice identified itself as Tim, who hated Tina for being a girl and who felt she deserved punishment for being female. He tormented Tina until she sought relief through external humiliation and abuse at the hands of a male with whom Tim, in his rage, identified. Over several sessions, Tim's role was renegotiated to be one of internal protector to Tina; this led her to stop seeking relationships with abusive others.

These are, of course, more extreme instances of this phenomenon, but they illustrate the notion that there is a continuum of the internal experience of the "internalized other." In abusive contexts where there is high potential for dissociation, the internalized other will take on a life of its own. The notion of impingement (McArthur, 1988) becomes important as individual authorship becomes a function of the capacity to individuate with a sense of personal agency. In the matrix of inter-action we are exploring, personal agency is directly attacked or engenders some form of rejection, as the goodness of self becomes a function of being a non-individuated compliant extension of the wants and needs of the other (Masterson, 1981). The pen of authorship often resides with the abusive and/or impinging other, who, dependent on his or her need to victimize and the enjoyment he/she derives from it, seeks to destroy the child's capacity to generate a viable sense of self.

Take, for example, the case of Gina, whose primary internal image was that of herself in a cage with her brother and father leering and circling the cage. One of her more poignant experiences in childhood was the death of the one person who valued her, an old man down the street. Several days after the funeral, her brother took her to the grave, raped her, spit in her face, and said, "Now he hates you, too." Or what of Joan, whose father molested her through age 18, aided by the fact that she dissociated and "went away," resulting in complete amnesia for the events. One of her father's favorite practices with his child was to pull out a medical book with multiple pictures of deformed women and make her look at these while intoning. "You look a lot like that, you know. No one will ever want something like you."

How can a child emerge from these circumstances with other than a sense of powerlessness? These children do not develop stories about themselves as bad. These stories are developed for them by others with a high need to victimize and humiliate in order to compensate for their own internal bankruptcy as human beings. They "impinge" on the child in order to empower themselves through the victimization, with the attendant desire to instill in the child a sense that something about him or her is causal in what is happening.

It is important to realize in this matrix of interaction that the child is bound to this dyad. In order to get whatever "good" there is from the other, the child must reduce himself or herself to an extension of what the other wants and needs; the child's sense of self is forfeited to the other. The child is taught that he/she is causal in what happened, or that his/her perceptions of what happened are not to be trusted (Is this real?). The abusive other also establishes an internalized sense of presence engendering a sense of fear, guilt, and shame if the child does attempt to individuate. Such "internalized other" opposition is paramount in such cases and must be depotentiated. Its presence may involve an attack by critical, demeaning internalized voices; or a projectively-based fear that the therapist will ridicule and attack one for being sad or needy; or a fearful look on a client's face as she scans the office anxiously because her mother wouldn't like her talking about her in this way.

The difficulties inherent in the empowerment of such folk are further compounded by their internalized sense of shame about themselves and their sense of "badness." They are unable to assimilate alternative perspectives of themselves that are completely incongruent with their "abuser/abused" internal images.

A poignant example of the above occurred in my office recently when I told a person with whom I was working to have a nice day. The next meeting she came back in confusion, knowing I had said something to her about the day but being unable to recall the word "nice" in relationship to "day." Her deep internal sense of undeservedness and sense of self as despicable, because she needed anything positive in her life, completely precluded her assimilation of anything positive from me or from anybody else.

As noted by Adams-Westcott and her colleagues in Chapter 13, the process of disqualification can render individuals incapable of languaging important elements of their experience. They are usually unable to feel a congruency with positive attributional statements about themselves due to an abiding sense of incompetency, undeservedness (due to their sense of badness), and an abiding sense of the presence of the devaluing other. Further, their internal representations of themselves preclude assimilation of anything good about themselves because of the cognitive dissonance that arises when presented with the spectre of such information.

The scope of any chapter is limited. My goal here has been to suggest a map of the internal representations that arise due to the external realities of the abused child's life. In joining the reality of the disconfirmed self, one enters into the landscape of exploited children who were never loved for themselves, while encountering issues ranging from multiple self-representations to the terrible nothingness of self-dissolution. The dilemma of such children is tragic; it is captured in the utterance of a woman who after seven years is still unable to accept the fact that her mother is dead: "If I admit my mother is dead, then I can never win the love of my mother, and if I can't win her love, then no one will ever love me, 'cause if you mother can't love you, who can?"

It has been said that a map is not the territory (Watzlawick, Weakland, and Fisch, 1974), but a good map accurately references the territory. Similarly, language not only constructs experience but also references the constructive processes through which we register our experiences. When such constructions constitute a mode of perception that has generalized across social circumstances, then theoretical language can serve a useful referential function; it provides a map of "reality." My argument becomes that the referential function is best used to describe a process of engagement, a mode of doing, rather than a classificatory label that reduces someone into a diagnostic object, i.e., borderline personality disorder. In so doing, I would like to argue against throwing out the baby (an understanding of the way children learn to structure their perception of themselves and others due to incongruencies inherent in impinging, abusive families) with the bathwater (of the pathologizing of clients with labels such as "borderline").

I have offered a partial map of the constructed "reality" of these individuals. It is an incomplete rendering, and little has been said about treatment implications. My hope is that others who are thinking about the generating of new possibilities, differences that make a difference, and new story lines in therapy will join those clients who have been "recruited" into this way of perceiving in exploring avenues of empowerment relative to the matrix I have described. I hope the map offered here will prove useful in formulating new means of effective therapeutic conversations to allow the release of such clients from the tyranny of both their shame and their continued victimization by internalized others, while supporting them in accepting and grieving for the reality of what fate bequeathed them as parents.

Commentary

Stephen Gilligan

> Life is understood backwards but is lived forwards.
>
> *Kierkegaard*

I WANT TO FIRST acknowledge the compassion and sensitivity Reese Price shows in his writings and as a therapist. His appreciation of the pain and struggle of his clients is impressive, as is his commitment to support them in "working through" their processes. He seems especially attuned to childhood traumas suffered by (apparently most, if not all) his clients, and suggests that such traumas create a "damaged self" that makes change or developmental growth quite difficult. This theoretical assertion gives rise to a therapy approach that emphasizes "joining the reality of the disconfirmed self" to explore "the landscape of exploited children who were never loved for themselves."

But therein lies the rub. Even if we took the traditional (though, to me, unhelpful) view of explaining a person's present in terms of a historical past, this "damaged child" metaphor is misleading in that it reduces an entire lifetime of experiences to a single frame of reference. As Michael Ventura (in Hillman and Ventura, 1992) cogently argues:

> . . . the concept of the inner child *represses our actual childhoods* and concentrates the fear, vulnerability, failure, and grief we feel as adults into an image that we can detach from our adult life — an image easily marketable and played upon . . . we project the needs of the present onto the past, then try to fill those needs in that projected past via the therapist. (Thus, in one move, not only is our actual childhood repressed by the ideal of the inner child, but the present is both repressed and diminished by being treated as merely a symptom caused by the past.)

287

Memory is mutable, as we all know. Our perceptions of the past change as we change. But to introduce the ideology of the inner child into how we remember is in effect to substitute *a fictional character* for ourselves. That is what therapists who use this method do to their client: they introduce a fictional character, the pure and wounded inner child, into the client's psyche; then this fictional character, like the protagonist of a novel, constellates one's memories around it, highlighting them to suit the theme of the character. A subtle, even insidious, transformation takes place. What happens to memories that don't fit this new character, events that are out of character, in which the ideal of the inner child could not have taken part? Those events lose importance, they fade, drained of *the ability to be remembered* because this creation through which we are now experiencing memory can't inhabit what happened. So parts of our life grow dimmer, dimmer, dimmer, until they disappear. This is what any ideology does — religious, political, psychological, feminist, mythological — when used as a lens for viewing one's life. The inner child is a fictional character produced by an ideology and introduced into one's memory, and like a computer virus, its ultimate result is to repress, distort, and eventually even erase memory. (pp. 73–74)

Ventura's comments could be applied to other "explanatory metaphors" used in psychotherapy, such as the historical past ("He's that way because of childhood experiences") and diagnostic categories ("She is that way because she's depressed"). When we give up our reliance on such metaphors, we are free to regard people in terms of their resources and their interests.

Consider, for example, the therapy that Milton Erickson (reported in Zeig, 1980) did with the "African Violet Queen of Milwaukee." She was a 52-year-old wealthy spinster who lived alone in her big house in Milwaukee. She ventured out of the house only to attend church services, and her relatives grew increasingly concerned that she was depressed and suicidal. Her nephew, a physician who knew Erickson, asked him to visit the woman during an upcoming trip to Milwaukee in hopes of somehow helping her.

Erickson arranged to meet the woman in her home. From talking with her and touring the home, he observed that (1) she was very isolated and emotionally flat, with a passive and obedient response style, (2) she expressed a deep sense of commitment to her church community (even though she didn't actively participate in it), and (3) she grew some beautiful African violet plants in the sunroom of her house. True to his commitment to work with what the client offered, Erickson grew curious about how the latter two values might be used to increase the woman's participation in the community.

He got the woman to agree to raise many more African violets. He then directed her to give one of these plants to individuals or families in her church community each time they experienced an important transitional event such as a birth, death, illness, marriage, and so on. As Erickson reported, she followed these instructions and became "too busy to be depressed." Furthermore, she became quite active in the community and earned the appreciation and attention of many people. In fact, when she died over 20 years later, she was mourned and lovingly remembered as the "African Violet Queen of Milwaukee."

What's remarkable to me about this case is how Erickson appreciated the woman in terms of her actual life space. Instead of reducing her to some diagnostic label or metaphorical description, he approached her as a unique person with many distinct values and interests. He demonstrated that while persons stuck in problems typically restrict their attention to a single frame, therapists searching for solutions must widen their lens to include many other aspects of the person as well. Often this is not easy, for such information may not be given in the person's presentation; however, it is essential if the person is to get back to playing with a full deck in the game of life. Therapy becomes a conversation that uses these additional values to allow new ways of being to develop.

In closing, I want to emphasize that in such an approach, it is perfectly legitimate to make room for a person's past experiences. The important thing is to appreciate that they have neither fixed meaning nor causal potency. With that in mind, therapy can continue to focus on whatever works for each individual.

REFERENCES

Clarkson, P. (1988). Ego state dilemmas of abused children. *Transactional Analysis Journal, 18*, 85–93.

Hillman, J., & Ventura, M. (1992). *We've had a hundred years of psychotherapy and the world's getting worse.* New York: HarperCollins.

McArthur, D. S. (1988). *Birth of self in adulthood.* Northvale, NJ: Aronson.

Masterson, J. F. (1976). *Psychotherapy of the borderline adult.* New York: Brunner/Mazel.

Masterson, J. F. (1981). *Narcissistic and borderline disorders: An integrated developmental approach.* New York: Brunner/Mazel.

Miller, A. (1983). *For your own good.* New York: Farrar, Straus, Giroux.

O'Hanlon, W. H. (1990). Personal communication.

Watzlawick, P., Beavin, J. B., & Jackson, D. D. (1967). *Pragmatics in human communication: A study of interactional patterns, pathologies and paradoxes.* New York: Norton.

Watzlawick, P., Weakland, J., & Fisch, R. (1974). *Change: Principles of problem formation and problem resolution.* New York: Norton.

White, M. (1988, Summer). The externalizing of the problem. *Dulwich Centre Newsletter.*

Zeig, J. (1980). *A teaching seminar with Milton H. Erickson, M.D.* New York: Brunner/Mazel.

15

INVITATIONS TO NEW STORIES:
USING QUESTIONS TO EXPLORE
ALTERNATIVE POSSIBILITIES

Jill Freedman
Gene Combs

A NUMBER OF years ago, when we were using more ideas from strategic therapy than we use now, we saw a family who came to therapy because Kathy, the 12-year-old-daughter, would not go to school. She didn't like it that her classmates at the girls' school she attended were showing increasing interest in boys, alcohol, and drugs. She had the idea that if she started thinking about any of these girls when she was involved in an activity, she would somehow become like them. This fear led to some problematic behaviors. For example, if she found herself thinking about one of her classmates while she was putting on a shoe, she took it off and put it on again. She would repeat this behavior until she was positive that she had completed it with none of her classmates in mind. She approached opening and closing doors, turning on and off lights, and a number of other activities in the same way. Because these girls surrounded Kathy in the classroom, she had to contend not only with her thoughts but also with the possibility of hearing their voices or seeing one of them while she was opening her desk or changing into gym shoes. She therefore found it intolerable to be in the classroom and refused to go to school.

We had met with Kathy and her parents five times with little change in her situation when they let us know that the two older children were home from school for Christmas vacation. We arranged for the whole family to come in, splitting the group for the first part of the session, with one of us (JF) seeing the siblings and one of us (GC) seeing the parents.

In the session with the siblings I learned that the parents both smoked heavily and that all the children, especially Kathy, were very worried about the effects of the smoking on their parents' health. Kathy was terrified that they would die.

I was struck by this discussion about the parents' smoking because Kathy seemed more actively involved than at any other point in therapy. I asked her, "Who would be in greater danger – your parents if they continue smoking or you if you go to school?" When she answered, "Mom and Dad," I began to wonder if Kathy would be willing to make a bargain, going to school in return for her parents' quitting smoking. To test my idea, I inquired further: "Are you the kind of person who will take a risk for the welfare of someone you care about?" She said that she was, and her brother and sister agreed, citing an incident in which she had rescued a neighbor's toddler from a locked bathroom through a small second-floor window. "Would it help you to do something that seemed dangerous if you knew that it was really benefitting someone important to you?" She said that it would. I asked, "How would it help?" and she answered that the benefit would put things in perspective. It would no longer seem so dangerous. I asked, "Could you go to school if you knew it might save your parents' lives?" She unhesitatingly answered, "Yes." I asked, "What would you do if you looked at someone and thought you might become like them?" She answered, "Just concentrate on the work and on being there." I asked, "Even if it is really difficult, if you agree to do something are you a person of your word?" She said she was.

During a break we (GC and JF) conferred and agreed that the parents were very committed to doing whatever it would take to get Kathy back in school, so we were hopeful that they would be willing to give up smoking. When we met together with the whole family, we stated that we all knew how important the parents thought it was that Kathy go to school. They had already put a lot of time and energy into this. We said we had just discovered how important it was to Kathy that her parents quit smoking and that she was willing to put time and energy into making that happen. We then proposed the trade, and asked Kathy if she would go to school if her parents would quit smoking. Beaming, she said she would. We asked the parents if they would quit smoking if Kathy went to school. They too agreed.

When we met again two weeks later we were shocked to learn what had happened. Both parents were still smoking, but Kathy had gone to school every day since our meeting. Kathy continued going to school and her parents continued smoking. Although she still wanted them to quit smoking, she never threatened to stop going to school. The repetitive behavior seemed to just disappear. We found this extremely puzzling.

It wasn't until about six months later that we found a way of thinking about what had happened that made sense to us. We began wondering if in the mental search involved in answering my (JF) questions Kathy had experienced a different way of being. That is, when I asked, "What would you do if you looked at someone and thought you might become like them?" Kathy vividly imagined herself in the context of school, concentrating on the work without fear taking over her experience. Her answer, "Just concentrate on the work and being there," implied just such an experience. She must have experienced herself as someone who can take risks and can handle being in dangerous situations by focusing on the task at hand rather than the danger. In answering the questions, she entered a different reality than the one she usually inhabited. She experienced herself as someone who could go to school. So she did.

We wondered what would have happened if we hadn't been so sure of the parents' willingness to do whatever it took to help Kathy go back to school. If we had asked them questions similar to the ones we asked Kathy, might they have entered into a different experience of themselves, one in which they were already nonsmokers?

This incident was a turning point in our way of thinking about and practicing therapy. Our background in Ericksonian approaches grounded us in the importance of associational searches, experiential learning, and alternative realities. However, we had not experienced or thought about questions in this arena. We became fascinated with the notion of questions as invitations to alternative experience – to new realities where people can meaningfully encounter new possibilities and new knowledge. We began to think of questions as a way of *generating experience* rather than as a way of gathering information.

QUESTIONS AS INTERVENTIONS

Other authors (e.g., Fleuridas, Nelson, and Rosenthal, 1986; Lipchik and de Shazer, 1986; O'Hanlon and Weiner-Davis, 1989; Penn, 1985; Tomm, 1987a, 1987b, 1988; White, 1988)* have discussed the idea that questions, traditionally thought of as functioning to gather infor-

---

*The work of Michael White and of Karl Tomm has been especially inspirational and influential to us as we develop our ideas about questions and how to use them in therapy.

mation, can also be viewed as interventions. This idea may have been expressed first by the Milan team (Selvini Palazzoli, Boscolo, Cecchin, and Prata, 1980) when they asked whether change could occur solely through their interview process, which consisted largely of circular questions, without a final intervention.

Karl Tomm (1988) has described four main categories of interventive questions: lineal, circular, strategic, and reflexive. We are most interested in *reflexive* questions, about which he says:

> One major presupposition behind these questions is that the therapeutic system is coevolutionary and what the therapist does is to trigger reflexive activity in the family's preexisting belief systems. The therapist endeavors to interact in a manner that opens space for the family to see new possibilities and evolve more freely of their own accord. (1988, p. 9)

We believe that, although our intent was different, the effect of the questions that facilitated the change in Kathy was reflexive. They invited her to compare beliefs and meanings from different domains to experience herself as a person who could go to school.

What we address in this paper is a specific function of reflexive questions, one that we believe deserves emphasis: *inviting people into a vivid, robust experience of alternative possibilities*. In our own work and in supervising other therapists, we have found reflexive questions to be more effective when we plan with this function in mind.

THE NARRATIVE METAPHOR

Shortly after our discoveries with Kathy and her family, we became acquainted with the text or *narrative* analogy through the work of Michael White (1988, 1989; White and Epston, 1990). Drawing from the work of social scientists such as Clifford Geertz (1983, 1986) and Jerome Bruner (1986, 1987), White and Epston argue for "a therapy of literary merit." They compare a life story with a literary text and discuss the notion that in reading any "actual" text a reader constructs a "virtual" text, filling in gaps and implications with details, events, and meanings so that a story that is unique to that reader during that reading emerges. This notion is an assertion that to "read" a text is actually to "write" it and that each "rereading" offers a context for "rewriting." Psychotherapy then can be considered as an opportunity for people to reauthor their lives.

Gregory Bateson (1972, 1979) believed that people make meaning by situating events and ideas in stories. The narrative metaphor expands Bateson's notion by asserting that people can change the stories they tell themselves about their lives by recovering events at odds with the dominant story and performing meaning on those events as a way of authoring new stories. These new stories can then change people's ideas about themselves and about what is possible for them. Using this metaphor we can look back at what Kathy did as a process of reauthoring her life.*

QUESTIONS TO ELICIT
EXPERIENCE OF NEW STORIES

We have found these two ideas—that questions can be used to generate experience and that people make sense of their lives by organizing their experience into stories—extremely helpful in guiding the questions we ask. The idea of using questions to generate experience reminds us to ask questions that require internal involvement and exploration to find their answers. The narrative metaphor guides us in asking questions that invite amplification of answers so that the experience generated has a past and a future, characters, a context, and meaning—in other words, so that it's a story.

It is important to remember that what we are after in asking questions is the elicitation of meaningful new experience for clients. To be effective, we must attend closely to family members as they answer each question, noting their responses and adjusting the process so as to elicit involvement at an experiential level. No question, no matter how creative and well-planned, is guaranteed to be interesting or meaningful to a given client. Conversely, questions that seem trivial to a therapist sometimes evoke compelling experiences for a client. As Karl Tomm says, " . . . the *actual* effect of any particular intervention with a client is *always* determined by the client, not the therapist. The intentions and consequent actions of the therapist only trigger a response; they never determine it" (1987a, pp. 4–5). So, as we ask each question, we note closely how the family or individual responds and adjust our verbal and nonverbal behavior accordingly.

We've developed some categories that we find useful in formulating these kinds of questions. They are by no means complete, but they are a useful starting place. The three main categories are: *opening space questions, story development questions,* and *meaning questions.*

---

*We can also look at the story of Kathy's therapy and our ideas about it as a new experience in our lives, helping to forge a new story about ourselves as therapists.

OPENING SPACE QUESTIONS

We have found four areas of inquiry that seem particularly useful in opening space for recovering and generating alternative experience and knowledge. They are *exceptions, point of view, time,* and *circumstance.* Our intention in asking these questions is to recover and develop experiences within these realms that are at odds with the dominant story. The following are examples of these types of questions.

Exceptions*

In describing the narrative metaphor we stated that people can change their "self stories" by recovering events at odds with dominant stories and performing meaning on the exceptional events. Asking questions to identify exceptions to the problem description is a straightforward way of recovering such events.** The following questions invite people to *recover experiences at odds with the dominant story*:

- When was the last time that the arguing could have taken control of your relationship but didn't?
- Even though you don't usually succeed at this sort of thing, have you ever surprised yourself by succeeding a little bit?
- In what situations do you all co-operate as a family?

Questions such as these invite people to sort through their personal experiences in a different way — they are invited to notice events that do not fit the dominant story, rather than continuing to accumulate evidence of the dominant story. In highlighting different events, they are opening space for the authoring of new stories.

Point of View

We cannot really step outside of ourselves (see Rorty, 1991a, 1991b), but asking questions about other points of view can be a way of eliciting experience of what Karl Tomm calls "internalized others." Having

---

*This term, popularized by the Brief Family Therapy Center team (de Shazer, 1985), is what we use to refer to what Michael White (1988) has called "unique outcomes." Unique outcomes are "those outcomes that contradict aspects of the problem-saturated description." (p. 8)

**People often spontaneously mention exceptions when describing the problem. In such cases, rather than asking an *opening space* question we can simply respond to what they have mentioned. For example, if someone says, "Once in a while we do this well, but usually . . . (and then proceeds to describe the dominant story) . . . " we can be curious about the "once in a while" part just as we would be curious about the answer to an *exceptions* question.

an experience of an internalized other or altering one's point of view by the attempt to stand in another person's shoes offers the possibility of new perceptions, new feelings, and new conclusions. These questions suggest *exploration of other people's realities*:

- What would your father say about this dilemma?
- Can you understand how from my point of view you are ready to take on this responsibility?
- Who in the family is most hopeful that you will succeed? . . . Who next?

In order to answer these questions, people experience other points of view. These then add new dimensions of experience, knowledge, and possibility.

Time

Michael White and David Epston write:

> Social scientists became interested in the text analogy following observations that, although a piece of behavior occurs in time in such a way that it no longer exists in the present by the time it is attended to, the meaning that is ascribed to the behavior survives across time. (1990, p. 9)

In asking opening space questions about time we are interested in directing attention to pieces of behavior that could carry different meaning into the present.

One use of questions about time is to *elicit knowledge of competence from the past* that can be incorporated to change current self-image or functioning:

- At what time in your life would you have been most confident that you could have accomplished this?
- When were the two of you able to communicate in a way that was satisfying?
- At what point did you know that your partner was someone you wanted to share your life with?

These questions tend to bring forth internal experiences (memories) of behaviors and knowledge that may be currently relevant.

Questions can also be used to *invite attention to improvement over time* as a way of changing self-image and bringing forth knowledge of continuing change:

- Is this motivation to do something different a growing thing or has it been fairly steady?
- When you look back and see how far you've come, what do you discover about yourself?
- How is what you are doing now different from what you used to do?

These questions tend to open space to notice trends and movement. Other questions may be oriented to the future. Peggy Penn has suggested that

> ... if you ask a family member a hypothetical question regarding future events, because the event is only now being considered, the system is free to create a new map. Then the communication of these new ideas about the future becomes important information introduced back into the present "time" of the system. (1985, p. 300)

Future questions can invite clients to *rehearse positive occurrences in the future*:

- After this problem is resolved, what might your family be doing differently?
- How will you know when it's time to end therapy?
- If we think of this accomplishment as the beginning of a trend, what do you think the next step will be?

It is sometimes easier for people to recognize alternatives when they are considering the future than when they are living in the dominant story through which they experience the present. Once an alternative possibility is experientially recognized in the future, it may open space for thinking differently about present possibilities.

Future questions can also motivate change by *extending a negative reality into the future to emphasize it*:

- If the problem continues into the future, continuing to get worse, what will be happening ten years from now?
- If bulimia continues to control more and more of your life, what effect will this have on your future?
- In what ways will your life be different when your kids go away to school if the problem has not been resolved than if it has been resolved?

Michael White refers to these kinds of questions as a way of collapsing time, which " . . . exposes the trend and enables family members to challenge any future invitations to acclimatise to the influential nature of the problem" (1987, p. 53).

Circumstance and Explanation
of Circumstance

Although problems are often born of particular circumstances, in the generalizations that are made in storying lives descriptions of people often become problem-saturated. Another way of opening space for people to see their capabilities and possibilities beyond the problem-saturated dominant story is by using questions inviting *explorations of hypothetical circumstances*.

In composing these questions we try to choose circumstances that may elicit responses that could be useful in the current situation. The following questions are examples:

- If one of your children had been born with a serious illness, how do you think you would have pulled together to face the crisis?
- If keeping your job depended on you and your wife learning to communicate with each other, what would you be doing differently?
- Suppose that one night, while you were asleep, there was a miracle and this problem was solved. How would you know? What would be different?*

One way to open space for the listener to experience present circumstances differently and perhaps even to respond differently is to consider different explanations for the circumstances. These questions ask the listener to consider *new explanations of present circumstances*:

- If you were to discover with certainty that your mother works overtime not to avoid your Little League games but to provide the things you want for your future, how would that knowledge change things for you?
- If your daughter revealed that secretly she does not feel disdain towards you but in fact hopes to be like you when she's an adult, what difference would that make?

*This is the "miracle question" of the Brief Family Therapy Center team (de Shazer, 1988, p. 5).

- If you were to discover that your poor job performance is a reflection not of your worth but of being in the wrong job, what might you be prompted to do?

Our hope in asking these questions is not to convince people of any particular hypothetical explanation, but rather to open space for experiential exploration of alternative explanations, ones that might include new possibilities and new knowledge.

STORY DEVELOPMENT QUESTIONS

Once space opens for a person or family to experience an alternative possibility, we find it useful to switch to questions that invite the development of a story around that possibility. The experience can then become connected to the past and the future, to a particular context, and to people. It can become a part of one's life instead of an isolated experience. As such it is more likely to have an effect on self-image and future possibilities.

Consider the question cited under *explorations of hypothetical circumstances*: "If one of your children had been born with a serious illness, how do you think you would have pulled together to face the crisis?" This question invites a feeling of motivation or commitment or perhaps a glimmer of the ability to work hard. If we follow it by asking, "And what would each of you have done to support each other as you faced the crisis?" the couple might begin to actually imagine the words, looks, and actions they would exchange in functioning as a team. If we then ask, "Who in your current life would be most affected if you were to develop such a relationship?" this new possibility may become attached to other people and the problem may be seen in a more relational context. We could continue asking questions to develop the story:

- What do you think would stand out for that person as the most important change in your relationship with her or him?
- How would that make a difference for her or him?
- What is the effect on your future of knowing that you can make that kind of difference?

As people answer these questions, the initial possibility becomes a story that extends far beyond the first experience of answering, "If one of your children had been born with a serious illness, how do you think you would have pulled together to face the crisis?"

My (GC) mother was an editor of the school paper when she was in college, and she told me many more times than she needed to that any good news story answered six questions: "Who?" "What?" "When?" "Where?" "Why?" and "How?" We find this rule of thumb useful in formulating story development questions, although we don't use all of these questions in each instance. We ask "'Why?" least often, but it can be useful in inviting an experience of motivation. We particularly like "How?" questions, maybe because we are so fascinated with the creative ways that people do things that we only find out about when we ask, "How?" This question invites people to notice their own competence and enter an experience so that they can specify details. In so doing they become their own models and instructors.

In general, we ask story development questions as long as they seem relevant to the issues at hand and are responded to with interest and new information.

MEANING QUESTIONS

Opening space questions allow glimpses of alternative possibilities. Story development questions invite people to experientially situate themselves within those possibilities. As a new story becomes "real" for a family or individual, focusing on the meaning of that story helps assure that the story is an experience that matters. Here are some examples of meaning questions:

- What does that mean to you?
- What does this new perspective tell you about yourself?
- What does finding out that your spouse appreciates this about you let you know about your relationship?
- Now that you see your family in this way what do you know about your relationships to one another that you didn't know before?

Meaning questions work more directly with beliefs than the other two types of questions. They invite people to examine the implications of the emerging story within the domain of values and beliefs.

USING ALL THREE TYPES OF
QUESTIONS TOGETHER

A sequence of questions, developing from and building on subsequent answers, is more effective than any single question in evoking a robust experience of an alternative possibility. To give a flavor of how these questions can work together, we'll go back to the first set of examples under *time*, this time following an opening space question with story development and meaning questions, noting the question category after each question:

> At what time in your life would you have been most confident that you could have accomplished this? (*opening space*) What did you know about yourself then that perhaps you have lost track of since then? (*meaning*) What experience was most important in supporting that belief in yourself? (*story development*) How did you prepare yourself for that experience? (*story development*) Where did that experience happen? (*story development*) When did you first realize the importance of that experience? (*story development*) Who else knew about that experience at the time? (*story development*) How did it affect them? (*story development*) What did it mean to them? (*meaning*) What details of that experience stand out for you now? (*story development*) What does that time in your life tell you about yourself? (*meaning*) How is that knowledge important in beginning this accomplishment now? (*story development*) If the you from that experience was doing this now, how would she proceed? (*story development*) What would be your next step in making this beginning? (*story development*) What would it mean to your coworkers when they see you taking that step? (*meaning*) Who else might appreciate this accomplishment? (*story development*)

We hope that as you read the preceding questions you constructed your own imaginary dialogue, filling in the client's responses to each question. As you did, you probably noticed that the conversation could take many possible turns. It is unlikely that each question in any predetermined list will follow a person's last response smoothly. In practice, each question must emerge from the dialogue of the moment, and sometimes it is not a question that is called for, but a nod, a smile, or a statement.

Questions with exactly the same wording as the ones we have been describing can be asked with the intention of eliciting a particular response. Such questions can be therapeutic, but they risk closing down creativity rather than opening space for new experiences. They also risk bringing forth a relationship in which people look to a therapist rather than to their own experience for answers. Both of these factors work against the kind of experiential involvement in new possibilities for which we are arguing.

What is important is not the elegance of each question but the quality of each client's experience. Therapists using questions to facilitate experience of alternative possibilities must attend carefully to their moment-by-moment relationship with clients. Questions work best to help people experience new stories as "real" when therapists ask them with an attitude of curiosity, celebrating their lack of precognition rather than bemoaning it (Anderson and Goolishian, 1991). With such an attitude, therapists find the emerging stories as suspenseful, exciting, and meaningful as do their clients. Perhaps that's the reason we find ourselves working more and more in this fashion.

Commentary

Jeff Chang

WHAT IS THERE to be added to the literature on the questioning process? We already know about circular questioning (Fleuridas, Nelson, and Rosenthal, 1986), future oriented questioning (Penn, 1985), purposeful solution-focused (Lipchik and de Shazer, 1986) or solution-oriented (O'Hanlon and Weiner-Davis, 1989) questions, intentionality in the use of various sorts of questions (Tomm, 1987a, 1987b, 1988), and questions based on Michael White's cybernetic model (White, 1988). As a field, we seem preoccupied with questions. The idea that questions are interventions, not merely information-gathering techniques, is not new. Do we need another paper on questioning? These were my thoughts as I began to dig into Jill Freedman and Gene Combs' offering to this volume.

These thoughts spring from some musings that I've had lately, the stuff of lunch bag seminars and coffee room conversations. Our field (whatever that means: brief-constructionist-systemic therapy or, as Bill O'Hanlon [1992] has called us, "fourth wavers") has adopted the metaphor of "therapy as conversation" wholeheartedly. The pioneering work of Harlene Anderson and Harry Goolishian (1988) started us in this direction, and the field has followed. The process of narrative development through therapeutic conversation has more recently been operationalized in a variety of ways (e.g., de Shazer, 1991; White and Epston, 1990). No matter how you slice it, therapists of our ilk are essentially wordsmiths. We are immersed in a language-based description of therapy (Real, 1990). The title of this volume bears witness to this trend. Our preoccupation with the minutiae of the questioning process reflects this as well.

Let us step back to view our own development as a field. In tracing the evolution of systemic/constructionist therapies, Real (1990) has distinguished three stages. In the first, the expanded strategic phase, represented by the early work of the Milan associates, the central metaphor for therapy was that of a game. In the Batesonian information-based phase, the central metaphor was that of double description; the central task for therapy was introducing new information into the system, i.e., "news of difference." Seeing where we've come from, using the conversation metaphor as a third stage to describe therapy has its merits. It evokes an experience of collaboration and seems preferable to simply seeing therapy as a game to be won or as the process of perturbing systems or introducing new information to passive receptors.

However, I've wondered whether the metaphor of therapy as conversation is an unnecessarily limiting one. Although it does imply collaboration, I would suggest — and others would seem to agree — that this metaphor tends to suggest that therapy is just words and does not adequately reflect the need for clients to experience themselves and their situation differently. For instance, Goldner (1990) has pointed out the inadequacy of the conversation metaphor when applied to the task of altering the experience of both genders concerning men's violence toward women. White and Epston (1990, p. 14, footnote) state the term conversation is not "sufficient as a description of an approach to the restorying of experience." Our field's preoccupation with verbiage in general, and the questioning process in particular, reflects a lack of attention to experience. Many times I've heard the comment "What a great question!" in response to an intervention that triggered a useful response in a client, as if it were the question alone that had determined the client's experience. For me, "therapy as conversation" falls short of capturing the essence of what we do.

So I embarked upon reading this chapter with a sense of uncertainty about whether I would find anything really different from what I've read before. The subtitle of the paper, "Using questions to explore alternative possibilities" sounded language-bound. I thought I would be reading about more ways to ask the same questions. That misconception was quickly dispelled. Freedman and Combs call us to strategize about our questioning with the aim of "inviting people into vivid, robust experience of alternative possibilities." They anchor their readers in this task by reminding us periodically that this is the principle which guides their questioning. However, it is not experience for its own sake that they are advocating. Their use of White and Epston's (1990) text analogy amplifies their emphasis on the experiential; alternative experiences are broadened into new stories as clients are invited to actively read and reauthor the stories that are their lives. While the paper offers a practical guide for the structuring and sequencing of various sorts of questions within an interview, they avoid "cookbook-ishness" by inviting us to respect and listen to our clients and attend to the process in interviews.

I see Freedman and Combs' paper as reflecting (and contributing to) a movement in our field away from a fixation on language and conversation, toward a renewed respect for the experiential. I do not think that we are going full circle, back to the days of encounter groups and gestalt therapy and experience for its own sake. Psychotherapy has evolved from a past focus, through a present, here-and-now focus, to a future focus (O'Hanlon, 1991). It appears that we fourth wavers are moving to a place of valuing the experiential — calling forth past and present experience in order to rewrite the future, rather than ignoring the experiential domain, or worse yet, dismissing it. As one who has operated solely in the domain of language, I have come to have a new respect for pathways to experience other than language. Art, music, and movement provide wonderful pathways to "vivid, robust experience." As an unabashed fourth waver, I have found that when I shed my excess theoretical baggage I have much in common with therapists who follow other pathways to experience, particularly when they, too, shed their excess theoretical baggage. Perhaps therapists of the "fifth wave" will preserve the collaborative aspect of the conversation metaphor but include other pathways to experience.

REFERENCES

Anderson, H., & Goolishian, H. A. (1988). Human systems as linguistic systems: Preliminary and evolving ideas about the implications of clinical theory. *Family Process, 27* (4), 371–393.

Anderson, H., & Goolishian, H. (1991, July). The client is the expert: A not-knowing approach to therapy. In *A collaborative language systems approach to therapy: New directions in theory and practice.* A reader pepared by Friends of the Houston–Galveston Institute.

Bateson, G. (1972). *Steps to an ecology of mind.* New York: Ballantine Books.

Bateson, G. (1979). *Mind and nature: A necessary unity.* New York: Dutton.

Bruner, J. (1986). *Actual minds, possible worlds.* Cambridge, MA: Harvard University Press.

Bruner, J. (1987). Life as narrative. *Social Research, 54* (1).

de Shazer, S. (1985). *Keys to solution in brief therapy.* New York: Norton.

de Shazer, S. (1988). *Clues: Investigation solutions in brief therapy.* New York: Norton.

de Shazer, S. (1991). *Putting difference to work.* New York: Norton.

Fleuridas, C., Nelson, T. S., & Rosenthal, D. M. (1986). The evolution of circular questions: Training family therapists. *Journal of Marital and Family Therapy, 12,* 113–127.

Geertz, C. (1983). *Local knowledge: Further essays in interpretive anthropology.* New York: Basic Books.

Geertz, C. (1986). Making experiences, authoring selves. In V. Turner & E. Bruner (Eds.), *The anthropology of experience.* Chicago: University of Illinois Press.

Goldner, V. (1990). *Feminism and system practice: Two critical traditions in transformation.* Conference sponsored by the Family Theapy Program, Faculty of Medicine, University of Calgary, November 1990.

Lipchik, E., & de Shazer, S. (1986). The purposeful interview. *Journal of Strategic and Systemic Therapies, 5,* 88–99.

O'Hanlon, W. H. (1991). *Solution oriented approaches with children, adolescents, and their families.* Workshop sponsored by Alberta Children's Hospital, Calgary, Alberta, November 1991.

O'Hanlon, W. H. (1992). Not systemic, not strategic: Still clueless after all these years. *Journal of Strategic and Systemic Therapies, 10,* 105–110.

O'Hanlon, W. H., & Weiner-Davis, M. (1989). *In search of solutions: A new direction in psychotherapy.* New York: Norton.

Penn, P. (1985). Feed-forward: Future questions, future maps. *Family Process, 24* (3), 229–310.

Real, T. (1990). The therapeutic use of self in constructionist/systemic therapy. *Family Process, 29,* 355–272.

Rorty, R. (F1991a). *Objectivity, relativism, and truth: Philosophical papers, Volume 1.* New York: Cambridge University Press.

Rorty, R. (1991b). *Essays on Heidegger and others: Philosophical papers, Volume 2.* New York: Cambridge University Press.

Selvini Palazzoli, M., Boscolo, L., Cecchin, G., & Prata, G. (1980). Hypothesizing-circularity-neutrality: Three guidelines for the conductor of the session. *Family Process, 19,* 7–19.

Tomm, K. (1987a). Interventive interviewing: Part I. Strategizing as a fourth guideline for the theapist. *Family Process, 26,* 3–13.

Tomm, K. (1987b). Interventive interviewing: Part II. Reflexive questioning as a means to enable self-healing. *Family Process, 26* (2), 167–183.

Tomm, K. (1988). Interventive interviewing: Part III. Intending to ask lineal, circular, strategic, or reflexive questions? *Family Process, 27* (1), 1–15.

White, M. (1987). Family therapy and schizophrenia: Addressing the 'in-the-corner' lifestyle. *Dulwich Centre Newsletter,* Spring.

White, M. (1988). The process of questioning: A therapy of literary merit? *Dulwich Centre Newsletter,* Winter, 8–14.

White, M. (1989). The externalizing of the problem and the re-authoring of lives and relationships. *Dulwich Centre Newsletter,* Summer, 3–20.

White, M., & Epston, D. (1990). *Narrative means to therapeutic ends.* New York: Norton.

16

LANGUAGE SOLUTIONS FOR
MIND–BODY PROBLEMS

James L. Griffith
Melissa Elliott Griffith

HOW DO WE TALK about mind and body in a manner that invokes the power of the spoken word to heal the body? A father whispers soft words to his little girl as she lies in his arms gasping with asthma. Her wheezing eases with the comfort she feels. An executive says to his wife, "Everything I can see about this job looks great, but my ulcer tells me differently." At dinner with her family, a mother vents her bitterness about the treatment she has received from her neurologist. After many expensive tests showed normal findings, he told her that the pains and numbness that had frightened her were due to stress and "all in your head." All about us we see evidence that mind and body are far more intimate in everyday life, for good and for bad, than our scientific rationality leads us to expect. Too often indeed, with our migraine headaches, ulcers, and painful muscle spasms, we know how mental pain can bring bodily illness. Yet this intimacy ought to open a potential path through which the spoken word can also bring healing to the ill body.

The deep, unspoken metaphors that underlie our scientific descriptions of mind and body give rise to an image of the body as a machine, amazingly complex, but a machine nonetheless, with the mind as its operator. The mind drives the body as if it were an automobile. This dualistic view of mind and body has underwritten remarkable biomedical achievements through which physicians can trouble-shoot diseased bodies with the precision of a good mechanic. Drugs can be swallowed that destroy cancers, kidneys can be transplanted from the dead to the living, and surgical repair of a fetus still in the uterus permits a baby to be born who otherwise would not have survived. All this has been accomplished within a world view that splits body from mind, seeing the body as made up of parts whose rule-driven operations permit us to manipulate their functions at will (Kleinman, 1986).

But this biomedical perspective does not provide a place for patients presenting bodily symptoms, but whose physiology is found to be normal, or less diseased than the complaints should indicate, after running the gamut of medical testing. Its rationalistic tradition is scandalized by the large numbers of patients whose distress in living is most evidenced by bodily symptoms they experience. In medical circles, such patients are called "hysterics," "the worried well," "hypochondriacs," "crocks," "gomers," and other names that capture the aversion felt towards those whose problems do not fit the accepted model (Ford, 1983). In the formal discourse of medicine, patients who show no evidence of physiological disease on medical tests and examinations are said to have a *somatoform disorder* (*DSM-III-R*, 1987; Ford, 1983). Patients who show clear evidence of physiological disease upon examination, but whose illness is largely attributed to exacerbation by psychological factors, are said to have a *psychophysiological disorder*.* Such patients are considered by medical doctors to have "mental" or psychiatric problems. But psychiatrists and psychologists, as "mental specialists" within the biomedical tradition, find themselves equally at a loss because the patients hold a firm conviction that their problems are "physical," not mental. Despite its dramatic accomplishments, biomedical technology, including that of psychiatry, offers little of use for these headaches, GI symptoms, and muscle aches and pains, and the afflicted patients feel betrayed (Kleinman, 1986).

By the decade of the 1970s, however, a convergence of two independent lines of thought about language, mind, and body suggested that a radical alternative to the biomedical perspective could be proposed.

Seventy years ago Martin Heidegger (1962a, 1962b, 1971) began a search to discover how the meaning of human experience emerged from acts of everyday living. His work carried him to places in human experience prior to the separation of subject from object, and mind from body, by language. Heidegger's work, and that of Merleau-Ponty

---

*Psychophysiological disorders have been renamed the cumbersome term *Psychological Factors Affecting Physical Symptoms* in the current *DSM-III-R*. We will continue to use the former name here.

(1968), Gadamer (1976), and other phenomenologists who extended it (see Palmer, 1969), asserted that both human thought and human action are shaped to a depth we cannot fathom by the language, customs, and social institutions that are handed to us in our historical moment. Their work, termed *philosophical hermeneutics*, showed how the mind-body division underlying modern medicine is a socially negotiated interpretation rather than a reflection of an objective reality that stands outside human experience (Messer, Sass, and Woolfolk, 1988). From this perspective, biomedical science has remained largely ignorant of its own status as one of many traditions, rather than the only valid tradition and a "mirror of reality." It has also been unaware of the extent to which its language is embodied not in its abstract concepts and printed words, but in the specific acts of clinicians talking and interacting with colleagues and patients. Thus, a biomedical clinician and a patient with a somatoform problem each come from a language tradition that is foreign to that of the other in how mind and body are distinguished. Even if they use the same words, the clinician and the patient in this context may have no shared language.

The contributions of hermeneutic philosophy to understanding mind-language-body relationships were generally not noted by clinicians working with patients and their problems. However, cognitive scientists in the 1970s arrived at a similar set of conclusions from an entirely different direction, and their work is more easily accessible to the medical science community. Humberto Maturana and Francisco Varela (1987; Varela, 1979; also see Efran, Lukens, and Lukens, 1990), neurobiologists from Chile, set upon the task of understanding the biology of cognition using current neuroanatomical, neurophysiological, and neuropsychological data. Their interest centered upon how both "mental events" and "physical events" existed in relationship as descriptions drawn from two different language domains. What was "language" that it could constitute both the mental world and the physical world? Staying true to their mission to provide scientific explanations in terms of structural mechanisms, Maturana and Varela (1987) described language as the generation of consensual behaviors by two beings who were structurally coupled, i.e., the behavior by one prompts behavior by the other in a recursive pattern that keeps the two in a stable interaction. To illustrate the biology of human language, they used the example of *trophallaxis*, the mechanism of communication among social insects:

> There is a continuous flow of secretions between the members of an ant colony through sharing of stomach contents each time they meet . . .

[which] results in the distribution, throughout the population, of an amount of substances (among them, hormones) responsible for the differentiation and specification of roles. Thus, the queen is a queen as long as she is fed in a certain way and certain substances that she produces are distributed among the colony members. Remove the queen from her location, and immediately the hormonal imbalance that her absence causes will result in a change in the feeding of the larvae which develop into queens. (1987, p. 186)

Just as the social organization of the ant colony is maintained through the mutual interchange of saliva, so among humans our social organization is maintained through the mutual interchange of language.

Both hermeneutic philosophy and cognitive science view language as located in the consensual behavioral interactions between persons, not inside "the mind" of either (Winograd and Flores, 1987). Language is not a vehicle that carries abstract communications back and forth between individual minds; it is a coordination of bodily states within members of a social group that preserves the structural integrity of both the social group and the individual group members.

PSYCHOTHERAPY AS A
BIOLOGICAL PHENOMENON

The view of language derived from cognitive science and the hermeneutic philosophers provides an alternative to traditional mind-body dualism for designing psychotherapeutic approaches to mind-body problems. From this perspective psychotherapy for a mind-body problem should use as its unit of treatment the social group of persons engaged in language around the mind-body problem, what Anderson and Goolishian (1988) have termed the *problem-organized system*. Typically, but not always, this is a group of family members. In this view, a *metaphor* is a linguistic unit of coordination of biological states among members of a social group. A *story* is a linguistic unit of coordinated social behavior over time. Coordination of biological states among members of a social group occurs through the back-and-forth telling and listening to personal stories.

Psychotherapy begins by creating a biological context favorable for telling, listening to, and reflecting upon first-person narratives about the problem. This context is revealed in the bodily states of session participants, including autonomic nervous system activity (sweating, pupil size, tremor), posture, rate and depth of breathing, state of muscle tone, and so forth. Bodily states organized around a readiness to respond to threat (suspicion, blame, fear, shame, or alienation) obstruct this process. Thus the therapist uses language to facilitate bodily states of caring, sharing, trusting, or listening. To promote the latter, a number of steps can be taken:

1. The therapist follows the bodily signs among therapy participants to guide how quickly the dialogue moves into novel or threatening topics. Body posture, breathing pattern, direction of gaze, facial expression, and tone of voice for each participant indicate either openness and permission to move more quickly or alarm and a request to slow down or temporarily stop. Andersen (1991) has suggested that the pace of the interview should move no faster than the most hesitant participant.

2. The therapist couples his or her own body with that of the therapy participants. This is perhaps done most effectively by coordinating one's breathing with that of the other with whom one is in dialogue (Andersen, 1991). It can be similarly helpful to assume matching body postures, volume of speech, or rate of speech.

3. The therapist takes responsibility for his or her own bodily readiness for dialogue by selecting presuppositions in language that foster curiosity, openness, and respect towards the person presenting a mindbody problem (Griffith and Griffith, 1991). We find three assumptions to be useful for facilitating dialogue with a patient presenting a somatoform problem.

First, a psychotherapy session is an alien environment for a person presenting a somatic symptom. This is especially true when a patient has first sought treatment from a medical doctor who refers the person for psychotherapy. Psychotherapy is a place where therapist and participants are expected to seek explanations for problems within a psychological domain, whereas a person asking a medical clinician for help is distinguishing problem explanations within a physiological domain.

Second, terrible bodily symptoms arise when there is a terrible life dilemma but the kind of conversation needed for its resolution somehow cannot occur. This assumption enables the therapist to be alert to the existence of an unspoken dilemma, curious about what has blocked the needed conversation, and empathic with the experience of entrapment by the symptomatic person.

A third premise is that the conversations needed to resolve this dilemma are blocked because either (a) the dominant narratives organizing the actions of those persons involved in the problem forbid dialogue about the problem; or (b) external constraints (such as political oppression, threat of family violence, cultural or religious practices) explicitly forbid conversation about the dilemma. This assumption guides the therapist to search for constraints that limit the possibilities for dialogue, rather than to search for how the symptom may be rewarding the patient, as is characteristic of some other therapy approaches.

Lena, a 28-year-old woman, had been referred by her family physician, who had treated her incapacitating headaches with a variety of standard headache regimens. Her headaches had persisted despite the treatments. Now the physician worried about her risk of addiction to narcotics if he gave her the stronger drugs that she requested. She refused for three months his suggestions that she seek a psychiatric evaluation. But when he continued to insist, she finally agreed to meet with a psychiatric consultant.

As her story unfolded, she told of marrying at an early age in order to leave a home full of alcoholism and verbal abuse. Her husband was a kind man who provided her with a stable family life and a good income. Their lives as a couple were busily centered around leading activities for young people in their church. But, she confessed tearfully, she did not feel he really "knows who I am," and she felt unsure of her love for him. If she were to speak about these concerns to him, she feared he would see her as an "ingrate" after all he had given her. He would be deeply wounded, and the conflict this might start could destroy the example of marriage that they wanted to provide for the young people in their church. Yet if she did not speak, she would feel that she was "living a lie," betraying both herself and her husband. She saw herself as now receiving a deserved punishment for having "abandoned" her family years earlier when it was so troubled and so much in need.

The therapist searches for the embodied language that coordinates bodily states. The speaking of functional language, with which we carry out everyday affairs, is typically coupled with a strong silencing of accompanying bodily states. Functional language seeks to shape the behavior of others rapidly and efficiently to further one's own objectives. While functional language has utility in securing food, shelter, and desired social positions, it sacrifices opportunities for coordinating bodyhoods with the other in dialogue. This functional language is often characterized as "speaking from the head" rather than "speaking from the heart."

But a therapist can usually pick out, interspersed between the lines of this functional language, remnants of a personal language that continues to speak from the body. To do so, one listens for idiosyncratic use of speech that is recurrent and for root metaphors from which the person's linguistic distinctions flow. These metaphors and phrases tend to mark the living presence of important narratives that constitute one's sense of self. These are the joints between idea and bodyhood.

These metaphors and phrases become the cornerstones upon which the subsequent dialogue of the therapy is built. The language of the therapy is thus constructed anew within each therapy using the patient's and other therapy participants' language as the building blocks, rather than importing a professional language the therapist has learned within his or her professional community. For example, if a symptomatic patient has used the expression "ingrate" three times in different sentences, the therapist can ask: What does "ingrate" mean? When you say "ingrate," is it like having a cousin who always asks for help in crises but is never available when you ask for help, or is it different from that? What were your key life experiences that taught you what "ingrate" means?

In this asking of questions and comparing of metaphors, there emerges a *conversational domain*, a consensual domain of language within which both therapist and patient feel mutually understood (Anderson and Goolishian, 1988; Pask, 1976; Varela, 1987). When the therapist and other session participants understand the first-person narratives that anchor the meaning of "ingrate" in the experience of the speaker, then "ingrate" has entered the conversational domain of the therapy. This language powerfully coordinates bodily states of those in dialogue.

> The therapist asked Lena, "What are the important stories of your life that connect with 'He doesn't know who I really am?'"
> Lena, still weeping, spoke disgustedly about her own mother who, with Lena and her brother from an earlier marriage, had married Lena's stepfather. Almost immediately the mother began secret extramarital affairs with a variety of men. From her grade school years on, Lena knew about her mother's secret life. When she had once hinted to her mother that her own marriage was unhappy, her mother explicitly suggested that Lena keep her husband for support, but look for passion elsewhere. Lena had always seen her mother as "abandoning" the marriage, "living a lie," and an "ingrate" for accepting her stepfather's home and money and then betraying his trust. Her deepest fear was that

she would end up like her mother. Now she was furious with her mother for suggesting that Lena also choose a double-life as a solution.

In the therapy with Lena, the meanings of "abandoning," "living a lie," "ingrate," and "doesn't know who I really am" are tied tightly to these self-narratives. Their meanings are individual, in some ways differing from the standard definitions of the words. These metaphors are also tied tightly to her bodily states.

WORKING WITH STORIES THAT
COORDINATE BODILY STATES

Although questions are asked during the therapy that seek to expand meaning of the metaphors and narratives, the therapist works to remain within the conversational domain as it has evolved. It helps to use the same language for describing and explaining the problem (to oneself or to colleagues) as one uses when speaking with clients in session. It is also helpful if the therapist can remember that, while he or she may be an expert about how language is used in dialogue, he or she still may not be able to supply workable answers for a patient's life dilemmas (Andersen, 1991).

This conversational domain allows therapy participants to publicly tell their personal stories of the problem. When such a dialogical context has been absent, this alone may be sufficient for the problem to spontaneously resolve.

The therapist followed Lena's body closely, pacing her speech and breathing, asking questions that opened space for still more stories: If Lena forsook a marriage of romance and passion to be faithful as a good wife and good mother in a stable home, what stories in her life would shape the future in years ahead? If she were to live out this future, then look back upon the life she had chosen, how would she feel?

Lena told stories of "invisibility," how as a six-year-old child, she had looked around her world and said, "There is no place for me here!" She was like the Little Mermaid, seeing and loving, but unseen and untouched. In brief moments of sexual passion, she sometimes now glimpsed the union she sought. But there was a gulf she could feel between herself and her husband that could not be crossed. The therapist did not explain or interpret or make an assignment, but listened and asked questions about the specific language Lena offered. She sought only to understand Lena's dilemma in Lena's language, within Lena's stories.

Lena chose to continue psychotherapy and eventually worked with her husband in a productive couples therapy. But she dated a dramatic improvement in her head pain to the first psychotherapy consultation when she first made understandable to another human being the dilemma that oppressed her. The headaches henceforth had not continued as a focus of therapy.

The important life dilemmas are those we feel in our bodies. Closely held, they cannot be articulated in the functional language of public life. Their language is spoken in self-narratives that exist at the junctures of mind and body. When a dilemma cannot find resolution because the needed dialogue is prohibited, then providing a safe place where the words can be spoken can, as with Lena, be sufficient to free the body from its pain.

More often than not, however, establishing a conversational domain is essential but not sufficient for resolution of a mind-body problem. The narratives available for guiding actions of the patient and other therapy participants may be inadequate for designing an effective solution. Narratives of fear, shame, blame, or despair may obscure awareness of skills and resources that otherwise might successfully resolve the problem. A dominant self-derogating narrative may overshadow others that hold greater promise for providing a problem solution. The therapist must therefore possess skills for expanding old narratives, retrieving alternative hidden narratives, and creating conditions that give birth to new narratives (White, 1988a, 1988b; White and Epston, 1990).

This process of narrative expansion/retrieval/creation proceeds best when the therapist primarily asks questions rather than makes declarative statements. The therapist is not an instructor, and questions must be asked from a position of genuine curiosity. This is possible when the therapist adopts a position of *therapeutic noncertainty* (Griffith and Griffith, 1991), making an active effort to maintain awareness of not understanding and not knowing. As Anderson and Goolishian (1988) have suggested, questions must be asked from a "not knowing" position if they are to invite creation of new meaning.

Therapist interpretations as used in psychodynamic psychotherapy are rarely, if ever, useful, because by definition they arise within the conversational domain of the professional community to which the therapist belongs, but of which the patient and other therapy participants are not members. The therapist can, however, offer ideas provided by his or her life experiences or those from other patients with similar problems. A variety of ideas, including ideas from the professional scientific communities, can be offered "cafeteria-style," provided the therapist watches to see which are selected as useful by patients and other therapy participants and then follows their selection (Griffith, Griffith, and Slovik, 1990).

> John H., a middle-aged engineer, described how discouraged he had become because he was once again having abdominal pain. He had worked to change his "Type A behavior" so that he would have no more ulcers. Until today he had believed that significant strides had been made in changing his thinking habits and pace of living. With the return of the aching, he wondered whether his efforts had accomplished anything at all.
>
> By the midpoint of the session, however, John was describing new "pressure" that had been building ever since he gained a new position that enabled him to work closely with his boss, whom he admired. He was constantly afraid that he would make a mistake in front of his boss. John quickly made a connection between this feeling-state and how he often had felt in the presence of his father, a perfectionistic, critical, and humorless man who John had both emulated and feared. However, this conscious insight did little to change the "pressure" and his bodily pain.
>
> In the dialogue, the therapist and John together had identified "gaining a sense of humor about oneself" as a cutting edge of John's personal growth that was leading him into new territory along a path never traversed by his father. Perhaps he could work upon this with his boss by deliberately making a small, but embarrassing, error each day in the presence of his boss and using the experience to practice laughing at himself. If he tried it as an experiment, was it possible that he might discover something new about himself?
>
> John was intrigued by the idea and agreed to try it, even though he felt somewhat threatened. On his return, he described how he had carried out the task and that, as a bonus, the feeling of "pressure" had dissipated with his ulcer pain.

The behavioral task, the "intentional error," is a commonly prescribed paradoxical assignment strategic therapists use to disrupt the stability of overregulated behaviors (Fisch, Weakland, and Segal, 1983). Here, the task was not made as an assignment, but rather as a collaboratively constructed exercise that John could use as a resource if he so wished. The task was subordinated to a specification of meaning governed by the self-narratives of John's life story. The participation of the therapist was more in the manner of a financial consultant discussing options for how John might wish to invest his money than in the manner of a physician prescribing pills to be taken for an illness.

CHANGING BODYHOOD TO CREATE NEW POSSIBILITIES FOR LANGUAGE

The discussion thus far has centered upon the use of language to create new possibilities for bodyhood that free it from suffering that had existed. We can take the discussion full circle by asking how we might create new possibilities for language through changing bodyhood.

The question of psychopharmacological treatment has been avoided by many nonpsychiatric clinicians, even though most therapists work with clients who take psychotropic medications, and most refer some clients to physicians specifically to be prescribed medications for anxiety, depression, or psychosis. It has been always been difficult, however, for clinicians who work with language within a psychological domain, whether psychoanalysis or strategic therapy, to conceptualize a generative relationship between language-based and physiology-based therapies (Griffith et al, 1991).

If we view language from a biological standpoint as a way of living in physiological community with self and others, a clearer relationship between physiology and psychology becomes visible. We speak about this relationship in terms of *selection* and *constraint* that holds between physiological and psychological domains as language domains (Chiari and Nuzzo, 1988). A particular physiological state selects a domain of states within which psychological phenomena can be observed, and a particular psychological state selects a domain of states within which physiological phenomena can be observed. The physiological domain thus constrains the psychological, and vice versa. Neither the physiological nor the psychological domains are reducible to the other, but they do intersect in language, in that each exist as language domains and do not exist apart from how we can describe them in language.

Thus far we have spoken about a therapy approach in which a therapist's language can bring resolution to bodily suffering. Similarly, the removal of physiological constraints can create new possibilities in a psychological domain. For example, the noradrenergic system is the specific brain system that is often the focus of intervention in pharmacological treatment of anxiety and depression symptoms. This system is so named due to its reliance upon norepinephrine as its neurotransmitter, the chemical with which it communicates with other brain systems (Nieuwenhuys, 1985). The cell bodies from which the fiber network constituting the noradrenergic system emerges lie deep in the brain stem and only number 20,000 out of a trillion nerve cells in the brain (Jacobs, 1986; Kandel, 1985). Yet these few neurons give off long fibers that branch again and again and again, so that eventually every area of the cerebral cortex, as well as the limbic system, cerebellum, and much of the spinal cord, is richly innervated. This system is a phylogenetically old system, meaning that its structure in the brain of a rat looks much like that in a dog and much like that in a human (Nieuwenhuys, 1985). This suggests that the noradrenergic system plays a fundamental, but simple, role in the overall functioning of the brain. We may liken it to the lightswitch in a room, whose design has changed little over the years, although the designs of other electrical equipment in the room, such as tape recorders, stereos, computers, and televisions, have become progressively more complex and sophisticated.

The noradrenergic system appears to be an alarm system that signals the presence of novelty or threat in the environment (Clark, Geffen, and Geffen, 1987; Jacobs, 1986). When it discharges, it shifts the orientation of information processing systems throughout the brain to focus upon scanning perceptual fields for a potential threat, and it initiates a behavioral readiness to run or to fight. In contrast, the noradrenergic system grows relatively quiescent when an animal (or human) shows consummatory and grooming behaviors—eating and drinking, grooming self or other, or resting. It falls completely silent during the intensely inwardly directed, creative state of dreaming that occurs during rapid eye movement sleep (Jacobs, 1986).

Judging from these observations, we can surmise that physiological states associated with a strong readiness to respond to environmental threat, evidenced by high activation of the noradrenergic system, select a domain of psychological states within which reflective listening and generation of new meaning are unlikely to occur. Conversely, a state of low activation of the noradrenergic system, as in a hypnotic induction when the soft, rhythmic words of the hypnotist lull the noradrenergic system into an idling mode, selects a domain of psychological states favorable for reflective listening and generation of new meaning. Similar or complementary descriptions can be made about other brain systems that appear to regulate behavioral states—the cholinergic, serotonergic, dopaminergic, histaminic systems, in particular – although the noradrenergic system is a bit better understood at present than the others. Each of these systems appears to operate by a feed-forward mechanism that biases which environmental sensations receive preferential access to the brain, and how that information is processed, as well as which repertoires of behavioral responses are initiated.

When a person presents a problem such as recurrent panic attacks, his or her noradrenergic system is set at a very high level of activation, establishing a brain readiness for noticing and rapidly responding to environmental events that could be potential threats. Since many life events are intrinsically ambiguous in their meaning, this early-warning system is constantly setting off alarms in the person with panic attacks. With some patients, this low threshold for alarm appears to be a learned behavior; with others it appears to result from an inborn instability in the neurochemical system. In either case, the medications effective in stopping panic symptoms – such as alprazolam, imipramine, and phenelzine – are all shown to turn down, directly or indirectly, the level of activation of the noradrenergic system (Charney et al., 1990).

Most therapists working with patients debilitated by panic attacks know how little room there is for therapeutic dialogue. Such patients typically are convinced that their palpitating hearts, sweaty palms, tremors, and feelings of dread all signal the onset of a dire illness. They focus only upon these bodily symptoms, search for medical treatment to stop them, and avoid situations, such as shopping malls, elevators, and churches, that may trigger them. Yet when medications raise the threshold of brain mechanisms for triggering panic behavior, new possibilities appear for open and reflective conversation.

In psychotherapy, we can best think about this turning down of the level of activation of a brain system as selecting an alternative set of states within which desired psychological phenomena, such as reflective listening, can occur. The state of activation of the noradrenergic system does not prescribe that reflective listening will occur, nor can an understanding of reflective listening be reduced to an understanding of the noradrenergic system. The state of activation of the noradrenergic system does strongly condition whether reflective listening is permitted to occur. Changing bodyhood thus creates new possibilities for change through language.

Paul G. was a 62-year-old man who arrived at our psychiatry inpatient unit covered with scratches and bruises from struggling with family members who brought him against his will due to their concern over his level of agitation and threats of suicide. On the unit, he constantly paced, struggled to open the doors, and brooded endlessly over his conviction that he had cancer which was untreatable. Efforts to engage him in dialogue failed, unless participating at the periphery of his monologue about terminal illness.

In the context of other depressive symptoms, a previous occurrence of severe depression, and a family history of depressions and suicide among his siblings, a psychiatric diagnosis of major depression with psychotic features was made. After three days treatment with antipsychotic medication, he became able to converse about present life events. After fifteen days treatment with antidepressant medication, his black mood, impaired sleep and appetite, and high anxiety began to improve. By this time he had told how he recently had become worried about his wife's health and an adult child who had financial problems. He had been unable to fend off requests by friends that he assume leadership for a civic function that he felt inadequate to manage. He began working in therapy to identify how his fears had led him into a vulnerable place where his depression was reactivated.

DISCUSSION

Current psychological treatments for somatic symptoms are based upon language that objectifies the body. These treatments seek to extend successes of biomedical science that applied a physical sciences model of inquiry and understanding to biological systems of the body. These successes resulted in remarkably effective treatments for diseased body organs and organ systems, whether from bacterial infections, myocardial infarction, or high blood pressure. Most research in psychiatry and psychology seeking to define treatments for patients diagnosed with somatoform disorders and psychophysiological disorders has attempted to apply the same approaches in treating these somatic symptoms.

We are exploring an alternative understanding of language as a dynamic coupling of bodyhoods that provides a social matrix within which we live as human beings. This approach uses new or expanded language that, through its coordination of bodyhoods, ends bodily suffering for the patient. It avoids linguistic distinctions, such as subject/object, mind/body, and mental/physical, when they are used to construct a reality in which the body is experienced as external to self, as we experience the machines we use in daily life.

If the modern American automobile mechanic is an apt metaphor for biomedical clinicians, then the Native American healer may be an apt metaphor for a language systems clinician (Torrey, 1986). Through a rhythmic dance of words that joins the body of the one who is ill, the therapist and therapy participants search for a story that will bring healing. Like the shaman who may offer peyote, the therapist may offer the pharmacological fruits of biomedical science to change the body so it can tell a better story with which to live. These ways acknowledge, as did Heidegger (1971), that, "Language is the house of Being. Man dwells in this house."

Commentary

Gene Combs
Jill Freedman

WHILE "Language Solutions for Mind-Body Problems" addresses a more circumscribed group of people and problems than many of the other papers in this collection, it offers ideas about language, narrative, conversation, and the social construction of realities that have general applicability. We will begin by responding to some of the Griffiths' ideas about working specifically with so-called mind-body problems, and then move into discussing some of their notions that we believe are more generally applicable.

Much of the Griffiths' day-to-day work as therapists takes place in the territory where the domains of medicine and psychotherapy overlap. To further their work as translators and mediators between these two domains, they utilize Maturana and Varela's definition of language as "a coordination of bodily states within members of a social group." While this focus on biological states risks a perpetuation of the "mind-body problem" by overly reifying the body side of the equation, the emphasis on the social group provides balance. This redefinition of language is at the heart of their "language solution." It invites us to think about mind not as a thing that inhabits, controls, or is in conflict with a body, but (à la Bateson) as a process that could easily involve several bodies. With this view, the domain of language becomes more important than either the domain of mind or that of body. The mind-body "problem" tends to dissolve. Neat!

We missed the voices of Harry Goolishian and Harlene Anderson at the Therapeutic Conversations conference. They have been in the forefront of advancing the acceptance of language-based approaches to psychotherapy, and their presence would have greatly enriched our conversations. Consequently, we are glad to see the Griffiths including ideas from Goolishian and Anderson at several points in their paper. The first of these is their emphasis on the *problem-organized system* as the appropriate unit of treatment. Goolishian and Anderson have long stated that it makes more sense to work with neither the "identified patient" nor the family of that person, but with the group of people engaged in language around a particular problem. The Griffiths use the notion of the problem-organized system to invite people to think of "psychophysiological" and "somatoform" problems not as things that reside in particular minds or bodies but as processes that have emerged in language among several people. When people accept such an invitation, arguments about whether the problem resides in the mind or the body become irrelevant. Neat again!

So, the Griffiths expand the conventional medical-model playing field in two directions. Their focus on bodily states as the stuff which mind, through language, is coordinating makes language an important part of the territory. Their focus on the problem-organized system invites us to consider the social system as part of the field of play. We are invited to think about mind-language-body-social network problems, with language and the social network becoming more figural than mind and body. The question for a therapist then becomes not "Is the problem in the mind or the body?" but "How can I invite the social network engaged in problematic conversation into more useful conversations?" At this point their ideas begin to have general applicability for all psychotherapists, as all psychotherapy could be thought of as the process of finding workable answers to the latter question.

Their definition of language as the coordination of bodily states leads the Griffiths to say that "psychotherapy begins by creating a biological context favorable for telling, listening to, and reflecting upon first-person narratives about the problem." The recommendations that they make about how to create such a biological context — attending to body posture, breathing pattern, voice tone, coordinating one's breathing with that of the other, etc. — are ones that we learned from the work of Milton Erickson. In the Ericksonian world, they are considered to be primary ways of meeting people at their model of the world. It is very interesting to us that the Griffiths, who have not immersed themselves in Erickson's work, have found such similar ideas through their own experience and their immersion in philosophical hermeneutics, cognitive science, and the work of Harry Goolishian and Harlene Anderson, Michael White, and particularly Tom Andersen.

A delightful thing about how the Griffiths approach the ideas that we would call "meeting people at their model of the world," is that they describe them in very human and compassionate, rather than technical, terms.

They then go on to suggest listening for idiosyncratic and recurring use of speech and root metaphors and using these in constructing the language of therapy. They write: "The language of the therapy is thus constructed anew within each therapy using the patient's and other therapy participants' language as the building blocks, rather than importing a professional language the therapist has learned within his or her professional community." This idea, again, is central to Ericksonian work, in which the therapy is regularly built on the uniqueness of a client and that uniqueness is often found in people's use of metaphor and language.

Once a context favorable for exchanging stories about the problem has emerged, we would characterize the therapy described in this paper as a therapy of *meaning* – not of universal or general meaning, but of particular, local, personal meaning. Therapists and clients are engaged in conversation to explore and expand the meaning of particular words and stories, of particular bodily states, and that expansion of meaning is for the whole problem-organized system, not just the "psyche" of the client.

The Griffiths clearly illustrate this process in their story of Lena and the gradual but profound expansion of the meaning of concepts such as "ingrate," "living a lie," and "abandoning." They focus on the expansion of meaning that occurs as they work together with Lena to establish a "conversational domain" where Lena's private dilemma becomes a public and interpersonal story. The importance of this is undeniable, and sometimes it is all that is needed, but they go on to say that establishing a conversational domain is not always a sufficient condition for psychotherapy.

When good conversation isn't enough all by itself, some new stories can be a big help, and the Griffiths illustrate how new narratives can be developed as the conversation continues. Drawing on the work of Michael White and David Epston, they say "It is important . . . that the therapist possess skills for expanding old narratives, retrieving alternative narratives that had been hidden, and creating conditions that give birth to new narratives." We wholeheartedly agree with both the attitude and the method that they recommend for practicing these skills.

Bringing the voices of Goolishian and Anderson into our conversation again, they stress the importance of a "not knowing" attitude. There is a profound difference in the process of a therapy conducted through questions asked with true curiosity and that of a therapy conducted through questions that are primarily rhetorical or instructive in their nature. Curiosity protects therapists from the belief that they can be detached, objective experts or authorities and allows them to function as contributing, collaborative members of the problem-dissolving system.

With the Griffiths' variety of ideas as a guide and the permission to have a "not knowing" attitude, the realm of "mind-body problems" becomes a less daunting and more inviting place for psychotherapists to visit.

REFERENCES

American Psychiatric Association (1987). *Diagnostic and statistical manual of mental disorders, third edition—revised.* Washington: Author.

Andersen, T. (Ed.) (1991). *The reflecting team: Dialogues and dialogues about the dialogues.* New York: Norton.

Anderson, H., & Goolishian, H. A. (1988). Human systems as linguistic systems: Preliminary and evolving ideas about the implications for clinical theory. *Family Process, 27*: 371–393.

Charney, D. S., Woods, S. W., Nagy, L. M., Southwick, S. M., Krystal, J. H., & Heninger, G. R. (1990). Noradrenergic function in panic disorder. *Journal of Clinical Psychiatry, 51* (12, suppl. A), 5–11.

Chiari, G., & Nuzzo, M. L. (1988). Embodied minds over interacting bodies: A constructivist perspective on the mind-body problem. *Irish Journal of Psychology, 9*: 91–100.

Clark, C. R., Geffen, G. M., & Geffen, L. B. (1987). Catecholamines and attention, II: Pharmacological studies in normal humans. *Neurosciences & Behavioral Reviews, 11*: 353–364.

Efran, J., Lukens, M. D., & Lukens, R. J. (1990). *Language, structure, and change: Frameworks of meaning in psychotherapy.* New York: Norton.

Fisch, R., Weakland, J. H., & Segal, L. (1983). *The tactics of change: Doing therapy briefly.* San Francisco: Jossey-Bass.

Ford, C. V. (1983). *The somatizing disorders: Illness as a way of life.* New York: Elsevier.

Gadamer, H-G. (1976). *Philosophical hermeneutics.* Berkeley: University of California Press.

Griffith, J. L., & Griffith, M. E. (1991). Owning one's epistemological stance in therapy. Unpublished manuscript.

Griffith, J. L., Griffith, M. E., Meydrech, E., Grantham, D., & Bearden, S. (1991). A model for psychiatric consultation in systemic therapy. *Journal of Marital and Family Therapy, 17*: 291–294.

Griffith, J. L., Griffith, M. E., & Slovik, L. S. (1990). Mind-body problems in family therapy: Contrasting first- and second-order cybernetics approaches. *Family Process, 29*: 13–28.

Heidegger, M. (1962a). *Being and time.* (J. Macquarrie & E. Robinson, Trans.). New York: Harper & Row.

Heidegger, M. (1962b). Letter on humanism. (E. Lohner, Trans.). In W. Barrett & H. D. Aiken (Eds.), *Philosophy in the twentieth century.* New York.

Heidegger, M. (1971). *On the way to language.* (P. D. Hertz, Trans.). San Francisco: Harper & Row.

Jacobs, B. L. (1986). Single unit activity of locus coeruleus neurons in behaving animals. *Progress in Neurobiology, 27*: 183–194.

Kandel, E. R. (1985). Nerve cells and behavior. In E. R. Kandel & J. H. Schwartz (Eds.), *Principles of neural science, 2nd edition.* New York: Elsevier.

Kleinman, A. (1986). Some uses and misuses of social science in medicine. In D. W. Fiske & R. A. Shweder (Eds.), *Metatheory in social science.* Chicago: University of Chicago Press.

Maturana, H. R., & Varela, F. J. (1987). *The tree of knowledge: The biological roots of human understanding.* Boston: Shambhala.

Merleau-Ponty, M. (1968). *The visible and the invisible.* Evanston, IL: Northwestern University Press.

Messer, S. B., Sass, L. A., & Woolfolk, R. L. (Eds.) (1988). *Hermeneutics and psychological theory.* New Brunswick, NJ: Rutgers University Press.

Nieuwenhuys, R. (1985). *Chemoarchitecture of the brain.* New York: Springer-Verlag.

Palmer, R. E. (1969). *Hermeneutics: Interpretation theory in Schleiermacher, Dilthey, Heidegger, and Gadamer.* Evanston, IL: Northwestern University Press.

Pask, G. (1976). *Conversation theory: Applications in education and epistemology.* New York: Elsevier.

Torrey, E. F. (1986). *Witchdoctors and psychiatrists: The common roots of psychotherapy and its future.* Northvale, NJ: Aronson.

Varela, F. J. (1979). *Principles of biological autonomy.* New York: Elsevier-North Holland.

White, M. (1988a). The externalizing of the problem and the re-authoring of lives and relationships. *Dulwich Centre Newsletter,* Summer.

White, M. (1988b). The process of questioning: A therapy of literary merit? *Dulwich Centre Newsletter,* Winter.

White, M. & Epston, D. (1990). *Narrative means to therapeutic ends.* New York: Norton.

Winograd, T., & Flores, F. (1987). *Understanding computers and cognition: A new foundation for design.* Reading, MA: Addison-Wesley.

17

BEWARE THE SIRENS' SONG:
THE AGS COMMISSION MODEL

Ernst Salamon
Klas Grevelius
Mia Andersson

THERE IS A long-standing proposition that normal life crises in individuals, families and other systems can trigger disabling psychiatric symptoms. We believe that such symtoms are often exacerbated by common health interventions, a phenomenon known as "iatrogenic injury." In our view, iatrogenic injury stems from the many guilt-imposing explanations and insulting suggestions advanced in the course of mental health practice. Under the weight of such explanations and suggestions, innate healing powers are stifled or paralyzed.

We have observed that many health professionals mistrust their clients' desire and capacity for change. Seeking shortcomings and difficulties, professionals become blind to resources and possibilities. We believe that this mistrust and bias permeates much of professional training and is equally injurious to clients, their resource systems,

The authors want to acknowledge some dear friends and colleagues: Imelda McCarthy has generously helped us with the translation and edition of this paper, and has together with her teammates, Nollaig Byrne and Philip Kearney, lovingly encouraged, aided, and supported us for many years in the development of our work; Bill O'Hanlon and Karl Tomm have kindly assisted in both the clarification and promotion of our model; Lynn Hoffman was the tender midwife of our team and spurred us to go our own way; Reese Price and Steven Gilligan vigorously cut down this paper to appropriate size while succeeding to distill the essence of our ideas.

and professionals. We refer to this phenomenon as "consultogenic injury."

In the last few years growing numbers of therapists have come to emphasize health and strength in people rather than deficit and weakness. They believe in the release of innate resources, rather than repair by external, all-knowing experts. There is an emerging confidence in the family's and other social systems' healing powers, rather than regarding these as pathogenic sources. These therapists emphasize love and strength, rather than bonds and constraints.

At the AGS Institute in Stockholm, we see ourselves as being part of this movement. We favor therapy methods that build on mutual respect and confidence between the helpseekers and therapists. One such method is our AGS Commission model, which views the person(s) coming for help as being the sole source(s) of information as to *what* the goal of therapy shall be, *how* that goal might be achieved, and *when* and *if* that goal has been achieved (O'Hanlon, 1990).

THE SIRENS' SONG

Ulysses, in the Greek epic which bears his name, is confronted with evil Sirens. The song of the Sirens is said to have erased all other intentions in the minds of those who heard it, lulling its listeners into full absorption in the song, and thereby towards disaster. The title of this paper refers to that saga. We see it as a metaphor for the plight of persons who appear to be governed by powers beyond their control.

Lately, we have used this metaphor to illustrate our own situation as consultants and therapists as much as to highlight the situations of our clients. How easy it is, like Ulysses, when tempted by the song of the Sirens, to lose one's intended course of helping the right person with the right thing. Karl Tomm (1986) has pointed out that we as therapists often carry a strong desire to help everyone who appears to suffer. We believe that such a desire often counteracts our possibilities of helping at all, because it tempts us to try to help the wrong person with the wrong thing in the wrong context. Humberto Maturana (see Andersson, 1991) warns about the imposition of one's will on another, about what he calls "the passion to change the other," rather than to invite the other to an exchange. Inspired by Maturana, we (Andersson, 1990) coined the expression "the passion to help," a passion which we perceive as a common stumbling block in therapy.

During all our activities, we have continuously been in search of methods that are both effective in dissolving problems and fit our high demands for respect and care of the persons who seek our help. A recurrent problem that we have struggled with is that we have far too often lost track of the needs of the person initially seeking our help. When we do this we find ourselves in opposition to her and her commission. It could be a parent seeking our help with worries about a child, or a social worker trying to get our help with a problem with a client, or a manager consulting us on her dissatisfaction with her team. Time after time we have found ourselves disapproving of the commission given to us, and taking sides with the child against the parent, or the client against the social worker, or the team against the manager. Time and again, we discovered that this way of investing our loyalty did not in the end satisfy anyone.

As the years pass we have more and more clearly come to see this phenomenon of trying to help the wrong person with the wrong thing as the most common reason for failures in therapy. The big problem has been that, even when we are aware of this trap, we keep falling into it. We have realized that to avoid this, we would need to make a major change in our mode of work. Little by little we have created a model that directs our focus and efforts to the needs of the person(s) who has commissioned us. The result of this change is the AGS Commission Model. It is a tool that we have created in order to distinguish and study the relationships that emerge when people, on a professional basis, help other people to get rid of their problems. To give an idea about what values we strive for in our model, we want to quote a few lines from the Danish philosopher Søren Kierkegaard (1851):

> That if real success is to attend the effort to bring a man to a definite position, one must first of all take pains to find HIM where he is and begin there.
>
> Any one who has not mastered this is himself deluded when he proposes to help others. In order to help another effectively I must understand more than he—yet first of all surely I must understand what he understands. If I do not know that, my greater understanding will be of no help to him. If, however, I am disposed to plume myself on my greater understanding, it is because I am vain and proud, so that at bottom, instead of benefiting him, I want to be admired. But all true effort to help begins with self-humiliation: the helper must first humble himself under him he would help, and therewith must understand that to help does not mean to be sovereign but to be a servant.
>
> If you cannot do that, then you cannot help him at all.

Our definition of characteristics of a professional context within which the above needs to occur is constituted by a *commissioner*, who executes services for revenue; a *commission-giver*, who orders the service and pays for it; and a *commission*, which represents the service that both parties mutually agree on. We have found it useful to apply these categories in our undertakings as psychotherapists. They provide us with both a practical and an ethical guide to our work.

The English term "commission" is defined in the dictionary as "a warrant granting certain powers and imposing certain duties." As we see it, we need some powers to accomplish our mission. These powers arc provided to us by a commission-giver. They may include, for instance, a right to ask questions and get answers on private, delicate matters, a right to assign different tasks to be carried out between sessions, a right to videotape, etc. The powers given to us by the commission-giver in order to help may also be turned against him or her. That "power corrupts" is a well-known fact, and we have to use all means available to prevent ourselves from abusing the confidence the commission-giver has placed in us. We have found that the use of the above-mentioned vocabulary is helpful in this regard.

- By regarding ourselves as commissioners, we put ourselves in a serving position towards the commission-giver.
- We get our authorization from the commission-giver, and he or she is the one who defines the goal and approves of the means for the commission.
- The commission-giver is the one who decides when the commission ends and whether it has been executed in a satisfactory way.
- Our task as commissioners is to carry out the commission with loyalty to the commission-giver, who is the one we openly strive to satisfy.

THE NOTION OF A "PROBLEM"

In the Stockholm airport there is a tunnel leading from the domestic hall to the parking garage. At the end of the tunnel, there is a huge advertisement for a consulting company with the text: "Give us the problem!" Is a problem something that you can give away to someone and thereby get rid of it? Well, the concept "problem" is often used as if that were the case, which is undoubtedly an attractive thought.

In Sweden the concept "problem" with the accompanying words— "drinking problem," "emotional problem," etc. – are widely used within psychiatric and social work. When we started to describe our work in writing, we did so in terms of helping clients to solve their "problems." However, we discovered in our theoretical discussions that we had a problem with the concept "problem." We found that it stood for different phenomena depending on the speaker and the intention of the speaker. After many failures, we succeeded in defining the concept "problem" in a way that satisfied us. Our definition has not only demarcated and made us aware of what we are doing, but has also been an important step in the development of our model. Here is our definition:

> A problem is a person's wish for a change that he or she does not know how to achieve.

In everyday language the word "problem" denotes a difficulty which is perceived as painful or unpleasant. Thus it usually denotes a negative state and has a negative connotation. But there is also a more positive aspect of the concept "problem." We first came across that when some of our trainees defined the word "problem" as "that which makes us do something." They advanced the notion that a problem is the engine that activates a person to change – and hopefully improve – his or her life.

CHANGE AND ITS REALIZATION

Imagine watching a man stepping out into a street and walking towards the other side. When he reaches the middle of the street he stops, turns 180 degrees, and walks back to the side from where he started. Why do we perceive such an event as a change of mind indigenous to the walker? We *expected* that he would cross the *entire* street. We presuppose a certain pattern, which exists in our minds, but which we perceive as inductively derived expectation. It seems that deviation from our expectations is perceived as a change. In everyday life we do not make these concepts explicit; rather, we reify them and regard them as "reality." An experience of change is thus personal, and depends on the expectations of the observer. Humberto Maturana (1983) points out that the observer unilaterally distinguishes and decides when a change has occurred.

This could be more simply expressed as follows: The observer has a preconceived notion of the occurrence of certain fluctuations within the phenomenon in question, which are perceived as "no change." Other shifts, however, are not allowable within the frame of the expected but are defined as "change." This leads us to the following definition of "change":

> Change is a course of events in the being of a phenomenon that is not embraced within the frame of the observers' expectations as belonging to that phenomenon.

One day a young woman came to our institute and asked for help with her depression. She had made a suicide attempt and had one unsuccessful attempt at therapy behind her. Klas agreed to see her a few times and do some exploration to find out what we could do for her.

During the third session Klas had a splitting headache. The young woman cried as usual, and told about her meaningless life. As usual, Klas could not make any sense out of her stories. Finally he told her that his headache was getting so bad that if she did not come to the point and tell him why she was so miserable, they could stop right there.

The young woman was quiet for a short time, as if holding her breath, and then she said: "Okay. It is the horse. I know that I am crazy!" She took out a bunch of photos from her handbag. They were all of her horse. The horse had died a year and a half earlier, and everybody told her that one cannot mourn for a horse like that.

"At last you are telling me what's really going on!" said Klas. "Of course you can mourn the loss of a horse as much as the loss of a human being. I know a lot about mourning, and there is nothing wrong with you." A few sessions later the young woman and Klas ended their contract. She was still in grief, but no longer thought that she was crazy and in need of therapy. Not only had changes occurred in the woman's grief behavior, but there was change in her classification of it. When her expectations of what represented acceptable grief behavior expanded to include her unresolved sadness over the loss of a horse, she no longer regarded herself as mad, but sad.

THE CONCEPTS OF
LOYALTY AND CURIOSITY

In our model we are openly and explicitly loyal to the commission-giver. This distinguishes our model from other family therapy models (e.g., Selvini Palazzoli et al., 1980), where it is considered to be important that the therapist take a neutral stance relative to the parties involved. We feel that a stance of neutrality objectifies the persons we are trying to help, reducing them to objects for strategic manipulation rather than partners in a mutual undertaking.

Another element that we regard as a prerequisite for our work at the AGS Institute is that we have positive sentiment towards our commission-givers. We have found that a positive interest is necessary for us to be genuinely curious in a nonjudgmental fashion. Only then can we be totally honest to our commission-giver and receive honesty in return. For instance, we have long had a rule of thumb never to ask questions about a phenomenon we are critical about, or of a person with whom we are not at ease. When we are critical we prefer to express our points of view in declarative sentences rather than hiding them behind seemingly neutral questions.

We regard curiosity to be the driving force behind all exploration. Eli Wiesel (1986) stated that "The opposite of love is not hate, the opposite of love is indifference." We continue this line of thought: The opposite of love is indifference, and the opposite of indifference is curiosity. Then, curiosity is love! This reasoning has helped us to ask questions that we could not conceive of asking previously. As long as we are sure that the curiosity is there, that we are genuinely and positively interested in understanding, then we can ask whatever comes to our minds and use all of our intuition and empathy.

The commission-giver presents us with a desired change that he or she does not know how to achieve. The commission-giver's actions, or lack thereof, directed towards achieving the desired change can at first appear absurd. Earlier we often found ourselves spontaneously disliking some behavior or judging our commission-giver negatively. Now when this happens we immediately interrupt the interview and talk to each other about our negative feelings and judgments so we can deepen our stance of curiosity.

For example, the father of a young bulimic woman was sitting with his evening paper open in front of him during most of the first interview. Mia was interviewing. She continued her task as if she did not notice the paper. She was then called out for a conference and was asked for her reactions to the father. Ernst and Klas were very irritated, but Mia felt she was not disturbed by the father's behavior. After some discussion it became clear, however, that Mia was also very critical towards the father's behavior. She perceived it as a provocation from the father. However, fearing that she would anger or embarrass the father, she had not been able to face those feelings and approach the issue during the interview.

The next step for the team was to discuss the possible positive interpretations of the paper reading. Mia suddenly remembered our repeated experience that most parents of mentally ill children embrace the idea that they are to blame for the illness of their child. It is not difficult to understand that the best thing a loving parent can do in such a situation is to stay as passive as possible. In this light the father's reading appeared as a sign of engagement and caring. Now we could view the father in a positive light despite his behavior. Mia could go back into the room and ask him why he seemingly did not take part in the conversation. She was curious again and could continue the exploration. Never again did we see that paper!

THE TRIAD

In our everyday work, our commission-giver is usually a person or persons who want our help to solve a problem. Such a relationship may be regarded as a dyadic relation between two parties, where one party, the commissioner, helps the other party, the commission-giver, for payment. Using the AGS commission model, however, we often regard treatment and consultation as a *triadic* process, including a third party, the target person. The target person is the one targeted by the commission-giver for change; he/she may be the commission-giver or some other person. The commission-giver determines the commission, and ultimately decides both what measures are to be taken by whom and whether or not they aim at him/herself or someone else.

One common situation is that the target person does not agree with the commission-giver about the definition of the problem and/or the goals of the consultation. The target person, for example, may not see any need for change. In such a situation we explain to the target person that the person who turned to us for help is our commission-giver. We have taken on the task of helping her or him with her or his concerns. We then inform the target person that it is not necessary for us that he/she agree with the commission-giver's definition of the problem. It is not even necessary that he/she come to our meetings. In some situations we might even choose not to invite the target person. We further explain that in some instances our efforts to help the commission-given may be facilitated if the target person chooses to attend.

An example of this approach was with a young man named Karl, who had been diagnosed with schizophrenia. During the initial telephone interview the father was asked why he had waited so long to call us. He answered that Karl was only now motivated for treatment. This change of attitude had happened in connection with his latest stay in the hospital.

A couple of months passed before we saw them for the first

exploratory session. We started by telling everybody present about the information we had received, and asked Karl if he was still interested in treatment. He answered that this was no longer the case. He no longer had any problems that he felt he needed our help with.

We asked Karl if he would be willing to help us in trying to help his father. We made clear that this meant that we would take a commission from this father. Our aim would be to assist his father with his problems as he saw them. We explained that our standpoint was that we would not try to help Karl with anything unless he was in agreement. Our communication to Karl was: "What we can do is to help your father to get rid of his problems. The theme for our discussions will be his worries that you might become a chronic schizophrenic. For the time being it would help us if you took part in the sessions, but this is not a necessary condition for us to help your father. However, we advise you to attend the sessions and at least hear the discussions that will focus on your father's wishes to see changes in you."

Karl accepted our invitation to attend and seemed to be satisfied with the role assigned to him. Eight months (and eight sessions) later, the commission-giver was satisfied and the commission was over. The father had stopped worrying, since Karl's "schizophrenic" behavior had changed.

All cases, of course, do not involve an actual triad. Sometimes the commission-giver and the target person are one and the same. When this occurs, our model calls for an assessment of the situation to determine whether the seriousness of the difficulty necessitates the presence of a third person whom our initial commission-giver can designate. This is advisable when the initial commission-giver is unable to stand alone against illness or a compulsion that seems stronger than the commission-giver. In those cases the metaphor of Ulysses seeking the aid of this crew in lashing him to the mast of the ship so he would not surrender himself to the Sirens' song is appropriate. In those cases where the individual is unable to stand alone, close and trusted persons are asked to take over the responsibility of the commission-giver and execute what we used to call "loving control."

STEPS IN THE MODEL

Having presented our general framework, we would like to briefly describe the basic steps we take in implementing it. The phases are presented in Figure 1. The time span that the different phases cover may very, but overall the table shows the approximate relative time that the different parts take and the general course of a consultation. The first phase is an exploration of the *"presented commission,"* which represents what the commission-giver asks from us in the first contact and his/her presented reasons for seeking help at this time. At the same time we get ideas of our own about what has lead the commission-giver to seek us out. These ideas we call the *"hypothetical commission."* The presented commission and the hypothetical commission are often the same; when they are not we have found it extremely important to further negotiate the commission.

The exploration of the problem includes an assessment of commission-givers' capability to carry out the necessary measures to be taken. We also explore the obstacles that have stopped commission-givers from carrying out their own ideas of solution. When the commission-givers are the target person's parents, our experience tells us that the incapability and the obstacles mostly stem from their burden of guilt and confusion. Not until we have brought order into their confusion and challenged their paralyzing guilt are they ready to set about starting the process of change.

The first phase of the exploration includes an exploration of the following areas:

* Earlier experience of treatment and diagnoses by all concerned parties,
* Why earlier treatments were not successful,
* Extrinsic sources of motivation represented by concerned significant others,
* Their confidence in us,
* The severity of the crisis,
* Causal explanations of the problem,
* Guilt and shame issues,
* Ideas of their own resources and ability to help.

An effect of the first phase of the exploration is that the commission-giver clearly defines both the problem and the goal. The goal definition includes a behaviorally based outline of what changes the commission-giver wants to bring about. In our view, the commission-giver seeks an answer to the question of how to get out of a difficult situation. The question, however, is often distorted and obscured by previous iatrogenic injuries. In such cases it is desirable that the pre-

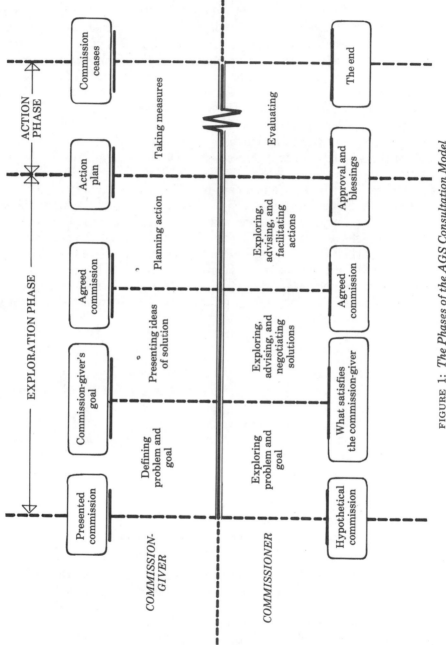

FIGURE 1: *The Phases of the AGS Consultation Model*

sented problems are clarified and reformulated into an overarching "*key question*" to enable an effective search for an answer.

At the AGS Institute we regard the therapeutic conversation to be as much a forum for our clients to interview us as for us to interview them. We encourage our commission-givers to question us at any time, and in our questioning and answering we are careful to be as open and honest toward our commission-givers as we would like them to be toward us. An important principle in all our work is to explain carefully what we do, why we do it, and for whom we do it. The resultant therapeutic conversation emerges as an alternate questioning and answering from both the commissioner and the commission-giver. The search for a key question, and a satisfactory answer to the problem, becomes like a mutual research project between the parties. We often find that when the key question is clarified, the commission-givers find their own solution to the problem.

The search for a key question is highlighted in the following case example, where a man requested a consultation with Ernst. In the present commission the man asked whether Ernst could help him to sort out his feelings about the relationship he had with his parents. The conversation moved from an account of the relationship between his parents, through an account of the relationship between himself and his parents, through an account of the relationship between his sister and the parents. Finally the conversation moved to the wife's ideas about the influence of the relationship between the man's parents and himself on the relationship between himself and his wife.

At this point, Ernst used an intervention borrowed from the work of Bill O'Hanlon (1991). The man was asked how the problem would appear if it were filmed by a video camera in his everyday life. The man began to talk again about his and his wife's feelings, and Ernst amended his question to include an old style movie camera without sound recording facilities. The man sat quietly for a while, pondering on the question, before he finally answered. He said, "The film would show a typical evening scene in my home. I go to bed and my wife stays up watching television in the living room, until she falls asleep on the sofa. She does that to avoid a situation where I might try to approach her. She does not want to have sex with me anymore."

The consultation ended after an hour. At that time, Ernst and his commission-giver had agreed to investigate the following key question: "How could he make his wife desire him (in the broad sense of the word) again?" The commission-giver decided to try out a few ideas of his own before he returned to Ernst. He seemed revived and eager to get started.

A lot of effort is put into exploring all the ideas of change that commission-givers have not dared to try earlier. We explore their most feared expectations of what would happen if they actually did carry out these ideas. In this phase we may also start to give advice, couched in the commission-giver's representations of "reality." When we have ended the negotiations about ideas of solutions, we have come to the *agreed commission*, which states what should be achieved and how. Care is taken to foresee possible obstacles in order to create readiness for emergencies due to unpredictable circumstances.

When the overall plan is ready, we give commission-givers the task of designing the final action plan by working on the practical details at home and then coming back to us with suggestions and questions. When suitable, we suggest that they gather resource persons at one or several meetings to arrange the necessary support, allocation of tasks, and coordination of actions.

The target person is invited to take part in the planning only if commission-givers think that it would be helpful. If it is possible to adjust the plan to fit the target person's wishes without reducing its effect, we encourage this. We warn commission-givers, however, that the target person's illness may seduce them to hand over some of the responsibility for carrying out the plan to the target person. We cannot stress the danger of the illness enough; under no circumstances should it be given any chance to sabotage the plan. Talking in this way separates the illness from the person, acting as a counterforce to the evil intentions commonly ascribed to patient and family alike in psychiatric facilities.

When the target person shows a willingness to cooperate, we welcome his/her cooperation but without giving him/her any responsibility that could undermine the plan. Before carrying out the plan, we usually ask the target person to submit to it when it is set in action. We are willing to discuss any modifications of the plan that would not endanger it, if it helps make it more workable. At the next session, when the commission-givers present their plan, we estimate both how solid it is and how willing the commission-givers are to carry it out in spite of the pain that the target person's agony and protests may cause them.

Once the plan is ready, we "bless" it and wish them good luck. In the cases where we have some reservations about the plan, we remind them that every case is unique, and therefore one or more failures are no catastrophe, as every experience serves to yield more information. Even when we believe in the plan, we talk about the possibility that it might not yield an immediate result and about our experience of occasional relapses. If the plan proves to be completely inefficient, we suggest a step back to a third phase of the exploration and have a new plan outlined.

When the commission-givers have found a way that works, we emphasize that time will take its course, and that there is not much more we can do for them other than to continue to evaluate and give more advice if needed. The commission-givers may call us on the telephone as often as they want to get answers to their questions and other advice.

When the commission-givers finally think that the route to change is sure and come to us for the last session, their commission to us ceases. We evaluate our work according to the problem definition and the criteria for change set by the commission-givers. When we part, the commission-givers have confidence that they can use their plan again if needed. By definition they no longer have their former problem, since they now know how to achieve the desired change. Often the commission-givers ask if they can come back on a priority basis if the change is not stable. We promise this, but to date this promise has never been called upon. Thus the commission comes to an end.

Commentary

Reese Price

IN RESPONDING to the AGS Institute's model for consultation, I would like to agree wholeheartedly with their emphasis on health, strength, innate resources, and love. I think more and more we are recognizing that the expectancy sets we carry into our therapies are powerful, self-fulfilling prophecies that can weigh the outcome in a favorable or unfavorable direction. To believe and communicate that a person or a family can make a difference in their own lives creates the expectancy that change will be achieved.

I also liked the notion that a passion to change the other is not a worthwhile endeavor. The notion of a wish to serve and humility before the commission-giver opens the door to a collaborative framework. Ericksonian notions of joining the client's reality while accepting and utilizing what is found there are very much in line with this spirit of cooperation, as are many of the ideas presented at this conference. The attendant notions of loyalty rather than neutrality towards the commission-giver, the need for positive sentiment, and an intense curiosity about the reality of the other are also all worthwhile. This is particularly true of curiosity, as within the confines of this state of orientation internal metacommentary about one's work drops out as one is caught up in fascination with all the different ways "reality" can be structured. In curiosity there is no judgment, only a desire to know and understand. When tempered by compassion, I can think of no better stance from which a therapist can operate in joining with another person(s) around the theme of change.

Technically, I liked the authors' notion of a key question that allows for an effective search for an answer. The negotiating of a clearly defined tack is often a prerequisite to effective therapeutic conversation. I am reminded of Milton Erickson's reputed definition of therapy as two people sitting down and trying to find out what the hell one of them wants.

Finally, I would like to turn to the metaphor of the Sirens' Song and its effect on Ulysses, as well as its connection to the authors' notion of the target person operating under the influence of mental illness as a compulsion. This notion of influence, while separating the person from the defined "problem," would appear to dovetail nicely on many levels with the work of Michael White, Karl Tomm, and David Epston. As such, the notion of commission and the consultive relationship developed around this term as explicated by these authors leaves us with a different angle from which to consider therapeutic conversations structured along these lines.

REFERENCES

Andersson, M. (1990). *To help or not to help: That is the question.* Ethics, Epistemology and New Methods Conference, Paris, October, 1990.

Andersson, M. (1991). Hur ser du på terapeutens arbete, Humberto? (How do you see the task of the therapist, Humberto?) Interview with Humberto Maturana, *Svensk Familjeterapi,* Stockholm, no. 1/91.

Kierkegaard, S. (1859). *The point of view for my work as an author.* Translated by Walter Lowrie, New York: Harper Torchbooks, Harper and Row, 1962.

Maturana, H. R. (1983). What is to see? *Arch. Biol. Med. Exp. 16,* 255-269, Chile.

O'Hanlon, W. H. (1990). Establishing the agenda: Approaches to schizophrenia, a solution-oriented approach. *The Family Therapy Networker,* November/December.

O'Hanlon, W. H. (1991). Possibility therapy. Seminar arranged by the AGS-Institutet, Stockholm, September, 1991.

Selvini Palazzoli, M., Boscolo, L., Cecchin, G., & Prata, G. (1980). Hypothesizing-circularity-neutrality: Three guidelines for the conductor of the session. *Fam. Processes, 19,* (1), 7-19.

Tomm, K. (1986). Seminar arranged by the AGS-Institutet, Stockholm, November 1986.

Wiesel, E. (1986, November). TV-interview by Erwin Leiser. Swedish television.

INDEX